Internet of Things

Internet of Things

Dr. Jeeva Jose
Associate Professor, Department of Computer Applications
Baselios Poulose II Catholicos College (BPC)
Piravom - 686 664, Ernakulam District, Kerala, India

KHANNA BOOK PUBLISHING CO. (P) LTD.
Publisher of Engineering and Computer Books
4C/4344, Ansari Road, Darya Ganj, New Delhi-110002
Phone : 011-23244447-48 **Mobile:** +91-99109 09320
E-mail : contact@khannabooks.com
Website : www.khannabooks.com

Dear Readers,

To prevent the piracy, this book is secured with HIGH SECURITY HOLOGRAM on the front title cover. In case you don't find the hologram on the front cover title, please write us to at contact@khannabooks.com or whatsapp us at +91-99109 09320 and avail special gift voucher for yourself.

Specimen of Hologram on front Cover title:

Moreover, there is a SPECIAL DISCOUNT COUPON for you with EVERY HOLOGRAM.

How to avail this SPECIAL DISCOUNT:

Step 1: Scratch the hologram
Step 2: Under the scratch area, your "coupon code" is available
Step 3: Logon to www.khannabooks.com
Step 4: Use your "coupon code" in the shopping cart and get your copy at a special discount
Step 5: Enjoy your reading!

ISBN: 978-93-86173-59-1

Internet of Things
by Jeeva Jose

First Edition: 2018
Reprint: 2022, 2023, 2025, **2026**

To view complete list of books, Please scan the QR Code:

Published by:
Khanna Book Publishing Co. (P) Ltd.
CIN: U22110DL1998PTC095547

Visit us at: **www.khannabooks.com**
Write us at: **contact@khannabooks.com**

Printed in Bharat.

Preface

Internet of Things (IoT) is a network of physical devices like vehicles, home appliances etc. embedded with electronics, software, sensors and actuators having connectivity for these "Things" to connect each other and exchange data.

The 'Thing" in IoT can be any object that has an IP address and has the ability to collect and transfer data over a network without manual assistance. The embedded technology in these objects help them to interact internally and externally.

When devices can represent themselves digitally, they can be controlled from anywhere. The connectivity helps us to capture more data from many places, ensuring more ways of increasing efficiency as well as improving IoT security. IoT is a transformational force that can help companies to improve performance through IoT analytics and security to deliver better results. Businesses in the utilities, insurance, manufacturing, transportation, infrastructure, retail sectors, oil & gas etc. can reap the benefits of IoT by helping them to take more informed decisions. IoT platforms can help organizations to reduce cost through improved process efficiency, asset utilization and productivity. The growth and convergence of data processes and "things" on the Internet would make such connections more relevant, creating more opportunities for people, business and industries.

The applications of IoT can be found in all areas of life. IoT helps to make cities smart by monitoring and allocation of parking spaces. Other applications of IoT in smart cities include monitoring of vibrations as well as material conditions of buildings, bridges or historical monuments for identifying their structural conditions. Sound monitoring in real time, measurement of the energy radiated by cell stations or WiFi routers is another application. Monitoring of vehicles and pedestrian levels help to optimize driving and walking routes. Intelligent and weather adaptive lighting in street lights is another application of IoT. Waste management by detection of rubbish levels in containers to optimize the trash collection routes, Intelligent highways with warning messages and diversions according to climate conditions or unexpected events like accidents is another potential application of IoT.

IoT helps to make environment smart by early forest fire detection, air pollution control by monitoring emissions of factories, vehicles etc. on real time basis. Monitoring of snow level, soil moisture, vibrations, earth density etc. helps to forecast dangerous patterns in land conditions for preventing landslides and avalanche. Distributed control in specific places of tremors helps for early detection of earthquake.

IoT helps in remote real time monitoring of potable water, chemicals in rivers, swimming pool, pollution levels in the sea, water leakages, river floods etc. and take suitable actions. IoT helps in energy consumption, monitoring and management like monitoring of water, oil and gas levels in storage tanks and dams as well as optimization of performance in solar energy plants. Security & emergencies team can get IoT support for access control to restricted areas and detection of people in unauthorized areas.

Retail business can use IoT for monitoring of storage conditions along the supply chain and product tracking for traceability, payment processing in public transport, gyms, theme parks, etc. This also helps in getting advices in the point of sale according to customer habits, preferences, presence of allergic components or expiry dates, control of rotation of products in shelves and warehouses to automate restocking processes. IoT in logistics is applied for monitoring of vibrations, container openings or cold chain maintenance, search of individual items in big surfaces like warehouses, warning emission on containers, storing inflammable goods close to others containing explosive material, control of routes followed for delicate goods like medical drugs, jewels or dangerous merchandises.

IoT helps industrial control by machine auto-diagnosis, assets control, monitoring of toxic gas or oxygen levels inside factories to ensure safety, control of temperature inside industrial or medical fridges having sensitive merchandise, monitoring of ozone levels, asset location by using ZigBee and RFID/NFC tags. For vehicle auto-diagnosis, information collection can be done for real time alarms to emergencies or provide advice to drivers.

In agriculture, IoT helps for monitoring soil moisture, control micro-climate conditions to maximize the production as well as quality of fruits and vegetables. Selective irrigation using IoT in dry zones help to reduce the water required. IoT helps to study weather conditions in fields to forecast rain, drought, snow or wind changes. IoT have application in Hydroponics to control the exact conditions of plants grown in water to get the highest efficiency crops.

IoT helps in animal farming by control of growing conditions of the offspring to ensure its survival and health. Tracking the location and identification of animals grazing in open pastures is another application of IoT.

In home automation, IoT helps for energy and water supply consumption monitoring to obtain advice on how to save cost and resources., switching on and off remotely appliances to avoid accidents and save energy, detection of windows and doors openings and violations to prevent intruders.

The components of an IoT system consists of sensors, network, single board computers, micro controllers, software and actuators. This book explains different types of sensors, actuators and network protocols. Raspberry Pi and its programming using Python is well explained. Programming with Arduino board is also explained in detail. A reader who has basic knowledge about sensors, networking and actuators will find this book effective for learning Internet of Things.

Annexure

Below are the expansion of abbreviations used in this book.

Abbreviation		Expansion
RFID	:	Radio-Frequency IDentification
NFC	:	Near-Field Communication
M2M	:	Machine-to-Machine Communication
CPS	:	Cyber-Physical Systems
WoT	:	Web of Things
IoT	:	Internet of Things
REST	:	Representational State Transfer
API	:	Application Programming Interface
WSN	:	Wireless Sensor Network
WLAN	:	Wireless Local Area Network
BLE	:	Bluetooth Low Energy
WWW	:	World Wide Web
HTTP	:	Hyper Text Transfer Protocol.
MQTT	:	Message Queuing Telemetry Transport
CoAP	:	Constrained Application Protocol
ULA	:	Unique Local Address
IKEv2	:	Internet Key Exchange version 2
DHCPv6	:	Dynamic Host Configuration Protocol version 6
SLAAC	:	StateLess Address Auto Configuration
RA	:	Router Advertisements
VPN	:	Virtual Private Network
PI	:	Provider Independent
AS	:	Autonomous System
DSL	:	Digital Subscriber Line
OSI	:	Open System Interconnection
ISDN	:	Integrated Services Digital Network
UDP	:	User Datagram Protocol
DTLS	:	Datagram Transport Layer Security

TCP	:	Transmission Control Protocol
JSON	:	JavaScript Object Notation
CBOR	:	Concise Binary Object Representation
DHCP	:	Dynamic Host Configuration Protocol
SSL	:	Secure Sockets Layer
XML	:	Extensible Markup Language
TLS	:	Transport Layer Security
MAC	:	Media Access Control
IOE	:	Internet of Everything
API	:	Application Program Interface
AMQP	:	Advanced Message Queuing Protocol
ECN	:	Electronic Communications Networks
DSCP	:	Differentiated Services Code Point
TTL	:	Time-to-Live
IETF	:	Internet Engineering Task Force
PDU	:	Protocol Data Unit
XMPP	:	Extensible Messaging and Presence Protocol
RFC	:	Remote Function Call
SASL	:	Simple Authentication and Security Layer
BPSK	:	Binary Phase-Shift Keying
CSMA-CA	:	Carrier Sense Multiple Access/Collision Avoidance
P2P	:	Peer To Peer
AODV	:	Ad hoc On-Demand Distance Vector
RREQ	:	Route REQuest
RERR	:	Route ERRor

Contents

1 INTRODUCTION TO INTERNET OF THINGS

1.1 Introduction

Internet of Things (IoT) is presently a hot technology worldwide. Government, academia and industry are involved in different aspects of research, implementation and business with IoT. IoT cuts across different application domain verticals ranging from civilian to defense sectors. These domains include agriculture, space, healthcare, manufacturing, construction, water and mining, which are presently transitioning their legacy to support IoT. Today it is possible to envision pervasive connectivity, storage and computation, which in turn gives rise to build different IoT solutions. IoT-based applications such as Innovative Shopping System, Infrastructure Management in both urban and rural areas, Remote Health Monitoring & Emergency Notification Systems and Transportation Systems are gradually relying on IoT based systems. Therefore, it is very important to learn the fundamentals of this emerging technology.

The Internet of Things (IoT) is the network of physical devices, vehicles, home appliances and other items embedded with electronics, software, sensors, actuators and network connectivity which enables these objects to get connected and exchange data. Each thing is uniquely identifiable through its embedded computing system but is able to inter-operate within the existing Internet infrastructure. *Internet of Things can also be defined as an Internet technology connecting devices, machines and tools to the Internet by means of wireless technologies like Bluetooth, WiFi, ZigBee etc.*

The IoT allows objects to be sensed or controlled remotely across existing network infrastructure, creating opportunities for more direct integration of the physical world into computer-based systems and resulting in improved efficiency, accuracy and economic benefit in addition to reduced human intervention. IoT also results in unification of technologies such as low power embedded systems, cloud computing, big data, machine learning and networking. The two solutions for the networking technologies in IoT are either to expand the existing network or to build a separate network from the scratch. Following Figure 1.1 gives an overview of objects connected to Internet of Things.

Fig.1.1: Overview of Internet of Things

The concept of the **Internet of Things** became popular in 1999, through the Auto-ID Center at MIT and related market-analysis publications. Radio-frequency identification (RFID) was seen by Kevin Ashton (one of the founders of the original Auto-ID Center) as a prerequisite for the Internet of Things at that point. If all objects and people in daily life were equipped with identifiers, computers could manage and store them. Besides using RFID, the tagging of things may be achieved through such technologies as near field communication, barcodes, QR codes and digital watermarking. Other IoT enabling technologies are nanotechnology, sensors and smart networks. Presently we are heading into a new era of ubiquity where the "users" of the Internet will be counted in billions. Humans may become the minority as generators and receivers of traffic. Instead most of the traffic will flow between among devices and all kinds of "things" thereby creating a much wider and more complex Internet of Things.

1.2 Characteristics of IoT

The fundamental characteristics of IoT are as follows.

Interconnectivity: With regards to IoT, anything can be interconnected with the global information and communication infrastructure.

Things related services: IoT is capable of providing "thing" related services within the constraints of things, such as privacy protection and semantic consistency among physical things and their associated virtual things. In order to provide "thing" related services within the constraints of things, both the technologies in physical world and information world will be changed.

Heterogeneity: The devices in the IoT are heterogeneous based on different hardware platforms, applications and networks. They can interact with other devices or service platforms through different networks. IoT may comprise of sleeping nodes, mobile devices and non-IP devices.

Dynamic changes: The state of device change dynamically, e.g., sleeping and waking up, connected and/or disconnected as well as the context of devices including location and speed. Moreover, the number of devices can be changed dynamically.

Enormous scale: The number of devices that need to be managed and that communicate with one another will be at least in an order of magnitude larger than the devices connected to the current Internet. The management of generated data and their interpretation for application purposes will be more critical. This relates to semantics of data, as well as efficient data handling.

Safety: We gain benefits from IoT, but we must not forget about safety. IoT must be designed with safety in mind. This includes the safety of our personal data and the safety of our physical devices. Securing the endpoints, the networks and the data moving across all of it means creating a security paradigm in IoT.

Connectivity: Connectivity enables network accessibility and compatibility. Accessibility is found on a network while compatibility provides the common ability to consume and produce data. The intermittent connectivity is desirable in IoT as when the device is no longer in use, the connection can be detached whereas the device needs to be connected when it wants to generate, transfer or receive data.

Naming and Addressing: The names and addresses of devices connected to Internet of Things should be unique. Efficient and unambiguous addressing mechanisms should be deployed for devices connected in IoT. Moreover the conversion and translation of addresses from one network to the other should take place efficiently.

1.3 Applications of IoT

The applications of IoT are found in almost all domains of life. It includes business, manufacturing, healthcare, retail, security, transport and other domains. The applications of IoT in key areas are explained in the following description.

Smart Home: In this concept, it is possible to switch on air conditioning before reaching home or switch off lights even after we have left home. Similarly we can unlock the doors to friends for temporary access even when we are not at home. Thus IoT is building products to make our life simpler and convenient. Smart Home has become the revolutionary ladder of success in the residential spaces and it is predicted Smart Homes will become as common as smart phones. The cost of owning a house is the biggest expense in a homeowner's life. Smart Home products are promised to save time, energy and money. With Smart Home companies like Nest, Ecobee, Ring and August, to name a few, will become household brands and are planning to deliver a unique experience.

Wearables: Wearables have experienced an explosive demand in markets all over the world. Companies like Google, Samsung, etc. have invested heavily in building such devices. Wearable devices are installed with sensors and software which collect data and information about the users. This data is later pre-processed to extract essential insights about user. These devices broadly cover fitness, health and entertainment requirements. The pre-requisite for Internet of Things technology for wearable applications is to be highly energy efficient or ultra-low power and small sized.

Connected Cars/Smart Cars: The automotive digital technology has focused on optimizing vehicle's internal functions. But now, this attention is growing towards enhancing the in-car experience. A connected car is a vehicle which is able to optimize it's own operation, maintenance as well as comfort of passengers using onboard sensors and Internet connectivity is ensured. Similarly a smart car can identify the behavior of another car coming in its opposite direction. For example, if a car coming in opposite direction switches on the indicator to the left, our car understands it and takes action accordingly. Most of the large automobile manufacturers as well as some brave startups are working on connected car and smart car solutions. Major brands like Tesla, BMW, Apple, Google are working on bringing the next revolution in automobiles.

Smart Industry: Smart Industry is the new buzz in the industrial sector, also termed as Industrial Internet of Things (IIoT). It is empowering industrial engineering with sensors, software and big data analytic to create brilliant machines. The driving philosophy behind IIoT is that, smart machines are more accurate and consistent than humans in communicating through data. This data can help companies in picking up inefficiencies and problems sooner. IIoT holds great potential for quality control and sustainability. Applications for tracking goods, real time information exchange about inventory among suppliers and retailers and automated delivery will increase the supply chain efficiency.

Smart Cities: Smart City is another powerful application of IoT generating curiosity among world's population. Smart surveillance, automated transportation, smarter energy management systems, water distribution, urban security and environmental monitoring are examples of Internet of Things applications for Smart Cities. IoT will solve major problems faced by the people living in cities of pollution, traffic congestion and shortage of energy supplies etc. Products like cellular communication enabled Smart Belly trash will send alerts to municipal services when a bin needs to be emptied. By installing sensors and using web applications, citizens can find free available parking slots across the city. Also, the sensors can detect meter tampering issues, general malfunctions and any installation issues in the electricity system.

Smart Agriculture: With the continuous increment in world's population, demand for food supply is extremely raised. Governments are helping farmers to use advanced techniques and researches to increase food production. Smart farming is one of the fastest growing fields in IoT. Farmers are using meaningful insights from the data to yield better return on investment. Sensing for soil moisture and nutrients, controlling water usage for plant growth and determining custom fertilizer are some simple usages of IoT.

Smart Retail: The potential of IoT in the retail sector is enormous. IoT provides an opportunity to retailers to get connected with the customers to enhance the in-store experience. Smart phones will be the way for retailers to remain connected with their consumers even out of store. Interacting through Smart phones and using beacon technology can help retailers serve their consumers in a better manner. They can also track consumer's path through a store and improve store layout and place premium products in high traffic areas.

Energy Management: Power grids of the future will not only be smart enough but also highly reliable. Smart Grid concept is becoming very popular all over the world. The basic idea behind the smart grids is to collect data in an automated fashion and analyze the behavior of electricity consumers and suppliers for improving efficiency as well as economics of electricity usage. Smart Grids will also be able to detect sources of power outages more quickly and at individual household levels like nearby solar panel, making possible distributed energy system.

Smart Healthcare: Connected healthcare yet remains the sleeping giant of the Internet of Things applications. The concept of connected healthcare system and smart medical devices bear enormous potential not just for companies, but also for the well-being of people in general.

Research shows IoT in healthcare will be massive in coming years. IoT in healthcare is aimed at empowering people to live healthier life by wearing connected devices. The collected data will help in personalized analysis of an individual's health and provide tailor made strategies to combat illness. In smart healthcare, devices are connected to hospitals, doctors and relatives to alert them of medical emergencies and take preventive or necessary measures.

Smart Poultry and Farming: Livestock monitoring is about animal husbandry and cost saving. Using IoT applications to gather data about the health and well being of the cattle, ranchers know early about the sick animal which can be pulled out and help prevent large number of sick cattle. With the help of collected data, ranchers can increase the poultry production.

Smart Dust: This consists of sensors at the nanotechnology level that can be deployed in the millions to billions, with a myriad of applications. They are computers smaller than a grain of sand and can be sprayed or injected almost anywhere to measure chemicals in the soil or to diagnose problems in human body. These devices are the wave of the future for anything from global weather management and smart city monitoring to war theater mapping and internal medicine. They are a single package with sensing, computation, communication and power to collect data and report it back to home base.

Other applications of IoT include smart parking for vehicles, detecting and regulating traffic congestion, smart lighting of cities, waste management, detection of river floods, landslides and earthquakes in advance, monitoring of snow level, measuring and control air and water pollution, forest fire detection, detection of leakages in a water transmission system, identification of radiation levels, explosives and hazardous gases and smart rescue systems. Figure 1.2 shows the IoT market share in various domains.

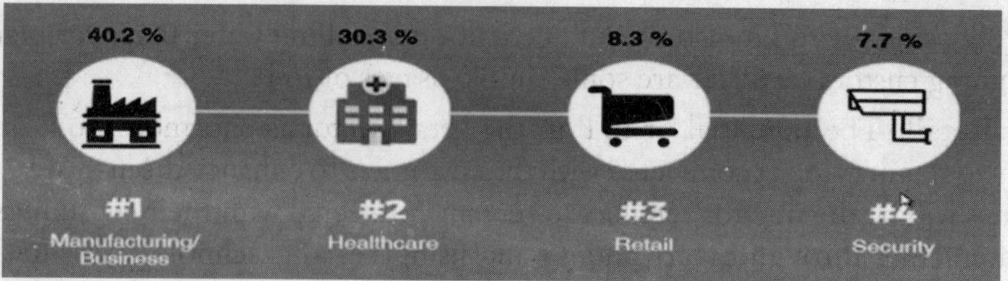

Fig.1.2: IoT Market Share in Various Domains

1.4 IoT Categories

Internet of Things can be classified into two categories: Industrial IoT and Consumer IoT. Figure 1.3 shows the components in Industrial IoT and Consumer IoT.

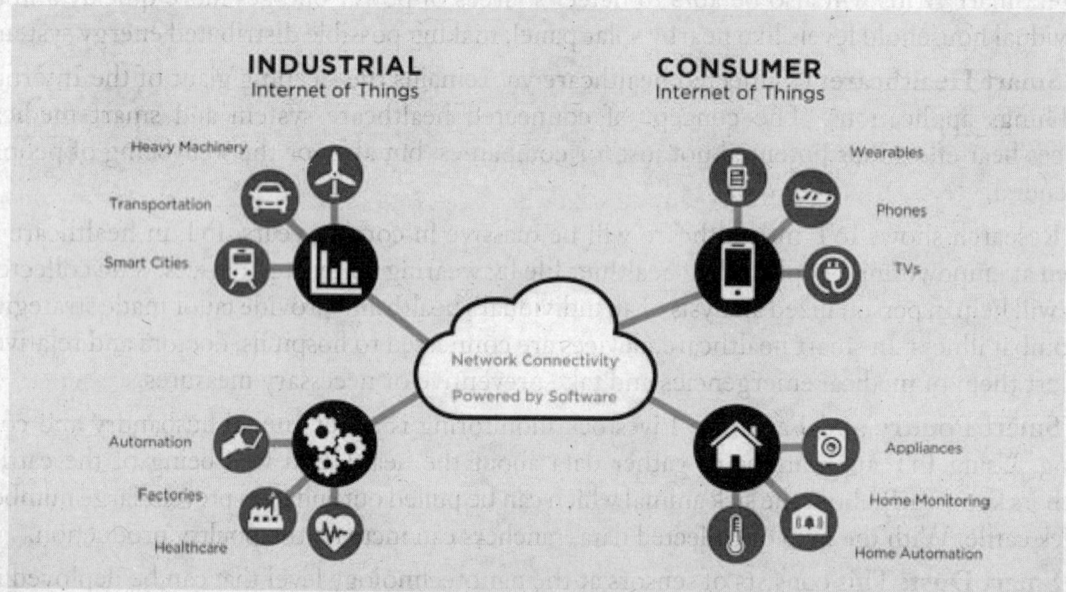

Fig.1.3: Components in Industrial IoT and Consumer IoT

Industrial IoT: If our factory equipment has sensors connected to Internet, then it is part of Industrial IoT (IIoT). In an Industrial IoT, a device connects to both an IP network and the global Internet. Connectivity between the nodes is done using regular as well as industry specific technologies. The IoT is important but not critical, while the IIoT failure often results in life-threatening or other emergency situations. IIoT provides an unprecedented level of visibility throughout the supply chain. Individual items, cases, pallets, containers and vehicles can be equipped with auto-identification tags and tied to GPS-enabled connections to continuously update location and movement. The IoT generates medium or high volume of data, while IIoT generates massive amount of data (a single turbine compressor blade can generate more than 500GB of data per day) so includes Big Data, Cloud Computing, Machine

Learning as necessary computing requirements. In future, the IoT will continue to enhance our lives as-consumers while IIoT will enable efficient management of entire supply chain.

Consumer IoT: If our thermostat or refrigerator is connected to the Internet, then it is part of the consumer IoT. IoT devices communicate within the locally networked devices and communication to outside Internet is done through a gateway. Local communication is done mostly via Bluetooth, ZigBee or WiFi. The consumer IoT has an impact on end consumers. Consumer IoT refers to the use of 'smart' objects, which are everyday things from cars and home appliances to athletic shoes and light switches that can connect to the Internet, transmitting and receiving data and connecting the physical world to the digital world. It is mostly about human interaction with objects. Devices can alert users when certain events or situations occur or monitor activities. Google Nest sends an alert when temperature in the house is dropped below 68 degrees is an example of Consumer IoT. Similarly a garage door sensors alert the user with sound when opened, turn up the air conditioner and turn on the driveway lights half an hour before you arrive at your home, a meeting room that turns off lights when no one is using it and an air conditioner switches off when windows are open are all examples of Consumer IoT.

1.5 IoT Enablers and Connectivity Layers

IoT enablers can be looked upon based on three factors namely (a) Implementation Perspective (b) Connectivity Methods (c) Enabling Technologies. Figure 1.4 shows various IoT enablers.

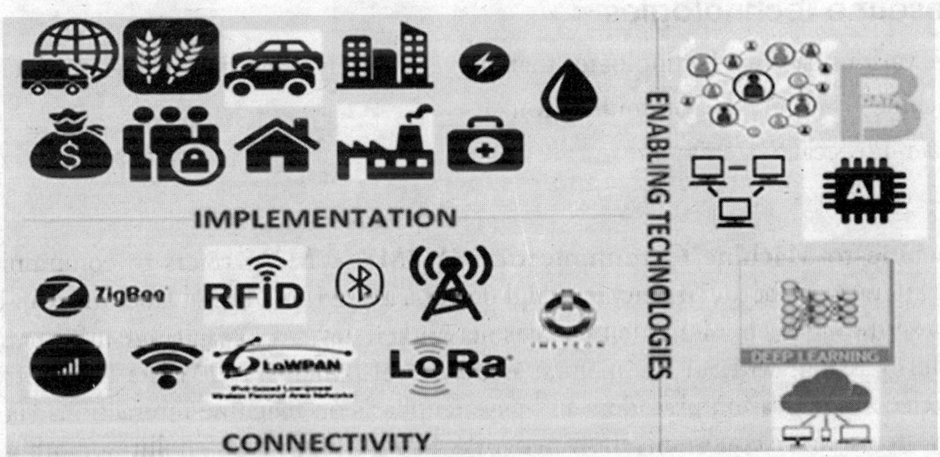

Fig.1.4: IoT Enablers

The implementation perspective includes smart industries, smart homes, smart factories, smart vehicles, smart healthcare etc. Connectivity methods in Internet of Things include ZigBee, RFID, Bluetooth, WiFi, 6LoWPAN, LoRa etc. Enabling technologies include cloud computing, artificial intelligence, big data, machine learning, deep learning, fog computing etc. The connectivity methods and enabling technology will be explained in the forthcoming Chapters. Figure 1.5 shows the connectivity layers in IoT.

Fig.1.5: Connectivity Layers in IoT

The top level is the services layer comprises of various implementation entities like smart industries, smart homes, smart factories, smart vehicles, smart healthcare etc. The layer below the services layer is the local connectivity layer consisting of various technologies like RFID, Bluetooth, WiFi, 6LoWPAN, LoRa etc. Below the local connectivity layer comes the global connectivity layer which comprises of gateways to connect to the Internet and the bottom layer forms the Internet. The local connectivity is offered by various service providers and IoT management takes place at the bottom layer.

1.6 Baseline Technologies

There are various baseline technologies that are very closely related to IoT. They include

(a) Machine-to-Machine Communication

(b) Cyber-Physical Systems

(c) Web of Things

(a) **Machine-to-Machine Communication (M2M)** — M2M refers to communications and interactions between machines and devices. (M2M) is a broad label that can be used to describe any technology that enables networked devices to exchange information and perform actions without the manual assistance of humans. M2M is a term introduced by telecommunication providers and pays emphasis on machine interactions via one or more telecom or communication networks like 3G, 4G, 5G, satellite or other public networks. This technology forms the basis for IoT. However IoT has a broader scope than M2M, since it comprises of a broader range of interactions including interactions between devices/things, things and people, things with applications and people with applications. It also enables the composition of workflows comprising all of the above interactions.

In product restocking, for example, a vending machine can message the distributor when a particular item is running low. M2M communication is an important aspect of warehouse management, remote control, robotics, traffic control, logistic services, supply chain management, fleet management and tele-medicines. Key components of an M2M system include sensors, RFID, a Wi-Fi or cellular communications link and autonomic computing software programmed to help a networked device interpret data and make decisions. The most well-known type of M2M communication is telemetry, which has been used since the early part of the last century to transmit operational data. Pioneers in telemetries first used telephone lines and later used radio waves to transmit performance measurements gathered from monitoring instruments in remote locations. The Internet and improved standards for wireless technology have expanded the role of telemetry from pure science, engineering and manufacturing to everyday used products like home heating units, electric meters and Internet-connected appliances. Products built with M2M communication capabilities are often marketed to end users as being "smart."

Currently, M2M does not have a standardized connected device platform and many M2M systems are built to be task or device specific. It is expected that M2M becomes more pervasive, vendors will need to agree upon standards for device-to-device communications.

(b) **Cyber-Physical Systems** — Cyber-Physical Systems (CPS) represent the next generation embedded intelligent ICT systems that are interconnected, interdependent, collaborative, autonomous and provide computing and communication, monitoring/control of physical components/processes in various applications. Future CPS needs to be scalable, distributed, decentralized allowing interaction with humans, environment and machines while being connected to Internet or to other networks. Adaptability, reactivity, optimality and security are features to be embedded in such systems, as the CPS is now forming an invisible 'neural network' of the society.

Cyber-Physical systems are systems that integrate computing elements with the physical components and processes. The computing elements coordinate and communicate with sensors, which monitor cyber and physical indicators and actuators, which modify the cyber and physical environment. Cyber-Physical systems use sensors to connect all distributed intelligence in the environment to gain a deeper knowledge of the environment, which enables more accurate actions and tasks. Common applications of CPS typically fall under sensor-based communication-enabled autonomous systems. For example, many wireless sensor networks monitor some aspects of the environment and relay the processed information to a central node. Other types of CPS include smart grid, autonomous automotive systems, medical monitoring, process control systems, distributed robotics, and automatic pilot avionics.

(c) **Web of Things** — The Web of Things (WoT) is a term used to describe approaches, software architectural styles and programming patterns that allow real-world objects to be part of the World Wide Web. Similarly to what the Web (Application Layer) is to the Internet (Network Layer), the Web of Things provides an Application Layer that simplifies the creation of Internet of Things applications. Rather than re-inventing completely new standards, the Web of Things reuses existing and well-known Web standards used in the programmable Web (e.g., REST, HTTP, JSON), semantic Web (e.g., JSON-LD, Microdata, etc.), the real-time Web (e.g., WebSockets) and the social Web (e.g., OAuth or social networks).

From a developer's perspective, the WoT enables access and control over IoT resources and applications using mainstream Web technologies like HTML 5.0, Javascript, Ajax, PHP etc. The approach to build WoT is therefore based on Representational State Transfer (REST) principles and REST APIs, which enable both developers and deployers to benefit from the popularity and maturity of Web Technologies. Building the WoT has various security and scalability issues which are needed to be addressed for achieving an efficient WoT. One of the early prototypes of the Web of Things is the "Energie Visible" project in which sensors are capable of monitoring and controlling the energy consumption of household appliances. They offered their functionality through a RESTful API. This API is then used to create a physical Mashup. Nimbits is an open source data historian server built on cloud computing architecture that provides connectivity among devices using data points.

ThingSpeak is an open source Internet of Things platform created by Hans Scharler to collect, analyze and to act on data generated by sensors and actuators. EVRYTHING is a platform for making unconnected products and connected devices as part of the Web based on Web of Things architecture. Figure 1.6 shows the terminological interdependence among various technologies.

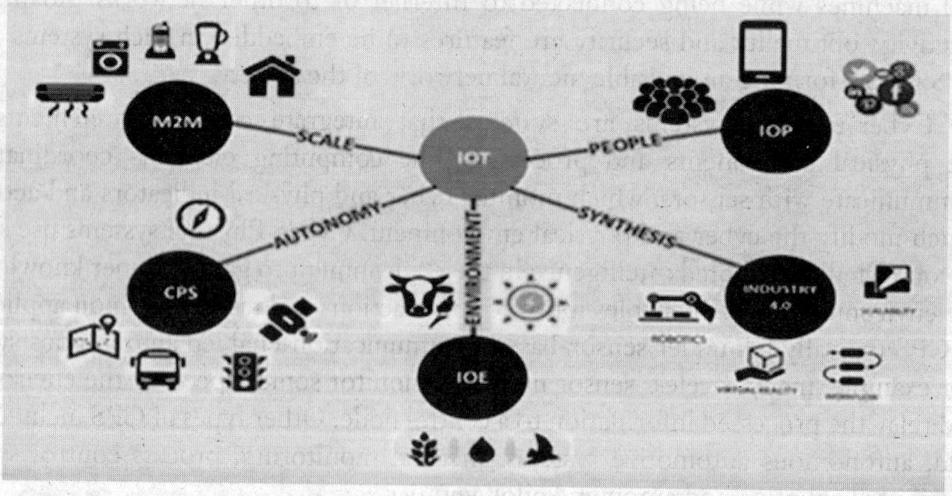

Fig.1.6: Terminological Interdependence among Technologies

1.7 Sensors

A sensor is a device that detects and responds to some type of input from the physical environment. The specific input could be light, heat, motion, moisture, pressure, or any one of a great number of other environmental phenomena. The output is generally a signal that is converted to human-readable display at the sensor location or transmitted electronically over a network for reading or further processing. Examples of sensors include infrared sensor, ultrasonic sensor, camera sensor, smoke detection sensor, temperature sensor, humidity sensor etc. Real world examples for sensing include the conversion of heat into electrical signals in a temperature sensor or atmospheric pressure converted to electrical signals in a barometer. Figure 1.7 shows a temperature sensor with three pins for sensing the temperature.

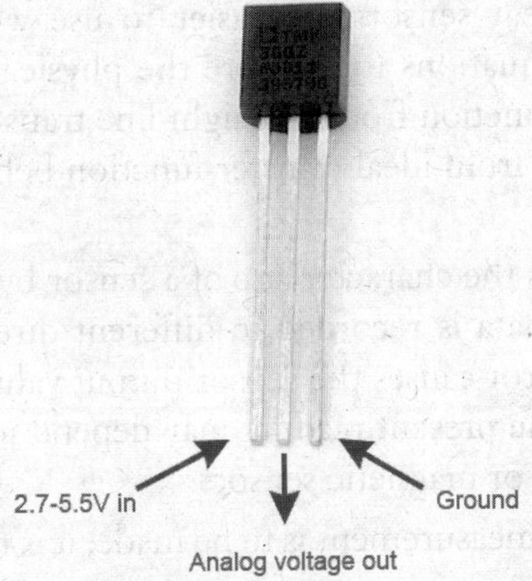

Fig.1.7: Temperature Sensor

1.7.1 Characteristics of a Sensor

Range: Every sensor has a range in which they work with an acceptable error. If the input is not in range, then the output is unpredictable.

Drift: If the output signal slowly changes or varies for the same input over a long period, this is called as drift. The drift will cause an error in the measured value. The drift may result from ageing of the sensor, temperature variance or physical changes in the sensor.

Sensitivity: Sensitivity is defined as the change in output per unit change in input of the property being measured. The sensitivity of the sensor may be constant or linear for the entire range of sensor or vary exponentially if the sensor is a non-linear sensor. The sensitivity of a sensor under real conditions may differ from the value specified. This is known as sensitivity error. If the output signal differs from the correct value by a constant, the sensor is said to have an offset error or bias.

Selectivity: Selectivity is the ability of the sensor to measure a target property in the presence of other properties. The sensor should only be sensitive to the measured property and should be insensitive to any other property likely to be encountered in its application. For example, if an oxygen sensor does not react to other gasses like CO_2 then it has good selectivity.

Resolution: The resolution of a sensor is the smallest change it can detect in the quantity that it is measuring. The resolution of a sensor with a digital output is usually the smallest resolution the digital output it is capable of processing. The more the resolution of a sensor, the more accurate is its precision. A sensor's accuracy does not depend upon its resolution.

Response and Recovery Time: The response time is the time taken by the sensor for its output to reach 95% of its final value when it is exposed to a target material. The Recovery Time is defined conversely.

Linearity: If the sensitivity of the sensor is constant for the range, then it is called as linearity of the sensor. The linear sensors are easier to use while the non-linear sensors require complex mathematical equations to measure the physical property. Non-linearity is the deviation a sensor's transfer function from a straight line transfer function. This is defined by the amount the output differs from ideal transfer function behavior over the full range of the sensor.

Hysteresis: The hysteresis is the characteristic of a sensor by which the sensor produces a different set of outputs if the data is recorded in different directions (increasing input or decreasing input). A hysteresis error causes the sensor output value to vary depending on the sensor's previous input values. The present reading may depend upon past input values. This usually happens in analog sensors or magnetic sensors.

Calibration: If a meaningful measurement is to be made, it is necessary to tune the output of the sensor with accurately known input.

Full-Scale Output: The full-scale output is the difference between the output for maximum input and the output for minimum input. The full scale range of a sensor defines the maximum and minimum values of the measured property. Since the range of the output signal is always limited, the output signal will eventually reach a minimum or maximum value, when the measured property exceeds the limits.

Precision: The precision of a sensor is its ability to produce same output when repeatedly measured for the same input. The precision is determined using statistical analysis like standard deviation.

Accuracy: The accuracy of a sensor defines how close the output is to the real value. The accuracy defines the maximum error the sensor may produce.

If the sensor has a digital output, the output is essentially an approximation of the measured property. Such an error is called quantization error. If the signal is monitored digitally, the sampling frequency can cause a dynamic error, or if the input variable or added noise changes periodically at a frequency proportional to the multiple of the sampling rate, aliasing errors may also occur.

1.7.2 Classification of Sensors

Sensors can be classified into two broad categories based on output and based on the type of data measured. Figure 1.8 shows the classification of sensors.

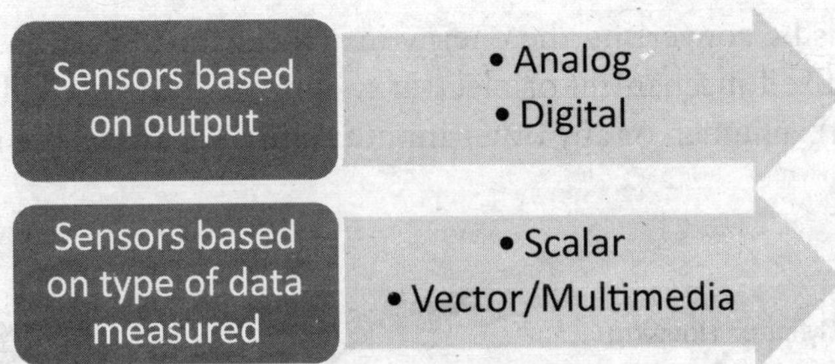

Fig.1.8: Classification of Sensors

Analog Sensors: They produce a continuous output signal or voltage which is generally proportional to the quantity being measured. Physical quantities such as temperature, speed, pressure, displacement, strain etc. are all analog quantities as they tend to be continuous in nature. For example, the temperature of a liquid can be measured using a thermometer or thermocouple (eg: geysers) which continuously responds to temperature changes as the liquid is heated up or cooled down.

Digital Sensors: They produce discrete digital output signals or voltages that are a digital representation of the quantity being measured. Digital sensors produce a binary output signal in the form of a logic "1" or logic "0" (ON and OFF). Digital sensors have been developed to overcome the traditional disadvantages of analog sensors. Digital sensors are mainly used in water, waste water and industrial processes. They measure parameters such as pH, conductivity, dissolved oxygen, ammonium, nitrate, Strong Acidic Citiation and turbidity. A digital sensor system also consists of the sensor itself, a cable and a transmitter.

Scalar sensors: These are the sensors that produce output signal or voltage which is generally proportional to the magnitude of the quantity being measured. Physical quantities such as temperature, color, pressure, strain etc. are all scalar quantities as only their magnitude is sufficient to convey the information. For example, the temperature of a room can be measured using a thermometer or thermocouple which responds to temperature changes irrespective of the orientation of the sensor or its direction.

Vector Sensors: Vector sensors produce output signal or voltage which is generally proportional to the magnitude, direction as well as the orientation of the quantity being measured. Physical quantities such as sound, image, velocity, acceleration, orientation etc. are all vector quantities as only their magnitude is not sufficient to convey the complete information. For example, the acceleration of a body can be measured using an accelerometer, which gives the component of acceleration of the body with respect to x, y, z co-ordinate axes.

1.8 Actuators

An actuator is a component of a machine or system that moves or controls the mechanism or the system. It is the mechanism by which a control system acts upon an environment. An actuator requires a control signal and a source of energy. Upon receiving the control signal, the actuator responds by converting the energy into mechanical motion. The control system can be simple (*eg.* a fixed mechanical or electric system), software-based (*eg.* a printer driver, robot control system), a human or any other input. Figure 1.9 shows the image of an oil based hydraulic actuator.

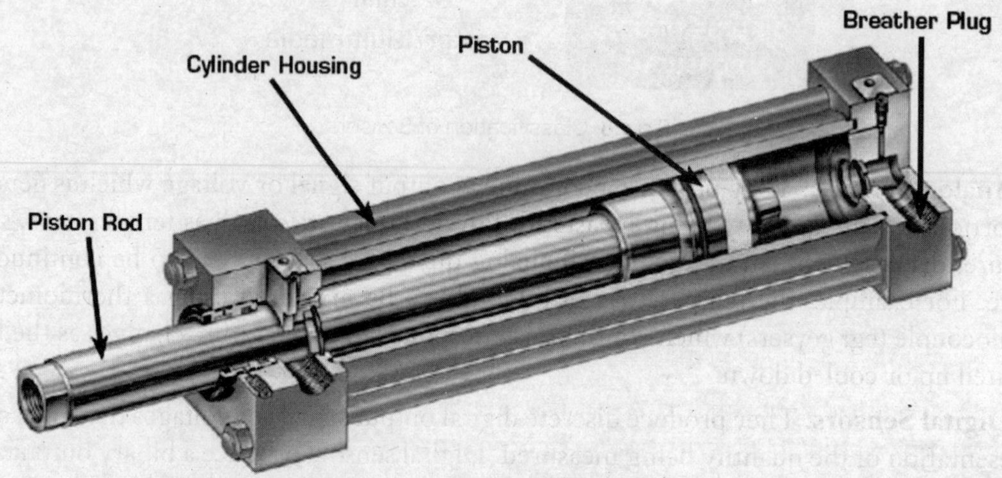

Fig.1.9: Oil based Hydraulic Actuator

1.8.1 Types of Actuators

Based on the technology used, actuators are classified into several categories as follows.

- Hydraulic Actuators
- Pneumatic Actuators
- Electrical Actuators
- Thermal/Magnetic Actuators
- Mechanical Actuators
- Soft Actuators

Hydraulic Actuators: A hydraulic actuator consists of a cylinder or fluid motor that uses hydraulic power to facilitate mechanical operation. The mechanical motion is converted to linear, rotary or oscillatory motion. Since liquids are nearly impossible to compress, a hydraulic actuator exerts considerable force. The actuator's limited acceleration restricts its usage. Examples for hydraulic actuator is the hydraulic brake in a vehicle.

Pneumatic Actuators: A pneumatic actuator converts energy formed by vacuum or compressed air at high pressure into either linear or rotary motion. Examples for pneumatic actuators are rack and pinion actuators which are used for valve controls of pipes. They are responsible for converting pressure into force. The advantage is pneumatic energy quickly responds to starting and stopping signals. The power source does not need to be stored in reserve for operation. Pneumatic actuators enable large forces to be produced from relatively small pressure changes. For example, pneumatic brakes are very responsive to small changes in pressure applied by the driver.

Electric Actuators: An electric actuator is generally powered by a motor that converts electrical energy into mechanical torque. The electrical energy is used to actuate equipment such as solenoid valves which control the flow of water in pipes in response to electrical signals. This is considered as one of the cheapest, cleanest and speedy actuator types available. Examples of electric actuator is a solenoid based electric bell ringing mechanism.

Thermal or Magnetic Actuators: These types of actuators can be actuated by applying thermal or magnetic energy. They tend to be compact, lightweight, economical and with high power density. These actuators use shape memory materials such as shape memory alloys. Example of a thermal actuator is a thermostat and that of a magnetic actuator is an electro magnet.

Mechanical Actuators: A mechanical actuator converts rotary motion into linear motion to execute some movement. It involves gears, rails, pulleys, chains and other devices to operate. Examples of mechanical actuators are the rack & pinion mechanism and crank shaft acting as mechanical actuator.

Soft Actuators: Soft actuators are polymer based which are designed to handle fragile objects like fruit harvesting in agriculture or manipulating the internal organs in biomedicine. Soft actuators produce flexible motion due to the integration of microscopic changes at the molecular levels into a macroscopic deformation of the actuator materials. They typically address the challenging tasks in robotics. The functions of Shape Memory Polymer Actuator are similar to our muscles. Even they provide a response to a range of stimuli such as light, electrical, magnetic, heat, pH, and moisture changes. Shape memory polymers exhibit surprising features such as low density, high strain recovery, biocompatibility and biodegradability. Photo polymers or light activated polymers are a special type of shape memory polymers that are activated by light stimuli. These actuators have instant response and can be controlled remotely using the variation of light frequency or intensity without any physical contact.

1.9 IoT Components and Implementation

Before Internet of Things is implemented we need to know the functional components of IoT. They can be classified as shown in Figure 1.10. The functional components include the following.

- Devices (Things): Various devices connected to IoT forms the components for interaction and communication with other IoT devices. It may include various mobile, non-mobile devices fitted with sensors.
- Local Network: This is the component for processing and analysis of local operations
- Internet: This is the outside network through which the data is transferred for remote processing and analytics.

- Back-end services: Components for handling Web services of applications comprising of processors, servers etc. Based on the data received some actuators may be activated
- Applications: This includes various applications for communications, processing, analytics and storage.
- User Interface: This is the interface between humans and machines to access IoT.

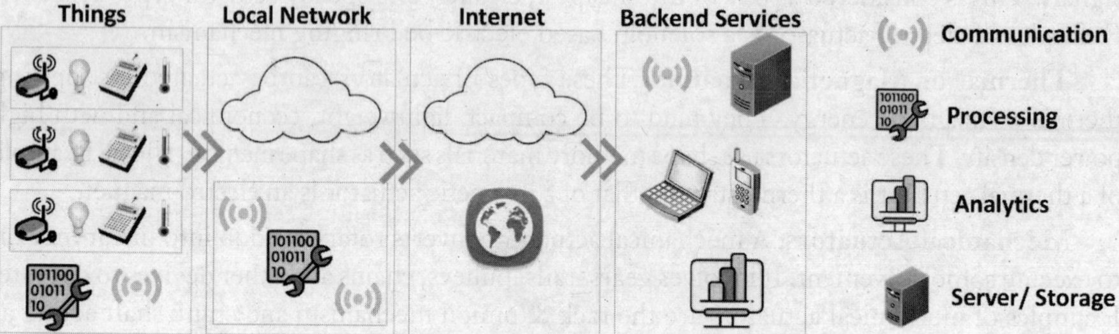

Fig.1.10: Functional Components of IoT

Now we will see the implementation of Internet of Things. Figure 1.11 shows an example for IoT implementation. On one end, we have various devices which include processors, sensor fitted equipments, radios etc which senses the data. They can also be called IoT nodes. These devices can talk to each other but they are under the jurisdiction of a gateway.

This gateway takes care of the addressing of the devices in that particular local area network. From the gateway, the sensor data passes through a proxy server to reach the Internet. Then the data passes through a Web socket. From the Web socket, the data moves on to the cloud server. It is in this cloud server back-end processing and analytics take place. Based on the analytics and inferences, the actuation takes place on the sensed data. Actuation for example may be lighting a lamp or turning off a motor or fan etc.

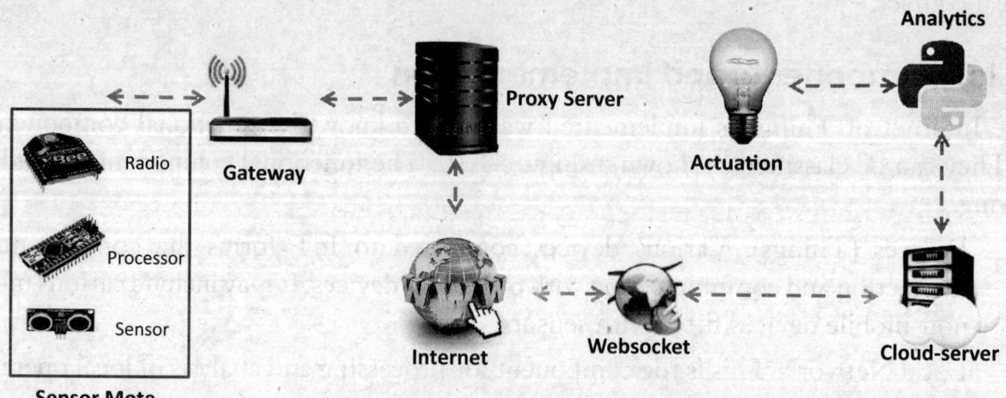

Fig.1.11: Implementation of IoT

1.9.1 Service Oriented Architecture

The service oriented architecture has four layers namely sensing layer, network layer, service layer and interface layer. Figure 1.12 shows the diagrammatic representation of service oriented architecture in IoT.

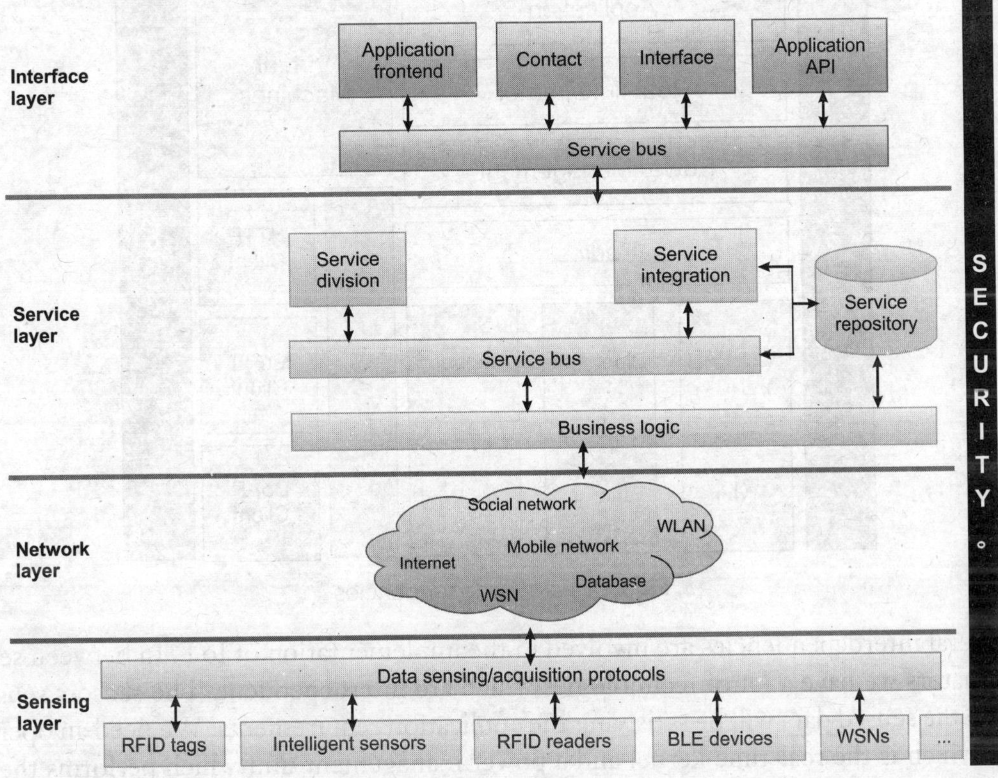

Fig.1.12: Service Oriented Architecture

The bottom most layer is the sensing layer whose prime responsibility is data sensing or taking care of the acquisition protocols. Various sensing devices like RFID tags, intelligent sensors, RFID readers, Bluetooth Low Energy (BLE) devices, wireless sensor networks etc constitute the sensing layer. The network layer above the sensing layer comprises of wireless sensor networks, Internet, mobile networks, databases, social networks and wireless LANs. The service layer comprises of the business logic, service repository, service division and service integration. The application front end, contract, API and interface forms the top most layer called the interface layer. Security is a matter of concern in all layers from top to bottom.

1.9.2 IoT Interdependencies

IoT comprises of a large number of entities like embedded devices, sensors, actuators, power management, real-time kernel, virtual machines, WWW, various clients like HTTP client, MQTT client, CoAP client etc., connectivity technologies like 6LowPan, Bluetooth, Zigbee,

WiFi, Ethernet and Low Range WiFi (LoRWiFi). Figure 1.13 shows the interdependencies between various components in IoT.

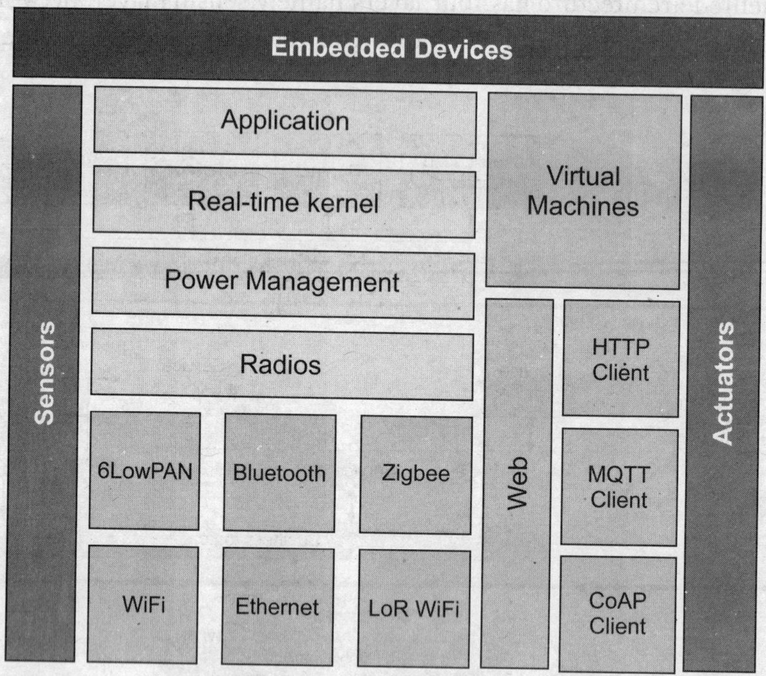

Fig.1.13: IoT Interdependencies

Several interdependencies are involved in the implementation of IoT. In between sensors and actuators we have a lot of technologies which are interdependent. The sensors sense the data and the sensed data will be satisfying the application requirements. We need an operating system which is the real-time kernel and a power management unit which performs the duty cycling of sensors. This determines how much time the sensors will be in active state, how much time will be in sleep state, how to power the sensors, how much power will be consumed, whether it can be optimized and so on. Various radios like 6LowPAN, Bluetooth, Zigbee, WiFi, Ethernet and LoR WiFi are the connectivity technologies that help to communicate the sensed data to other nodes. Virtual machines take care of the virtualization of the nodes. Different application level protocols like HTTP client, MQTT client and CoAP client help for the functioning of IoT. All these together constitute the horizontal embedded devices.

1.10 Challenges for IoT

When it comes to developing Internet of Things devices inside a laboratory, network connectivity is not a major issue. With only a few devices backed up by a server, connectivity has a very low latency and is seamless. But deploying the same IoT application on a global scale, with thousands or maybe even millions of users accessing it simultaneously, it is completely different. The Internet isn't only one network, and there are many considerations like cell towers, connectivity, firewalls, and proxy servers that can cause problems with connectivity. Following are the most discussed challenges in IoT.

Security: Security is a crucial issue on the Internet, and it is probably the most significant challenge for the IoT. When we increase the number of connected devices, the number of opportunities to exploit vulnerabilities through poorly designed devices can expose user's data to theft, especially when the data streams are left with inadequate protection. In certain cases, it may even harm the safety and health of people.

Data encryption is one method of providing data security in IoT. Internet of Things collects tons of data. Data retrieval and processing is integral part of the whole IoT environment. Most of this data is personal and needs to be protected through encryption. To address this IoT security issue we can use Secure Sockets Layer protocol or SSL wherever our data is present online. Websites already use SSL certification to encrypt and protect the user's data online. This is only half part of the equation and other half is to protect the wireless protocol side. While data is being transferred wirelessly it needs encryption as well. Sensitive data like locations need to be available and it is to be concerned with the user and no one else. Therefore make sure we use a wireless protocol with inbuilt encryption.

Data authentication is another method of providing security in IoT environment. After successful encryption of data, chances of device itself being hacked still exist. If there is no way to establish the authenticity of the data being communicated to and from an IoT device, security is compromised. For instance, say we built a temperature sensor for smart homes. Even though we encrypt the data it transfers. There is no way to authenticate the source of data then anyone can make up fake data and send it to your sensor instructing it to cool the room even when its freezing or vice versa. Authentication issues may not be upfront but they definitely pose a security risk.

Side-channel attack is yet another security issue in IoT. Encryption and authentication both are in place. Still it leaves scope for side channel attacks. Such attacks focus less on the information and more on how that information is being presented. For instance if someone can access data like timing information, power consumption or electromagnetic leak, all of this information can be used for side channel attacks.

Hardware security issues are another problem faced by IoT. With all the hype and sudden interest in IoT devices chipmakers like ARM and Intel are reinforcing their processors for more security with every new generation but the realistic scenario doesn't seem to ever close that security gap. The problem is with modern architecture of the chips made specifically for the IoT devices, the prices will go up making them expensive. Also the complex design will require more battery power which is definitely a challenge for IoT applications. Affordable wearable IoT devices won't use such chips meaning there is need for better approach.

Privacy: The Internet of Things presents some unique challenges when it comes to privacy and a lot of that goes far beyond the data privacy issues that exist currently. Much of this is due to the trouble of integrating devices into the environments without people using them consciously. This is becoming even more prevalent when it comes to consumer devices, such as tracking devices for cars and phones and also smart TVs. Vision features and voice recognition are now being integrated into smart TVs. These features can listen continuously to conversations or look for activity and transmit data selectively to cloud services for processing. These cloud services may sometimes even include third parties. The collection of all this information faces a number of regulatory and legal challenges.

Apart from this, there are a number of IoT scenarios that involve the data collection and the deployment of devices with a global or multinational scope that crosses cultural and social boundaries. If we are to realize the opportunities of the Internet of Things, strategies are going to have to be developed that respect the individual privacy choices while fostering innovation for new services and technologies.

Scalability: With exponential growth, the ability to manage efficiently those devices becomes paramount. Our business needs to be able to monitor the operation of its devices and add to its system as device functionality matures and networks evolve.

When deploying an IoT system, we have to keep in mind both current and future needs. If our system is not scalable, then it will not be able to accommodate future expansion when shifts in technology occur. This leaves businesses with unusable systems and devices that must either be replaced or augmented, and both are expensive prospects. The network can adapt when failures occur and remain mostly operational until the issue is repaired. For example, 2G technology is still being used in more than half of the world's mobile connections, and unless the companies still utilizing this technology are prepared for the network's impending sunset, they will likely find themselves with millions of useless devices on their hands in the not-so-distant future. Make sure our plans incorporate long-term support for devices based on technology projections in IoT.

Bandwidth Management: The number of devices connected to IoT network is skyrocketing. This is going to be a massive change to Internet. If we have more IoT devices trying to report data over a low bandwidth link than it is capable of carrying, then to ensure that the most important data gets through, we are going to filter out the less important data and compress the remaining data down. Hopefully the data will then fit within the available bandwidth. The obvious pitfall of this approach is the possibility of filtering out the important data if you have many IoT devices. The problem going forward with the IoT is every solution is going to be different and require different approaches to solve the network latency and bandwidth problems and therefore, it is difficult to make sweeping solution statements.

Interoperability: At the most basic level, the Internet of Things (IoT) is connectivity among people, processes and things. While this is as vast when spanning all industries, the enterprise and consumers, one of the central-most challenges in IoT is the enablement of seamless interoperability between each connection. These issues include the following.

- Different devices or equipments that are not made by the same manufacturer cannot be integrated.

- Different operating systems: inability to run on the same operating systems
- Different versions or times of purchase: devices that weren't made or purchased at the same time.
- Different/incommunicable types of connectors or connectivity frameworks (e.g. devices)
- Different/inconsistent communication protocol standards (i.e. rules)
- Lack of programs needed to connect the devices

Data Storage: The Internet of Things will have a huge impact on storage – the sheer volume of data, the radically different types of data created and the storage needed. Machine-generated data comes in two distinct types, creating two entirely different challenges. First, there is large-file data, such as images and videos captured from smart phones and other devices. This data type is typically accessed sequentially. The second data type is very small, for example, log-file data captured from sensors. These sensors, while they are small in size, can create billions of files that must be accessed randomly. There can be no single method to deal with the data generated by things, not least because there is such a wide variety of data generators and data types. For those planning storage for an IoT project, the first task is to determine the types of data the project will generate. It is also clear that data volumes are large and growing, that the data centre needs to adapt to deal with them and cloud-based storage may be one solution – but not the only one.

Data Analytics: The analysis of Internet of Things (IoT) data is quickly becoming a mainstream activity. With many data sources, it is often quite an effort to gather the source data required for analysis. It is necessary to identify what information is available, how it is formatted, and also to reconcile data from different sources that often contained similar information, but have inconsistencies in how it is provided.

Another challenge is to determine the proper frequency of sensor readings. For example, a temperature sensor may spit out a reading every millisecond. However, in most cases, receiving data at that cadence is overkill. That overkill has a price due to the cost of storing the extra data and the cost and complexity of analyzing masses of data that aren't valuable. As a result, it is necessary to determine what cadence actually has value for the problem you're tackling. If we're monitoring a car engine, readings once per second might be more than enough. The point is that we have to assess each metric and determine what you need through some experiments. Then, filter the data down to the proper level. Otherwise, we'll be overwhelmed with data and meaningful patterns will be that much harder to identify.

Another challenge is to identify complex patterns over time. The heart of many IoT analytics need to identify complex patterns or trends that occur over time. Classic time series and forecasting models are oriented towards identifying a trend and then extending it to forward. When analyzing IoT data, in contrast, we are often interested in deviations from normal rather than projecting the expected. After identifying what is normal we must work to find abnormal patterns that are of importance. However, there are multiple ways that abnormal patterns might evolve. Sudden increases in temperature would naturally draw interest. But, the impacts of a very small rise in temperature that either persists for an extended period or that comes and goes with increasing frequency is different. There is much complexity in the identification of these time-based patterns.

Next challenge is how to handle interactions between terms in a model. With sensor data, this process is much more difficult. The problem is that there can be lags between impacts. For example, temperature may start rising in advance of pressure rising. To identify the interactions between various sensor readings require complicated analysis to determine not just what metrics might interact, but also over what time frame and with what lag. This makes the analysis difficult.

Finally there exist challenges in accounting for errors and missing readings. Sensors aren't always reliable. Any analytics process must build in checks and balances to account for missing data or data that is in error. For example, if an engine sensor says temperature spiked from 300 to 1,000 degrees in one second, there is a good chance that the reading was an error. If the next reading is back to normal, it is easy to flag and correct the error. But, what about if a sensor gets moved into an improper position or breaks and bad readings continue? What if a sensor fails to transmit at all for a period of time? Our analytics processes must include logic to identify suspected errors or transmission gaps and to handle those scenarios. We don't want a multitude of warning lights or messages alerting to a problem if it is really a data issue.

Standards: A lack of documented or standard best practices has had a much larger impact on Internet of Things devices that goes well beyond simply limiting their development and potential. An absence of standards may well enable inappropriate behavior by IoT devices. Without the right standards to guide and regulate manufacturers, developers may design products that operate in any number of disruptive ways online without regard for their impact. If they are configured or designed poorly, these devices may have negative consequences for networking resources they connect to and, in the broader picture, the Internet itself. A lot of this is caused by cost constraints as well as the need to develop products and get them to market before their competitors. When we add the difficulties of configuring and managing a large number of IoT devices, the need for standardization of methods, interfaces, configuration tools, and thoughtful design, along with IPv6 adoption, which is essential for the future.

Regulation: Just like privacy, there are a number of legal and regulatory questions that surround the Internet of Things. This also needs some thoughtful consideration. Legal issues concerning Internet of Things devices aren't limited to potential violations of civil rights because of law-enforcement surveillance. Other issues that must be considered are cross-border data flow, legal liability when it comes to unintended use, privacy lapses and security breaches. Also, technology is advancing at a much faster pace than regulatory policies and the agencies charged with setting and supervising IoT guidelines cannot keep up with the pace of technology.

1.11 Conclusion

This Chapter gives an introduction to Internet of Things. The characteristics of IoT, applications of IoT, various categories of IoT including consumer IoT and industrial IoT is explained. Further the different IoT enablers - implementation perspective, connectivity methods & enabling technologies and connectivity layers – services layer, local connectivity and global connectivity are illustrated with diagrams. Important baseline technologies closely related to Internet of Things like Machine-to-Machine communication, Cyber-Physical systems and Web of Things are explained in this Chapter. Sensors which provide data or input to IoT network with its characteristics are described. The different types of sensors – analog, digital, scalar and vector sensors are illustrated with examples. Another important component of IoT network is the actuator that needs to take actions according to the sensed data. Various types of actuators based on the technology used – hydraulic, pneumatic, electrical, thermal/ magnetic, mechanical and soft actuators are illustrated. The components of IoT and how IoT is implemented is explained with necessary diagrams. The service oriented architecture and dependencies between various components in IoT are described. Finally, the challenges faced in IoT implementation and how it could be mitigated is discussed in detail. After reading this Chapter, the reader will get a clear idea about the basic concepts in IoT. In the forthcoming Chapters, we will have a detailed study of all the components discussed in this Chapter.

2 IOT NETWORKING

2.1 Connectivity Terminologies

The number of IoT connected devices will increase drastically in near future. The reason is the integration of existing devices, smart devices as well as constrained nodes in a singular framework. There will be need for the integration of various connectivity features such as cellular, Wi-Fi, Ethernet with upcoming ones such as Bluetooth Low Energy (BLE), Dash7, Instead, IEEE 802.15.4 etc. We need to understand the basic connectivity terminologies in Internet of Things before going with network configurations and various protocols used in IoT. Following are the connectivity terminologies used in IoT.

IoT Node- These are machines, things or computers connected to other nodes inside a LAN via the IoT LAN. This node may be sometimes connected to the Internet through a WAN directly.

IoT LAN- Local Area Network or LAN is short to medium range, where distances can be up to hundreds of meters, such as home automation or sensors that are installed within a factory production line that communicate over Wi-Fi with a gateway device that is installed within the same building. It is an organization wide network which may or may not be connected to Internet. Figure 2.1 shows the architecture of IoT LAN where L represents a node in the Local Area Network.

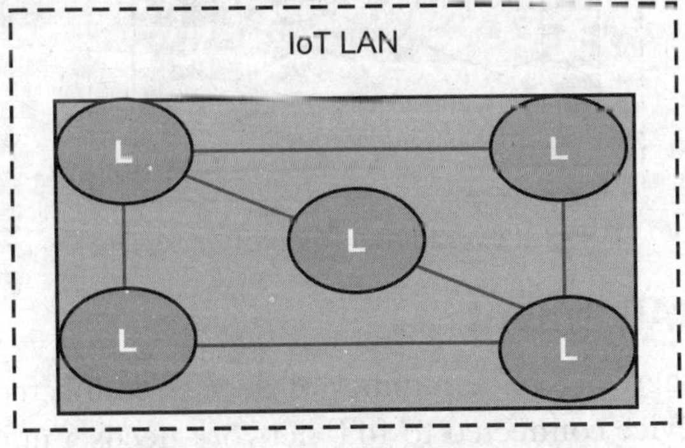

Fig.2.1: Architecture of IoT LAN

IoT WAN- Wide Area Networks or WAN is the connection of various network segments organizationally and geographically wide which connects to the Internet. It may consist of several LANs. Each node in a LAN will have a unique address but another node in a different LAN may have the same address. Different LANs are connected to WAN via gateways. Figure 2.2 shows the architecture of IoT WAN and IoT Gateway, where LU represents Locally Unique address.

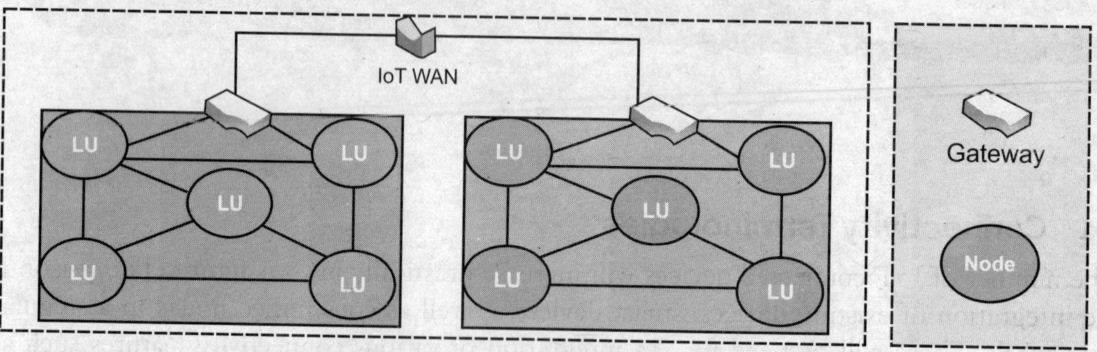

Fig.2.2: Architecture of IoT WAN and IoT Gateway

IoT Gateway-This is a router connecting the IoT LAN to a WAN or to the Internet. It can implement several LANs and WANs. The main responsibility of IoT gateways is to forward packets between LAN and WAN on the IP layer.

IoT Proxy-This performs active application layer functions between IoT nodes and other entities. Figure 2.3 shows the architecture of IoT Proxy, where LU represents Locally Unique address.

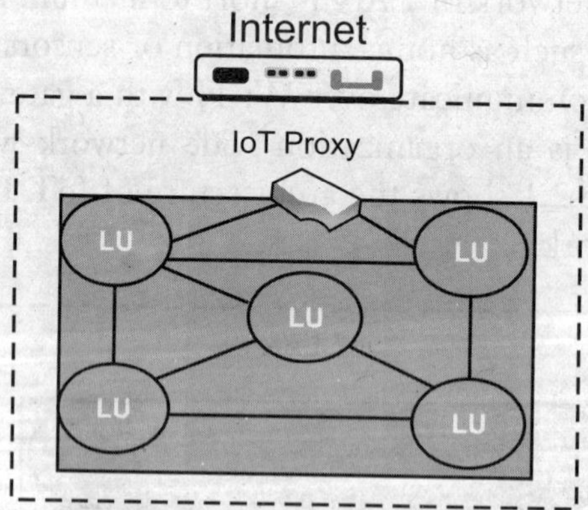

Fig.2.3: Architecture of IoT Proxy

2.2 Gateway Prefix Allotment

In IoT addressing, since there are huge number of devices connected, we need to conserve the address space. Each device connected to IoT network needs a unique IP address. Nodes within a gateway's jurisdiction have addresses that are valid within the gateway's domain only.

The same addresses may be repeated in the domain of another gateway. The gateway has a ***unique network prefix*** which can be used to identify them globally. This strategy saves a lot of unnecessary address wastage although the nodes have to communicate to the Internet via the gateway.

One of the strategies of address conservation in IoT is to use local addresses which exist uniquely within the domain of the gateway. Figure 2.4 shows the diagram of gateway prefix allotment. In Figure 2.4, the nodes that come under the jurisdiction are denoted using circles. The network connected to the internet has routers with their set of addresses and ranges. These routers have multiple gateways connected to them which can forward packets from the nodes to Internet only via the routers. These routers assign prefixes to gateways under them so that the gateways can be identified with them.

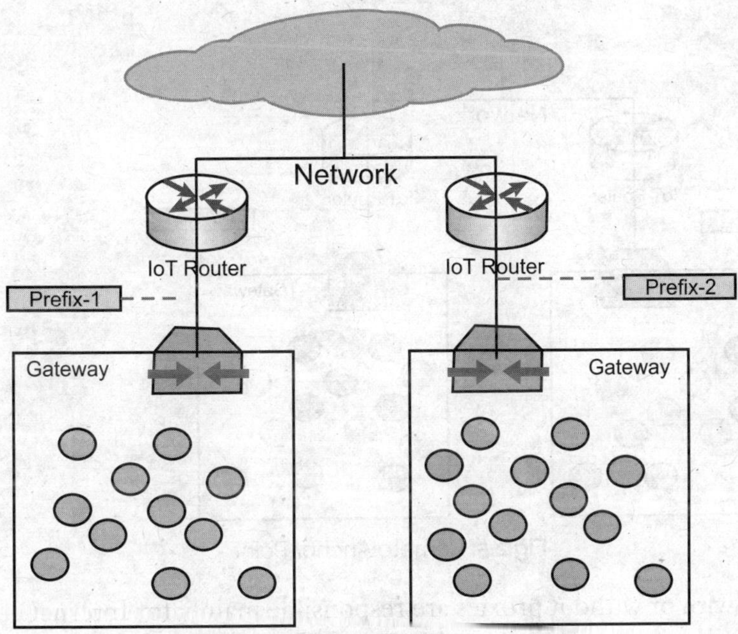

Fig.2.4: Gateway Prefix Allotment

2.3 Impact of Mobility on Addressing

There is a great impact on IoT addressing as devices move in a network. Consider Figure 2.4 for gateway prefix allotment. The network prefix changes from 1 to 2 due to the movement making the IoT LAN safe from changes due to movements. IoT gateway WAN address changes without change in IoT LAN address. This is achieved using Unique Local Address (ULA).

The gateways assigned with prefixes are attached to a remote anchor point by using various protocols such as mobile IPv6 and are immune to changes of network prefixes. Figure 2.5 shows the diagram of remote anchor point.

The address of the nodes within the gateways remain unchanged as the gateways provide them with locally unique address and the change in gateway's network prefix doesn't affect them. Sometimes there is a need for the nodes to communicate directly to the Internet. This is achieved by tunneling. In tunneling, the nodes communicate to a remote anchor point instead of channeling the packets through the routers. This is achieved by using tunneling protocols such as Internet Key Exchange version 2 (IKEv2).

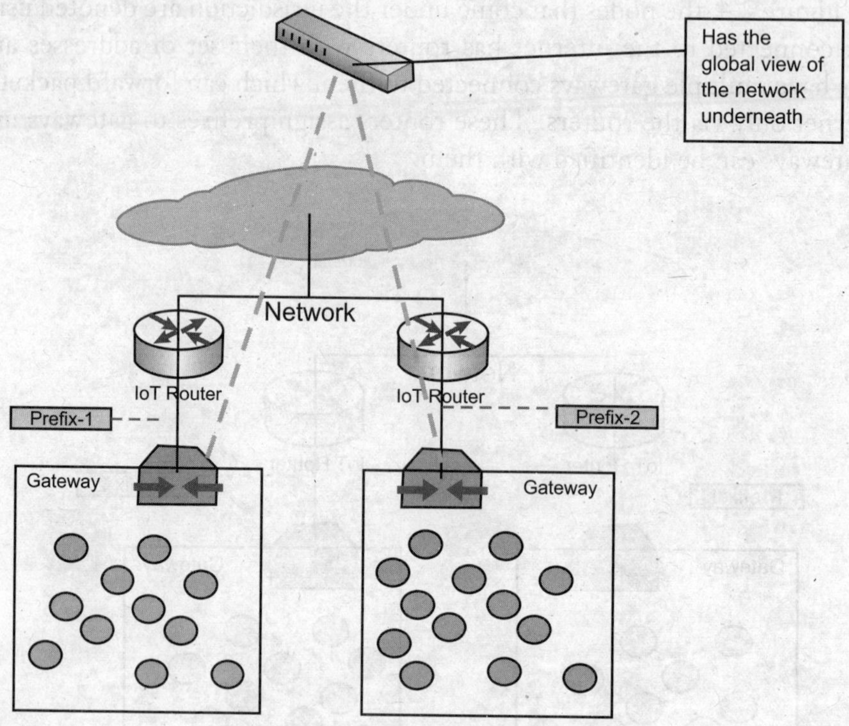

Fig.2.5: Remote Anchor Point

IoT gateways with or without proxies are responsible mainly for Internet connectivity and IoT LAN intra-connectivity. Upstream address prefixes are obtained using mechanisms like Dynamic Host Configuration Protocol version 6 (DHCPv6). The Dynamic Host Configuration Protocol version 6 (DHCPv6) is a network protocol for configuring Internet Protocol version 6 (IPv6) hosts with IP addresses, IP prefixes and other configuration data required to operate in an IPv6 network. It is the IPv6 equivalent of the Dynamic Host Configuration Protocol for IPv4. We will discuss more about IPv4 and IPv6 later in this Chapter. After obtaining upstream address prefixes, it is then delegated to the nodes using stateless addressing (SLAAC). SLAAC provides the ability to address a host based on a network prefix that is advertised from a local network router via Router Advertisements (RA).

Unique Local Addresses (ULA) is maintained independently of globally routable addresses in the case where internal address stability is of prime concern. Despite providing address stability, ULA cannot communicate directly with the Internet or the upper layers which is solved by an application layer proxy. Application layer proxies may be additionally configured to process data, rather than just passing it. In nodes with no support for computationally intensive tasks, IoT proxy gathers data sent to the link-local multicast address and routes them globally.

2.4 Multihoming

Multihoming is the practice of connecting a host or a computer network to more than one network. This can be done in order to increase reliability or performance, or to reduce cost. There are several different ways to perform multihoming.

(a) **Host multihoming**: In this a single host may be connected to multiple networks. For example, a mobile phone might be simultaneously connected to a Wi-Fi network and a 3G network, and a desktop computer might be connected to both a home network and a VPN. A multihomed host usually is assigned multiple addresses, one per connected network.

(b) **Classical multihoming**: In classical multihoming, a network is connected to multiple providers, and uses its own range of addresses (typically from a Provider Independent (PI) range). The network's edge routers communicate with the providers using a dynamic routing protocol, typically Border Gateway Protocol (BGP), which announces the network's address range to all providers. If one of the links fail, the dynamic routing protocol recognizes the failure within seconds or minutes, and reconfigures its routing tables to use the remaining links, transparently to the hosts. Classical multihoming is costly, since it requires the use of address space that is accepted by all providers, a public Autonomous System (AS) number, and a dynamic routing protocol. Since multihomed address space cannot be aggregated, it causes growth of the global routing table.

(c) **Multihoming with multiple addresses**: In this approach, the network is connected to multiple providers, and assigned multiple address ranges, one for each provider. Hosts are assigned multiple addresses, one for each provider. Multihoming with multiple addresses is cheaper than classical multihoming, and can be used without any cooperation from the providers (e.g. in a home network) but requires additional technology in order to perform routing.

In case of small IoT LANs where allotment of address prefixes is not feasible and possible, a proxy based approach is used to manage multiple IP addresses. And map them to link local addresses. In another approach, gateway based approach is used for assigning link local addresses to the nodes under it. Providing source addresses, destination addresses and routing information to the multihomed nodes is the real challenge in multihoming networks.

2.5 Deviations from Regular Web

In this section, we will have a comparison of the communication networks in Web and communication networks in IoT. The various layers in ISO/OSI layer and communication layers in IoT have many similarities. But there are differences in the protocols used at various layers of IoT. Figure 2.6 shows the comparison of the protocols of IoT stack and Web stack.

We have already seen the four layers of IoT in Chapter 1. The four layers include the sensing layer, network layer, service layer and interface layer. The sensing layer in IoT is equivalent to physical layer and data link layer of OSI reference model. The protocols used in IoT are IEEE 802.15.4 MAC and IEEE 802.15.4 PHY/Radio for this layer while protocols for OSI layer are Ethernet, DSL, ISDN, Wireless LAN, Wi-Fi. Similarly in the network layer, the protocols used are IPv6 and 6LowPAN in IoT whereas the protocols used in OSI are IPv4, IPv6 and IPSec. Again the protocols used in service layer in IoT are UDP and DTLS while the protocols in transport layer for web are TCP and UDP. The application layer in OSI is similar to the interface layer in IoT. The protocols used in IoT and web are different as they are intended for different purposes. Unlike web stack, we can see in addition to the protocols in IoT, there is a management component in IoT stack. This is essential because there are a large number of devices, networks and other resources which needs to be managed efficiently.

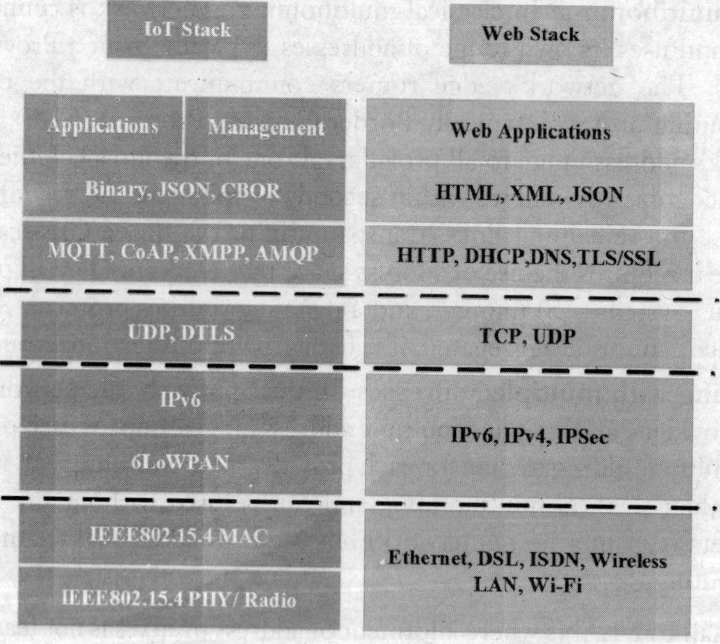

Fig.2.6: Comparisons of IoT and Web Stacks

2.6 IoT Identification and Data Protocols

The Internet of Things covers a huge range of industries and use cases that scale from a single constrained device up to massive cross-platform deployments of embedded technologies and cloud systems connecting in real-time. There are all together numerous legacy and emerging communication protocols that allow devices and servers to talk to each other in new, more interconnected ways. Rather than trying to fit all of the IoT protocols on top of existing architecture models like OSI Model, we have broken the protocols into the following layers to provide some level of organization.

Infrastructure (ex: 6LowPAN, IPv4/IPv6, RPL)

Identification (ex: EPC, uCodc, IPv6, URIs)

Comms / Transport (ex: Wi-Fi, Bluetooth, and LPWAN)

Discovery (ex: Physical Web, mDNS, DNS-SD)

Data Protocols (ex: MQTT, CoAP, AMQP, Websocket, Node)

Device Management (ex: TR-069, OMA-DM)

Semantic (ex: JSON-LD, Web Thing Model)

Multi-layer Frameworks (ex: Alljoyn, IoTivity, Weave, Homekit)

In this Chapter we will be discussing about infrastructure protocols like IPv4, IPv6 and data protocols like MQTT, CoAP, AMQP etc. Other commonly used protocols will be discussed in the upcoming Chapter.

2.6.1 IPv4

Internet Protocol Version 4 (IPv4) is the fourth revision of the Internet Protocol and a widely used protocol in data communication over different kinds of networks. IPv4 is a connectionless protocol used in packet-switched layer networks, such as Ethernet. It provides the logical connection between network devices by providing identification for each device. There are many ways to configure IPv4 with all kinds of devices – including manual and automatic configurations – depending on the network type.

IPv4 is based on the best-effort model. This model guarantees neither delivery nor avoidance of duplicate delivery. These aspects are handled by the upper layer transport. IPv4 is defined and specified in IETF publication RFC 791. It is used in the packet-switched link layer in the OSI model. IPv4 uses 32-bit addresses for Ethernet communication in five classes: A, B, C, D and E. Classes A, B and C have a different bit length for addressing the network host. Class D addresses are reserved for multicasting, while class E addresses are reserved for future use.

Class A has subnet mask 255.0.0.0 or /8, B has subnet mask 255.255.0.0 or /16 and class C has subnet mask 255.255.255.0 or /24. For example, with a /16 subnet mask, the network 192.168.0.0 may use the address range of 192.168.0.0 to 192.168.255.255. Network.hosts can take any address from this range; however, address 192.168.255.255 is reserved for broadcast within the network. The maximum number of host addresses IPv4 can assign to end users is 232. IPv6 presents a standardized solution to overcome IPv4's limitations. Because of its 128-bit address length, it can define up to 2,128 addresses.

Presently, the Internet is mainly IPv4 based with little or no IPv6 uplink facilities or support. Due to the lack of a universal solution to IPv6, lots of un-optimized solutions are being used for IoT deployment. These makeshift solutions mainly address IPv6 to IPv4 translation, IPv6 tunneling over IPv4 and application layer proxies like data relaying. Figure 2.7 shows an IPv4 header format.

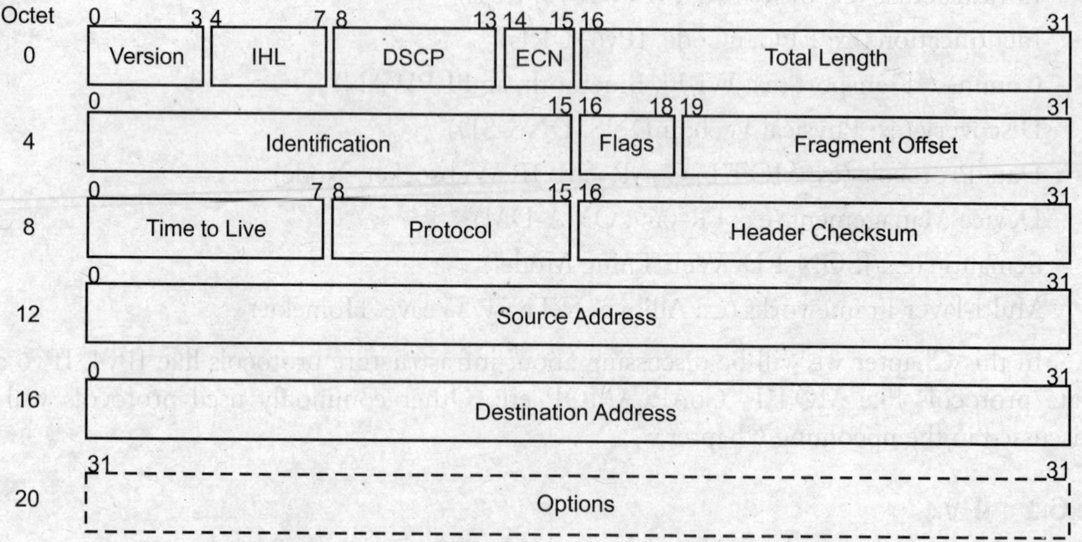

Fig.2.7: IPv4 Header Format

IPv4 header includes several relevant information as follows.

Version: Version no. of Internet Protocol used (e.g. IPv4).

IHL: Internet Header Length. Gives the length of entire IP header.

DSCP: Differentiated Services Code Point. This is a type of service.

ECN: Explicit Congestion Notification. It carries information about the congestion seen in the route.

Total Length: Length of entire IP Packet (including IP header and IP Payload).

Identification: If IP packet is fragmented during the transmission, all the fragments contain same identification number. This is to identify original IP packet they belong to.

Flags: As required by the network resources, if IP Packet is too large to handle, these 'flags' tells if they can be fragmented or not. In this 3-bit flag, the MSB is always set to '0'.

Fragment Offset: This offset tells the exact position of the fragment in the original IP Packet.

Time to Live: To avoid looping in the network, every packet is sent with some TTL value set, which tells the network how many routers (hops) this packet can cross. At each hop, its value is decremented by one and when the value reaches zero, the packet is discarded.

Protocol: Tells the Network layer at the destination host, to which Protocol this packet belongs to, i.e. the next level Protocol. For example protocol number of ICMP is 1, TCP is 6 and UDP is 17.

Header Checksum: This field is used to keep checksum value of entire header which is then used to check if the packet is received error-free.

Source Address: 32-bit address of the Sender (or source) of the packet.

Destination Address: 32-bit address of the receiver (or destination) of the packet.

Options: This is optional field, which is used if the value of IHL is greater than 5. These options may contain values for options such as security, record route, time stamp, etc.

IPv4 emphasizes more on reliable transmission, as is evident by fields such as type of service, total length, identification, fragment offset, TTL and checksum fields.

2.6.2 IPv6

IPv6 (Internet Protocol version 6) is a set of specifications from the Internet Engineering Task Force (IETF) that's essentially an upgrade of IP version 4 (IPv4). The basics of IPv6 are similar to those of IPv4 -- devices can use IPv6 as source and destination addresses to pass packets over a network, and tools like ping work for network testing as they do in IPv4, with some slight variations. The most obvious improvement in IPv6 over IPv4 is that IP addresses are lengthened from 32 bits to 128 bits. This extension anticipates considerable future growth of the Internet and provides relief for what was perceived as an impending shortage of network addresses. IPv6 also supports auto-configuration to help correct most of the shortcomings in version 4, and it has integrated security and mobility features.

IPv4 is Internet Protocol version 4 and it describes what the numbers used by every device that connects to the Internet must look like (for example, 192.168.0.254). Based on this model, the early Internet architects made an estimated 4.3 billion numbers available and at the beginning of the Internet age, that number probably seemed inexhaustible. However, over the last couple of decade's network, cloud, and mobile technologies have rapidly reduced the number of available IP addresses as each new technology added devices to the global Internet. When the IP addresses inventory first began to shrink and it appeared the IPv4 supply of numbers were being consumed at a higher than expected rate, plans were devised to transition to a new protocol called IPv6 that would provide for a significantly larger supply of numbers. Although implementing IPv6 would solve a problem that has been known for over a decade, no one has been in a hurry to adopt the new standard.

The reason for this is that to make the switch to IPv6 would require anyone who connects to the Internet to move from the IPv4 protocol to IPv6. IPv4 and IPv6 are not compatible and finding ways to run both protocols without affect users, businesses, and service providers. Still, the transition to IPv6 will solve the problem of running out of available IP addresses. The number of IPv4 addresses in the pool is 232 or 4,294,967,296 (approximately 4.29 billion). Switching to IPv6 would make 2128 or 340 Undecillion (or 340,282,366,920,938,000,000,000,000,000,000,000,000) addresses available. With so many addresses available, it would be unlikely that a transition of this type would ever need to happen again.

Figure 2.8 shows the IPv6 header format.

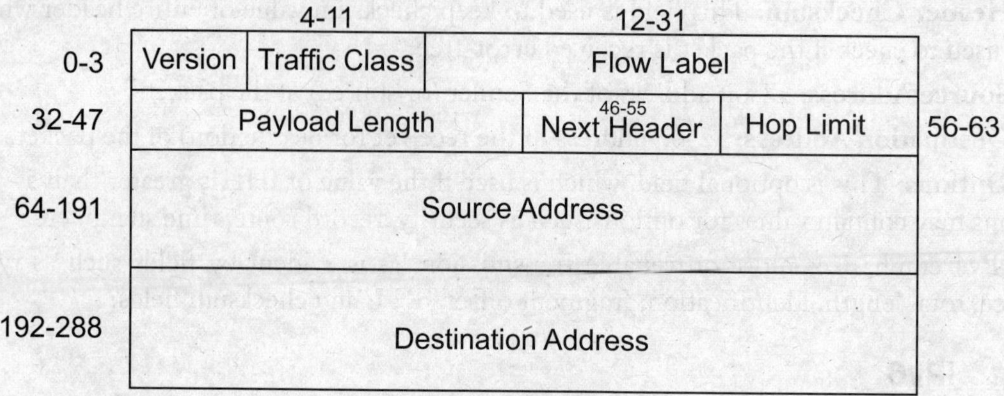

Fig.2.8: IPv6 Header Format

IPv6 header includes several relevant information as follows.

Version (4-bits): It represents the version of Internet Protocol, i.e. 0110.

Traffic Class (8-bits): These 8 bits are divided into two parts. The most significant 6 bits are used for Type of Service to let the router known what services should be provided to this packet. The least significant 2 bits are used for Explicit Congestion Notification (ECN).

Flow Label (20-bits): This label is used to maintain the sequential flow of the packets belonging to a communication. The source labels the sequence to help the router identify that a particular packet belongs to a specific flow of information. This field helps avoid re-ordering of data packets. It is designed for streaming/real-time media.

Payload Length (16-bits): This field is used to tell the routers how much information a particular packet contains in its payload. Payload is composed of Extension Headers and Upper Layer data. With 16 bits, up to 65535 bytes can be indicated; but if the Extension Headers contain Hop-by-Hop Extension Header, then the payload may exceed 65535 bytes and this field is set to 0.

Next Header (8-bits): This field is used to indicate either the type of Extension Header, or if the Extension Header is not present then it indicates the Upper Layer PDU. The values for the type of Upper Layer PDU are same as IPv4's.

Hop Limit (8-bits): This field is used to stop packet to loop in the network infinitely. This is same as TTL in IPv4. The value of Hop Limit field is decremented by 1 as it passes a link (router/hop). When the field reaches 0 the packet is discarded.

Source Address (128-bits): This field indicates the address of originator of the packet.

Destination Address (128-bits): This field provides the address of intended recipient of the packet.

IPv6 header structure is simpler as it mainly focuses on the addressing part of the source and destination. It is concerned more with addressing than with reliability of data delivery. A comparison of IPv4 and IPv6 is given in Figure 2.9.

	IPv4	IPv6
Developed by	IETF 1974	IEF 1998
Length (bits)	32	128
No: of addresses	2^{32}	2^{128}
Notation	Dotted Decimal	Hexadecimal
Dynamic allocation	DHCP	SLAAC/DHCPv6
IPSec	Optional	Compulsory
Header Size	Variable	Fixed
Header Checksum	Yes	No
Header Options	Yes	No
Broadcast Addresses	Yes	No
Multicast Address	No	Yes

Fig.2.9: IPv4 versus IPv6

2.6.3 MQTT

MQTT or Message Queuing Telemetry Transport is an ISO standard (ISO/IEC PRF 20922). It is a publish-subscribe-based light weight messaging protocol used in conjunction with TCP/IP protocol. It works on top of the TCP/IP protocol. It is designed for connections with remote locations or the network bandwidth is limited. MQTT was introduced by IBM in 1999 and standardized by OASIS in 2013. It is designed to provide connectivity mostly embedded between applications and middlewares on one side and networks & communications on the other side. Figure 2.10 shows the components of MQTT.

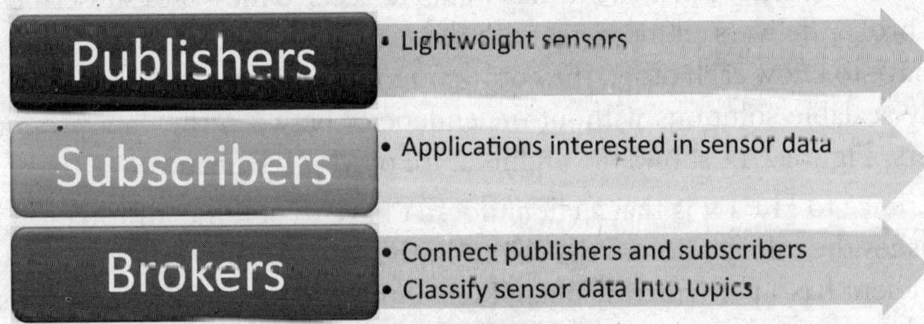

Fig.2.10: Components of MQTT

Publishers are usually light weight sensors and subscribers are applications which are interested in sensor data. A topic to which a client/subscriber is subscribed is updated in the form of messages and distributed by the message broker. MQTT client can be any device, from a micro controller to a fully-fledged server, which runs the MQTT library and is connected to MQTT broker over any network. MQTT client libraries are available across a wide variety of programming language platforms like C, C++, C#, Java, JavaScript, Android, iOS etc. A message broker controls the publish-subscribe messaging pattern. Brokers connect publishers and subscribers. MQTT Broker is responsible for receiving all messages, filtering, decision making and sending messages to subscribed clients. MQTT is based on TCP/IP, hence both client and broker is expected to have TCP/IP stack.

Methods in MQTT

MQTT methods are also referred to as verbs. MQTT defines methods to indicate desired actions to be performed on identified resources. Resources can be files or the outputs of an executable program found on a server.

(a) **Connect** – Waits for connection to be established with the server.

(b) **Disconnect** – Waits for the MQTT client to finish any work, which needs to be done and for the TCP/IP session to disconnect.

(c) **Subscribe** – Requests the server to let the client subscribe to one or more topics.

(d) **Unsubscribe** – Requests the server to let the client unsubscribe from one or more topics.

(e) **Publish** – Publishes the data from sensors or end devices. Returns immediately to application thread after passing request to the MQTT client.

Working of MQTT

The protocol uses a publish/subscribe architecture in contrast to HTTP with its request/response paradigm. Publish/Subscribe is event-driven and enables messages to be pushed to clients. The central communication point is the MQTT broker, which is in charge of dispatching all messages between the senders and the rightful receivers. Each client that publishes a message to the broker includes a topic into the message. The topic is the routing information for the broker. Each client that wants to receive messages subscribes to a certain topic and the broker delivers all messages with the matching topic to the client. Therefore the clients don't have to know each other, they only communicate over the topic. This architecture enables highly scalable solutions without dependencies between the data producers and the data consumers. Figure 2.11 shows the architecture of MQTT protocol.

The difference to HTTP is that a client doesn't have to pull the information it needs, but the broker pushes the information to the client, in the case there is something new. Therefore each MQTT client has a permanently open TCP connection to the broker. If this connection is interrupted by any circumstances, the MQTT broker can buffer all messages and send them to the client when it is back online.

The central concepts in MQTT to dispatch messages are topics. A topic is a simple string that can have more hierarchy levels, which are separated by a slash. A sample topic for sending temperature data of the living room could be ***house/living-room/temperature***. On one hand the client can subscribe to the exact topic or on the other hand use a **wildcard**.

The subscription to ***house/+/temperature*** would result in all message send to the previously mentioned topic ***house/living-room/temperature*** as well as any topic with an arbitrary value in the place of living room, for example ***house/kitchen/temperature***. The plus sign is a single level wild card and only allows arbitrary values for one hierarchy. If you need to subscribe to more than one level, for example to the entire sub-tree, there is also a **multilevel wildcard (#)**. It allows subscribing to all underlying hierarchy levels. For example ***house/#*** is subscribing to all topics beginning with house.

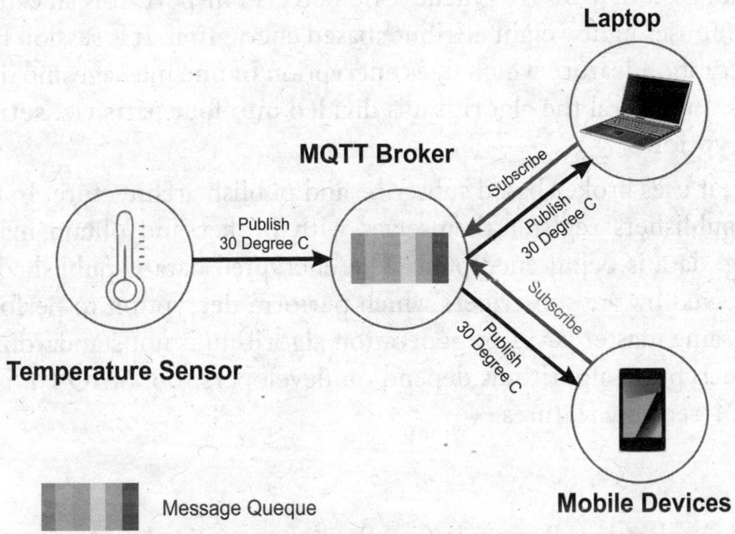

Fig.2.11: Architecture of MQTT

Applications of MQTT

There are several projects that implement MQTT. Facebook Messenger has used aspects of MQTT in Facebook Messenger for online chat. IECC Signaling Control System uses MQTT for communications within the various parts of the system and other components of the signaling system. It provides the underlying communications framework for a system that is compliant with the CENELEC standards for safety-critical communications. The EVRYTHNG IoT platform uses MQTT as an M2M protocol for millions of connected products. Amazon Web Services announced Amazon IoT based on MQTT. The Open Geospatial Consortium SensorThings API standard specification has a MQTT extension in the standard as an additional message protocol binding. It was demonstrated in a US Department of Homeland Security IoT Pilot. Ad fruit launched a free MQTT cloud service for IoT experimenters and learners called Ad fruit IO. Microsoft Azure IoT Hub uses MQTT as its main protocol for telemetry messages. XIM, Inc. launched an MQTT client called MQTT Buddy in 2017. It's a MQTT app for Android and iOS, but not F-Droid, users available in English, Russian and Chinese languages. Open-source software home automation platform Home Assistant is MQTT enabled and offers four options for MQTT brokers. Pimatic home automation framework for Raspberry Pi and based on Node.js offers MQTT plug in providing full support for MQTT protocol. McAfee Open DXL is based on MQTT with enhancements to the messaging brokers themselves so that they can intrinsically understand the DXL message format in support of advanced features such as services, request/response (point-to-point) messaging and service zones.

SMQTT

SMQTT stands for Secure Message Queue Telemetry Transport. It is an extension to simple MQTT protocol. It uses light weight attribute based encryption. It is session layer protocol. It has broadcast encryption feature which does encryption of one message and delivers the same to multiple nodes. In general the algorithm is divided into four parts viz. **setup, encryption, publish** and **decryption**.

Like MQTT, it uses broker based subscribe and publish architecture. In the setup phase, subscribers and publishers register themselves with broker and obtain master secret key. Before publishing, data is being encrypted. The encrypted data is published by the broker. This is being received by the subscribers which perform decryption to perform decoding of the data with the same master key. Key generation algorithm is not standardized and depends on developers. Encryption algorithms depend on developers too. SMQTT is proposed only to enhance MQTT security features.

2.6.4 CoAP

The Constrained Application Protocol (CoAP) is a specialized web transfer protocol for use with constrained nodes and constrained (e.g., low-power, lossy) networks. The nodes often have 8-bit microcontrollers with small amounts of ROM and RAM, while constrained networks such as IPv6 over Low-Power Wireless Personal Area Networks (6LoWPANs) often have high packet error rates and a typical throughput of 10s of Kbit/s. 6LoWPANs will be discussed in the next Chapter. The protocol is designed for machine- to-machine (M2M) applications such as smart energy and building automation.

Features of CoAP

Following are the features of CoAP.

(a) Overhead and parsing complexity.

(b) URI and content-type support.

(c) Support for the discovery of resources provided by known CoAP services.

(d) Simple subscription for a resource and resulting push notifications.

(e) Simple caching based on maximum message age.

CoAP provides a request/response interaction model between application end points. It supports built-in discovery of services and resources and includes key concepts of the Web such as URIs and Internet media types. CoAP is designed to easily interface with HTTP for integration with the Web while meeting specialized requirements such as multicast support, very low overhead and simplicity for constrained environments. In CoAP, client-server interaction is asynchronous over a datagram oriented transport protocol such as User Datagram Protocol (UDP). The Constrained Application Protocol (CoAP) is a session layer protocol designed by IETF constrained RESTful Environment (CORE) working group to provide light weight RESTful interface. REST is Representational State Transfer, which is the standard interface between HTTP client and servers.

Light weight applications such as those in IoT could result in significant overhead and power consumption by REST. CoAP is designed to enable low power sensors to use RESTful services while meeting their power constraints. Unlike HTTP which is built with TCP, CoAP is built with UDP and has a light mechanism to provide reliability.

CoAP Architecture

CoAP architecture contains four layers namely application, request/response, messages and UDP. Figure 2.12 shows various layers in CoAP.

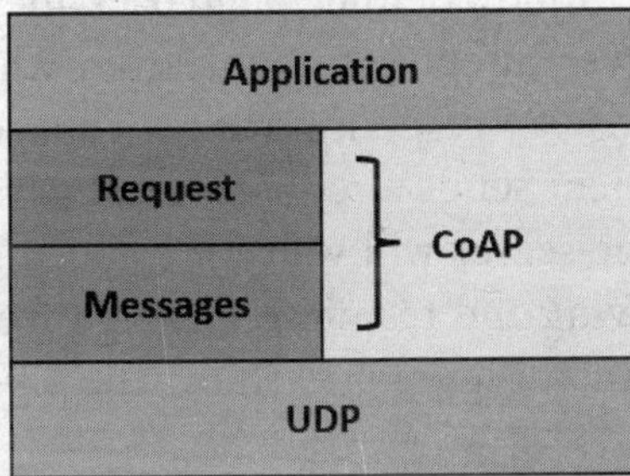

Fig.2.12: Layers in CoAP

The two main sub layers in CoAP are messaging and request/response sub layers. The messaging sub layer is responsible for reliability and duplication of messages while the request/response sub layer is responsible for communication. CoAP has four messaging modes.

1. Confirmable
2. Non-confirmable
3. Piggyback
4. Separate

Confirmable messaging mode represents reliable transmission whereas non-confirmable messaging mode represents unreliable transmission. Figure 2.13 shows the confirmable and non-confirmable messaging.

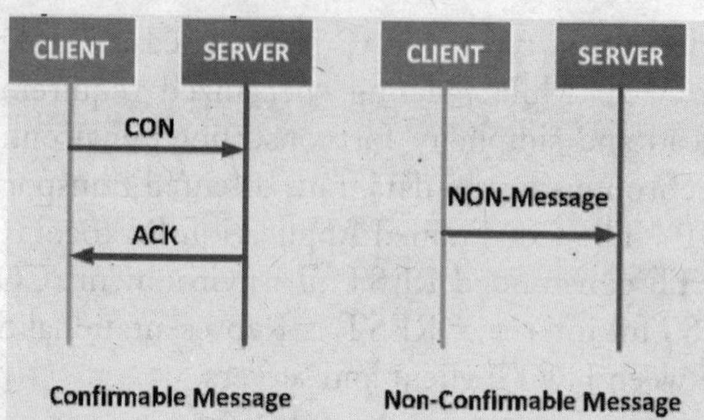

Fig.2.13: Confirmable and Non-confirmable Messaging

In confirmable messaging, the client keeps retransmission until it gets ACK with the same message ID. The client uses a default time out and decreases counting time exponentially when transmitting CON. If recipient fail to process message, it responses by replacing ACK with RST (Reset). In non-confirmable messaging, the client sends a message and does not wait for the acknowledgement. It doesn't need to be ACKed, but has to contain message ID for supervising in case of retransmission. If recipient fail to process message, server replies RST.

The request/response model follows either piggyback messaging or separate messaging. Piggyback is used for client/server direct communication where the client sends a request to the server. The server sends its response within the acknowledgement message. In separate messaging mode, the client sends a request to the server. The server sends back the acknowledgement separately. The server will wait for a specified time interval and then send the response message. On receiving the response message from the server, the client sends back acknowledgement to the server. Figure 2.14 shows the piggyback and separate messaging modes.

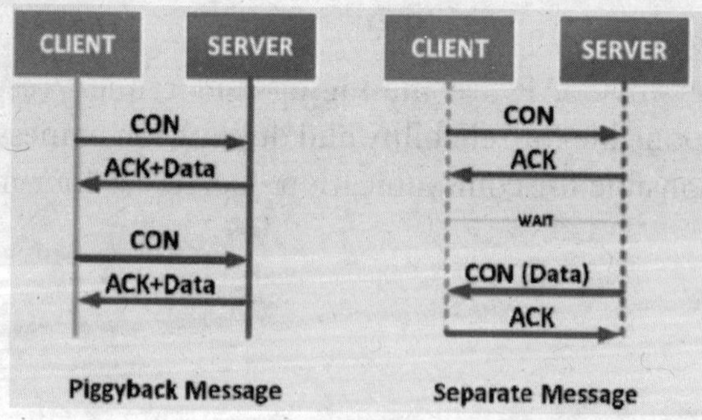

Fig.2.14: Piggyback and Separate Messaging

In piggybacking, client sends request using CON type or NON type message and receives response ACK with confirmable message immediately. For successful response, ACK contain response message (identify by using token), and for failure response, ACK contain failure response code. In separate message mode, if server receives a CON type message but not able to response this request immediately, it will send an empty ACK. In this case, client resends this message. When server is ready to response this request, it will send a new CON to client and client reply a confirmable message with acknowledgment. ACK is just to confirm CON message, no matter CON message carry request or response. Similar to HTTP, CoAP utilizes GET, PUT, PUSH and DELETE messages to retrieve, create, update and delete messages respectively.

2.6.5 XMPP

Extensible Messaging and Presence Protocol (XMPP) is a communication protocol for message-oriented middleware based on XML (Extensible Markup Language). It enables the real time exchange of structured yet extensible data between any two or more network entities. Designed to be extensible, the protocol has been used also for publish-subscribe systems, signaling for VoIP, video, file transfer, gaming, Internet of Things (IoT) applications such as the smart grid, and social networking services.

Unlike most instant messaging protocols, XMPP is defined in an open standard and uses an open systems approach of development and application, by which anyone may implement an XMPP service and interoperate with other organizations' implementations. Since this is an open standard, it supports M2M or peer-to-peer communications across a diverse set of networks. The XMPP network uses client server architecture. By design, there is no central authoritative server. XMPP provides for the discovery of services residing locally or across a network and the availability information of these services. This is well suited for cloud computing where virtual machines, networks and firewalls would otherwise present obstacles to alternative service discovery and presence based solutions. Figure 2.15 shows the architecture of XMPP.

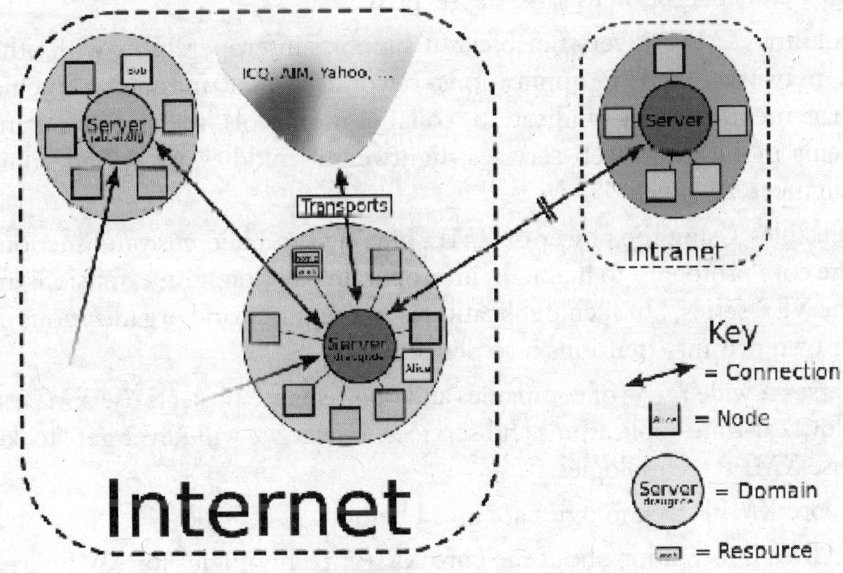

Fig.2.15: Architecture of XMPP

Following are the features of XMPP.

1. Proven – The first Jabber/XMPP technologies were developed by Jeremie Miller in 1998 and are now quite stable. Hundreds of developers are working on this technology. There are tens of thousands of XMPP servers running on the Internet today and millions of people use XMPP for instant messaging through public services such as Google Talk and XMPP deployments at organizations worldwide.
2. Decentralization – There is no central server. Anyone can run their own XMPP server. The architecture of the XMPP network is similar to email. This enables individuals and organizations to take control of their communications experience.
3. Open Standards – The XMPP protocols are free, open, public, and easily understandable. In addition, multiple implementations exist in the form clients, servers, server components, and code libraries. Since this is an open standard, no royalties or granted permissions are required to implement these specifications. The Internet Engineering Task Force (IETF) has formalized the core XML streaming protocols as an approved instant messaging and presence technology. The XMPP specifications were published as RFC 3920 and RFC 3921 in 2004 and the XMPP Standards Foundation continues to publish many XMPP Extension Protocols. In 2011 the core RFCs were revised, resulting in the most up-to-date specifications (RFC 6120, RFC 6121, and RFC 7622).
4. Security – Security in XMPP can be achieved by authentication, encryption etc. Any XMPP server may be isolated from the public network (e.g., on a company intranet) and robust security using SASL and TLS has been built into the core XMPP specifications. In addition, the XMPP developer community is actively working on end-to-end encryption to raise the security.
5. Flexibility- XMPP is very flexible as it supports interoperability with other machines and networks. XMPP applications beyond instant messaging include network management, content syndication, collaboration tools, file sharing, gaming, remote systems monitoring, web services, lightweight middleware, cloud computing, and much more.
6. Extensible- Using the power of XML, anyone can build custom functionality on top of the core protocols, to maintain interoperability. Common extensions are published in the XEP series, but such publication is not required and organizations can maintain their own private extensions if so desired.
7. Diverse- A wide range of companies and open-source projects use XMPP to build and deploy real-time applications and services. Hence we will never get "locked in" when we use XMPP technologies.

Some of the core XMPP technologies are given below.

Core — Gives information about the core XMPP technologies for XML streaming.

Jingle — Technology for multimedia signaling for voice, video, file transfer, and other applications.

Multi-User Chat — Provides flexible, multi-party communication.

PubSub — Supports alerts and notifications for data syndication, rich presence and more.

BOSH — This is an HTTP binding for XMPP (and other) traffic.

2.6.6 AMQP

Advanced Message Queuing Protocol (AMQP) is an open standard application layer protocol for message-oriented middleware. The defining features of AMQP are message orientation, queuing, routing (including point-to-point and publish-and-subscribe), reliability and security. Advanced Message Queuing Protocol (AMQP) is an open source published standard for asynchronous messaging by wire. AMQP enables encrypted and interoperable messaging between organizations and applications. The protocol is used in client/server messaging and in IoT device management. It is a binary application layer protocol.

AMPQ is cfficient, portable, multichannel and secure. The binary protocol offers authentication and encryption by way of SASL or TLS, relying on a transport protocol such as TCP. The messaging protocol is fast and features guaranteed delivery with acknowledgement of received messages. AMQP works well in multi-client environments and provides a means for delegating tasks and making servers handle immediate requests faster. Because AMQP is a streamed binary messaging system with tightly mandated messaging behavior, the interoperability of clients from different vendors is assured. AMQP allows for various guaranteed messaging modes specifying a message be sent.

1. At-most-Each message is delivered once or never. It is sent one time with the possibility of being missed.
2. At-least-once-Each message is certain to be delivered, but may do so multiple times. It guarantees delivery with the possibility of duplicated messages.
3. Exactly-once- Each message will always certainly arrive and do so only once. This guarantees a one-time only delivery.

AMQP Features

In addition to security, reliability, interoperability between protocols and devices, routing, queuing and open standard AMQP has certain important highlights. It includes the following.

(a) Targeted QoS (Selectively offering QoS to links)

(b) Persistence (Message delivery guarantees)

(c) Delivery of messages to multiple consumers.

(d) Possibility of ensuring multiple consumption.

(e) Possibility of preventing multiple consumption.

(f) High speed protocol.

AMQP Architecture

AMQP connects systems, feeds business processes with the information they need and reliably transmits onward the instructions that achieve their goals. AMQP connects across organizations, technologies, time and space. The architecture of AMQP is shown in Figure 2.16.

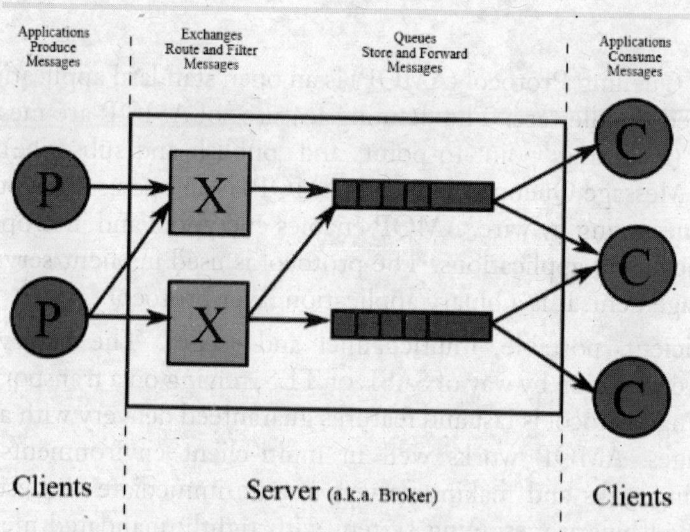

Fig.2.16: Architecture of AMQP

There are applications that produce messages on one end and applications that consume messages on the other end. In Figure 2.16, clients that produce messages are denoted as P and clients that consume messages are denoted as C and X represents exchanges, route and filter messages. The servers in between contains brokers which receives messages and routes them to queues. The queues store and forward messages to business clients. There will be separate queues for separate business processes. The consumer clients receive messages from these queues. In addition, there are bindings which are rules for distributing messages like who can access what message, destination of the message etc.

After receiving messages from the publishing clients, the exchanges process them and route them to one or more queues. The type of routing performed depends on the type of the exchange and there are currently four of them.

Direct Exchange: Direct exchange type involves the delivery of messages to queues based on routing keys. Routing keys can be considered as additional data defined to set where a message will go. Typical use case for direct exchange is load balancing tasks in a round-robin way between workers.

Fan-out Exchange: Fan-out exchange completely ignores the routing key and sends any message to all the queues bound to it. Use cases for fan-out exchanges usually involve distribution of a message to multiple clients for purposes similar to notifications: Sharing of messages (e.g. chat servers) and updates (e.g. news), Application states (e.g. configurations).

Topic Exchange: Topic exchange is mainly used for pub/sub (publish-subscribe) patterns. Using this type of transferring, a routing key alongside binding of queues to exchanges are used to match and send messages. Whenever a specialized involvement of a consumer is necessary (such as a single working set to perform a certain type of actions), topic exchange comes in handy to distribute messages accordingly based on keys and patterns.

Headers Exchange: Headers exchange constitutes of using additional headers (i.e. message attributes) coupled with messages instead of depending on routing keys for routing to queues. Being able to use types of data other than strings headers exchange allow differing routing mechanism with more possibilities but similar to direct exchange through keys.

In AMQP, basic unit of data is a ***frame***. There are nine AMQP frame types defined that are used to initiate, control and tear down the transfer of messages between two peers. They are the following.

1. Open (the connection)
2. Begin (the session)
3. Attach (initiate new link)
4. Transfer (for sending actual messages)
5. Flow (controls message flow rate)
6. Disposition(informs the changes in state of transfer)
7. Detach (terminate the link)
8. End (the session)
9. Close (the connection)

AMQP Applications

AMQP is ideal for several applications as follows.

1. Monitoring and globally sharing updates.
2. Connecting different systems and processes to talk to each other.
3. Allowing servers to respond to immediate requests quickly and delegate time consuming tasks for later processing.
4. Distributing a message to multiple recipients for consumption.
5. Enabling offline clients to fetch data at a later time.
6. Introducing fully asynchronous functionality for systems.
7. Increasing reliability and uptime of application deployments.

2.7 Conclusion

This Chapter gives an overview about IoT networking. This Chapter explains the connectivity terminologies, gateway prefix allotment, impact of mobility on addressing, multihoming and the differences of IoT stack and Web stack. Various IoT identification and data protocols like IPv4, IPv6, MQTT, CoAP, XMPP and AMQP are explained with its features, architecture and applications.

3 CONNECTIVITY TECHNOLOGIES

3.1 Introduction

In the previous Chapter, we have already discussed some important identification and data protocols like IPv4, IPv6, MQTT, CoAP, XMPP and AMQP. In this Chapter we will be discussing some other important communication protocols which have immediate importance to consumer and industrial IoTs. The connectivity technologies that will be discussed in this Chapter are IEEE 802.15.4, ZigBee, 6LoWPAN, Wireless HART, Z-Wave, ISA 100, Bluetooth, NFC and RFID. We will see each technology in detail.

3.2 IEEE 802.15.4

IEEE standard 802.15.4 intends to offer the fundamental lower network layers of a type of Wireless Personal Area Network (WPAN) which focuses on low-cost, low-speed ubiquitous communication between devices. It can be contrasted with other approaches, such as Wi-Fi, which offer more bandwidth and require more power. The emphasis is on very low cost communication of nearby devices with little to no underlying infrastructure, intending to exploit this to lower power consumption even more.

IEEE 802.15.4 was developed for low data rate monitoring and control applications with extended life, low power consumption uses. This standard uses only the first two layers (PHY, MAC). In addition to this, the Logical Link Control (LLC) and Service Specific Convergence Sub-layer (SSCS) are used to communicate with all upper layers. This protocol operates in the ISM band. The industrial, scientific, and medical radio band (ISM band) refers to a group of radio bands or parts of the radio spectrum that are internationally reserved for the use of radio frequency (RF) energy intended for scientific, medical and industrial requirements rather than for communications. Devices are conceived to interact with each other over a conceptually simple wireless network. The definition of the network layers is based on the OSI model; although only the lower layers are defined in the standard, interaction with upper layers is intended, possibly using an IEEE 802.2 logical link control sub-layer accessing the MAC through a convergence sub-layer. Implementations may rely on external devices or be purely embedded, self-functioning devices. Figure 3.1 shows the architecture of IEEE 802.15.4.

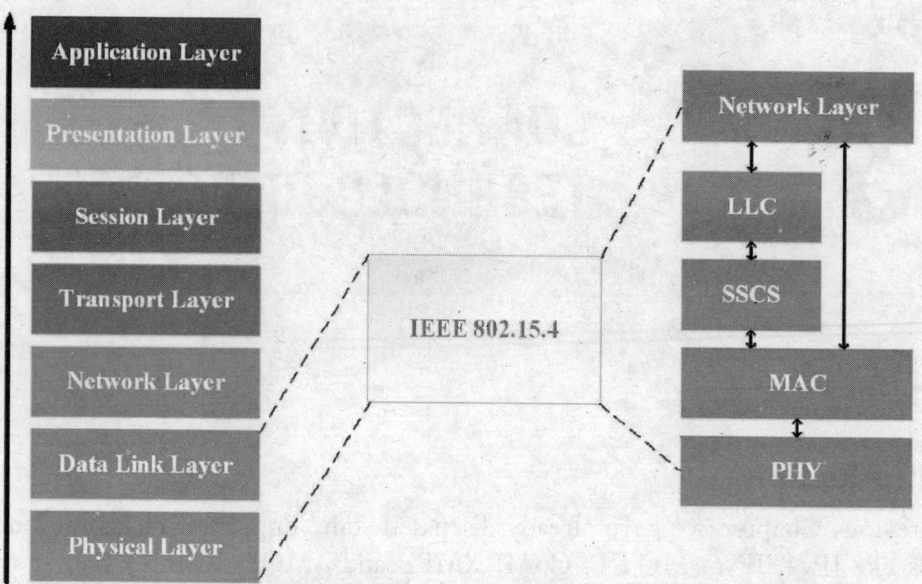

Fig.3.1: Architecture of IEEE 802.15.4

The standard uses Direct Sequence Spread Spectrum (DSSS) modulation. It is highly tolerant of noise and interference and offers coding gain to improve link reliability. Standard binary phase-shift keying (BPSK) is used in the two low-speed versions, while offset-quadrature phase-shift keying (O-QPSK) is used for the higher-data-rate version. O-QPSK has a constant wave envelope meaning that more efficient non-linear power amplification techniques can be used to minimize power consumption.

With regard to channel access, 802.15.4 uses carrier sense multiple access with collision avoidance (CSMA-CA). This multiplexing approach lets multiple users or nodes access the same channel at different times without interference. Most transmissions are short packets that occur infrequently for a very low duty cycle (<1 %), minimizing power consumption. The minimum power level defined is –3 dBm or 0.5 mW. Most modules use 0 dBm or 1 mW. However, some 20-dBm or 100-mW modules are available.

Transmission range varies considerably depending on the nature of the path that must for the most part be line of sight (LOS). Transmission power level and receiver sensitivity are also factors. Under the best conditions the range can be as great as 1000 meters with a clear outdoor path. Most applications cover a shorter range of 10 to 75 meters.

With regard to networking capability, 802.15.4 defines two topologies. One of them is a basic star topology given in Figure 3.2 (a). All communications between nodes must pass through the central coordinator node. A basic peer-to-peer (P2P) topology is also defined in IEEE 802.15.4 which is given in Figure 3.2(b). Any device may then talk to any other device. This basic topology may be expanded into other topologies in the upper network layers, such as the popular mesh topology.

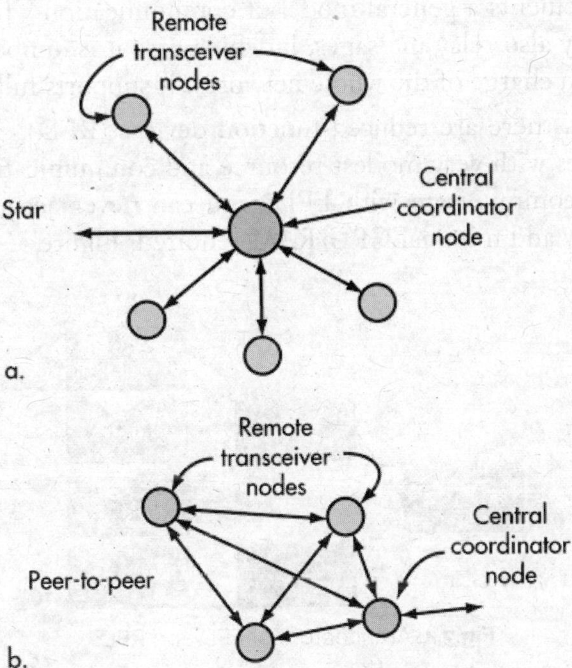

Fig.3.2: Star and Peer-to-Peer Topologies

There are different variants for IEEE 802.15.4. Figure 3.3 gives the different variants of IEEE 802.15.4.

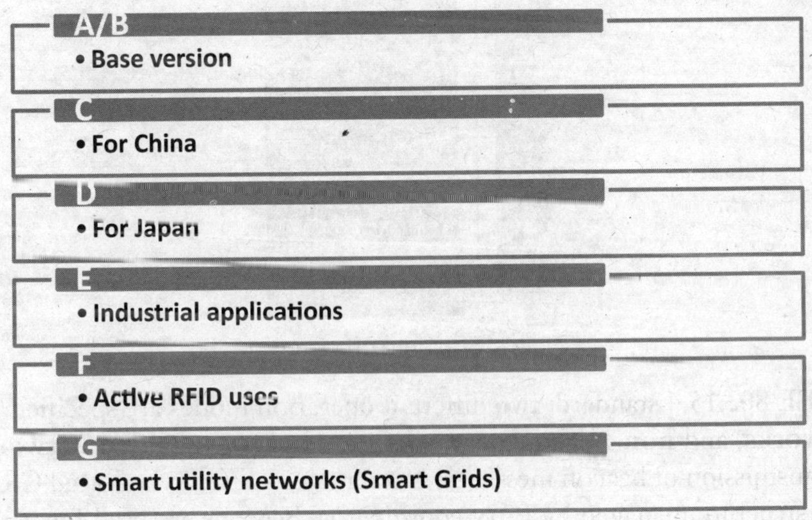

Fig.3.3: Variants of IEEE 802.15.4

IEEE 802.15.4 defines two types of network node. The first one is the full-function device (FFD). It can serve as the coordinator of a personal area network just as it may function as a common node. It implements a general model of communication which allows it to talk to any other device. It may also relay messages, in which case it is dubbed a coordinator (PAN coordinator when it is in charge of the whole network). It supports full protocol.

On the other hand, there are reduced-function devices (RFD). These are meant to be extremely simple devices with very modest resource and communication requirements. Due to this, they can only communicate with FFDs and can never act as coordinators. Power consumption is very low and minimal CPU/RAM required. Figure 3.4 shows architecture of FFD and RFD.

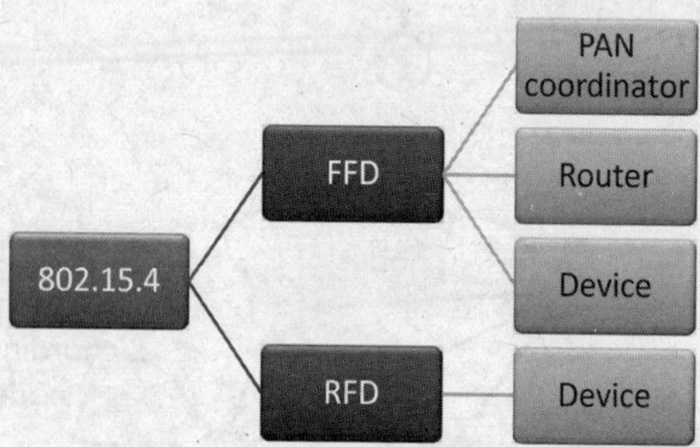

Fig.3.4: Architecture of FFD and RFD

Frames are the basic unit of data transport, of which there are four fundamental types (data, acknowledgment, beacon and MAC command frames), which provide a reasonable tradeoff between simplicity and robustness. Figure 3.5 shows the structure of a frame.

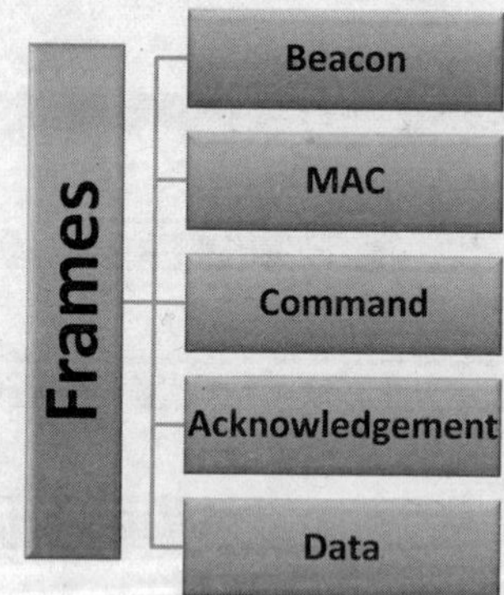

Fig.3.5: Structure of a Frame

In the IEEE 802.15.4 standard, two different operation modes are specified: the **beacon-enabled networks**, and **non-beacon networks**. In a **beacon-enabled network**, there will be periodic transmission of beacon messages. Data frames are sent via slotted CSMA/CA with a super frame structure managed by PAN coordinator. Beacons are used for synchronization and association of other nodes with the coordinator. The devices in a beacon-enabled network synchronize with each other and the beacon frame which is treated as synchronization signal also provides some extended features. On the other hand, a beacon-enabled device is hard to implement. High processing power is required to meet the constrained timing events and process the beacon packets. The scope of operation spans the whole network.

In **non-beacon enabled networks**, data frames are sent via un-slotted CSMA/CA. Beacons are used only for link layer discovery. Non-beacon enabled networks require both source and destination IDs. As 802.15.4 is primarily a mesh protocol, all protocol addressing must adhere to mesh configurations. In non-beacon enabled networks, there is decentralized communication amongst various nodes.

3.3 ZigBee

ZigBee is an IEEE 802.15.4 based specification for a suite of high-level communication protocols used to create personal area networks with small, low-power digital radios, such as for home automation, medical device data collection, and other low-power low-bandwidth needs. It is designed for small scale projects which need wireless connection. Hence, ZigBee is a low-power, low data rate, and close proximity (*i.e.*, personal area) wireless ad-hoc network.

It's low power consumption limits transmission distances to 10–100 meters line-of-sight, depending on power output and environmental characteristics. ZigBee devices can transmit data over long distances by passing data through a mesh network of intermediate devices to reach more distant ones. ZigBee is typically used in low data rate applications that require long battery life and secure networking. ZigBee networks are secured by 128 bit symmetric encryption keys. ZigBee has a defined rate of 250 Kbits/s, best suited for intermittent data transmissions from a sensor or input device.

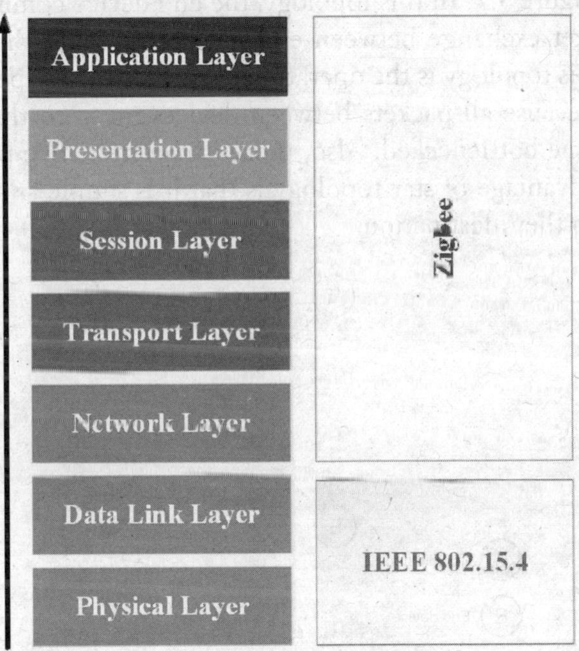

Fig.3.6: Structure of ZigBee

The most widely deployed enhancement to the 802.15.4 standard is ZigBee, which is a standard of the ZigBee Alliance. The organization maintains, supports and develops more sophisticated protocols for advanced applications. It uses layers 3 and above to define additional communication features as shown in Figure 3.6. It works with the 802.15.4 layers 1 and 2. These enhancements include authentication with valid nodes, encryption for security and a data routing and forwarding capability that enables mesh networking.

The ZigBee network layer uses Ad-hoc On Demand Distance Vector (AODV) routing. To find the final destination, The AODV broadcasts a route request to all of its immediate neighbours. The neighbours relay the same information to their neighbours eventually spreading the request throughout the network. Upon discovery of the destination, a low-cost path is calculated and informed to the requesting device via unicast messaging.

ZigBee has two important components. They are ZigBee Device Object (ZDO) and Application Support Sub-layer (APS). ZDO is responsible for device management, security and policies whereas APS is responsible for interfacing and controlling devices, bridge between network and other layers.

ZigBee Topologies

IEEE 802.15.4 offers star, tree, cluster tree, and mesh topologies. However, ZigBee supports only star, tree and mesh topologies. It uses an association hierarchy. A device joining the network can either be a router or an end device and routers can accept more devices.

Star Topology: The star topology consists of a coordinator and several end devices (nodes), as shown in Figure 3.7. In this topology, the end device communicates only with the coordinator. Any packet exchange between end devices must go through the coordinator. The disadvantage of this topology is the operation of the network depends on the coordinator of the network, and because all packets between devices must go through coordinator, the coordinator may become bottlenecked. Also, there is no alternative path from the source to the destination. The advantage of star topology is that it is simple and packets go through at most two hops to reach their destination.

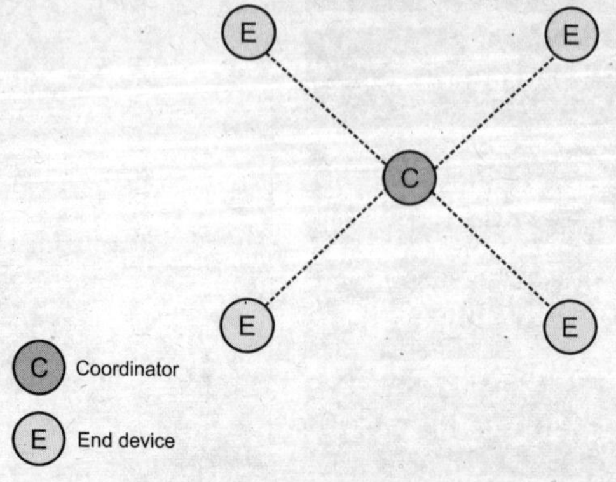

Fig.3.7: Star Topology

Tree Topology: In this topology, the network consists of a central node (root tree), which is a coordinator, several routers, and end devices, as shown in Figure 3.8. The function of the router is to extend the network coverage. The end nodes that are connected to the coordinator or the routers are called children. Only routers and the coordinator can have children. Each end device is only able to communicate with its parent (router or coordinator). The coordinator and routers can have children and, therefore, are the only devices that can be parents. An end device cannot have children and, therefore, may not be a parent. A special case of tree topology is called a cluster tree topology.

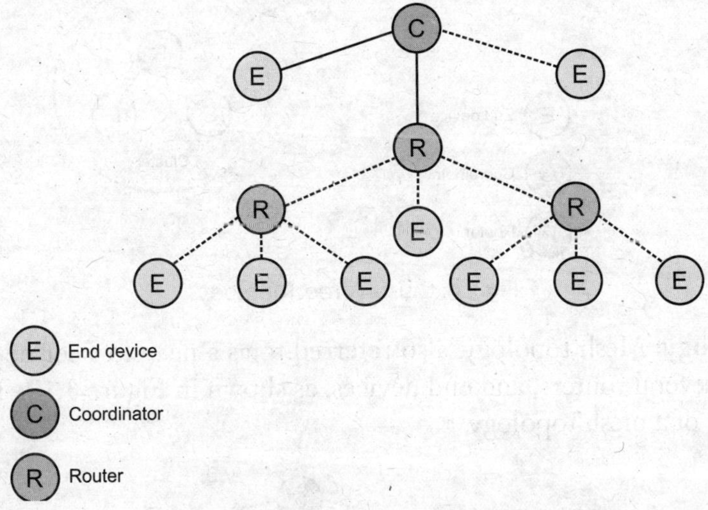

Fig.3.8: Tree Topology

The disadvantages of tree topology are—

a. If one of the parents becomes disabled, the children of the disabled parent cannot communicate with other devices in the network.

b. Even if two nodes are geographically close to each other, they cannot communicate directly.

Cluster Tree Topology: A cluster tree topology is a special case of tree topology in which a parent with its children is called a cluster, as shown in Figure 3.9. Each cluster is identified by a cluster ID. ZigBee does not support cluster tree topology, but IEEE 802.15.4 does support it.

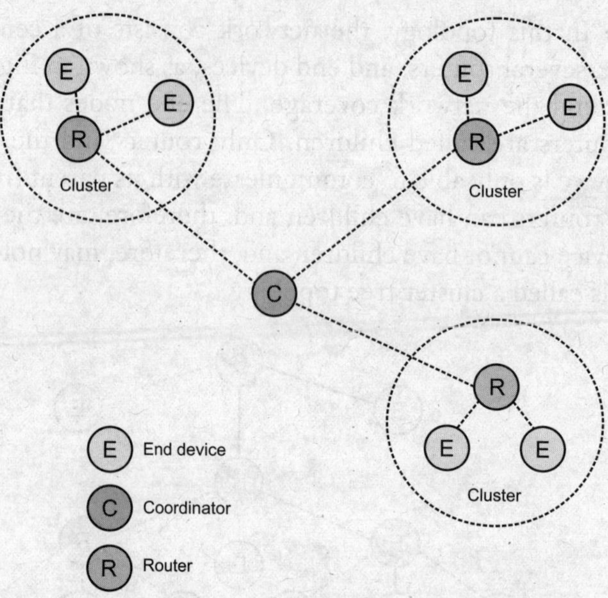

Fig.3.9: Cluster Tree Topology

Mesh Topology: Mesh topology, also referred to as a peer-to-peer network, consists of one coordinator, several routers, and end devices, as shown in Figure 3.10. The following are the characteristics of a mesh topology.

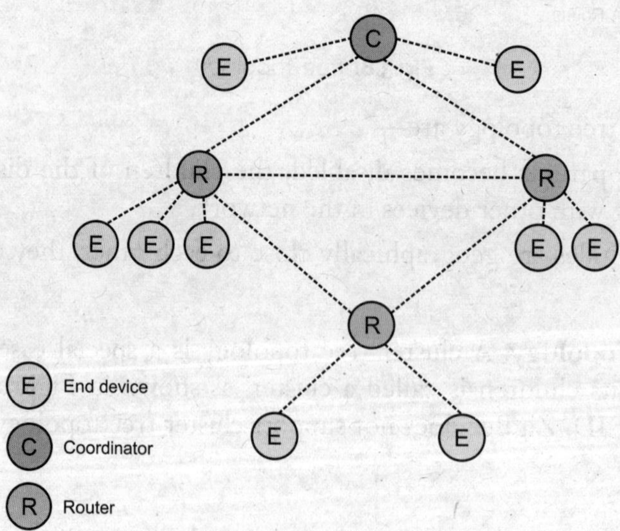

Fig.3.10: Mesh Topology

a. A mesh topology is a multi-hop network. Packets pass through multiple hops to reach their destination.

b. The range of a network can be increased by adding more devices to the network.

c. It can eliminate dead zones.
d. A mesh topology is self-healing, meaning during transmission, if a path fails, the node will find an alternate path to the destination.
e. Devices can be close to each other so that they use less power.
f. Adding or removing a device is easy.
g. Any source device can communicate with any destination device in the network.

The disadvantages are compared with star topology, mesh topology requires greater overhead. Mesh routing uses a more complex routing protocol than a star topology.

ZigBee Device Types

ZigBee devices are of three kinds.

ZigBee Coordinator (ZC): The ZigBee Coordinator forms the root of the ZigBee network tree and might act as a bridge between networks. There is a single ZigBee coordinator in each network which originally initiates the network. It stores information about the network under it and outside it. It acts as a trust center and repository for security keys.

ZigBee Router (ZR): ZigBee Routers are capable of running applications as well as relaying information between nodes connected to it. Router can act as an intermediate router, passing on data from other devices.

ZigBee End Device (ZED): It contains just enough functionality to talk to the parent node (either the coordinator or a router). It cannot relay data from other devices. This relationship allows the node to be asleep a significant amount of the time thereby giving long battery life. A ZED requires least amount of memory and therefore can be less expensive to manufacture than a ZR or ZC.

Applications

ZigBee finds application in the following domains.

a. Building automation.
b. Remote Control (RF4CE or RF for consumer electronics).
c. Smart energy for home energy monitoring.
d. Healthcare for medical and fitness monitoring.
e. Home automation for control of smart homes.
f. Light link for control of LED lighting.
g. Telecom services.

3.4 6LoWPAN

6LoWPAN is an acronym of IPv6 over Low-Power Wireless Personal Area Networks. The 6LoWPAN concept originated from the idea that "the Internet Protocol could and should be applied even to the smallest devices," and that low-power devices with limited processing capabilities should be able to participate in the Internet of Things. It allows low power devices to connect to the Internet. 6LoWPAN was created by Internet Engineering Task Force (IETF). The 6LoWPAN protocol is based on IPv6 and operates in a fully asynchronous way. It adopts a mesh topology and uses a routing algorithm which does not take care of the sleeping node thus requiring approaches such as low-power listening for energy saving purpose.

The features of 6LoWPANs are the following:

a. It allows IEEE 802.15.4 radios to carry 128 bit addresses of Internet Protocol Version 6 (IPv6).
b. Header compression and address translation techniques allow the IEEE 802.15.4 radios to access the Internet.
c. IPv6 packets are compressed and reformatted to fit the IEEE 802.15.4 packet format.
d. Requires low bandwidth.
e. Consumes low power and typically battery operated.
f. Supports star and mesh topologies.
g. Relatively low cost with other technologies.

The 128 bits of IPv6 addresses are divided in two parts: The network prefix (64 bits) and the host address (64 bits). The 6LoWPAN header compression mechanism omits the 64 most significant bits (network prefix) because they're fixed for a given 6LoWPAN. Moreover, the 64 least significant bits can address very large address space (up to 1.84467441×1019). Therefore, 6LoWPAN provides options for compressing the host address (the common usage is 16 bits). In a nutshell, a 128-bit IPv6 address can be compressed down to 16 bits using 6LoWPAN. Figure 3.11 shows the packet format of 6LoWPAN.

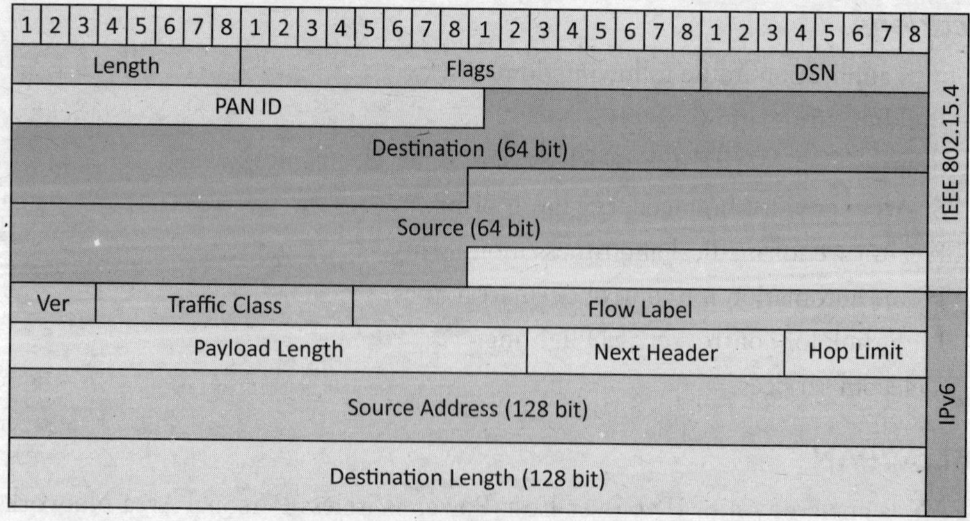

Fig.3.11: Packet Format of 6LoWPAN

Version	– 4-bit Internet Protocol version number = 6.
Traffic Class	– 8-bit traffic class field.
Flow Label	– 20-bit flow label.
Payload Length	– 6-bit unsigned integer. Length of the IPv6 header is in octets.
Next Header	– 8-bit selector. Identifies the type of header immediately following the IPv6 header. Uses the same values as the IPv4 protocol field.
Hop Limit	– 8-bit unsigned integer. Decremented by 1 by each node that forwards the packet. The packet is discarded if hop limit is decremented to zero.
Source Address	– 128-bit address of the originator of the packet.
Destination Address	– 128-bit address of the intended recipient of the packet (possibly not the ultimate recipient, if a routing header is present).

6LoWPAN Headers

There are 3 types of header for 6LoWPAN—Dispatch header, Mesh addressing header and Fragmentation header.

Dispatch Header

It is a 32-bit header. 0, 1 is the identifier for dispatch type. Dispatch initiates communication. This is a 6-bit and identifies the next header type. The Type Specific Header is determined by Dispatch header. Figure 3.12 shows the dispatch header.

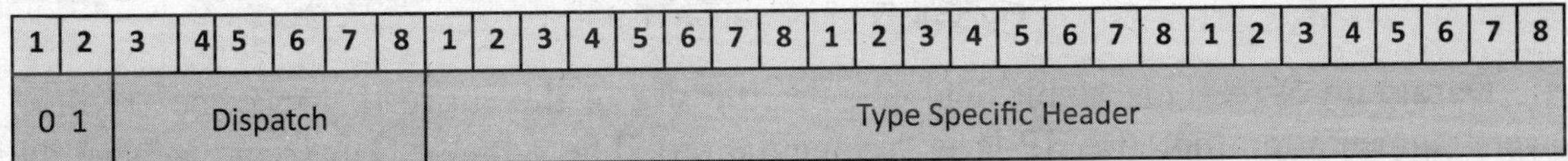

Fig.3.12: Dispatch Header

Mesh Addressing Header

It is a 32-bit header. 1, 0 is the identifier for mesh addressing header. V has 2 values 0 and 1. The value of V is 0, if originator is 64-bit extended address and 1 if 16-bit address. Similarly F has 2 values 0 and 1. The value of F is 0 if destination is 64-bit address and 1 if 16-bit address. Hops Left is decremented by each node before sending to next hop. Originator address is the source address and Final address is the destination address. Figure 3.13 shows the mesh addressing header.

Fig.3.13: Mesh Addressing Header

Fragmentation Header

In fragmentation header, the first fragment is 32 bits and the subsequent fragment is also 32 bits. If an entire payload (*e.g.*, IPv6) datagram fits within a single 802.15.4 frame, it is un-fragmented and the 6LoWPAN encapsulation should not contain a fragmentation header. If the datagram does not fit within a single IEEE 802.15.4 frame, it shall be broken into link fragments. As the fragment offset can only express multiples of eight bytes, all link fragments for a datagram except the last one must be multiples of eight bytes in length. The first link fragment shall contain the first fragment header and the second and subsequent link fragments (up to and including the last) shall contain a fragmentation header that conforms to the format shown in Figure 3.13.

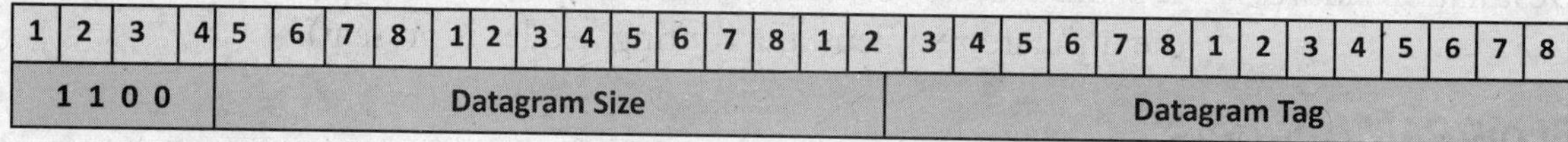

(a) First Fragment

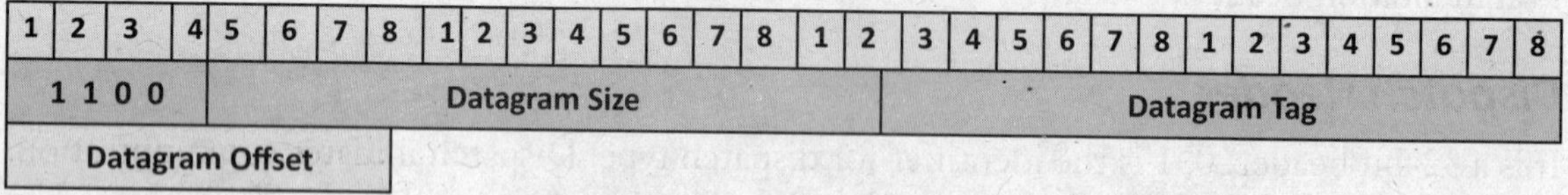

(b) Subsequent Fragment

Fig.3.14: Fragmentation Header

Datagram Size: This 11-bit field encodes the size of the entire IP packet before link-layer fragmentation (but after IP layer fragmentation). The value of Datagram Size shall be the same for all link-layer fragments of an IP packet. For IPv6, this shall be 40 octets (the size of the uncompressed IPv6 header) more than the value of Payload Length in the IPv6 header [RFC2460] of the packet. Note that this packet may already be fragmented by hosts involved in the communication, *i.e.*, this field needs to encode a maximum length of 1280 octets.

Datagram Tag: The value of Datagram Tag shall be the same for all link fragments of a payload (*e.g.*, IPv6) datagram. The sender shall increment Datagram Tag for successive, fragmented datagrams. The incremented value of Datagram Tag shall wrap from 65535 back to zero. This field is 16 bits long, and its initial value is not defined.

Datagram Offset: This field is present only in the second and subsequent link fragments and shall specify the offset, in increments of 8 octets, of the fragment from the beginning of the payload datagram. The first octet of the datagram (*e.g.*, the start of the IPv6 header) has an offset of zero; the implicit value of Datagram Offset in the first link fragment is zero. This field is 8 bits long.

6LoWPAN Routing

Routing is a two phased problem that is being considered for low-power IP networking. Mesh routing in the Personal Area Network (PAN) space and routing of packets between the IPv6 domain and the PAN domain. There are several protocols used but the commonly used ones are LOADng and RPL. Figure 3.14 shows the architecture of 6LoWPAN routing.

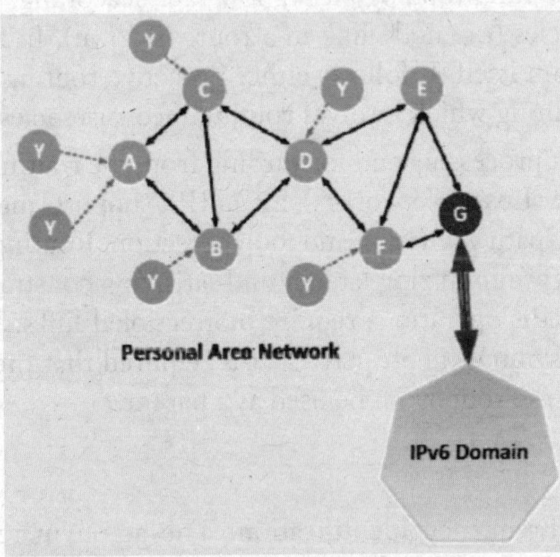

Fig.3.15: Architecture of 6LoWPAN Routing

In Figure 3.15, A, B, C, D, E and F constitutes the nodes in mesh networking and G is the gateway to IPv6 domain.

LOADng Routing: This is derived from Ad-hoc On-Demand Distance Vector (AODV), a routing protocol designed for wireless and mobile Ad-hoc networks. AODV protocol establishes routes to destinations on demand and supports both unicast and multicast routing. LOADng routing is extended for use in IoT. Basic operations of LOADng include the following.

a. Generation of Route Requests (RREQs) by a LOADng router (originator) for discovering a route to a destination.
b. Forwarding of such RREQs until they reach the destination LOADng router.
c. Generation of Route Replies (RREPs) upon receipt of an RREQ by the indicated destination and unicast hop by hop forwarding of these RREps towards the originator.
d. If a route is detected to be broken, a Route Error (RERR) message is returned to the originator of that data packet to inform the originator about the route breakage.
e. Optimized flooding is supported, reducing the overhead incurred by RREQ generation and flooding.
f. Only the destination is permitted to respond to an RREQ.

g. Intermediate LOADng routers are explicitly prohibited from responding to RREQs, even if they may have active routes to the sought destination.
h. RREQ/RREP messages generated by a given LOADng router share a single unique monotonically increasing sequence number.

RPL Routing: RPL stands for IPv6 Routing Protocol for Low-Power and Lossy Networks. This routing maintains routing topology using low rate beaconing. Beaconing rate increases on detecting inconsistencies (*e.g.* node/link in a route is down). In this, routing information is included in the datagram itself. It follows either proactive routing that maintains a routing topology or a reactive routing which resolves routing inconsistencies.

RPL separates packet processing and forwarding from the routing optimization objective, which helps in Low-power Lossy Networks (LLN). RPL supports message confidentiality and integrity. It supports data-path validation and loop detection. Routing optimization objectives include minimizing energy, minimizing latency and satisfying constraints with respect to node power, band width etc. RPL operations require bidirectional links. In some LLN scenarios, those links may exhibit asymmetric properties. It is required that the reachability of a router should be verified before the router can be used as a parent.

3.5 RFID

RFID stands for Radio-Frequency Identification. The acronym refers to small electronic devices that consist of a small chip and an antenna. The chip typically is capable of carrying 2,000 bytes of data or less. The RFID device serves the same purpose as a bar code or a magnetic strip on the back of a credit card or ATM card. It provides a unique identifier for that object. And, just as a bar code or magnetic strip must be scanned to get the information, the RFID device must be scanned to retrieve the identifying information.

Data read from RFID tags are stored in a database by the reader. As compared to traditional bar codes and QR codes, RFID data can be read outside the line of sight. RFID tag consists of an integrated circuit and an antenna. The tag is covered by a protective material which also acts as a shield against various environmental effects. Tags may be passive or active. Passive RFID tags are the most widely used. Passive tags have to be powered by a reader inductively before they can transmit information, whereas active tags have their own power supply. The applications of RFID can be found in various domains as follows.

- Inventory management
- Asset tracking
- Personnel tracking
- Controlling access to restricted areas
- ID badging
- Supply chain management
- Counterfeit prevention (*e.g.* In the pharmaceutical industry)

Working of RFID

RFID technology is derived from Automatic Identification and Data Capture (AIDC) technology. AIDC performs object identification, object data collection and mapping of the collected data to computer systems with little or no human intervention. AIDC uses wired communication. RFID uses radio waves to perform AIDC functions. At a simple level, RFID systems consist of three components: an RFID tag or smart label, an RFID reader, and an antenna. RFID tags contain an integrated circuit and an antenna, which is used to transmit data to the RFID reader (also called an interrogator). The reader then converts the radio waves to a more usable form of data. Information collected from the tags is then transferred through a communications interface to a host computer system, where the data can be stored in a database and analyzed at a later time. Figure 3.16 shows the working principle of RFID.

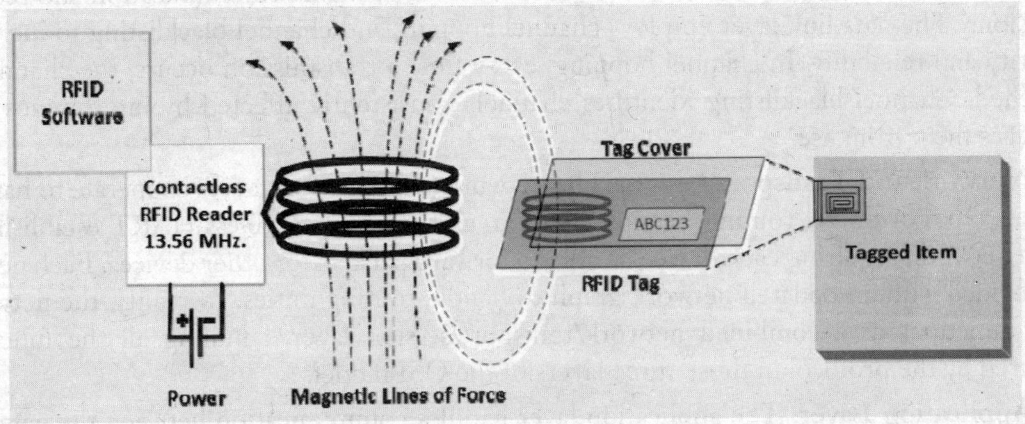

Fig.3.16: Working Principle of RFID

3.6 HART and Wireless HART

HART is the acronym for Highway Addressable Remote Transducer Protocol. Wireless HART is the latest release of HART protocol. HART standard was developed for networked smart field devices. The wireless protocol makes the implementation of HART cheaper and easier. HART encompasses the most number of field devices incorporated in any field network. Wireless HART enables device placements more accessible and cheaper such as the top of a reaction tank, inside a pipe or at widely separated warehouses. Figure 3.17 shows various layers in HART.

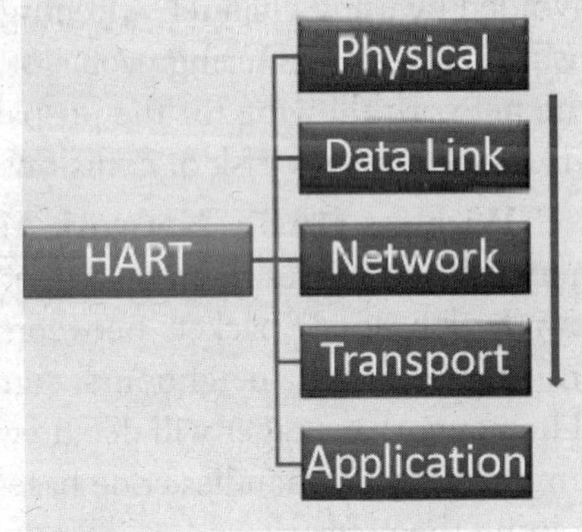

Fig.3.17: Various Layers in HART

HART includes five layers of the OSI model: physical layer, data link layer, network layer, transport layer, and application layer. The main difference between the wired and unwired versions is in the physical layer, data link layer and network layer. In fact, wired HART does't have a network layer.

Physical Layer: The physical layer of the protocol is derived from the IEEE 802.15.4 standard. Basically, it is a subset of the IEEE standard with modifications. It only operates in one of the bands specified in the IEEE 802.15.4 standard – the 2450MHz ISM band. The physical layer employs 15 channels of the band which the data link layer exploits to increase reliability. Several transceivers developed to meet the IEEE standard have also been approved for use with Wireless HART, reducing development time and cost.

Data Link Layer: The data link layer introduces the use of superframes and Time Dimension Multiple Access (TDMA) technology to provide collision free, deterministic communication. Timeslots 10ms in length are grouped into superframes. These superframes are used to control the timing of transmissions to insure reliable communication and reduce collisions. The data link layer employs channel hopping and channel blacklisting to increase security and reliability. In channel hopping, every time a transmission occurs, the channel is switched. Channel blacklisting identifies channels consistently affected by interference and removes them from use.

Network and Transport Layers: The network and transport layers cooperate to handle various types of traffic, routing, session creation, and security. Wireless HART establishes a mesh network, requiring each device be able to forward packets for other devices. Each device is provided with an updated network graph to handle routing duties. In reality, the network layer functions as a combined network/transport/session layer, handling all the function required by the protocol in those three layers of the OSI model.

Application Layer: The application layer handles communication between the gateway and devices through a series of commands and responses. This layer extracts the command from a message, executes the command and generates a response. At this level, there is really no difference between the wired and wireless versions of the HART protocol.

HART Congestion Control: Due to its restricted use in certain areas, HART is restricted to 2.4 GHz ISM band with channel 26 removed. Interference-prone channels are avoided by using channel switching after every transmission. Transmissions are synchronized using 10ms slots. During each slot, all available channels can be utilized by various nodes in the network allowing for the propagation of 15 packets through the network at a time, which also minimizes the risk of collisions.

Wireless HART Network Manager: The network manager supervises each node in a network and guides them on when and where to send packets. It allows for collision-free and timely delivery of packets between a source and destination. The network manager updates information about neighbours, signal strength and information needing delivery or receipt. The network manager will decide who will send, who will listen and at what frequency is each time-slot. It also handles code based network security and prevents unauthorized nodes from joining the network.

Wireless HART versus ZigBee

Wireless HART	ZigBee
A wireless HART node hops after every message, changing channels every time it sends a packet.	ZigBee does not feature hopping at all and only hops when the entire network hops.
At the MAC layer, wireless HART utilizes Time Division Multiple Access (TDMA) allotting individual time slots for each transmission.	ZigBee applies Carrier Sense Multiple Access with Collision Detection. (CSMA/CD)
Wireless HART represents a true mesh network where each node is capable of serving as a router so that if one node goes down, another can replace it ensuring packet delivery.	ZigBee utilizes a tree topology which makes nodes along the trunk critical.
Wireless HART devices are all backward compatible allowing for the integration of legacy devices as well as new ones.	ZigBee share the same basis for their physical layers, but ZigBee, ZigBee Pro, ZigBee RF4CE and ZigBee IP are otherwise incompatible with each other.

3.7 NFC

Near field communication, abbreviated NFC, is a form of contactless communication between devices like smart phones or tablets. Contactless communication allows a user to wave the smart phone over a NFC compatible device to send information without needing to touch the devices together or go through multiple steps setting up a connection. Fast and convenient, NFC technology is popular in parts of Europe and Asia, and is quickly spreading throughout the United States. Near field communication maintains interoperability between different wireless communication methods like Bluetooth and other NFC standards including FeliCa which is popular in Japan.

The NFC forum enforces strict standards that manufacturers must meet when designing NFC compatible devices. This ensures that NFC is secure and remains easy-to-use with different versions of the technology. Compatibility is the key to the growth of NFC as a popular payment and data communication method. It must be able to communicate with other wireless technologies and be able to interact with different types of NFC transmissions.

NFC's data transmission frequency is 13.56 MHz. NFC can transmit data at a rate of either 106, 212 or 424 Kbps. Tags typically store between 96 and 512 bytes of data. Communication range is less than 20 cms.

NFC finds application in various domains such as smart phone based payments, parcel tracking, information tags in posters and advertisements, computer game synchronized toys, low power home automation systems etc. The characteristics of NFC are the following.

Wireless Connection: It is similar to the connection of other technologies such as WiFi or Bluetooth but with a shorter range, generally between 10 and 20 centimetres. Its short range allows for avoiding possible security problems such as the reading of our transmission.

Connection Speed: It has almost immediate connection with a transfer rate that can reach 424 Kbit/s.

Autonomy: The chips included in NFC technology do not need to be connected to a main battery.

Working of NFC

NFC works on the principle of magnetic induction. Figure 3.18 shows the working of NFC. A reader emits a small electric current which creates a magnetic field that in turn bridges the physical space between the devices. The generated field is received by a similar coil in the client device where it is turned back into electrical impulses to communicate data such as identification number status information or any other information.

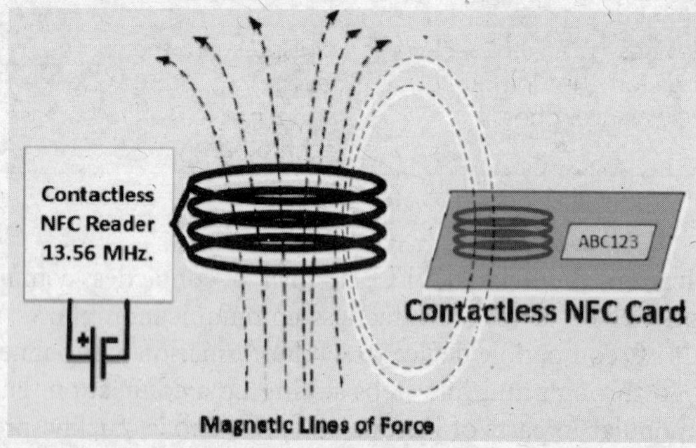

Fig.3.18: Working of NFC

Passive NFC tags use the energy from the reader to encode their response while active or peer-to-peer tags have their own power source.

NFC Types

There are two types of NFC devices–**passive devices** and **active devices.** Passive devices contain information which is readable by other devices. However, it cannot read information itself. NFC tags found in supermarket products are examples of passive NFC. Active devices are able to collect as well as transmit information. Smart phones are good examples of active devices. NFC tags are passive devices that can be used to communicate with active NFC devices (an active NFC reader/writer). The NFC tags can be used within applications such as posters and other areas where small amounts of data can be stored and transferred to active NFC devices. Within the poster the live area can be used as a touch point for the active NFC device.

The stored data on the NFC tag may contain any form of data, but common applications are for storing URLs from where the NFC device may find further information. NFC tags may also be used. The NFC tag is a passive device with no power of its own. Accordingly when one is used, the users touch an NFC enabled device onto the tag. A small amount of power is taken by the NFC tag from the reader/writer to power the tag electronics. The tag is then enabled to transfer a small amount of information to the reader/writer.

The data stored in the tag memory is transferred to the NFC enabled device. Normally there will be a small amount of data in the tag memory and this may be used to direct the device to a website URL.

Modes of Operation

There are three modes of operation for NFC. They are **reader/writer, peer-to-peer** and card **emulation**. The different operating modes are based on the ISO/IEC 18092 NFC IP-1 and ISO/IEC 14443 contactless smart card standards.

In **reader/writer** mode, the NFC device is capable of reading NFC Forum-mandated tag types, such as a tag embedded in an NFC smart poster. The reader/writer mode on the RF interface is compliant with the ISO 14443 and FeliCa schemes.

In **Peer-to-Peer** mode, two NFC devices can exchange data. For example, we can share Bluetooth or WiFi link set-up parameters or we can exchange data such as virtual business cards or digital photos. Peer-to-Peer mode is standardized on the ISO/IEC 18092 standard.

In **Card Emulation** mode, the NFC device appears to an external reader much the same as a traditional contactless smart card. This enables contactless payments and ticketing by NFC devices without changing the existing infrastructure.

3.8 Bluetooth

Bluetooth wireless technology is a short range communications technology intended to replace the cables connecting portable unit and maintaining high levels of security. Bluetooth technology is based on Ad-hoc technology also known as Ad-hoc Pico nets, which is a local area network with a very limited coverage. Bluetooth finds applications in audio players, home automation, smart phones, toys, hands free headphones and sensor networks.

Features of Bluetooth

1. Bluetooth offers a uniform structure for a wide range of devices to connect and communicate with each other.
2. Bluetooth technology has achieved global acceptance such that any Bluetooth enabled device, almost everywhere in the world, can be connected with Bluetooth enabled devices.
3. Low power consumption of Bluetooth technology and an offered range of up to ten meters have paved the way for several usage models.
4. Bluetooth offers interactive conference by establishing an Ad-hoc network of laptops.
5. Bluetooth usage model includes cordless computer, intercom, cordless phone and mobile phones.

Bluetooth technology operates in the unlicensed industrial, scientific and medical ISM band at 2.4 to 2.485 GHz. It uses spread spectrum hopping, full-duplex signal at a nominal rate of 1600 hops/sec. Bluetooth supports 1 Mbps data rate for version 1.2 and 3 Mbps data rate for version 2.0 combined with error data rate. Bluetooth operating range depends on the device. The transmit power and therefore range of a Bluetooth module is defined by its power class. There are three defined classes of power as given below.

Class Number	Max. Output Power (dBm)	Max. Output Power (mW)	Max. Range
Class 1	20 dBm	100 mW	100 m
Class 2	4 dBm	2.5 mW	10 m
Class 3	0 dBm	1 mW	100 cm

- Class 3 radios have a range of upto 1 meter or 3 feet.
- Class 2 radios are most commonly found in mobile devices having a range of 10 meters or 30 feet.
- Class 1 radios are primarily in industrial use cases having a range of 100 meters or 300 feet.

Bluetooth Connection

Every single Bluetooth device has a unique 48-bit address, commonly abbreviated BD_ADDR. This will usually be presented in the form of a 12-digit hexadecimal value. The most-significant half (24 bits) of the address is an organization unique identifier (OUI), which identifies the manufacturer. The lower 24-bits are the more unique part of the address. This address should be visible on most Bluetooth devices.

Creating a Bluetooth connection between two devices is a multi-step process involving three progressive states. Figure 3.19 shows the connection establishment in a Bluetooth.

Fig.3.19: Connection Establishment in Bluetooth

Inquiry – If two Bluetooth devices know absolutely nothing about each other, one must run an inquiry to try to discover the other. One device sends out the inquiry request, and any device listening for such a request will respond with its address, and possibly its name and other information.

Paging (Connecting) – Paging is the process of forming a connection between two Bluetooth devices. Before this connection can be initiated, each device needs to know the address of the other (found in the inquiry process).

Connection – After a device has completed the paging process, it enters the connection state. While connected, a device can either be actively participating or it can be put into a low power sleep mode.

- **Active Mode:** This is the regular connected mode, where the device is actively transmitting or receiving data.
- **Sniff Mode:** This is a power-saving mode, where the device is less active. It'll sleep and only listen for transmissions at a set interval (*e.g.* every 100 ms).
- **Hold Mode:** Hold mode is a temporary, power-saving mode where a device sleeps for a defined period and then returns back to active mode when that interval has passed. The master can command a slave device to hold.
- **Park Mode:** Park is the deepest of sleep modes. A master can command a slave to "park", and that slave will become inactive until the master tells it to wake back up.

When two Bluetooth devices share a special affinity for each other, they can be bonded together. Bonded devices automatically establish a connection whenever they are close enough. For example, when I start up my car, the phone in my pocket immediately connects to the car's Bluetooth system because they share a bond. No Unique Identifier interactions are required in this case. Bonds are created through one-time a process called **pairing**. When devices pair up, they share their addresses, names, and profiles, and usually store them in memory. They also share a common secret key, which allows them to bond whenever they're together in the future.

Pairing usually requires an authentication process where a user must validate the connection between devices. The flow of the authentication process varies and usually depends on the interface capabilities of one device or the other. Sometimes pairing is a simple "Just Works" operation, where the click of a button is all it takes to pair (this is common for devices with no UI, like headsets). Other times pairing involves matching 6-digit numeric codes. Older, legacy (v2.0 and earlier), pairing processes involve the entering of a common PIN code on each device. The PIN code can range in length and complexity from four numbers (*e.g.* "0000" or "1234") to a 16-character alphanumeric string.

Bluetooth Protocol Stack

The Bluetooth protocol stack allows devices to locate, connect and exchange data with each other and to execute interoperable, interactive applications against each other. Figure 3.20 shows the Bluetooth protocol stack.

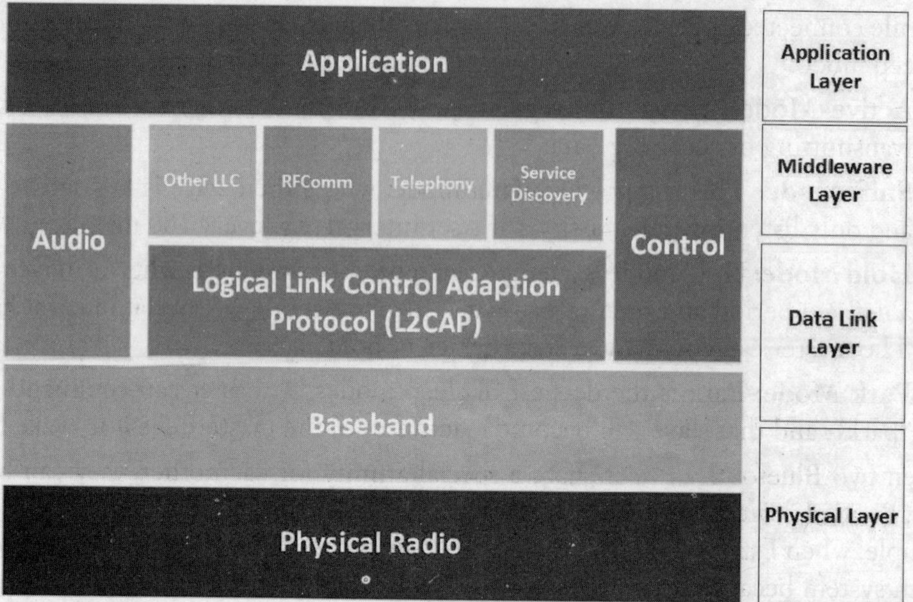

Fig.3.20: Bluetooth Protocol Stack

(a) Physical Radio and Baseband

The physical radio layer defines the requirements for a Bluetooth transceiver operating in the 2.4 GHz ISM band. The baseband layer describes the specification of the Bluetooth Link Controller (LC), which carries out the baseband protocols and other low-level link routines. It specifies piconet/channel definition, "low-level" packet definition and channel sharing. Physical radio and baseband forms the physical layer of the Bluetooth. Other services of this layer include error correction, data whitening, hop selection and Bluetooth security. The baseband layer is responsible for searching other devices, assigning master and slave roles. It manages link between devices and determines packet types supported for synchronous and asynchronous traffic.

(b) Logical Link Control Adaptation (L2CAP)

L2CAP is layered over the baseband protocol and resides in the data link layer. All data traffic is routed through this layer. This layer shields higher layers from details of lower layers. It segments larger packets from higher layers into smaller packets that can be easily handled by lower layers. It facilitates maintenance of desired grade of service in two peer devices.

This protocol is used to multiplex multiple logical connections between 2 devices. It provides connection-oriented and connection-less data services to upper layer protocols. (L2CAP) supports higher level protocol multiplexing, packet segmentation and reassembly and conveys quality of service information.

(c) RFComm

RFComm stands for Radio Frequency Communication. It is a cable replacement protocol used for generating a virtual data stream. It provides a virtual serial port for applications needed for scenarios like dial-up networking, etc. RFComm provides for binary data transport. It emulates EIA-232 (formerly RS-232) control signals over the Bluetooth baseband layer, *i.e.* it is serial port emulation. RFComm provides a simple, reliable data stream to the user similar to TCP. It supports up to 60 simultaneous connections between 2 Bluetooth devices.

(d) Service Delivery Protocol (SDP)

The Service Delivery Protocol (SDP) provides a means for applications to discover, which services are provided by or available through a Bluetooth device. It also allows applications to determine the characteristics of those available services. It addresses the unique characteristics of Bluetooth environment such as dynamic changes in the quality of services in Radio Frequency proximity of devices in motion. SDP can function over a reliable packet transfer protocol. It uses a request/response model.

(e) Telephone Control Specifications Layer (TCS) and Audio

This layer is designed to set up voice calls. It supports functions like call control and group management. TCS can also be used to set up data calls. TCS protocols are compatible with International Telecommunication Union (ITU) specifications. Bluetooth audio communication takes place at rate of 64Kbps.

(f) Application

This group of protocols consists of actual applications that make use of Bluetooth links and refers to software that exists above protocol stack. The Bluetooth does not define any application protocols nor does it specify any API. Bluetooth profiles are developed to establish a base point for use of a protocol stack to accomplish a given usage case.

Bluetooth Topology: Piconet and Scatternet

Bluetooth enabled electronic devices connect and communicate wirelessly through short range devices known as Piconets. Bluetooth devices exist in small ad-hoc configurations with the ability to act either as **master** or **slave** the specification allows a mechanism for master and slave to switch their roles. Point to point configuration with one master and one slave is the simplest configuration.

When more than two Bluetooth devices communicate with one another, this is called a **Piconet**. A Piconet can contain up to seven slaves clustered around a single master. The device that initializes establishment of the Piconet becomes the master. The master is responsible for transmission control by dividing the network into a series of time slots amongst the network members, as a part of **time division multiplexing** scheme.

The features of Piconets are as follows:

- Within a Piconet, the timing of various devices and the frequency hopping sequence of individual devices is determined by the clock and unique 48-bit address of master.
- Each device can communicate simultaneously with up to seven other devices within a single Piconet.
- Each device can communicate with several Piconets simultaneously.
- Piconets are established dynamically and automatically as Bluetooth enabled devices enter and leave Piconets.
- There is no direct connection between the slaves and all the connections are essentially master-to-slave or slave-to-master.
- Slaves are allowed to transmit once these have been polled by the master.
- Transmission starts in the slave-to-master time slot immediately following a polling packet from the master.
- A device can be a member of two or more Piconets, jumping from one Piconet to another by adjusting the transmission regime-timing and frequency hopping sequence dictated by the master device of the second Piconet.
- It can be a slave in one Piconet and master in another. It however cannot be a master in more than once Piconet.

Devices resident in adjacent Piconets provide a bridge to support inner-Piconet connections, allowing assemblies of linked Piconets to form a physically extensible communication infrastructure known as **Scatternet**. The Figure 3.21 shows the diagram of Piconets and Scatternet.

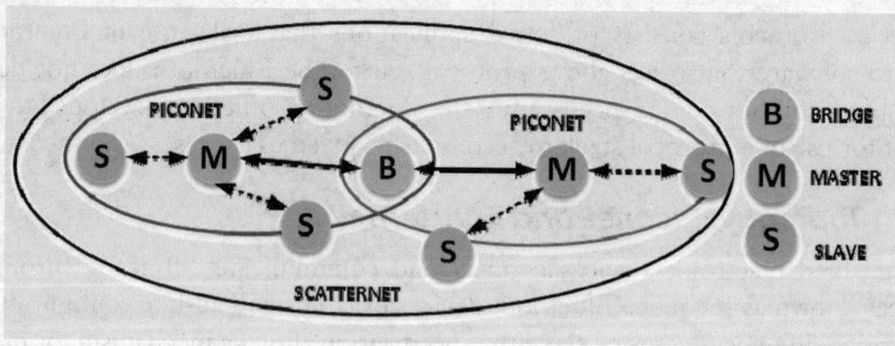

Fig.3.21: Diagram of Piconets and Scatternet

3.9 Z-wave

Z-wave (or Z wave or Zwave) is a protocol for communication among devices used for home automation. It uses RF for signaling and control. Z-wave was developed by Zensys, Inc. a start-up company based in Denmark. Z-wave was released in 2004. Based on the concepts of ZigBee, Z-wave strives to build simpler and less expensive devices than ZigBee.

Z-wave operates at 908.42 MHz in the US (868.42 MHz in Europe) using a mesh networking topology. A Z-wave network can contain up to 232 nodes, although reports exist of trouble with networks containing over 30-40 nodes. Z-wave operates using a number of profiles but the manufacturer claims they interoperate. When selecting products due care must be taken as some products from certain manufacturers are not compatible with other manufacturer's products.

Z-wave utilizes Gaussian Frequency Shift Keying (GFSK) modulation and Manchester channel encoding. In GFSK, baseband pulses are passed through a Gaussian filter prior to modulation. Filtering operation smoothens the pulses consisting of streams -1 and 1. This is known as pulse shaping. Pulse shaping limits the modulated spectrum width.

In data transmission, Manchester encoding is a form of digital encoding in which data bits are represented by transitions from one logical state to the other. This is different from the more common method of encoding, in which a bit is represented by either a high state such as +5 volts or a low state such as 0 volts. When the Manchester code is used, the length of each data bit is set by default. This makes the signal self-clocking. The state of a bit is determined according to the direction of the transition. In some systems, the transition from low to high represents logic 1, and the transition from high to low represents logic 0. In other systems, the transition from low to high represents logic 0, and the transition from high to low represents logic 1. The chief advantage of Manchester encoding is the fact that the signal synchronizes itself. This minimizes the error rate and optimizes reliability. The main disadvantage is the fact that a Manchester-encoded signal requires that more bits be transmitted than those in the original signal.

A central, network controller, device is required to setup and manage a Z-wave network. Each product in the home must be "included" to the Z-wave network before it can be controlled via Z-wave. Each Z-wave network is identified by a network ID and each device is further identified by a node ID. Figure 3.22 shows the architecture of Z-wave.

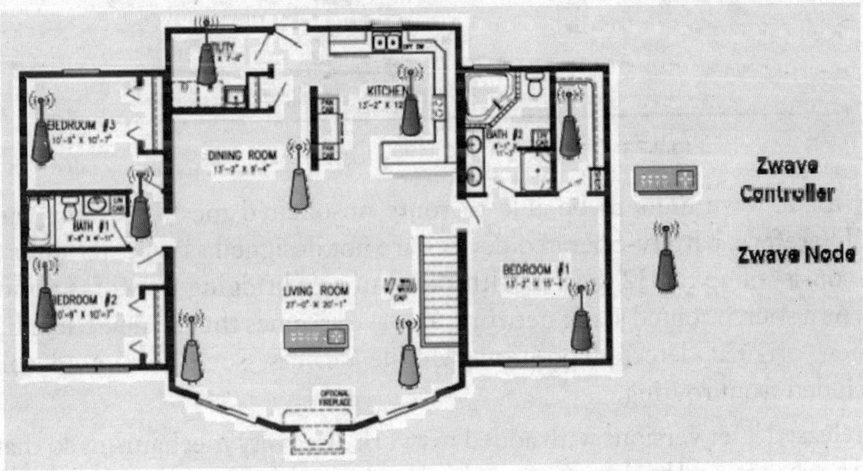

Fig.3.22: Architecture of Z-wave

The network ID (home ID) is the common identification of all nodes belonging to one logical Z-wave network. Network ID has a length of 4 bytes and is assigned to each device by the primary controller when the device is added into the network. Nodes with different network ID's cannot communicate with each other. The node ID is the address of the device/node existing within network. The node ID has a length of 1 byte.

Z-wave uses a source-routed mesh network topology and has one primary controller. Secondary controllers can exist, but are optional. Devices can communicate to one another by using intermediate nodes to route around and circumvent household obstacles or radio dead spots that might occur though a message called **"healing"**. Delays will be observed during the healing process. A message from node A to node C can be successfully delivered even if the two nodes are not within range, providing that a third node B can communicate with nodes A and C. If the preferred route is unavailable, the message originator will attempt other routes until a path is found to the "C" node. Therefore, a Z-wave network can span much farther than the radio range of a single unit. However, with several of these hops a slight delay may be introduced between the control command and the desired result. Figure 3.23 shows the direct path and healing path in Z-wave.

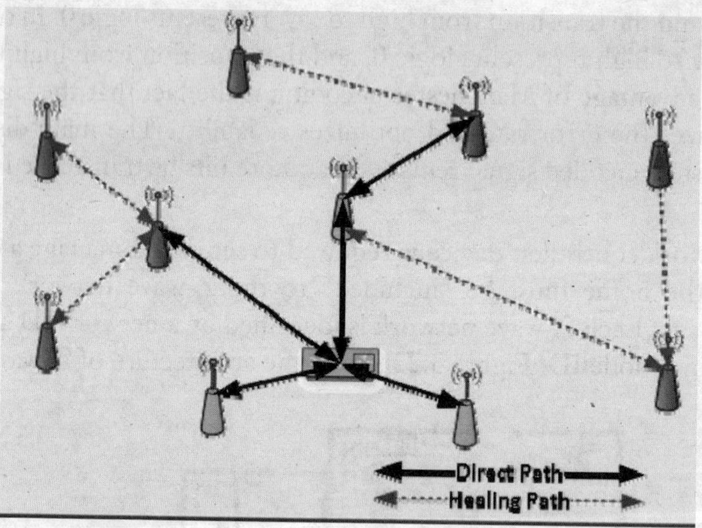

Fig.3.23: Direct Path and Healing Path in Z-wave

In order for Z-wave units to be able to route unsolicited messages, they cannot be in sleep mode. Therefore, battery-operated devices are not designed as repeater units. A Z-wave network can consist of up to 232 devices with the option of bridging networks if more devices are required. As a source routed static network, Z-wave assumes that all devices in the network remain in their original detected position. Mobile devices, such as remote controls, are therefore excluded from routing.

Z-wave released later versions with added network discovery mechanisms so that 'explorer frames' could be used to heal broken routes caused by devices that have been moved or removed.

A pruning algorithm is used in explorer frame broadcasts and is therefore supposed to reach the target device, even without further topology knowledge by the transmitter. Explorer frames are used as a last option by the sending device when all other routing attempts have failed.

Z-wave versus ZigBee

Z-wave	ZigBee
User friendly and provides a simple system that users can set up themselves.	Requires little power that devices can last upto 7 years on one set of batteries.
Ideal for someone with a basic understanding of technology who wants to keep their home automation secure, efficient, simple to use and easy to maintain.	Ideal for technology experts who want a system they can customize with their preferences and install themselves.
Expensive.	Cheaper than Z-wave.
Nine out of ten leading security and communication companies in the US use Z-wave in their smart home solutions.	ZigBee Alliance consists of nearly 400 member organizations that use, develop and Improve ZigBee's open standard wireless connection.

3.10 ISA 100.11A

ISA is the acronym for International Society of Automation. The official description is "Wireless Systems for Industrial Automation: Process Control and Related Applications". ISA 100.11 A is designed mainly for large scale industrial complexes and plants. More than 1 billion devices use ISA 100.11A. The features of this protocol includes flexibility, support for multiple protocols and applications, use of open standards, reliability which includes error detection channel hopping etc., determinism which includes TDMA, QoS support and security. Figure 3.24 shows the architecture of ISA 100.11A.

- ✓ RD=routing device
- ✓ NRD=Non-routing device
- ✓ H=Handheld device
- ✓ B=backbone device

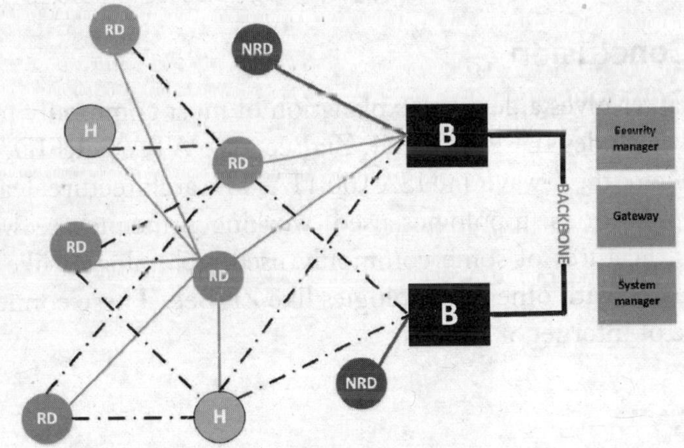

Fig.3.24: Architecture of ISA 100.11A

ISA 100.11 A is designed to support native and tunneled application layers. Various transport services including 'reliable', 'best effort', 'real-time' are offered. Network and transport layers are based on TCP or UDP/IPv6. Data link layer supports mesh routing and frequency hopping. Physical and Mac layers are based on IEEE 802.15.4. Topologies allowed in this protocol are star, tree and mesh. Permitted networks include radio link, ISA over Ethernet and field buses. Application support layer delivers communication services to user and management processes. This layer can pass objects, methods, attributes natively within the ISA 100.11A protocol. A tunneling mode is available to allow legacy data through the ISA 100.11A network.

Security is fully built-in to the standard. Authentication and confidentiality services are independently available for this standard. A network manager, manages and distributes the keys. There are twin security steps in each node. Data link layer encrypts each hop. Transport layer secures peer-to-peer communications. There are various usage classes associated with ISA 100.11A. It gives the category, class, application and description. Figure 3.25 shows the usage classes of ISA 100.11A.

Category	Class	Application	Description
Safety	0	Emergency action	Always critical
Control	1	Closed loop regulatory control	Often critical
	2	Closed loop supervisory control	Usually non-critical
	3	Open loop control	Human-in-the-loop
Monitoring	4	Alerting	Short term operational consequences
	5	Logging/Downloading	No immediate operation consequences

Fig.3.25: Usage Classes ISA 100.11A

3.11 Conclusion

This Chapter gives a detailed explanation of most commonly used connectivity technologies in IoT. It includes IEEE 802.15.4, ZigBee, 6LoWPAN, RFID, HART and Wireless HART, NFC, Bluetooth, Z-wave and ISA 100.11A. The architecture, features, various communication layers, applications, topologies used, working principle are well illustrated with necessary diagrams. Features of some commonly used technologies like wireless HART and Z-wave are compared with other technologies like ZigBee. These connectivity technologies form the backbone of Internet of Things.

4 WIRELESS SENSOR NETWORKS

4.1 Introduction

Wireless Sensor Networks (WSNs) consists of a large number of sensor nodes deployed over an area. Sensor nodes are capable of collaborating with one another and measuring the condition of their surrounding environments like light, temperature, sound, vibration etc. The sensed measurements are then transformed into digital signals and processed to reveal some properties of the phenomena around sensors. Sensor nodes find applications in various domains like temperature measurement, humidity level, lighting condition, air pressure, soil make-up, noise level and vibration.

These are similar to wireless ad hoc networks in the sense that they rely on wireless connectivity and spontaneous formation of networks so that sensor data can be transported wirelessly. The WSN is built of "nodes" from a few to several hundreds or even thousands, where each node is connected to one (or sometimes several) sensors. The sensor nodes in WSNs have short radio transmission range and hence intermediate nodes act as relay nodes to transmit data towards the destination node (sink node) using a multi-hop path. Figure 4.1 shows the multi-hop path in WSN.

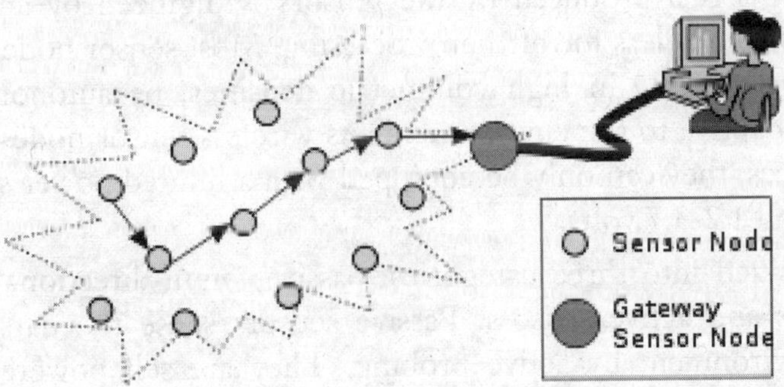

Fig.4.1: Multi-hop Path in WSN

Each such sensor network node has typically several parts: a radio transceiver with an internal antenna or connection to an external antenna, a microcontroller, an electronic circuit for interfacing with the sensors and an energy source, usually a battery or an embedded form of energy harvesting. Size and cost constraints on sensor nodes result in corresponding constraints on resources such as energy, memory, computational speed and communications bandwidth. The topology of the WSNs can vary from a simple star network to an advanced multi-hop wireless mesh network. The propagation technique between the hops of the network can be routing or flooding.

4.2 Components of a Sensor Node

The main components of a sensor node are a location finding unit which contains a transceiver, sensing unit which contains one or more sensors and an analog to digital converter (ADC), processor, storage or external memory and a power source. Figure 4.2 shows the architecture of a sensor node.

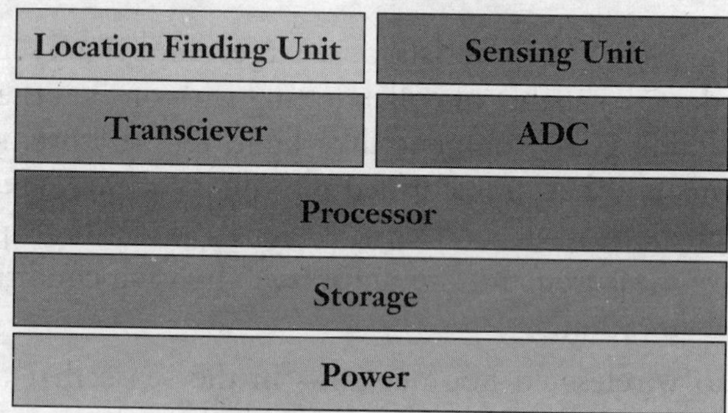

Fig.4.2: Architecture of a Sensor Node

Sensing unit: Sensors are used by wireless sensor nodes to capture data from their environment. They are hardware devices that produce a measurable response to a change in a physical condition like temperature or pressure. Sensors measure physical data of the parameter to be monitored and have specific characteristics such as accuracy, sensitivity etc. The continual analog signal produced by the sensors is digitized by an analog-to-digital converter and sent to controllers for further processing. Most sensor nodes are small in size, consume little energy, operate in high volumetric densities, be autonomous and operate unattended, and be adaptive to the environment. As wireless sensor nodes are typically very small electronic devices, they can only be equipped with a limited power source of less than 0.5-2 ampere-hour and 1.2-3.7 volts.

Sensors are classified into three categories: passive, omni-directional sensors: passive, narrow-beam sensors and active sensors. Passive sensors sense the data without actually manipulating the environment by active probing. They are self powered. The energy is needed only to amplify their analog signal. Active sensors actively probe the environment, for example, a sonar or radar sensor and they require continuous energy from a power source. Narrow-beam sensors have a well-defined notion of direction of measurement, similar to a camera. Omni-directional sensors have no notion of direction involved in their measurements.

Each sensor node has a certain area of coverage for which it can reliably and accurately report the particular quantity that it is observing. Several sources of power consumption in sensors are: signal sampling and conversion of physical signals to electrical ones, signal conditioning, and analog-to-digital conversion. Spatial density of sensor nodes in the field may be as high as 20 nodes per cubic meter.

Location Finding Unit and Transceiver

Location finding unit contains a transceiver which transmits or receives data. Sensor nodes often make use of ISM band, which gives free radio, spectrum allocation and global availability. The possible choices of wireless transmission media are radio frequency (RF), optical communication (laser) and infrared. Lasers require less energy, but need line-of-sight for communication and are sensitive to atmospheric conditions. Infrared, like lasers, needs no antenna but it is limited in its broadcasting capacity. Radio frequency-based communication is the most relevant that fits most of the WSN applications. WSNs tend to use license-free communication frequencies: 173, 433, 868, and 915 MHz and 2.4 GHz. The functionality of both transmitter and receiver are combined into a single device known as a transceiver. Transceivers often lack unique identifiers. The operational states are **transmit, receive, idle,** and **sleep.** Current generation transceivers have built-in state machines that perform some operations automatically.

Most transceivers operating in idle mode have a power consumption almost equal to the power consumed in receive mode. Thus, it is better to completely shut down the transceiver rather than leave it in the idle mode when it is not transmitting or receiving. A significant amount of power is consumed when switching from sleep mode to transmit mode in order to transmit a packet.

Processor

The processor processes data and controls the functionality of other components in the sensor node. While the most common processor is a microcontroller, other alternatives that can be used as a controller are a general purpose desktop microprocessor, digital signal processors etc. A microcontroller is often used in many embedded systems such as sensor nodes because of its low cost, flexibility to connect to other devices, ease of programming and low power consumption. A general purpose microprocessor generally has higher power consumption than a microcontroller, therefore it is often not considered a suitable choice for a sensor node. Digital Signal Processors may be chosen for broadband wireless communication applications, but in Wireless Sensor Networks the wireless communication is often modest: i.e., simpler, easier to process modulation and the signal processing tasks of actual sensing of data is less complicated. Therefore, the advantages of DSPs are not usually of much importance to wireless sensor nodes.

Storage or External Memory

From an energy perspective, the most relevant kinds of memory are the on-chip memory of a microcontroller and flash memory. Flash memories are used due to their cost and storage capacity. Memory requirements are very much application dependent. Two categories of memory based on the purpose of storage are: user memory used for storing application related or personal data and program memory used for programming the device. Program memory also contains identification data of the device if present.

Power Source

A wireless sensor node is a popular solution when it is difficult or impossible to run a mains supply to the sensor node. However, since the wireless sensor node is often placed in a hard-to-reach location, changing the battery regularly can be costly and inconvenient. An important aspect in the development of a wireless sensor node is ensuring that there is always adequate energy available to power the system. The sensor node consumes power for sensing, communicating and data processing. More energy is required for data communication than any other process. Power is stored either in batteries or capacitors. Batteries, both rechargeable and non-rechargeable, are the main source of power supply for sensor nodes. Current sensors are able to renew their energy from solar sources, temperature differences or vibration. Two power saving policies used are Dynamic Power Management (DPM) and Dynamic Voltage Scaling (DVS). DPM conserves power by shutting down parts of the sensor node which are not currently used or active. A DVS scheme varies the power levels within the sensor node depending on the non-deterministic workload. By varying the voltage along with the frequency, it is possible to obtain quadratic reduction in power consumption.

4.3 Modes of Detection

There are 4 modes by which sensors detect the objects or sense the data. They are as follows.

a. **Single Source Single Object Detection** – In this a single object will be detected by a single sensor node. The detected data will be sent to the sink node via the intermediate sensors. Figure 4.3 shows single source single object detection mode.

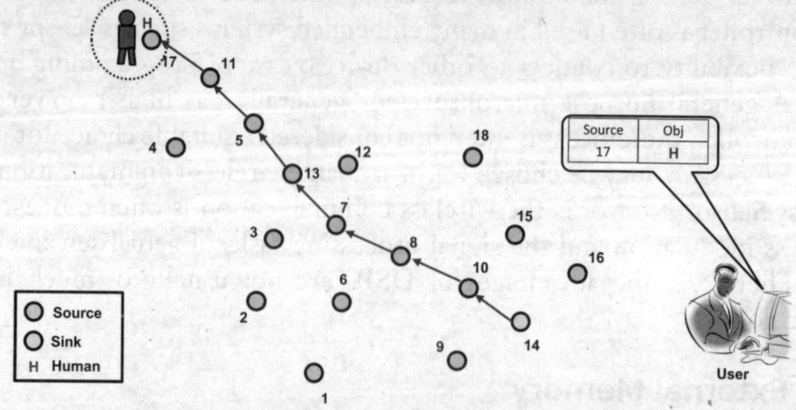

Fig.4.3: Single Source Single Object Detection

b. **Single Source Multiple Object Detection** – In this there will be a single source for detecting multiple objects. The detected data on reaching the sink node will identify the various objects. Figure 4.4 shows single source multiple object detection mode.

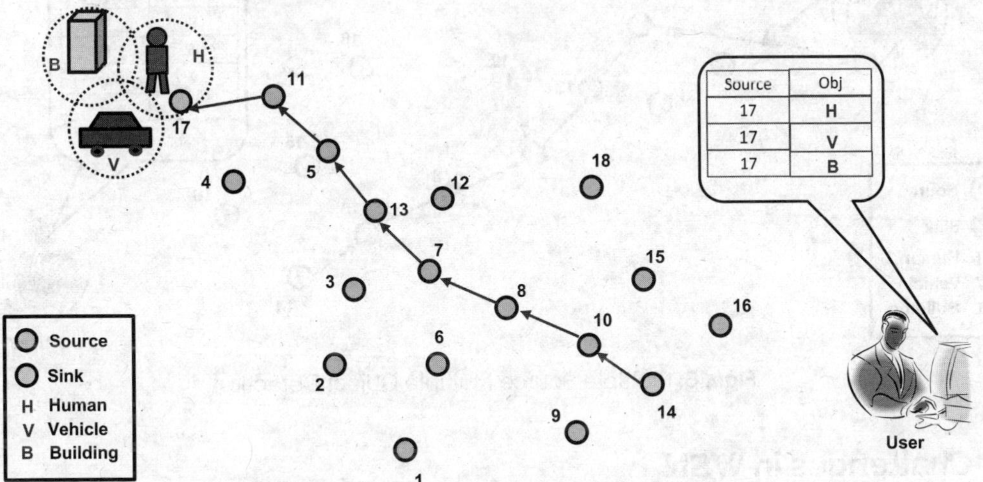

Fig.4.4: Single Source Multiple Object Detection

c. **Multiple Source Single Object Detection** – In this, same object will be detected by multiple sensors. This is expensive and can be applied for security critical applications. Figure 4.5 shows multiple source single object detection mode.

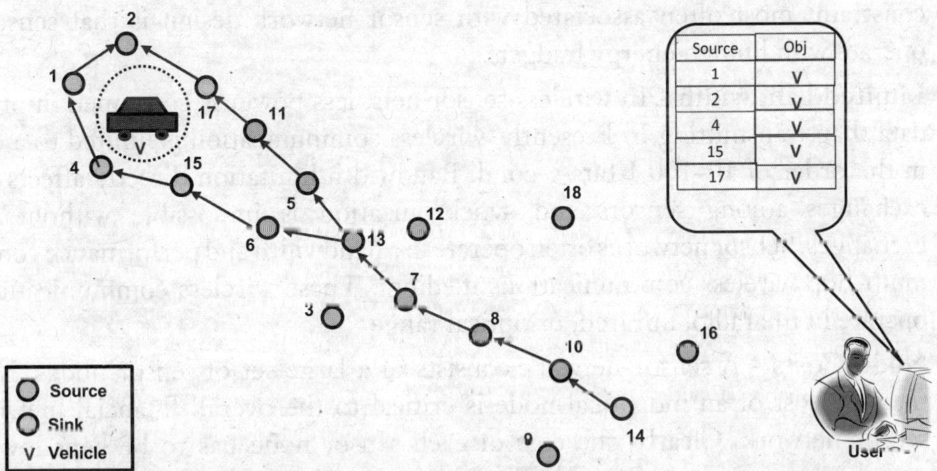

Fig.4.5: Multiple Source Single Object Detection

d. **Multiple Source Multiple Object Detection** – This mode of detection contains more than one object and more than one sensor. Each object may be detected by more than one sensor. Figure 4.6 shows multiple source multiple object detection mode.

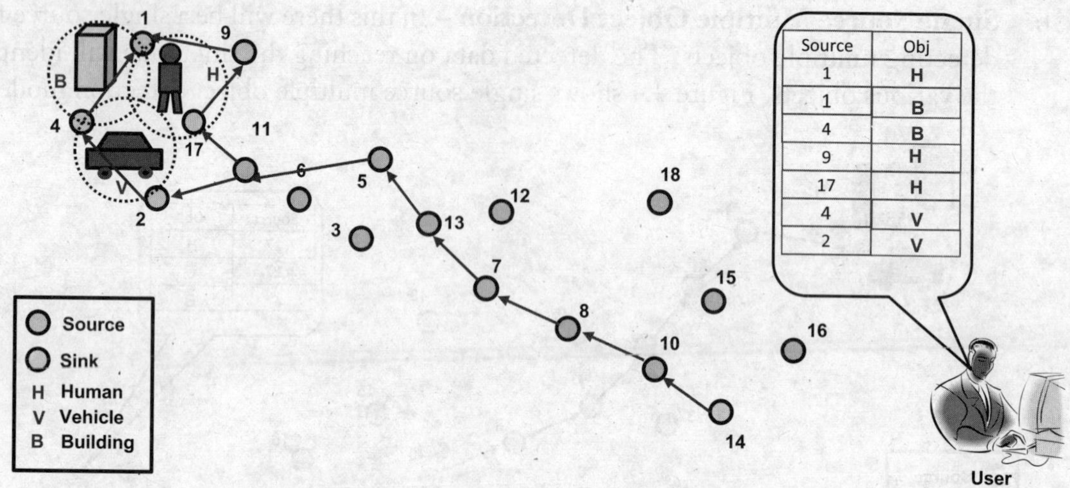

Source	Obj
1	H
1	B
4	B
9	H
17	H
4	V
2	V

Fig.4.6: Multiple Source Multiple Object Detection

4.4 Challenges in WSN

There are several challenges in WSN. They are the following.

a. **Energy Efficiency** - The first and often most important design challenge for a WSN is energy efficiency. Power consumption can be allocated to three functional domains: sensing, communication and data processing, each of which requires optimization. The sensor node lifetime typically exhibits a strong dependency on battery life. The constraint most often associated with sensor network design is that sensor nodes operate with limited energy budgets.

b. **Limited bandwidth** - In wireless sensor nets, less power is consumed in processing data than transmitting it. Presently, wireless communication is limited to a data rate in the order of 10–100 Kbits/second. Bandwidth limitation directly affects message exchanges among sensors and synchronization is impossible without message exchanges. Sensor networks often operate in a bandwidth and performance constrained multi-hop wireless communications medium. These wireless communications links operate in the radio, infrared, or optical range.

c. **Node Costs** - A sensor network consists of a large set of sensor nodes. It follows that the cost of an individual node is critical to the overall financial metric of the sensor network. Clearly, the cost of each sensor node has to be kept low for the global metrics to be acceptable. Depending on the application of sensor network, large number of sensors might be scattered randomly over an environment, such as weather monitoring. If the overall cost was appropriate for sensor networks and it will be more acceptable and successful to users which need careful consideration.

d. **Deployment** - Node deployment is a fundamental issue to be solved in Wireless Sensor Networks. A proper node deployment scheme can reduce the complexity of problems. Deploying and managing a high number of nodes in a relatively bounded environment requires special techniques. Hundreds to thousands of sensors may be deployed in a sensor region. There are two deployment models at present: (i) static deployment (ii) dynamic deployment. The static deployment chooses the best location according to the optimization strategy and the location of the sensor nodes has no change in the lifetime of the WSN. The dynamic deployment throws the nodes randomly for optimization.

e. **Design Constraints** - The primary goal of wireless sensor design is to create smaller, cheaper and more efficient devices. A variety of additional challenges can affect the design of sensor nodes and wireless sensor networks. WSN have challenges on both software and hardware design models with restricted constraints.

f. **Security** - One of the challenges in WSNs is to provide high security requirements with constrained resources. Many wireless sensor networks collect sensitive information. The remote and unattended operation of sensor nodes increases their exposure to malicious intrusions and attacks. The security requirements in WSNs are comprised of node authentication and data confidentiality. To identify both trustworthy and unreliable nodes from a security stand point, the deployment sensors must pass a node authentication examination by their corresponding manager nodes or cluster heads and unauthorized nodes can be isolated from WSNs during the node authentication procedure. As a consequence, sensor networks require new solutions for key establishment and distribution, node authentication and secrecy.

4.5 Sensor Web

The concept of the Sensor Web is a type of sensor network that is especially well suited for environmental monitoring. Sensor Web is also associated with a sensing system which heavily utilizes the World Wide Web. Figure 4.7 shows the architecture of Sensor Web.

Sensor Web is the combination of Service Oriented Architecture (SOA), grid computing and sensor networks. Various sensors and sensor nodes form a web view and are treated as available services to all the users who access the Web. Sensor Web brings the heterogeneous sensors into an integrated and uniform platform supporting dynamic discovery and access. A sample scenario would be the client (may be the researchers or other software, model and workflow system), who wants to utilize the information collected by the deployed sensors on the target application, such as weather forecast, tsunami or pollution detection. The client may query the entire sensor web and get the response either from real-time sensors that have been registered in the web or existing data from a remote database. The clients are not aware of where the real sensors are and what operations they may have, although they are required to set parameters for their plan and invoke the service (similar to when people perform a search on Google, filling in the search field and clicking the search button). The primary goal of the Sensor Web is to offer reliable and accessible services to the end-users. In other words, it provides the middleware infrastructure and the programming environment for creating, accessing and utilizing sensor services through the Web.

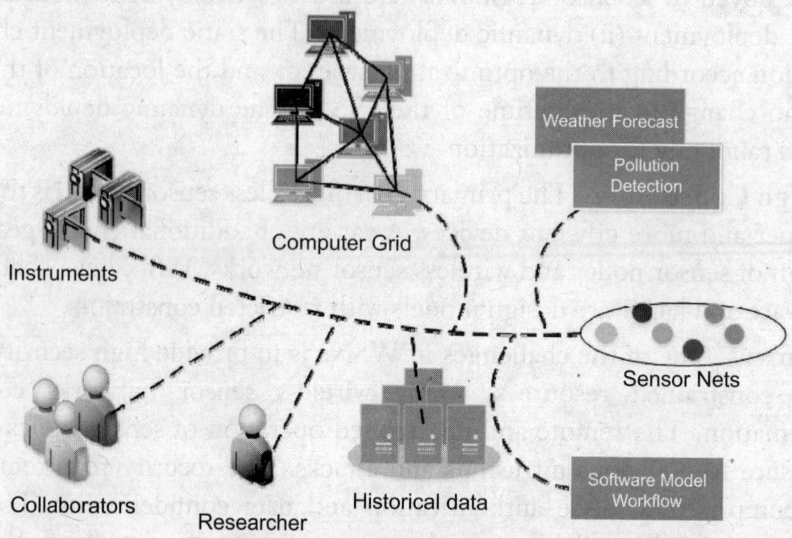

Fig.4.7: Architecture of Sensor Web

Sensor Web Enablement

The Sensor Web Enablement (SWE) becomes the de facto standard regarding Sensor Web development, understanding SWE is crucial for both researchers and developers. In general, SWE is the standard developed by Open Geospatial Consortium (OGC) that encompasses specifications for interfaces, protocols and encodings that enable discovering, accessing, obtaining sensor data as well as sensor-processing services. Figure 4.8 shows a typical collaboration within Sensor Web Enablement framework. The following are the primary specifications for SWE.

1. Sensor Model Language (SensorML) – Information model and XML encodings that describe either single sensor or sensor platform in regard to discover, query and control sensors.
2. Observation and Measurement (O&M) – Information model and XML encodings for observations and measurement.
3. Transducer Markup Language - TransducerML or TML is an OGC standard developed to describe any transducer (sensor or transmitter) in terms of a common model, including characterizing not only the data but XML formed metadata describing the system producing that data.
4. Sensor Observation Service (SOS) - Open interface for a web service to obtain observations and sensor and platform descriptions from one or more sensors.

5. Sensor Planning Service (SPS) – Service to help users build feasible sensor collection plan and to schedule requests for sensors and sensor platforms.
6. Sensor Collection Service (SCS) – Service to fetch observations, which conforms to the Observations and Measurement information model, from a single sensor or a collection of sensors. It is also used to describe the sensors and sensor platforms by utilizing SensorML.
7. Web Notification Service (WNS) – Service to manage client session and notify the client about the outcome of one's requested service using various communication protocols.

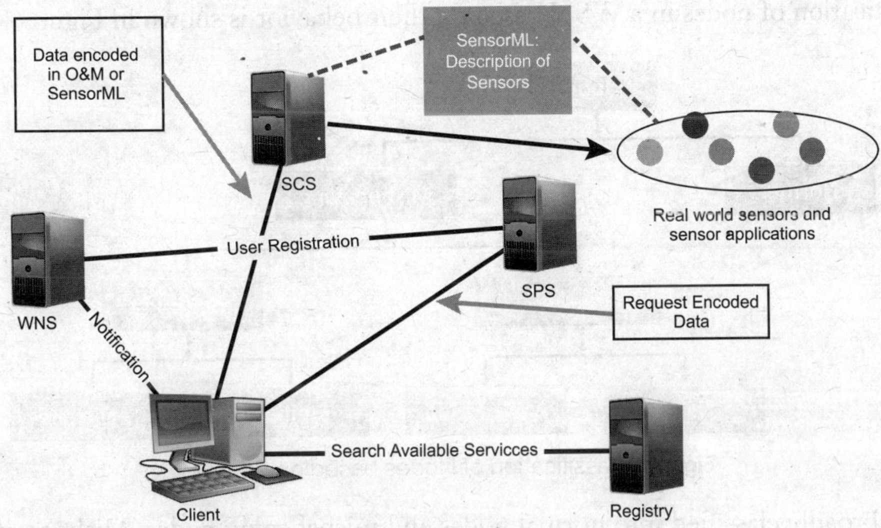

Fig.4.8: Sensor Web Enablement Framework

4.6 Cooperation

Cooperative communication is one of the promising techniques to enhance the performance of wireless networks. Nodes in a WSN communicate with other nodes with the help of intermediate nodes. These intermediate nodes act as relays. The extent of performance improvement needs to be carefully investigated, especially for wireless sensor networks, due to the overhead and energy costs involved with cooperation and the dependency on energy consumption models. Wireless nodes are energy constrained. Nodes may or may not cooperate in a communication in WSN. There are two extremities for cooperation. They are

a. **Total Cooperation** – If all relay requests from successor nodes are accepted, it is known as total cooperation. In this case the nodes will quickly exhaust limited energy.

b. **Total Non Cooperation** – In total non cooperation, no relay requests are accepted from the successor nodes. Here energy is conserved but the network throughput will go down rapidly.

There are several security challenges in cooperation. It is a challenge to enforce security in open, shared medium by the nodes which dynamically change its positions. There is no centralized network management or certification authority to implement security in WSN. Existence of malicious codes in software is yet another challenge. Nodes are prone to attacks, infiltration, eavesdropping and interference. Nodes can be captured, compromised or false routing information can be sent by the intruders thereby paralyzing the whole network. There is a chance of victimizing the cooperating node.

4.7 Behavior of Nodes in WSN

The nodes in a WSN can be classified according to the behavior they exhibit in a network. The classification of nodes in a WSN based on their behavior is shown in Figure 4.9.

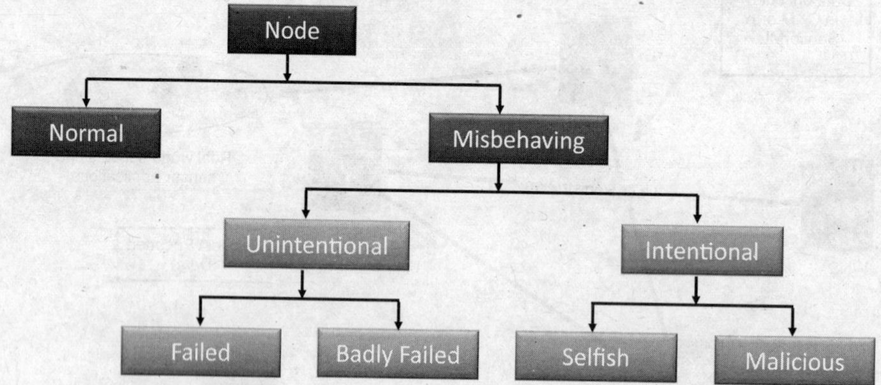

Fig.4.9: Classification of Nodes based on Behavior

Nodes are broadly classified into normal nodes and misbehaving nodes. Misbehaving may be intentional or unintentional. Intentional behavior can be due to selfish nodes or malicious nodes. Unintentional behavior may be due to failed nodes or badly failed nodes.

a. **Normal nodes**: These are nodes that work perfectly in ideal environment conditions.

b. **Failed nodes**: These are nodes that are unable to perform an operation. Failed nodes may arise due to power failures or adverse environmental conditions.

c. **Badly failed nodes**: They are similar to failed nodes but with a difference. They exhibit the features of failed nodes but they sometimes send false routing messages which are a threat to the integrity of the network.

d. **Selfish nodes**: They are named selfish because of their unwillingness to cooperate in a network transmission. These nodes utilize the network resources for its own profit but it refuses to share their personal resources for other nodes. Due to presence of selfish node in the network, the network is defective and the data communication between nodes is disrupted. Packet dropping is the main attack by selfish nodes.

e. **Malicious nodes**: These nodes aim to deliberately disrupt the correct operation of the routing protocol, denying network service if possible. Since it disrupts or undermines network protocols like routing and clustering, they are very dangerous and need to be detected as soon as possible to minimize the damage they can cause.

Some nodes in a WSN misbehave temporarily. Detection of such temporary misbehavior is required in order to preserve normal functioning of the network. This temporary misbehavior is known as **dumb behavior**. In the presence of adverse environmental conditions like high temperature, rainfall and fog, the communication range shrinks. In this scenario, a sensor node can sense its surroundings but it is unable to transmit the sensed data. When the environmental conditions resume favorably, these dumb nodes again work normally. Dumb behavior is temporal in nature.

Even though the dumb behavior is temporary, the presence of dumb nodes impedes the overall network performance. Detection of such dumb nodes and subsequently the re-establishment of network connectivity is crucial. The sensed information can only be utilized if the connectivity between each dumb node with other nodes in the network could be re-established. Connectivity Re-establishment in the Presence of Dumb nodes (CoRD) and Connectivity Re-establishment of lost connectivity using sensor nodes with Adjustable communication range (CoRAD) are two popular schemes that re-establish the connectivity between dumb nodes with others.

4.8 Information Theoretic Self Management of WSN

A Wireless Sensor Network (WSN) is deployed primarily with the interest of collecting information about an area of interest or some events of interest occurring in that area. A WSN transmits the sensed information to the end users in the form of data-packets. The number of packets is directly proportional to the transmission rate of the nodes in the WSN. There is a distributed self-management scheme for WSNs, named as Information Theoretic Self-Management (InTSeM), for WSNs. The scheme helps the nodes in the network to adapt themselves with the changes in their environment and to select an appropriate transmission rate using an information theoretic metric. This dynamic selection of transmission rate conserves the energy of nodes while maintaining the quality of data. Figure 4.10 shows the general framework of InTSeM.

The advantages of this InTSeM are the reduction of consumption of transmission energy of transmitters and receiving energy of relay nodes.

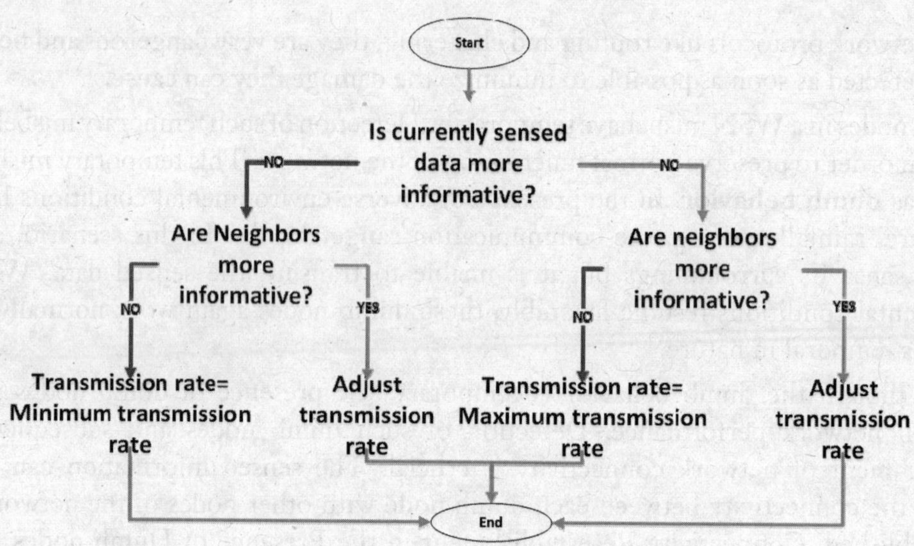

Fig.4.10: General Framework of InTSeM

4.9 Social Sensing in WSN

In a Wireless Sensor Network, an event of interest should be timely detected. The event should be monitored and disseminates the event data to the sink. It depends on event location, event area and event duration. In WSN, the data delivery models, such as periodic, event-driven, have implications on the overall network topology. A distributed event-aware topology management scheme for WSN named as Event-Aware Topology Management (EATM), periodically constructs the network topology on the basis of the current event state and the state of the nodes of the network. EATM partitions the network into clusters, and uses concepts intertwined with the concepts of Facility Location Theory, in a distributed manner, for reducing the energy dissipation of the event monitoring nodes by reducing their average transmission distance. EATM is able to conserve 15 % energy of event-monitoring nodes and enhances the network lifetime by at least 5 % time.

Wireless Sensor Networks are energy constrained. The social sensing based duty cycle management minimizes energy consumption in monitoring 'rare events' by reducing the period of 'ineffective sensing'. Ineffective sensing is defined as event monitoring or sensing, even if there is no event to monitor or sense. Existing schemes suffer from unnecessary energy consumption because of ineffective sensing. For example, the period and frequency of occurrence of an event in military applications is unpredictable and sometimes the delay between two consecutive occurrences is very large. We exploit the social sensing behavior of social networks for avoiding non-effective sensing by managing the duty cycle of a node in a sensor network. The challenges include distinguishing rare events and regular events and adapting the duty-cycle with the event occurrence probability. Figure 4.11 shows a typical example for social sensing in WSN.

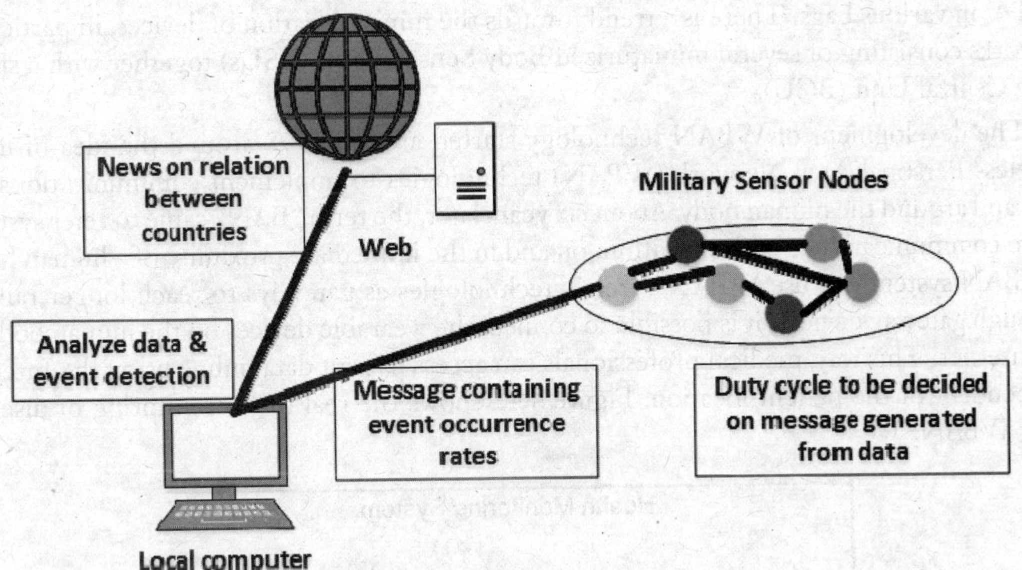

Fig.4.11: Social Sensing in WSN

In Figure 4.11, there is a network of military sensor nodes. These network nodes need to be more alert when there is a problem in the relationship between two countries. Whenever a local computer receives data about an incident that may affect the security of a country from Web or any social networking sites, it analyzes the data and passes the message to the military sensor nodes. Depending on the data received from the local computer, the duty cycle of the nodes are adjusted so that it sense the data frequently when a rare event is going to happen or slow down the sensing of the data otherwise. This mechanism can save a lot of energy.

4.10 Applications of WSN

Wireless Sensor Networks find application in several domains like mines, healthcare sectors, surveillance, agriculture etc. Wireless Sensor Networks can be used in a fire monitoring and alarm system (FMA) for underground Bord and Pillar based coal mines. It is not only capable of providing real-time monitoring and alarm in case of a fire, but also capable of providing exact fire location and spreading location by continuously gathering, analyzing and storing real time information. We will see the application of Wireless Sensor Networks in healthcare and agriculture in detail.

4.10.1 WSN in Healthcare

A Wireless Body Area Network (WBAN) or a body sensor network (BSN), is a wireless network of wearable computing devices. BAN devices may be embedded inside the body, implants, surface-mounted on the body in a fixed position. Wearable technology may be accompanied devices which humans can carry in different positions, in cloth's pockets, by hand or in various bags. There is a trend towards the miniaturization of devices, in particular, networks consisting of several miniaturized Body Sensor Units (BSUs) together with a single Body Central Unit (BCU).

The development of WBAN technology started around 1995 around the idea of using Wireless Personal Area Network (WPAN) technologies to implement communications on, near, and around the human body. About six years later, the term "BAN" came to refer systems where communication is entirely within, on and in the immediate proximity of a human body. A WBAN system can use WPAN wireless technologies as gateways to reach longer ranges. Through gateway devices, it is possible to connect the wearable devices on the human body to the Internet. This way, medical professionals can access patient data online using the Internet independent of the patient location. Figure 4.12 shows the real time monitoring of diseases using WBAN.

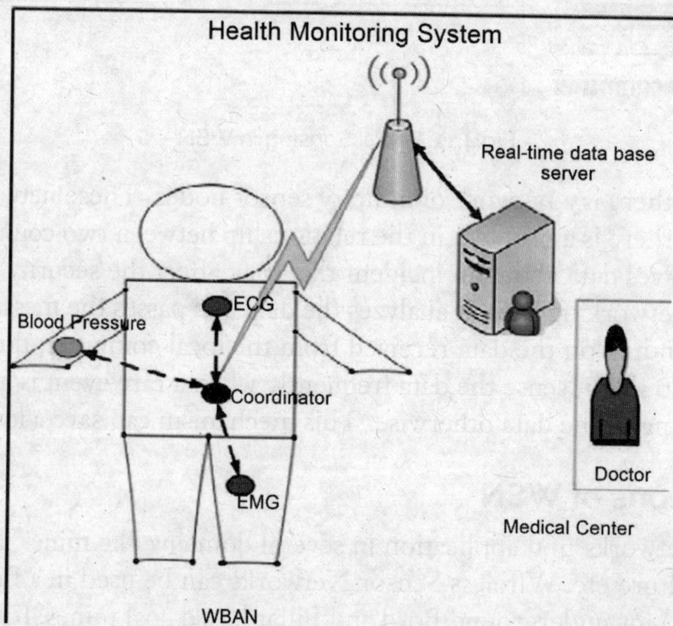

Fig.4.12: Real-time Monitoring of Diseases using WBAN

WBANs have recently gained popularity due to their ability in providing innovative, cost-effective and user-friendly solutions for continuous monitoring of vital physiological parameters of patients. WBANs are useful in monitoring chronic and serious diseases such as cardiovascular diseases and diabetes in elderly persons in a daily manner.

In a cloud-assisted Wireless Body Area Network (WBAN), health data of patients are transmitted from the Local Data Processing Units (LDPUs) to the health-cloud platform through a set of mobile monitoring nodes. In a post-disaster scenario, it is important that the data acquired by the body sensor nodes are aggregated in an efficient manner and channelized to the cloud platform with minimum delay. This includes ambulatory healthcare services where the health status of a patient is examined continuously over time, while the patient is being moved to the emergency healthcare center.

There are two fundamental research issues in this context – aggregation of health data transmitted by the LDPUs within the mobile monitoring nodes and channelization of the aggregated data by dynamic selection of the cloud gateways. Aggregation takes place at the mobile monitoring nodes, which makes the problem challenging due to reasons attributed to mobility and health data prioritization. Data aggregation among LDPUs is done in a "fair" manner following the "Theory of Social Choice". Body Area Network Data Aggregation Algorithm (Banag), generates a preference order for each patient, based on the severity and acuteness of his/her health. For each patient, an exigency factor, which measures health criticality, is also associated. In addition to the actual health condition, there exists indirect influence of external parameters such as age, height, weight and sex on health parameters. The challenge is to design a dynamic decision making model that can optimize the energy consumption of each physiological sensor.

Priority based time slot allocation in WBANs is quite useful. In medical emergency situation, it is important to discriminate the WBANs transmitting critical health data from the ones transmitting data of regular importance. Existing frequency division based transmission in a multi-source single-sink network results in flooding of the sink's receiver buffer. This leads to packet loss and consequent retransmission of the regenerated packets. Transmission priority of a Local Data Processing Unit (LPDU) is indifferent to the criticality of the health data that is being transmitted by the LDPU. Based on LDPU properties such as the criticality of health data, energy dissipation factor and time elapsed since last successful transmission, a fitness parameter is formulated which is a relative measure of node importance. The Priority based Allocation of Time Slots (PATS) algorithm allows the LDPUs to choose their strategies based on their fitness. LDPUs with higher fitness are given higher preference while ensuring minimum waiting time between successive transmissions of data packets.

4.10.2 WSN In Surveillance

Wireless Sensor Networks can be used in surveillance systems. This is known as **target tracking** or object tracking. It comprises of a WSN network containing cameras. This can be used in crowded places like railway stations, shopping malls, airports etc. When a suspicious object is detected by a sensor, it needs to track the trajectory of the object. This tracking can be of two types. First one is to keep on following the target as and when the target moves to know where it is moving using different sensors. This can be done in real time. The second one is to predict the trajectory of the target. There are three different problems of formulation in target tracking. They are a) Push based Formulation b) Pull based Formulation and c) Guided Formulation.

Push based formulation: Figure 4.13 shows an example for push based formulation. In push based formulation shown in Figure 4.13, an object (let it be a human) is sensed by three sensors. The arrows show the trajectory of the object. As the object moves, the nodes compute the position of the target and periodically notify the sink node. Sink node is the node that receives data from all other source nodes. A cluster structure is used in this case.

Poll based formulation: Figure 4.14 shows an example for poll based formulation. In this the nodes register the presence of the target to permit a low cost query. In other words each node sends poll information periodically to other nodes to see whether an object is present within its sensing range. Data reports are sent towards the sink only when there is a query to be answered. Tree structure is often used in this case.

Guided Formulation: Figure 4.15 shows a guided formulation. In this some nodes called beacon nodes define a trajectory to the target. The tracker follows this trail to intercept the target. Face structure is often used in this case.

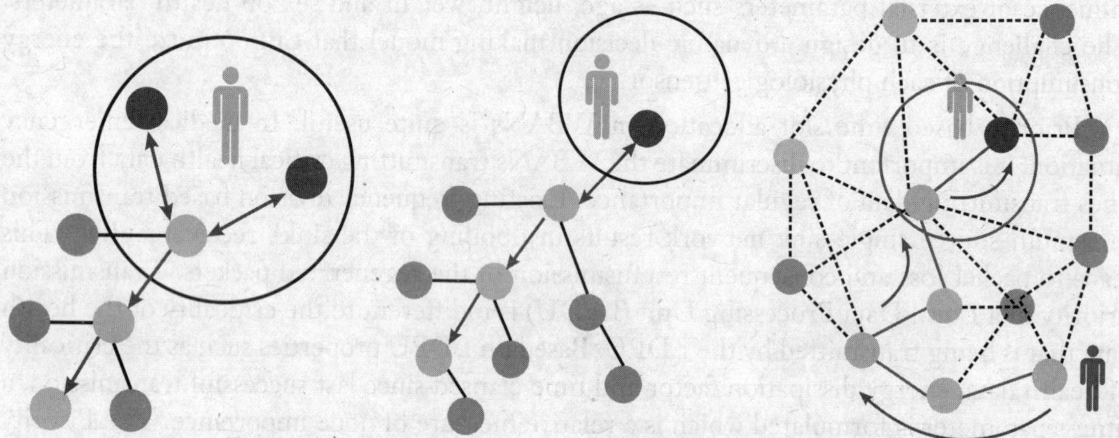

Fig.4.13: Push based Formulation **Fig.4.14:** Poll based Formulation **Fig.4.15:** Guided Formulation

Figure 4.16 illustrates the functioning of target tracking. Initially sensors detect an object in their sensing range. The next step is the cooperation of the nodes. Cooperation among nodes takes place due to several activities like aggregation of the data, relaying the information that has been received etc. Then the exact position of the target object needs to be computed. The position can be computed using several concepts like trilateration. In geometry, trilateration is the process of determining absolute or relative locations of points by measurement of distances, using the geometry of circles, spheres or triangles. Using this concept, we can compute the position of the object if we know the position of the sensors.

Next step is the prediction of the target object. There may be situations where large number of sensors start sensing which leads to issues like energy management. To deal with energy management, it needs to be identified the minimum number of sensors to be activated for tracking an object. This will help to put other sensors to sleep mode which conserves a lot of energy.

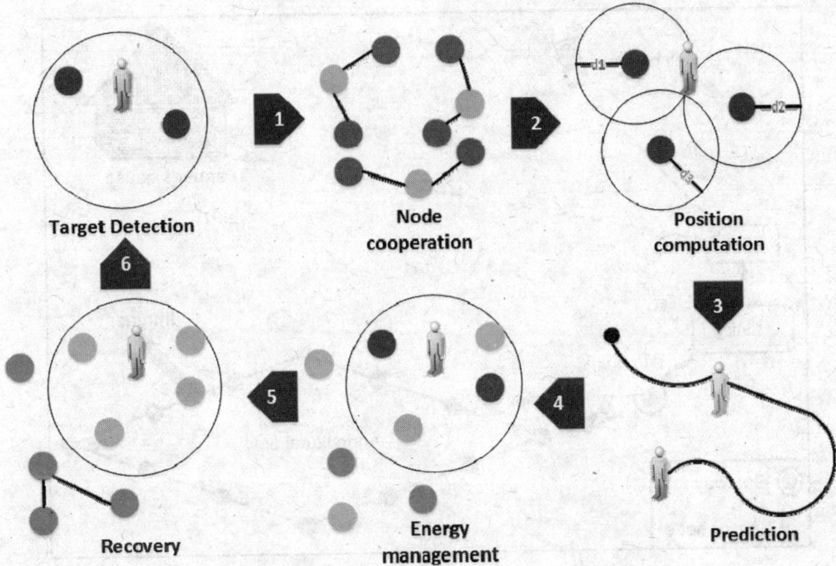

Fig.4.16: Functioning of Target Tracking

4.10.3 WSN in Agriculture

Wireless Sensor Networks are used in agriculture for intrusion detection, monitoring soil parameters like moisture content, mineral content etc. The information about the moisture content of the soil can be used for irrigation. Likewise the information about the mineral content of the soil can be used for applying manures and fertilizers. For intrusion detection, a set of sensory nodes are deployed over an agricultural field. Figure 4.17 shows the architecture of the sensing unit in an agricultural field.

Each of the sensing units is enabled with two types of sensors. a) Passive Infrared Sensors (PIR) b) Ultrasonic Sensors. When an intruder enters into the field, through the boundary or perimeter of the field, the PIR sensor detects the object. The ultrasonic sensor senses the distance at which the object is located. If an intrusion takes place, the farmer will be notified via cell phone or other means of communication. Figure 4.18 shows the layered architecture of the Intrusion Detection System.

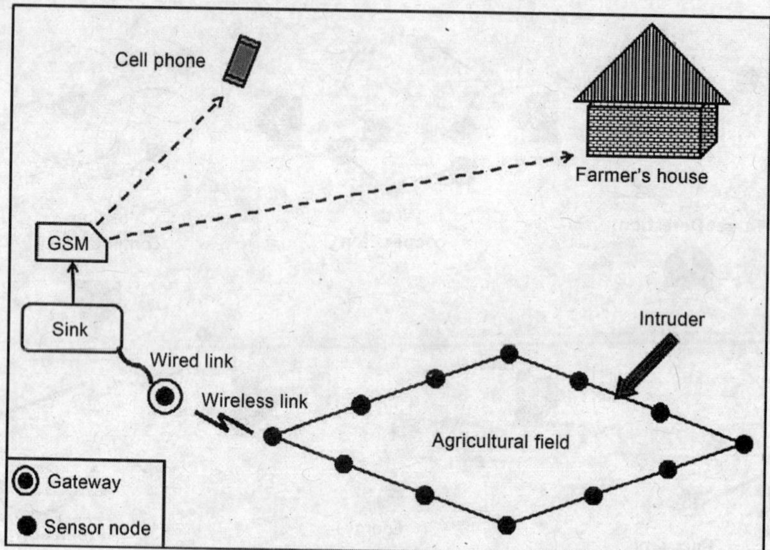

Fig.4.17: Architecture of Sensing Unit in an Agricultural Field

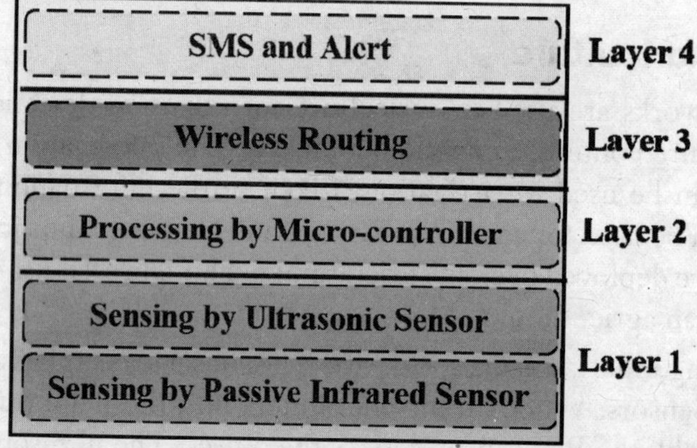

Fig.4.18: Layered Architecture of Intrusion Detection System

Layer 1 consists of the sensing by ultrasonic sensor and PIR sensor. Layer 2 comprises of processing the data by microcontroller. Layer 3 forms the wireless routing and finally at layer 4 SMS and alert messages will be sent to the farmer.

4.11 Wireless Multimedia Sensor Networks

Wireless Multimedia Sensor Networks (WMSNs) have emerged and shifted the focus from the typical scalar wireless sensor networks to networks with multimedia devices that are capable to retrieve video, audio, images, as well as scalar sensor data. WMSNs are able to deliver multimedia content due to the availability of inexpensive CMOS cameras and microphones coupled with the significant progress in distributed signal processing and multimedia source coding techniques. There are two types of sensor nodes.

a. Camera Sensor Nodes – These nodes capture multimedia content like audio and video data. These nodes are expensive and resource hungry with a directional sensing range. The sensing changes with direction.

b. Scalar Sensor Nodes – These nodes sense scalar data like temperature, light, vibration etc. This is low cost compared to camera sensor nodes. These nodes have an omni-directional sensing range where direction does not affect the sensing.

WMSNs consist of less number of camera sensor nodes and large number of scalar sensor nodes. WMSNs find application in security surveillance, wild habitat monitoring and environmental monitoring. In these types of applications camera sensor nodes can provide precise information than scalar sensor nodes. Video data are larger in size which require larger bandwidth and consumes high battery power. There are three types of architecture involved in WMSNs. Figure 4.19 shows the architecture of WMSN.

Figure 4.19(a) is a single tier flat architecture comprising of homogeneous sensors. A subset of the deployed sensors has higher processing capabilities and is thus referred to as processing hubs. The union of the processing hubs constitutes a distributed processing architecture. The multimedia content gathered is relayed to a wireless gateway through a multi-hop path. The gateway is interconnected to a storage hub that is in charge of storing multimedia content locally for subsequent retrieval. Clearly, more complex architectures for distributed storage can be implemented when allowed by the environment and the application needs, which may result in energy savings since by storing it locally, the multimedia content does not need to be wirelessly relayed to remote locations. The wireless gateway is also connected to a central sink, which implements the software front-end for network querying and tasking.

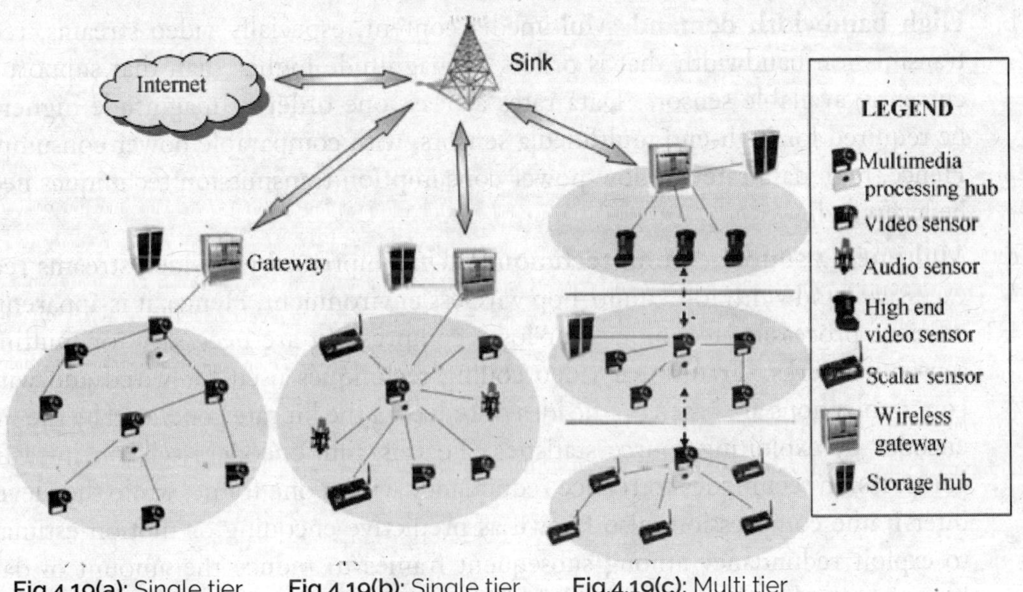

Fig.4.19(a): Single tier flat architecture

Fig.4.19(b): Single tier cluster architecture

Fig.4.19(c): Multi tier network

Fig.4.19: Architecture of WMSN

Figure 4.19(b) represents a single-tiered clustered architecture of heterogeneous sensors (only one cluster is depicted). Video, audio and scalar sensors relay data to a central cluster head, which is also in charge of performing intensive multimedia processing on the data (processing hub). The cluster head relays the gathered content to the wireless gateway and to the storage hub.

Figure 4.19(c) represents a multi-tiered network, with heterogeneous sensors. Each tier is in charge of a subset of the functionalities. Resource constrained, low-power scalar sensors are in charge of performing simpler tasks, such as detecting scalar physical measurements, while resource-rich, high-power devices are responsible for more complex tasks. Data processing and storage can be performed in a distributed fashion at each different tier.

Factors Influencing the Design of Multimedia Sensor Networks

a. **Application-specific QoS requirements**: The wide variety of applications envisaged on WMSNs will have different requirements. In addition to data delivery modes typical of scalar sensor networks, multimedia data include snapshot and streaming multimedia content. Snapshot type multimedia data contain event triggered observations obtained in a short time period. Streaming multimedia content is generated over longer time periods and requires sustained information delivery. Hence, a strong foundation is needed in terms of hardware and supporting high-level algorithms to deliver QoS and consider application-specific requirements. These requirements may pertain to multiple domains and can be expressed, amongst others, in terms of a combination of bounds on energy consumption, delay, reliability, distortion, or network lifetime.

b. **High bandwidth demand**: Multimedia content, especially video streams, require transmission bandwidth that is orders of magnitude higher than that supported by currently available sensors. Data rates at least one order of magnitude higher may be required for high-end multimedia sensors, with comparable power consumption. Hence, high data rate and low-power consumption transmission techniques need to be leveraged.

c. **Multimedia source coding techniques**: Uncompressed raw video streams require excessive bandwidth for a multi-hop wireless environment. Hence, it is apparent that efficient processing techniques for lossy compression are necessary for multimedia sensor networks. Traditional video coding techniques used for wired and wireless communications are based on the idea of reducing the bit rate generated by the source encoder by exploiting source statistics. To this aim, encoders rely on intra-frame compression techniques to reduce redundancy within one frame, while they leverage inter-frame compression (also known as predictive encoding or motion estimation) to exploit redundancy among subsequent frames to reduce the amount of data to be transmitted and stored, thus achieving good rate-distortion performance. Since predictive encoding requires complex encoders, powerful processing algorithms and entails high energy consumption, it may not be suited for low-cost multimedia sensors.

d. **Multimedia in-network processing**: WMSNs allow performing multimedia in-network processing algorithms on the raw data extracted from the environment. This requires new architectures for collaborative, distributed, and resource-constrained processing that allow for filtering and extraction of semantically relevant information at the edge of the sensor network. This may increase the system scalability by reducing the transmission of redundant information, merging data originated from multiple views, on different media, and with multiple resolutions. For example, in video security applications, information from uninteresting scenes can be compressed to a simple scalar value or not be transmitted altogether, while in environmental applications, distributed filtering techniques can create a time-elapsed image. Hence, it is necessary to develop application-independent architectures to flexibly perform in-network processing of the multimedia content gathered from the environment.

e. **Power consumption**: Power consumption is a fundamental concern in WMSNs, even more than in traditional wireless sensor networks. In fact, sensors are battery-constrained devices, while multimedia applications produce high volumes of data, which require high transmission rates and extensive processing. While the energy consumption of traditional sensor nodes is known to be dominated by the communication functionalities, this may not necessarily be true in WMSNs. Therefore, protocols, algorithms and architectures to maximize the network lifetime while providing the QoS required by the application are a critical issue.

f. **Flexible architecture to support heterogeneous applications**: WMSN architectures will support several heterogeneous and independent applications with different requirements. It is necessary to develop flexible, hierarchical architectures that can accommodate the requirements of all these applications in the same infrastructure.

g. **Multimedia coverage**. Some multimedia sensors, in particular video sensors, have larger sensing radii and are sensitive to direction of acquisition (directivity). Furthermore, video sensors can capture images only when there is unobstructed line of sight between the event and the sensor. Hence, coverage models developed for traditional wireless sensor networks are not sufficient for pre-deployment planning of a multimedia sensor network.

h. **Integration with Internet (IP) architecture**: It is of fundamental importance for the commercial development of sensor networks to provide services that allow querying the network to retrieve useful information from anywhere and at anytime. For this reason, future WMSNs will be remotely accessible from the Internet and will therefore need to be integrated with the IP architecture. The characteristics of WSNs rule out the possibility of all-IP sensor networks and recommend the use of application level gateways or overlay IP networks as the best approach for integration between WSNs and the Internet.

i. **Integration with other wireless technologies:** Large-scale sensor networks may be created by interconnecting local "islands" of sensors through other wireless technologies. This needs to be achieved without sacrificing on the efficiency of the operation within each individual technology.

4.12 Wireless Nanosensor Networks

With the rapidly changing environment of nanotechnology and progress in the field of nanotechnology, wireless nanosensor networks is gaining importance in wireless technology. In many applications like bio-medical, environmental and industrial, military nanosensor networks are finding the way to many solutions and paving the way to a better communication paradigm in today's scenario. There are mainly four communication strategies for communication between nano-machines. They are (a) acoustic (b) nano-mechanical (c) molecular and (d) electromagnetic.

Among these four communication strategies, molecular and electromagnetic communication falls into wireless communication.

Molecular communication is the transmission and reception of information encoded in molecules. In this, molecule is used as information. Information is packed into vesicles and gap junction works as mediator between cells and vesicles. One mode of direct communication involves the cell-to-cell transmission of molecules through channels in a specialized cell surface membrane structure called the gap junction.

Electromagnetic communication is defined as the transmission and reception of electromagnetic radiation from components based on various nanomaterial. A Wireless Nanosensor Network is composed by integrated nanomachines which interact through electromagnetic communication.

Main features of the Wireless Nanosensor Networks are: (i) size of the nano-devices are ranging from one to few hundreds of nanometers (ii) Graphene based nano-antennas are used that supports the electromagnetic communication in terahertz band (iii) bit rates are extremely higher(terabits/s) in WNSN (iv) very little transmission ranges (tens of millimeters). Due to size and energy constraint of nanodevices, it is not feasible to generate high power signals in the nanoscale at terahertz frequency.

Wireless Nanosensor Networks are composed by several elements like Nano-nodes, Nano-router, Nano-link, Nano-microinterface and gateway. Figure 4.20 shows the architecture of a Wireless Nanosensor Network.

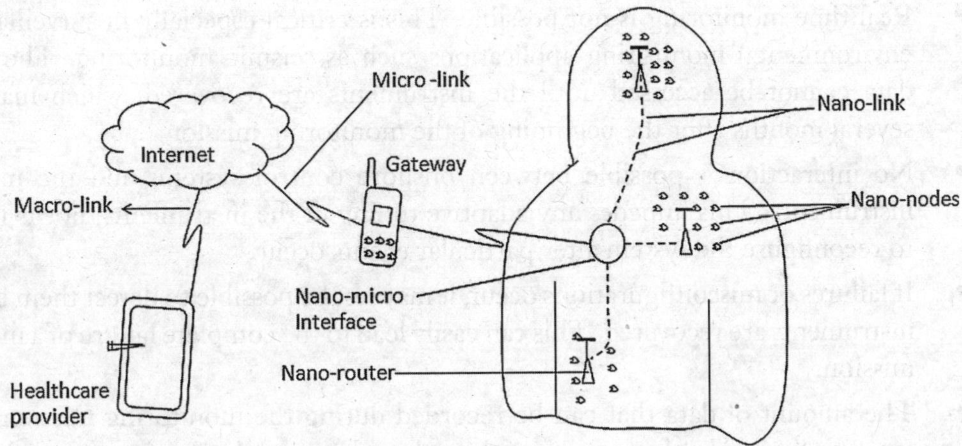

Fig.4.20: Architecture of a Wireless Nanosensor Network

4.13 Under Water Acoustic Sensor Networks

Wireless underwater acoustic networking is the enabling technology for these applications. Under Water Acoustic Sensor Networks (UW-ASN) consist of a variable number of sensors and vehicles that are deployed to perform collaborative monitoring tasks over a given area. To achieve this objective, sensors and vehicles self-organize in an autonomous network which can adapt to the characteristics of the ocean environment.

Ocean bottom sensor nodes are deemed to enable applications for oceanographic data collection, pollution monitoring, offshore exploration, disaster prevention, assisted navigation and tactical surveillance applications. Unmanned Underwater Vehicle or Autonomous Underwater Vehicles (UUVs, AUVs), equipped with underwater sensors, will also find application in exploration of natural undersea resources and gathering of scientific data in collaborative monitoring missions. To make these applications viable, there is a need to enable underwater communications among underwater devices. Underwater sensor nodes and vehicles must possess self configuration capabilities, i.e., they must be able to coordinate their operation by exchanging configuration, location and movement information, and to relay monitored data to an onshore station.

Acoustic communications are the typical physical layer technology in underwater networks. In fact, radio waves propagate at long distances through conductive sea water only at extra low frequencies (30-300 Hz), which require large antenna and high transmission power. Optical waves do not suffer from such high attenuation but are affected by scattering. Moreover, transmission of optical signals requires high precision in pointing the narrow laser beams. Thus, links in underwater networks are based on acoustic wireless communications. The traditional approach for ocean-bottom or ocean column monitoring is to deploy underwater sensors that record data during the monitoring mission and then recover the instruments. This approach has the following disadvantages:

- Real time monitoring is not possible. This is critical especially in surveillance or in environmental monitoring applications such as seismic monitoring. The recorded data cannot be accessed until the instruments are recovered, which may happen several months after the beginning of the monitoring mission.
- No interaction is possible between onshore control systems and the monitoring instruments. This impedes any adaptive tuning of the instruments, nor is it possible to reconfigure the system after particular events occur.
- If failures or misconfigurations occur, it may not be possible to detect them before the instruments are recovered. This can easily lead to the complete failure of a monitoring mission.
- The amount of data that can be recorded during the monitoring mission by every sensor is limited by the capacity of the onboard storage devices (memories, hard disks, etc.).

Therefore, there is a need to deploy underwater networks that will enable real time monitoring of selected ocean areas, remote configuration and interaction with onshore human operators. This can be obtained by connecting underwater instruments by means of wireless links based on acoustic communication. Many researchers are currently engaged in developing networking solutions for terrestrial wireless ad hoc and sensor networks. There exist many recently developed network protocols for wireless sensor networks. The unique characteristics of the underwater acoustic communication channel, such as limited bandwidth capacity and variable delays, require for very efficient and reliable new data communication protocols. Figure 4.21 shows the architecture of Under Water Acoustic Sensor Networks. Major challenges in the design of underwater acoustic networks are:

1. Battery power is limited and usually batteries cannot be recharged, also because solar energy cannot be exploited.
2. The available bandwidth is severely limited.
3. Channel characteristics, including long and variable propagation delays, multi-path and fading problems.
4. High bit error rates.
5. Underwater sensors are prone to failures because of fouling, corrosion, etc.
6. Oceanic forces may affect the node's mobility.

Many of the models developed are limited to only shallow depths and coastal areas. There is a physical mobility model named Oceanic Forces Mobility Model (OFMM) by incorporating important realistic oceanic forces imparted on nodes. In this model, nodes move in 3D column. Localization is another problem in UW-ASN.

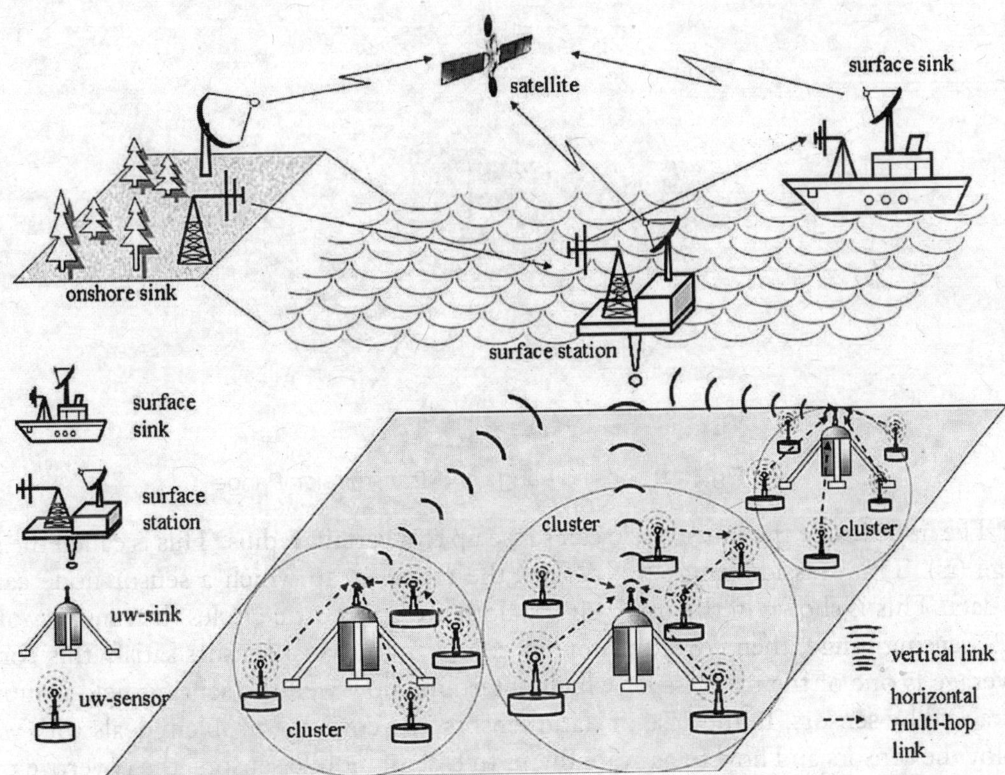

Fig.4.21: Architecture of Under Water Acoustic Sensor Networks

4.14 WSN Coverage

Sensing **coverage** and network **connectivity** are two of the most fundamental issues to ensure effective environmental sensing and robust data communication in a WSN application. Coverage implies whether the area-of-interest is covered satisfactorily. By connectivity, we mean whether all the nodes are connected in the network so that sensed data can reach the sink node. Sensor coverage studies how to deploy or activate sensors to cover the monitoring area. It includes a) **sensor placement** b) **density control**

Sensor placement means how sensors are to be placed so that the problem of coverage is properly addressed. By density control, it means the placement of minimal sensor nodes for coverage and connectivity. The cost and other overheads increase with increase in the number of nodes.

There are two modes of sensors. a)**static sensors** b)**mobile sensors**. The coverage and connectivity issues are different for static sensors and mobile sensors. In static sensors, the primary concern is the deployment of each and every node to have maximum coverage in a particular area. In mobile sensors, in addition to the deployment of sensors in an area, it should make sure that the coverage is also done with respect to time. Figure 4.22 shows the sensing range and transmission range.

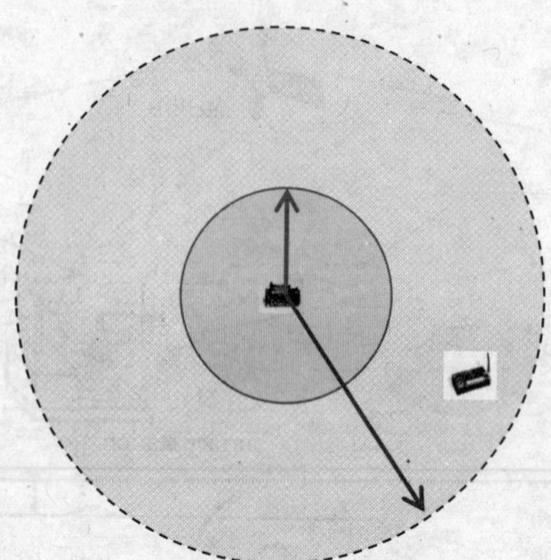

Fig.4.22: Sensing Range and Transmission Range

The node inside the inner circle can sense up to a certain radius. This is called the sensing range (rs). Transmission range (rt) defines the range up to which a sensor node can sense the data. This is shown in the outer circle. Both are concentric circles. If transmission range >= 2* sensing range, then coverage implies connectivity. Most sensors satisfy this condition. Coverage is one of the main issues which determine how well the sensing field is monitored or tracked by sensors. In the case of static sensors, the coverage problem deals with where to deploy the sensors and how to activate them. In case of mobile sensors, the coverage problem deals with the planning of the trajectory of the mobile sensors.

The purpose of deploying WSN is to collect relevant data for processing or reporting. There are two types of reporting. The first one is **event-driven** (e.g. forest fire monitoring). In this case the event is reported only when it happens. The second one is **on-demand** (e.g. inventory control system). In this the reporting takes place on receiving a demand. The objective of these types of reporting is to use a minimum number of sensors and maximize the lifetime.

The coverage algorithms are centralized, distributed or localized. In distributed coverage, nodes compute their position by communicating with their neighbors only. In centralized coverage, data is collected at a central point and global map is computed. Localized coverage is a special type of distributed coverage where only a subset of nodes in the WSN participates in sensing, communication and computation. The sensor deployment methods can be deterministic or random. The objective of the coverage problem is to maximize network lifetime or deploy minimum number of sensors.

A continuous region R is covered if there exists crossings in R and every crossing in R is covered. Crossings are intersection points between disk boundaries or between monitored space boundary and disk boundaries. A crossing is covered, if it is in the interior region of at least one node's coverage disk. Figure 4.23 shows the optimality conditions for placing the node.

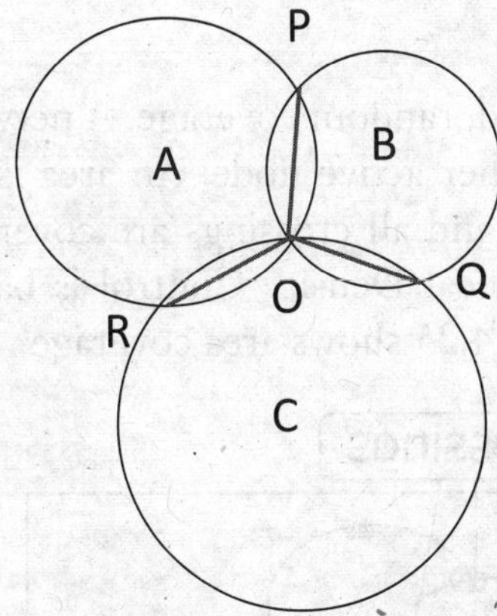

Fig.4.23: Optimality Conditions for Placing the Node

Optimality conditions for minimizing overlap while crossings are as follows.

- If nodes A and B are fixed nodes, then C should be placed such that OR=OQ.
- If nodes A, B and C all can change their locations, then OP=OR=OQ.
- If all nodes have the same sensing range, the distance between them is $\sqrt{3} \times rs$

Coverage problems in static WSNs can be classified as

- Point Coverage
- Area Coverage
- Barrier Coverage

Point Coverage

The objective of point coverage is to cover a set of points. Point coverage can be random point coverage or deterministic point coverage. In random point coverage, the sensors are distributed randomly so that every point must be covered by at least one sensor at all times. Figure 4.24 shows point coverage. The object inside the triangle is covered by 3 sensors.

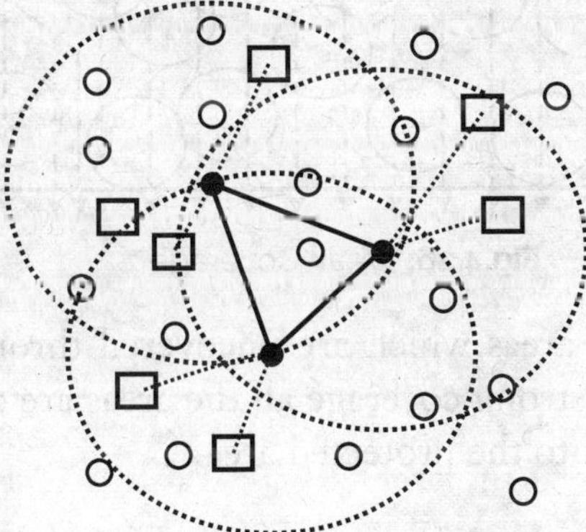

Fig.4.24: Point Coverage

Area Coverage

This is an energy efficient, connected, random coverage. A network is connected if any active node can communicate with any other active node. An area is completely covered, if there are at least two disks that intersect and all crossings are covered. The distributed localized algorithm called Optimal Geographical Density Control is based on area coverage will be discussed in the next section. Figure 4.25 shows area coverage.

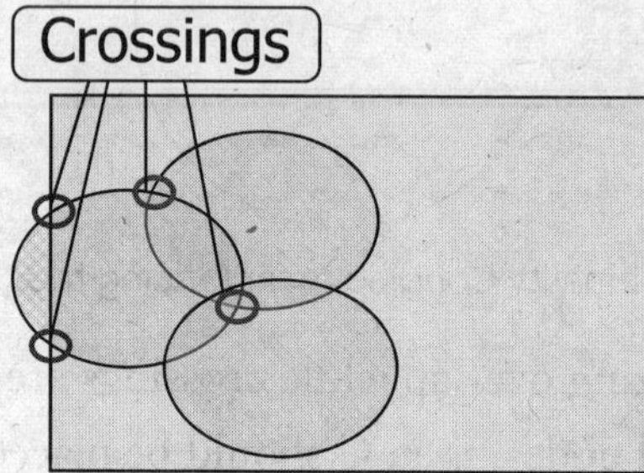

Fig.4.25: Area Coverage

Barrier Coverage

Barrier coverage is a critical issue in WSNs for security applications, which aims to detect intruders attempting to penetrate protected areas. In 1-barrier coverage, the coverage area will be covered by at least one sensor. In 2-barrier coverage, the coverage area will be covered by at least 2 sensors and in k-barrier coverage, the coverage area will be covered by at least k sensors. The following Figure 4.26 and Figure 4.27 show the weak coverage and strong coverage respectively in k-barrier coverage.

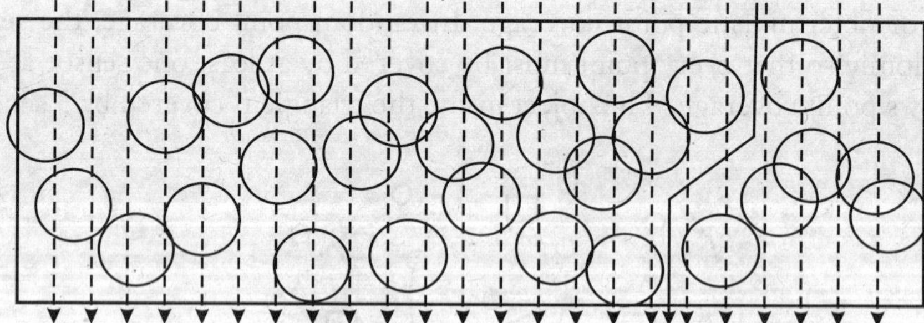

Fig.4.26: Weak Coverage

In weak coverage, there are areas which are uncovered through which an intruder can enter into the protected area. In strong coverage all the areas are covered so that there is not a chance for the intruder to get into the protected area.

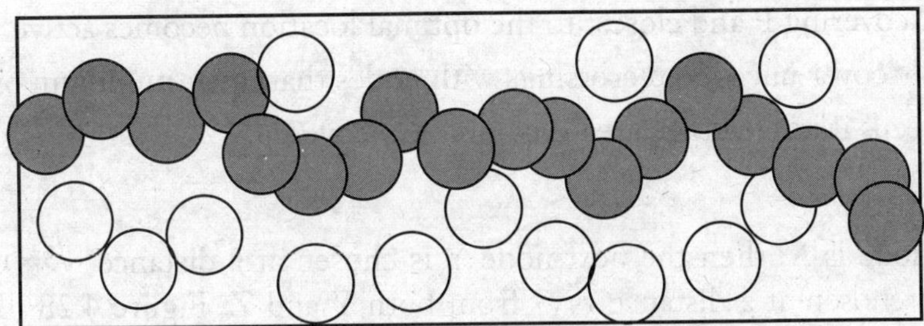

Fig.4.27: Strong Coverage

4.14.1 Optimal Geographical Density Control (OGDC) Algorithm

The OGDC algorithm is an advanced algorithm whose formal specification, simulation, and analysis pose a set of challenges, including the following.

1. Modeling and computing with geometric entities such as coverage areas, angles, and distances.
2. Modeling broadcast communication with limited range in a setting where a node does not know its neighbors, and where broadcast is subject to transmission delays.
3. Modeling time-dependent behavior such as use of timers, transmission delays and power consumption.
4. Modeling probabilistic behaviors. For example, sensor nodes volunteer to start with certain probabilities and different values are supposed to be "random values, drawn from a uniform distribution."
5. Simulating and analyzing systems with hundreds of sensor nodes scattered randomly in the sensing area.
6. Both correctness and performance are critical aspects that must be analyzed.

Algorithm

1. Begin
2. Node A volunteers as a starting node. It broadcasts a message containing ideal direction which is randomly selected.
   a. Each node voluntarily participates with probability P.
   b. It chooses a back off time randomly.
   c. If it does not hear anything from its neighbours, it declares itself as the starting node.
   d. It declares its position and preferred direction.
   e. On receiving message from a starting node, another node B closest to the ideal distance and angle becomes active.

3. A node C covering P and closest to the optimal location becomes active.
4. Repeatedly cover uncovered crossings with nodes that incur minimum overlap.
5. A node sleeps if its coverage area is completely covered.
6. End

If the initial node is X, then the next node Y is chosen at a distance $\sqrt{3} \times rs$. Similarly another node Z is chosen at a distance rs√3 from both Y and Z. Figure 4.28 illustrates the selection of nodes.

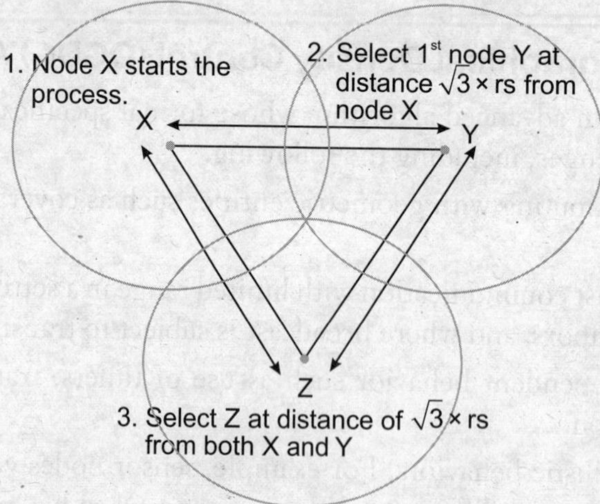

Fig.4.28: Selection of Nodes

Likewise the process continues until it covers uncovered crossings with nodes that incur minimum overlap. Output of OGDC algorithm is shown in Figure 4.29.

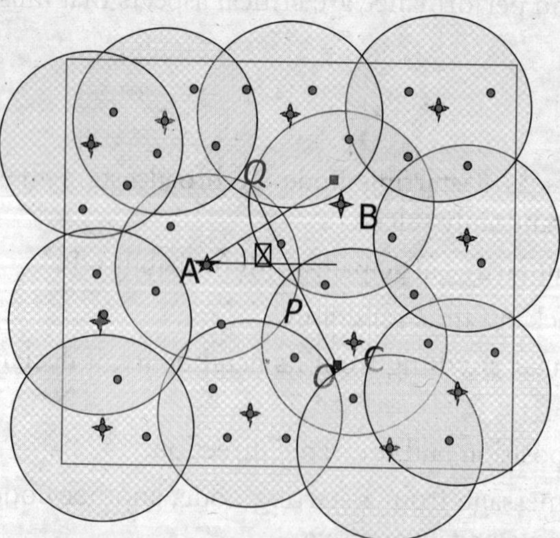

Fig.4.29: Output of OGDC Algorithm

4.15 Stationary WSN

Wireless Sensor Networks in which sensor nodes are static is known as Stationary Wireless Sensor Network. Figure 4.30 shows a Stationary Wireless Sensor Network.

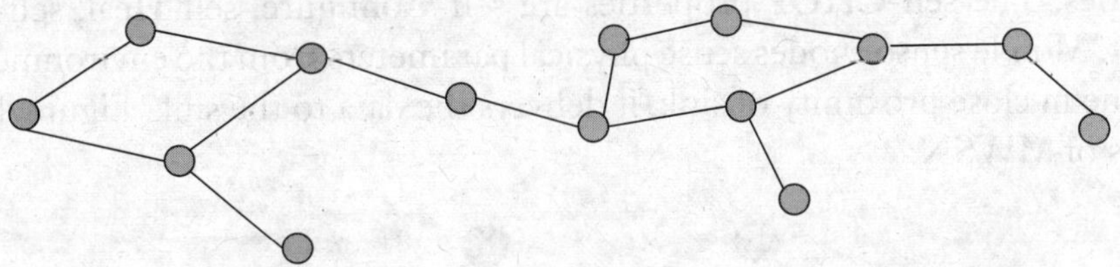

Fig.4.30: Stationary Wireless Sensor Network

The advantages of these types of networks are they can be easily deployed, easy topology maintenance and nodes can be placed at an optimized distance which reduces the total number of nodes. The disadvantages of Stationary Wireless Sensor Networks are that the topology cannot be changed automatically. Node failure may results in partition of networks. Figure 4.31 and Figure 4.32 shows the partition of networks which arises due to node failure.

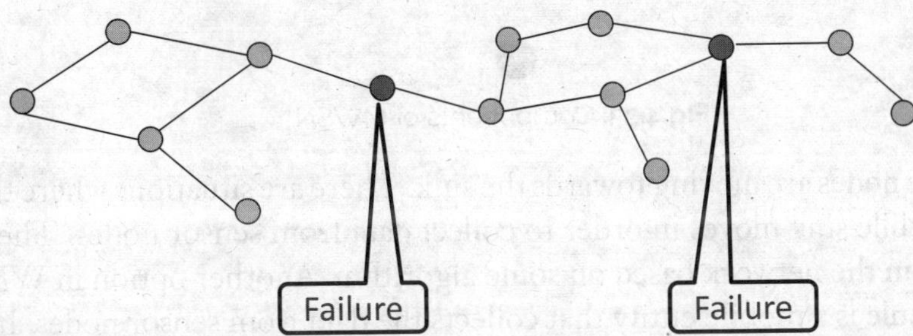

Fig.4.31: Node Failure

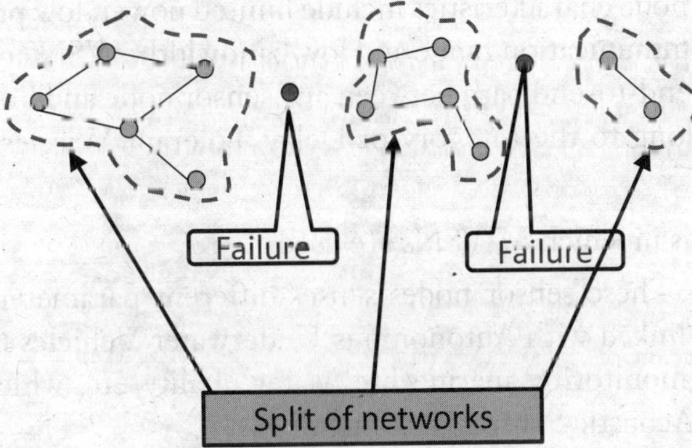

Fig.4.32: Split of Networks

To mobilize the sensor nodes the solution is to go for Mobile Wireless Sensor Networks (MWSN).

4.16 Mobile WSN

Mobile Wireless Sensor Network is Mobile Adhoc Network (MANET). This is an infrastructure-less network of mobile devices connected wirelessly which follow the self-**CHOP** properties. The self-CHOP properties are self-**C**onfigure, self-**H**eal, self-**O**ptimize and self-**P**rotect. Mobile sensor nodes sense physical parameters from the environment. When these nodes come in close proximity of sink, it delivers the data to the sink. Figure 4.33 shows the components of MWSN.

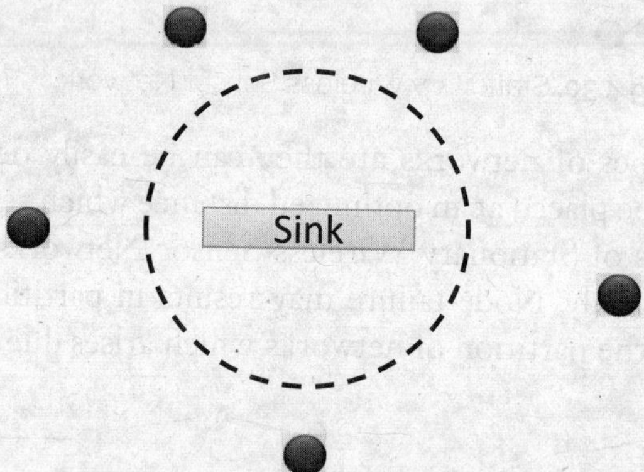

Fig.4.33: Components of MWSN

In this case the nodes are moving towards the sink. There are situations where the sink itself is mobile. The mobile sink moves in order to collect data from sensor nodes. The sink moves to different nodes in the network based on some algorithm. Another option in WMSN is data mules. The data mule is a mobile entity that collects the data from sensor nodes. It goes to the sink and delivers the collected data from different sensor nodes. Delay Tolerant Networks are those networks with intermittent connectivity, long or variable delay, asymmetric data rates and high error rates. The node characteristics include limited power, low processing capability, minimal storage, short communication range and low bandwidth. WSN and MWSN typically assume the availability of end-to-end path between any sensor node and base station. MWSNs which use data mules belong to the category of Delay Tolerant Wireless Sensor Networks (DT-WSNs).

There are various domains in which MWSNs are used.

Underwater MWSNs – These sensor nodes senses different parameters under the sea or water levels. This can be linked with Autonomous Underwater Vehicles (AUVs). They have various applications like monitoring marine life, water quality etc. which we have already discussed in Underwater Acoustic Sensor Networks.

Terrestrial MWSNs – They are sensor nodes which are typically deployed over land surface. This can be linked with Unmanned Aerial Vehicles (UAVs). Applications of terrestrial WMSNs include wildlife monitoring, surveillance, object tracking etc.

Aerial MWSNs – In this, nodes fly on air and sense data. It can sense both physical phenomena and multimedia data. Typical example for Aerial MWSN is Unmanned Aerial Vehicles (UAVs). The applications include surveillance, multimedia data gathering.

There are 3 possible entities that can act as mobile nodes in daily life. It can be **human, vehicles** or **mobile robots**. In the case of humans, it is difficult to predict mobility. The cell phone carried by humans can gather information and deliver data to an access point. In the case of vehicles, sensors may be equipped on it. These sensors sense data from different geographical locations and transmit to Road Side Unit (RSU). Mobile robots have controllable sensor nodes. They collect data by pre-defined instructions. It delivers the data to a specific unit.

Human centric sensing is gaining acceptance now-a-days. A large number of smart phones and PDAs are equipped with several sensors. Accelerometer and gyroscope are examples for this. Miniaturization and proliferation of such devices give rise to new sensing paradigms such as participatory sensing, people-centric sensing, and opportunistic sensing. The basic idea behind all these sensing are humans carry their devices and move around. Sensors embedded within the devices record readings. These sensory readings are then transmitted to a base station.

There are 3 distinct roles played by humans which are not necessarily mutually exclusive. They are **sensor targets, sensor operators** and **data source**. In sensor targets, the humans themselves are sensed. Personal health monitoring is an example for this. In sensor operators, humans use sensors and applications in smart phones and PDAs to sense surroundings. In data source, humans disseminate and collect data without actually using any sensor. The update posted in social networking sites is an example.

The goal of participatory sensing is not just to collect data, but allow common people to access data and share knowledge. The collected data provides quantitative information. For example carbon dioxide level in the atmosphere. The collected data should also contain endorsement of authenticity like geo-tagged location and timestamp. The challenges in human-centric sensing include energy of devices, participant selection and privacy of users.

4.17 Conclusion

This Chapter gives a detailed description of Wireless Sensor Networks. Various elements like components of a sensor node, modes of detection, challenges in WSN, sensor web, cooperation, behavior of nodes in WSN, Information theoretic self management of WSN, social sensing in WSN, applications of WSN which includes WSN in healthcare, WSN in surveillance, WSN in agriculture, Wireless Multimedia Sensor Networks, Wireless Nanosensor Networks, Under Water Acoustic Sensor Networks, WSN coverage, Optimal Geographical Density Control algorithm, stationary WSN and mobile WSN are explained in detail with supporting diagrams.

5 UAV NETWORKS & M2M COMMUNICATION

5.1 Introduction

This Chapter explains three important topics namely Unmanned Aerial Vehicle Networks (UAV), Machine to Machine Communication (M2M) and interoperability in Internet of Things. An Unmanned Aerial Vehicle (UAV), commonly known as a drone, is an aircraft without a human pilot aboard. UAVs are a component of an Unmanned Aircraft System (UAS) which include a UAV, a ground-based controller and a system of communications between the two. The flight of UAVs may operate with various degrees of autonomy: either under remote control by a human operator or autonomously by onboard computers.

Compared to manned aircraft, UAVs were originally used for missions too "dull, dirty or dangerous" for humans. While they originated mostly in military applications, their use is rapidly expanding to commercial, scientific, recreational, agricultural and other applications, such as policing, peacekeeping, surveillance, product deliveries, aerial photography, agriculture, smuggling and drone racing. Civilian UAVs now vastly outnumber military UAVs. They can be seen as an early commercial application of autonomous things, to be followed by the autonomous car and home robots.

There are single UAV systems as well as Multi-UAV systems. Multi-UAV systems can collaboratively complete missions more efficiently and economically as compared to single UAV systems. Multiple UAVs can cover a given area faster or take photos from different perspectives at the same time. The development of such multi-UAV systems is still at an early stage and, consequently, profound research efforts are needed. Table 5.1 gives a comparison of single UAV system and Multi-UAV systems.

Table 5.1: Comparison of Single UAV and Multi-UAV Systems

Features	Single UAV System	Multi-UAV System
Failures	High	Low
Scalability	Limited	High
Survivability	Poor	High

Speed of Mission	Slow	Fast
Cost	Medium	High
Bandwidth Required	High	Medium
Antenna	Omni-directional	Directional
Complexity of control	Low	High
Failure of co-ordinate	Low	Present

5.2 UAV Components

Manned and unmanned aircraft of the same type generally have recognizably similar physical components. The main exceptions are the cockpit and environmental control system or life support systems. Some UAVs carry payloads (such as a camera) that weigh considerably less than an adult human, and as a result can be considerably smaller. Though they carry heavy payloads, military UAVs with weapons are lighter than their manned counterparts with comparable armaments.

Small civilian UAVs have no life-critical systems and can thus be built out of lighter but less sturdy materials and shapes, and can use less robustly tested electronic control systems. For small UAVs, the quadcopter design has become popular, though this layout is rarely used for manned aircraft. Miniaturization means that less-powerful propulsion technologies can be used that are not feasible for manned aircraft, such as small electric motors and batteries.

Control systems for UAVs are often different than manned craft. For remote human control, a camera and video link almost always replace the cockpit windows; radio-transmitted digital commands replace physical cockpit controls. Autopilot software is used on both manned and unmanned aircraft, with varying feature sets. Figure 5.1 shows the architecture of UAV.

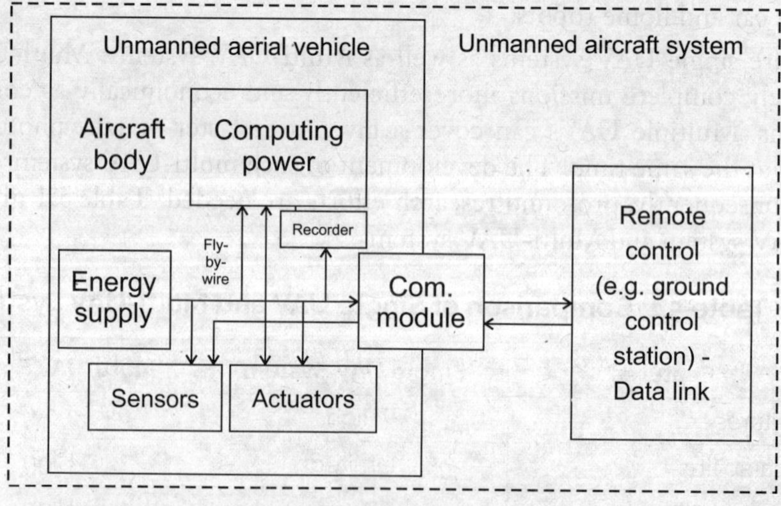

Fig.5.1: Architecture of UAV

Aircraft body

The primary difference for planes is the absence of the cockpit area and its windows. Tailless quadcopters are a common form factor for rotary wing UAVs while tailed mono and bi-copters are common for manned platforms.

Power supply and platform

Small UAVs mostly use lithium-polymer batteries (Li-Po), while larger vehicles rely on conventional airplane engines. Battery elimination circuitry (BEC) is used to centralize power distribution and often harbors a microcontroller unit (MCU). Costlier switching BECs diminish heating on the platform.

Computing module

UAV computing capability followed the advances of computing technology, beginning with analog controls and evolving into microcontrollers, then system-on-a-chip (SOC) and single-board computers (SBC). System hardware for small UAVs is often called the Flight Controller (FC), Flight Controller Board (FCB) or Autopilot.

Sensors

Position and movement sensors give information about the aircraft state. Exteroceptive sensors deal with external information like distance measurements, while exproprioceptive ones correlate internal and external states. Non-cooperative sensors are able to detect targets autonomously so they are used for separation assurance and collision avoidance. Degrees of freedom (DOF) refer to both the amount and quality of sensors on-board: 6 DOF implies 3-axis gyroscopes and accelerometers (a typical inertial measurement unit – IMU), 9 DOF refers to an IMU plus a compass, 10 DOF adds a barometer and 11 DOF usually adds a GPS receiver.

Actuators

UAV actuators include digital electronic speed controllers (which control the RPM of the motors) linked to motors/engines and propellers, servomotors (for planes and helicopters mostly), weapons, payload actuators, LEDs and speakers.

Software

UAV software called the flight stack or autopilot. UAVs are real-time systems that require rapid response to changing sensor data. Examples include Raspberry Pis, Beagleboards, etc. shielded with NavIO, PXFMini, etc. or designed from scratch such as Nuttx, preemptive-RT Linux, Xenomai, Orocos-Robot Operating System or DDS-ROS 2.0.

Loop principles

UAVs employ open-loop, closed-loop or hybrid control architectures. Open loop provides a positive control signal (faster, slower, left, right, up, down) without incorporating feedback from sensor data. Closed loop incorporates sensor feedback to adjust behavior (reduce speed to reflect tailwind, move to altitude 300 feet). The proportional–integral–derivative (PID) controller is common. Sometimes, feed forward is employed, transferring the need to close the loop further.

Flight controls

Flight control is one of the lower-layer systems and is similar to manned aviation: plane flight dynamics, control and automation, helicopter flight dynamics and controls and multi-rotor flight dynamics were researched long before the rise of UAVs. Automatic flight involves multiple levels of priority.

UAVs can be programmed to perform aggressive maneuvers or landing/perching on inclined surfaces and then to climb toward better communication spots. Some UAVs can control flight with varying flight models such as Vertical Take-Off and Landing (VTOL) designs. UAVs can also implement perching on a flat vertical surface.

Communications

Most UAVs use a radio frequency front-end that connects the antenna to the analog-to-digital converter and a flight computer that controls avionics. They are capable of autonomous or semi-autonomous operation. Radio allows remote control and exchange of video and other data. In military systems and high-end domestic applications, downlink may convey payload management status. In civilian applications, most transmissions are commands from operator to vehicle. Downstream is mainly video. Telemetry is another kind of downstream link, transmitting status about the aircraft systems to the remote operator. UAVs also use satellite "uplink" to access satellite navigation systems.

The radio signal from the operator side can be issued from either:

a. Ground control – a human operating a radio transmitter/receiver, a smart phone, a tablet, a computer, or the original meaning of a military Ground Control Station (GCS). Recently control from wearable devices, human movement recognition, human brain waves is also available.

b. Remote network system- such as satellite duplex data links for some military powers. Downstream digital video over mobile networks has also entered consumer markets, while direct UAV control uplink over the celullar mesh is under researched.

c. Another aircraft, serving as a relay or mobile control station – military manned-unmanned teaming (MUM-T).

5.3 UAV Networks

A network comprising of several UAVS are termed as UAV networks. There are several features for UAV networks which makes it suitable for IoT applications. At the same time there are several challenges for UAV networks.

5.3.1 Features

The advantages of UAV networks include high reliability, high survivability, single malfunction proof, cost effective, efficient and can be used for speeded up missions. Following are the features of UAV networks.

a. **Infrastructure-based or ad hoc** : Most of the available literature treats UAV networks as ad hoc networks. Depending on the application, the UAV network could have stationary, slow moving or highly mobile nodes. Many applications require UAV nodes to act as base stations in the sky to provide communication coverage to an area. Thus, unlike MANET and VANET ad hoc networks, the UAV networks could behave more like infrastructure based networks for these applications. These would have UAVs communicating with each other and also with the control center. Such a network would resemble the fixed wireless network with UAVs as base stations except that they are aerial. There is, however, a class of applications where the nodes would be highly mobile and would communicate, cooperate and establish the network dynamically in an ad hoc manner. In such a case the topology may be determined, and the nodes involved in forwarding data decided, dynamically. There are many issues that affect both UAV infrastructure based and UAV ad hoc networks. For example, replacing nodes by new nodes when they fail or their power gets exhausted.

b. **Server or client**: Another point of distinction is whether the node acts as a server or a client. In vehicular networks they are usually clients, in mobile ad hoc networks most of the time they would be clients and may also provide forwarding services to other clients' data. In UAV networks, the UAV nodes are usually servers, either routing packets for clients or relaying sensor data to control centers.

c. **Star or mesh**: Architecture of UAV networks for communication applications is an understudied area. The simplest configuration is a single UAV connected to a ground based command and control center. In a multi-UAV setting, the common topologies that can be realized are star, multi-star, mesh and hierarchical mesh.

d. **Large coverage area**: UAV networks especially multi-UAV networks can cover a large area compared to other kinds of networks. This makes it cost effective.

e. **Easily reconfigurable**: The nodes monitor their links and any failures trigger the reconfiguration process. The autonomous network reconfiguration system requires computational overhead and reasonable bandwidth. There are times when some of the UAVs could go out of service because of battery drain or communication failure.

In such cases the remaining nodes in the network re-organize and re-establish communication.

f. **Flexible deployment and management using SDN**: UAV networks apply the concept of Software Defined Networking (SDN) for flexible deployment and management of wireless environments. In networks like VANETs, the use of SDN can help in path selection and channel selection. This helps in reducing interference, improved usage of wireless resources including channels and routing in multi-hop mesh networks.

g. **Routing protocol should be adaptive**: Static protocols have static routing tables, which are computed and loaded when the task starts. These tables cannot be updated during an operation. Because of this constraint, these systems are not fault tolerant or suitable for dynamically changing environment. UAV systems need routing protocols that are adaptive in nature.

5.3.2 Challenges

UAVS pose a large number of challenges which are still undergoing researches to mitigate the challenges.

a. **Link failures**: The UAV networks constituted for various applications may vary from slow dynamic to the ones that fly at considerable speeds. The nodes may go out of service due to failure or power constraints and get replaced by new ones. Link disruption may frequently occur because of the positions of UAVs and ground stations. Additionally, the links could have high bit error rates due to interference or natural conditions. Links are prone to malfunction due to environmental effects like winds, rain etc.

b. **Huge power requirements**: Each drone needs to be powered by battery or other sources like solar energy. The power requirements are high since each node continuously monitors or senses data. In green networks, radios in the nodes may be automatically switched off for power conservations when the load is low.

c. **Change in network topology**: There will be frequent change in network topology due to several reasons like malfunctioning of UAVs, changes in the relative position of UAVs and intermittent link nature. The fluid topology, the vanishing nodes and finicky links would all challenge the designer to go beyond the normal ad hoc mesh networks.

d. **Lack of suitable routing algorithm**: The routing protocol cannot be a simple implementation of a proactive or a reactive scheme. The inter-UAV backbone has to repeatedly reorganize itself when UAVs fail. In some cases the network may get partitioned. The challenge would then be to route the packet from a source to a destination while optimizing the chosen metric. Another challenge would be to maintain users' sessions by transferring them seamlessly from an out of service

UAV to an active UAV. Several existing routing protocols have been in the zone of consideration of researchers and quite a few variations have been proposed. While newer protocols attempt to remove some shortcoming of the traditional ones, the field is still open.

In addition to the requirements present in the generic wireless mesh networks, e.g., finding the most efficient route, allowing the network to scale, controlling latency, ensuring reliability, taking care of mobility and ensuring required Quality of Service (QoS); routing in airborne networks requires location-awareness, energy-awareness, and increased robustness to intermittent links and changing topology. Designing the network layer for UAV networks is still one of the most challenging tasks. Although conventional ad hoc routing protocols are designed for mobile nodes, they are not necessarily suitable for airborne nodes because of varying requirements of dynamicity and link interruptions. Routing protocols that try to increase delivery ratio, reduce delays, scalability, loop freedom, energy conservation and efficient use of resources also needs to be resolved.

5.3.3 Topology

UAV network topology or configuration can be broadly classified into a) Star topology b) Mesh topology.

Star Topology

Star topology can be again classified as a) single star configuration b) multi-star configuration

In a single star configuration, each UAV is directly connected to the ground station. In a multi-star configuration, UAVs form multiple star topology. One node from each star topology group connects to the ground station. Star topology has high latency and highly dependent on ground station. Figure 5.2 (a) shows a single star configuration and Figure 5.2(b) shows a multi-star configuration.

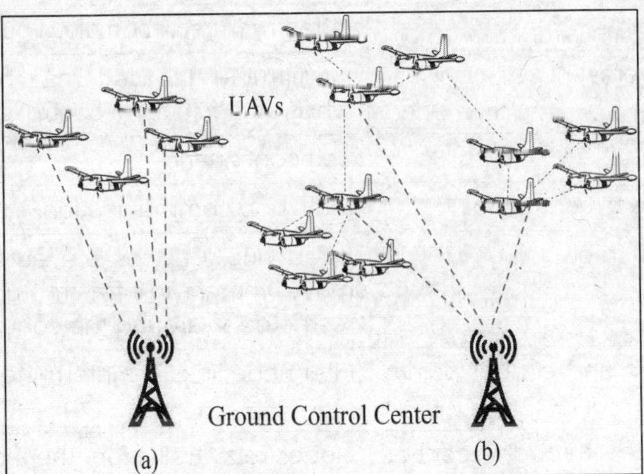

Fig.5.2: (a) Single Star Configuration (b) Multi-star Configuration

Mesh Topology

Mesh topology can be again classified as (a) flat mesh configuration (b) hierarchical mesh configuration. In a flat mesh configuration, all nodes are interconnected and one node will be connected to the ground station. In hierarchical mesh configuration, there will be several mesh groups and each mesh group will be at different hierarchy. One node from the mesh group at a lowest hierarchy will be connected to the ground station. Figure 5.3 (a) shows a flat mesh configuration and Figure 5.3(b) shows a hierarchical mesh configuration. Mesh configurations are flexible, reliable and more secure compared to star configurations. Table 5.2 shows a comparison between star network configuration and mesh network configuration.

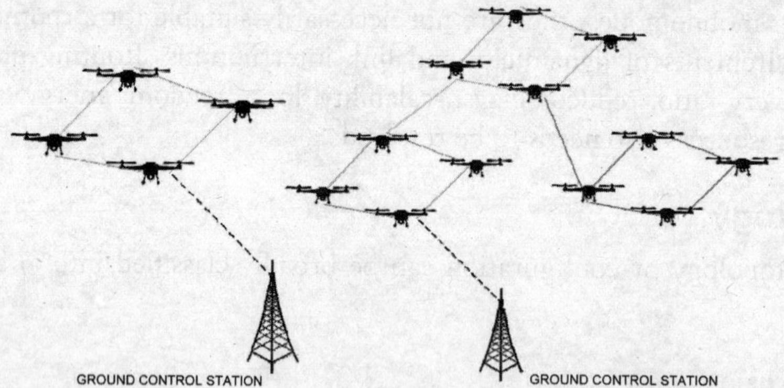

Fig.5.3: (a) Flat Mesh Configuration **Fig.5.3:** (b) Hierarchical Mesh Configuration

Table 5.2: Comparison between Star Network Configuration & Mesh Network Configuration

Star Network	Mesh Network
Connection is point-to-point.	Connection is multi-point to multi-point.
Infrastructure based.	Infrastructure based or ad hoc.
Central control point present.	Infrastructure based may have a control center while ad hoc has no control center.
Not self configuring.	Self configuring.
Single hop from node to central point.	Multi hop communication.
Devices cannot move freely.	In ad hoc, devices are autonomous and free to move whereas in infrastructure based, movement is restricted to around the control center.
Links between nodes and central points are configured.	Inter node links are intermittent.
Nodes communicate through central controller.	Nodes relay traffic for other nodes.

5.4 FANET

Flying Ad hoc Network (FANET) is a subclass of Mobile Ad hoc Network (MANET) and made up of a swarm of small flying vehicles enabled with camera, sensor and GPS system. In FANET, network formation will be using UAVs which ensures longer range, clearer line of sight propagation and environment resilient communication. UAVs may be in same plane or organized at varying altitudes. Besides self-control, each UAV must be aware of the other flying nodes of the FANET to avoid collision. These FANETS are popular for disaster time and post disaster emergency network establishment. There are situations such as flooding, war zone and rescue operations where traditional MANETs cannot be deployed because they uses ground moving nodes. FANETs can play significant role in those situations because they employ a swarm of UAVs to form ad hoc network. Figure 5.4 shows the architecture for FANET.

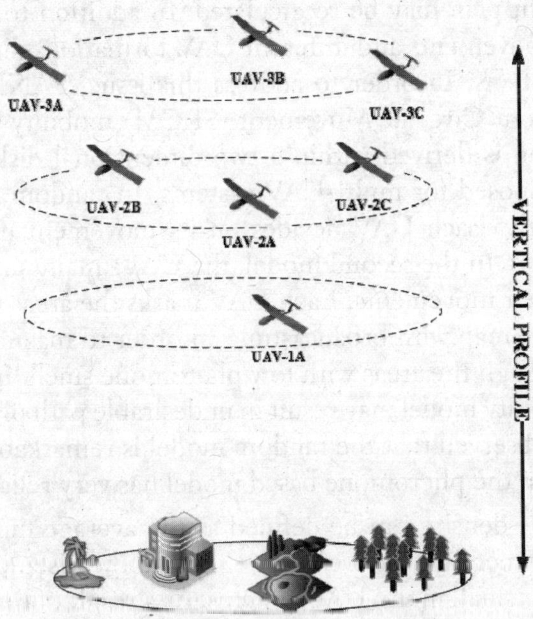

Fig.5.4: Architecture of FANET

5.4.1 Differences between FANET and the Existing Ad hoc Networks

Wireless ad hoc networks are classified according to their utilization, deployment, communication and mission objectives. By definition, FANET is a form of MANET and there are many common design considerations for MANET and FANET. In addition to this, FANET can also be classified as a subset of VANET, which is also a subgroup of MANET. FANET shares common characteristics with these networks, and it also has several unique design challenges. Following are the differences between FANET and other existing ad hoc networks.

Node Mobility: Node mobility related issues are the most notable difference between FANET and the other ad hoc networks. MANET node movement is relatively slow when it is compared to VANET. In FANET, the node's mobility degree is much higher than in the VANET and MANET. UAV has a speed of 30–460 km/h, and this situation results in several challenging communication design problems.

Mobility Model: While MANET nodes move on a certain terrain, VANET nodes move on the highways, and FANET nodes fly in the sky. MANETs generally implement the random waypoint mobility model, in which the direction and the speed of the nodes are chosen randomly. VANET nodes are restricted to move on highways or roads. Therefore, VANET mobility models are highly predictable. In some multi-UAV applications, global path plans are preferred. In this case, UAVs move on a predetermined path, and the mobility model is regular. In autonomous multi-UAV systems, the flight plan is not predetermined. Even if a multi-UAV system uses predefined flight plans, because of the environmental changes or mission updates, the flight plan may be recalculated. In addition to the flight plan changes, the fast and sharp UAV movements and different UAV formations directly affect the mobility model of multi-UAV systems. In order to address this issue, FANET mobility models are proposed. In Semi-Random Circular Movement (SRCM) mobility model, the approximate node distribution function is derived within a two dimensional disk region. There are two new mobility models proposed for multi-UAV systems. In random UAV movement model, UAVs move independently. Each UAV decides on its movement direction, according to a predefined Markov process. In the second model, the UAVs maintain a pheromone map, and the pheromones guide their movements. Each UAV marks the areas that it scans on the map, and shares the pheromone map with broadcasting. In order to maximize the coverage, UAVs prefer the movement through the areas with low pheromone smell. It was shown that the use of a typical MANET mobility model may result in undesirable path plans for cooperative UAV applications. It was also observed that the random model is remarkably simple, but it leads to ordinary results. However, the pheromone based model has very reliable scanning properties.

Node Density: Node density can be defined as the average number of nodes in a unit area. FANET nodes are generally scattered in the sky and the distance between UAVs can be several kilometers even for small multi-UAV systems. As a result of this, FANET node density is much lower than in the MANET and VANET.

Topology Change: Depending on the higher mobility degree, FANET topology also changes more frequently than MANET and VANET topology. In addition to the mobility of FANET nodes, UAV platform failures also affect the network topology. When a UAV fails, the links that the UAV has been involved in also fail and it results in a topology update. As in the UAV failures, UAV injections also conclude a topology update. Another factor that affects the FANET topology is the link outages. Because of the UAV movements and variations of FANET node distances, link quality changes very rapidly and it also causes link outages and topology changes.

Radio Propagation Model: Differences between FANET and the other ad hoc network operating environments affect the radio propagation characteristics. MANET and VANET nodes are remarkably close to the ground and in many case, there is no line-of-sight between the sender and the receiver. Therefore, radio signals are mostly affected by the geographical structure of the terrain. However, FANET nodes can be far away from the ground and in most of the cases, there is a line-of-sight between UAVs.

Power Consumption and Network Lifetime: Network lifetime is a key design issue for MANETs, which especially consist of battery-powered computing devices. Developing energy efficient communication protocols is the goal of efforts to increase the network lifetime. Especially, while the battery-powered computing devices are getting smaller in MANETs, system developers have to pay more attention to the energy efficient communication protocols to prolong the lifetime of the network. However, FANET communication hardware is powered by the energy source of the UAV. This means FANET communication hardware has no practical power resource problem as in MANET. In this case, FANET designs may not be power sensitive, unlike most of the MANET applications. However, it must be stated that power consumption still can be a design problem for mini UAVs.

Computational Power: In ad hoc network concept, the nodes can act as routers. Therefore, they must have certain computation capabilities to process incoming data in real-time. Generally, MANET nodes are battery powered small computers such as laptops, PDAs and smart phones. Because of the size and energy constraints, the nodes have only limited computational power. On the other hand, both in VANETs and FANETs, application specific devices with high computational power can be used. Most of the UAVs have enough energy and space to include high computational power. The only limitation about the computational power is the weight. By the help of the hardware miniaturization tendency, it is possible to put powerful computation hardware in UAV platforms. However, the size and weight limitation can still constitute serious constraints for mini UAVs that have very limited payload capacity.

Localization: Accurate geospatial localization is at the core of mobile and cooperative ad hoc networks. Existing localization methods include global positioning system (GPS), beacon (or anchor) nodes, and proximity-based localization. In MANET, GPS is generally used to receive the coordinates of a mobile communication terminal and most of the time, GPS is sufficient to determine the location of the nodes. When GPS is not available, such as in dense foliage areas, beacon nodes or proximity-based techniques can also be used. In VANET, for a navigation-grade GPS receiver, there is about 10–15 m accuracy, which can be acceptable for route guidance. However, it is not sufficient for cooperative safety applications, such as collision warnings for cars. Some researchers use assisted GPS (AGPS) or differential GPS (DGPS) by using some type of ground-based reference stations for range corrections with accuracy about 10 cm .

Because of the high speed and different mobility models of multi-UAV systems, FANET needs highly accurate localization data with smaller time intervals. GPS provides position information at one-second interval and it may not be sufficient for certain FANET protocols. In this case, each UAV must be equipped with a GPS and an inertial measurement unit (IMU) to offer the position to the other UAVs at any time. IMU can be calibrated by the GPS signal and thus, it can provide the position of the UAV at a quicker rate. The differences between MANET, VANET and FANET are outlined in Table 5.3.

Table 5.3 Differences between MANET, VANET and FANET

	MANET	VANET	FANET
Node mobility	Low	High	Very high
Mobility model	Random	Regular	Regular for predetermined paths, but special mobility models for autonomous multi-UAV systems.
Node density	Low	High	Very low
Topology change	Slow	Fast	Fast
Radio propagation model	Close to ground. LoS is not available for all cases.	Close to ground. LoS is not available for all cases.	LoS is available for most of the cases.
Power consumption and network lifetime	Energy efficient protocols	Not needed	Energy efficiency for mini UAVs but not needed for small UAVs.
Computational power	Limited	High	High
Localization	GPS	GPS, AGPS, DGPS	GPS, AGPS, DGPS, IMU

5.4.2 FANET Design Considerations

The distinguishing features of FANET impose unique design considerations. In this section, the most prominent FANET design considerations like adaptability, scalability, latency, UAV platform constraints and bandwidth requirements are discussed.

Adaptability: There are several FANET parameters that can change during the operation of a multi-UAV system. FANET nodes are highly mobile and always change their location. Because of the operational requirements, the routes of the UAVs may be different and the distance between UAVs cannot be constant. Another issue that must be considered is the UAV failures. Consequent to a technical problem or an attack against multi-UAV system, some of the UAVs may fail during the operation. While UAV failures decrease the number of UAVs, UAV injections may be required to maintain the multi-UAV system operation. UAV failures and UAV injections change the FANET parameters.

Environmental conditions can also affect FANET. If the weather changes unexpectedly, FANET data links may not survive. FANET should be designed so that it should be able to continue to operate in a highly dynamic environment. The mission may also be updated during the multi-UAV system operation. Additional data or new information about the mission may require a flight plan update. For example, while a multi-UAV system is operated for a search and rescue mission; after the arrival of a new intelligence report, the mission may be concentrated on a certain area and the flight plan update also affects FANET parameters. FANET design should be developed so that it can adjust itself against any changes or failures. FANET physical layer should adapt according to the node density, distance between nodes and environmental changes. It can scan the parameters and choose the most appropriate physical layer option. The highly dynamic nature of FANET environment also affects network layer protocols. Route maintenance in an ad hoc network is closely related to the topology changes. Thus, the performance of the system depends on the routing protocol in adapting to link changes. Transport layer should also be adapted according to the status of FANET.

Scalability: Collaborative work of UAVs can improve the performance of the system in comparison to a single-UAV system. In fact, this is the main motivation to use multi-UAV based systems. In many applications, the performance enhancement is closely related with the number of UAVs. For example, the higher number of UAVs can complete a search and rescue operation faster. FANET protocols and algorithms should be designed so that any number of UAVs can operate together with minimal performance degradation.

Latency: Latency is one of the most important design issues for all types of networks and FANET is not an exception. FANET latency requirement is fully dependent on the application. Especially for real-time FANET applications, such as military monitoring, the data packets must be delivered within a certain delay bound. Another low latency requirement is valid for collision avoidance of multiple UAVs. The packet delay behaviors are different for MANETs and FANETs and the protocols developed for MANET may not satisfy the latency requirements of FANET. New FANET protocols and algorithms are needed for delay sensitive multi-UAV applications.

UAV Platform Constraints: FANET communication hardware must be deployed on the UAV platform and this situation imposes certain constraints. The weight of the hardware is an important issue for the performance of the UAVs. Lighter hardware means lighter payload, and it extends the endurance. Another opportunity that comes with the lighter communication hardware is to deploy additional sensors on the UAV. If the total payload is assumed as constant and the communication hardware is lighter, more advanced sensors and other peripherals can be deployed. Space limitation is another UAV platform related constraints for FANET designs. Especially for mini UAVs, the space limitation is very important for communication hardware that must be fitted into the UAV platform.

Bandwidth requirement: In most of the FANET applications, the aim is to collect data from the environment and to relay the collected data to a ground base. For example, in surveillance, monitoring or rescue operations; the image or video of the target area must be relayed from the UAV to the command control center with a very strict delay bound and it requires high bandwidth. In addition, by the help of the technological advancements on sensor technologies, it is possible to collect data with very high resolution and this makes the bandwidth requirement much higher. The collaboration and coordination of multiple UAVs also need additional bandwidth resource. On the other hand, there are many constraints for the usage of available bandwidth such as: capacity of the communication channel, speed of UAVs, error-prone structure of the wireless links and lack of security with broadcast communication. A FANET protocol must satisfy the bandwidth capacity requirement so that it can relay very high resolution real time image or video under several constraints.

5.4.3 FANET Communication

There are several types of communication involved in FANET. Figure 5.5 shows different types of communication in a FANET.

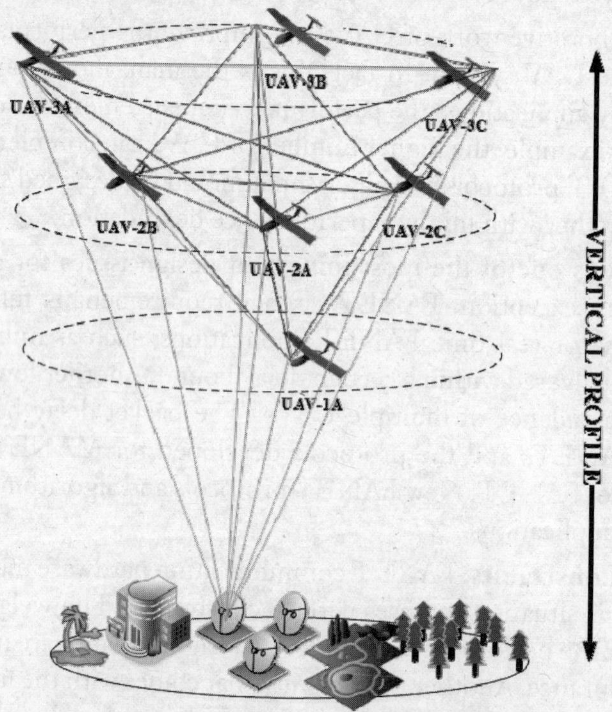

Fig.5.5: Different Types of Communication in FANET

- Inter-plane Communication – In Figure 5.5 there are three planes for FANET. The communication between UAVs in one plane and UAVs of another plane is called inter-plane communication.
- Intra-plane Communication – The communication between UAVs of the same plane is known as intra-plane communication.
- Ground Station Communication – This is the communication between UAVs of any plane to the ground or base station.
- Ground Sensor Communication - This is the communication between UAVs in any plane to the sensors on the ground.

- FANET-VANET Communication – The FANETs could communicate with the Vehicular Ad hoc Networks (VANET) on the ground.

Air-to-Air (A2A) links are used for data delivery among UAVs. Heterogeneous radio interfaces can be considered in A2A links such as XBee-PRO (IEEE 802.15.4) and Wi-Fi (IEEE 802.11). The ground networks can be stationary WSNs, VANETS or control stations. UAV-WSN link-up may be used for collaborative sensing as well as data muling. UAV-VANETs link-up may be used for visual guidance, data muling and coverage enhancement.

5.4.4 Gateway Selection in FANETs

Main communication requirements of UAV networks are the following.

1. Sending back the sensor data.
2. Receiving the control commands.
3. Cooperative trajectory planning.
4. Dynamic task assignment.

The number of UAV ground remote connections should be controlled to avoid interference. Reduced nodes in the UAV network should act as gateways to allow communication between all UAV and the ground. Entire UAV network coverage area is divided into sub-areas as shown in Figure 5.6.

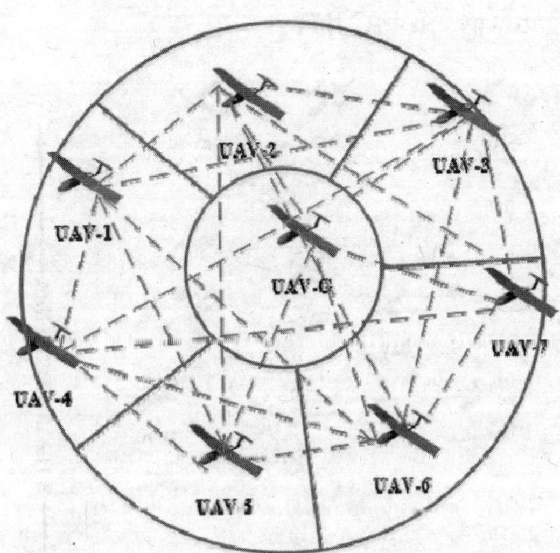

Fig.5.6: Sub-areas in Network Coverage Area

Sub-area collectively covers the entire communication area. The size of the sub-area to be controlled is adjusted dynamically. The adjustments are based on UAV inter-connections and derived metrics. The derived metrics are optimized for several iterations till optimum state is achieved. Gateway selection is initiated by selection of the most stable node in the sub-area. Figure 5.7 illustrates the selection of most stable node in a sub-area.

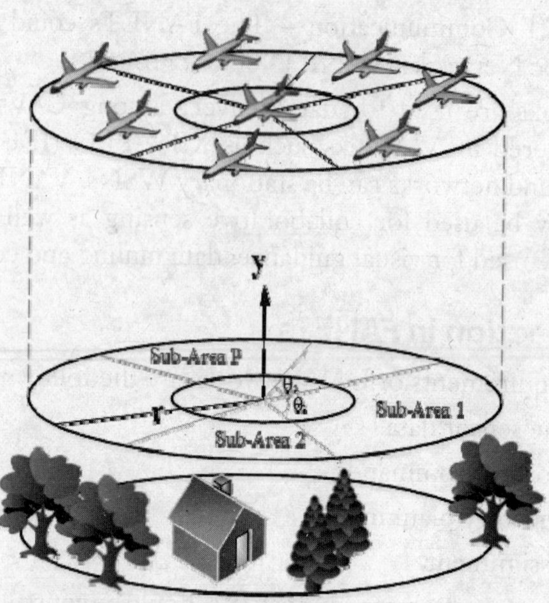

Fig.5.7: Selection of Most Stable Node in Sub-area

Consecutively, the partition parameters are optimized according to topology. Each UAV acquires the information of all UAVs within its 2 hops. There are layered gateways in FANETs. Figure 5.8 shows layered gateways in FANET.

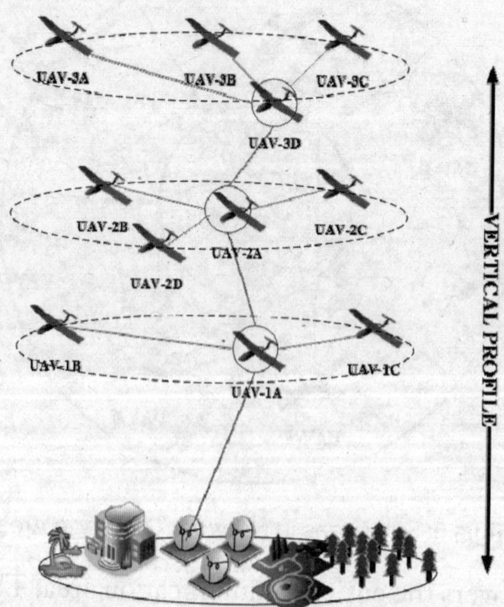

Fig.5.8: Layered Gateways in FANET

In a multi-layered UAV topology, there will be one gateway in each layer. The gateways from each layer communicate forwarded information between layers as well as from ground control. This will increase the delay between ground control and higher layers. This topology is not suitable for time-critical relaying tasks. For communication between FANETs and VANETs there are several links like Air-to-Air (A2A), Air-to-Vehicle (A2V) and Vehicle-to-Vehicle (V2V) links. Figure 5.9 shows various links in FANET and VANET. These links can be for surveillance, guidance, exploration or data transfer.

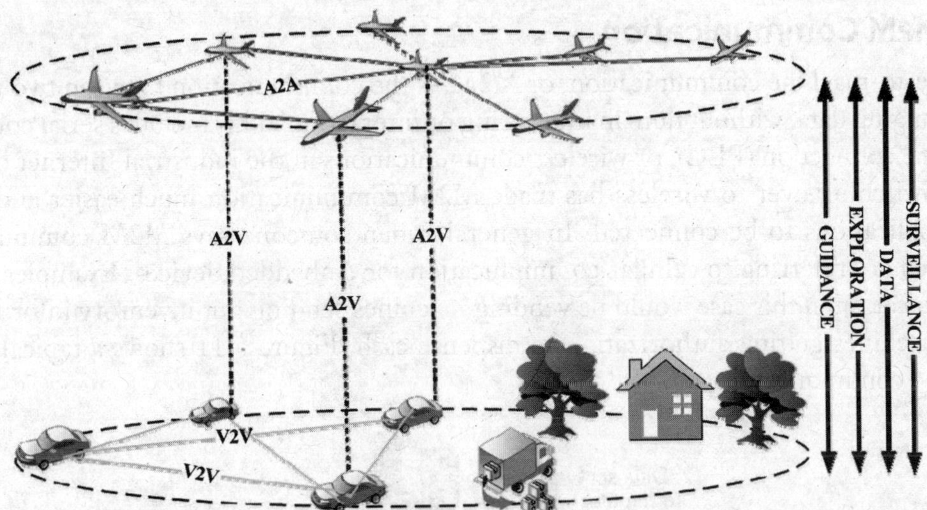

Fig.5.9: Various Links in FANET and VANET

In FANET-VANET communication, a mesh network can be formed in aerial plane. There can be several links between UAVs and ground network. Figure 5.10 shows different communications in FANET and VANET. Various communications like request, scheduling, control, sensing, navigation, data relay etc. can take place between FANETs and VANETs.

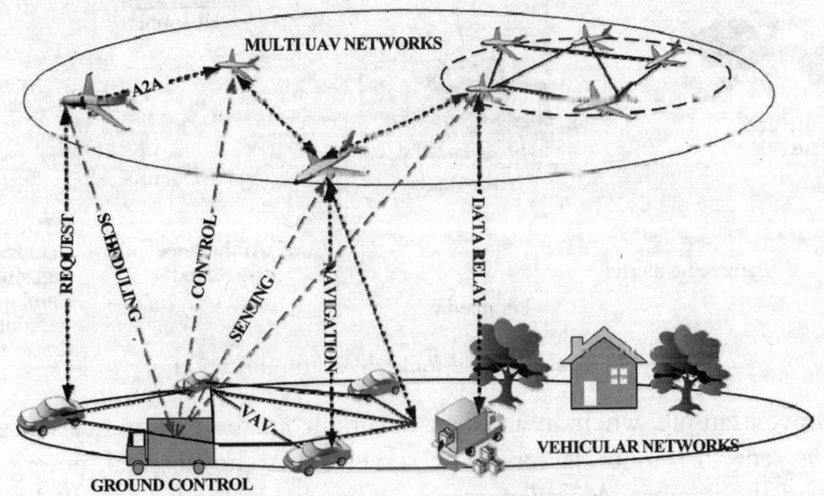

Fig.5.10: Communications in FANET and VANET

The control of trajectory is important for increasing the throughput. UAVs with queue occupancy above a threshold, experiences congestion resulting in communication delay. In such situations, the control station instructs UAVs to change centers of trajectory. Commands will be given to UAVs based on traffic at communication links that are busy. To provide enhanced coverage, UAVs may be commanded to change the radius of their trajectories.

5.5 M2M Communication

Machine-to-machine communication, or M2M, is the communication between two machines or exchanging data, without human interfacing or interaction. This includes serial connection, powerline connection (PLC), or wireless communications in the industrial Internet of Things (IoT). Switching over to wireless has made M2M communication much easier and enabled more applications to be connected. In general, when someone says M2M communication, they often are referring to cellular communication for embedded devices. Examples of M2M communication in this case would be vending machines sending out inventory information or ATM machines getting authorization to dispense cash. Figure 5.11 shows a typical example for M2M communication.

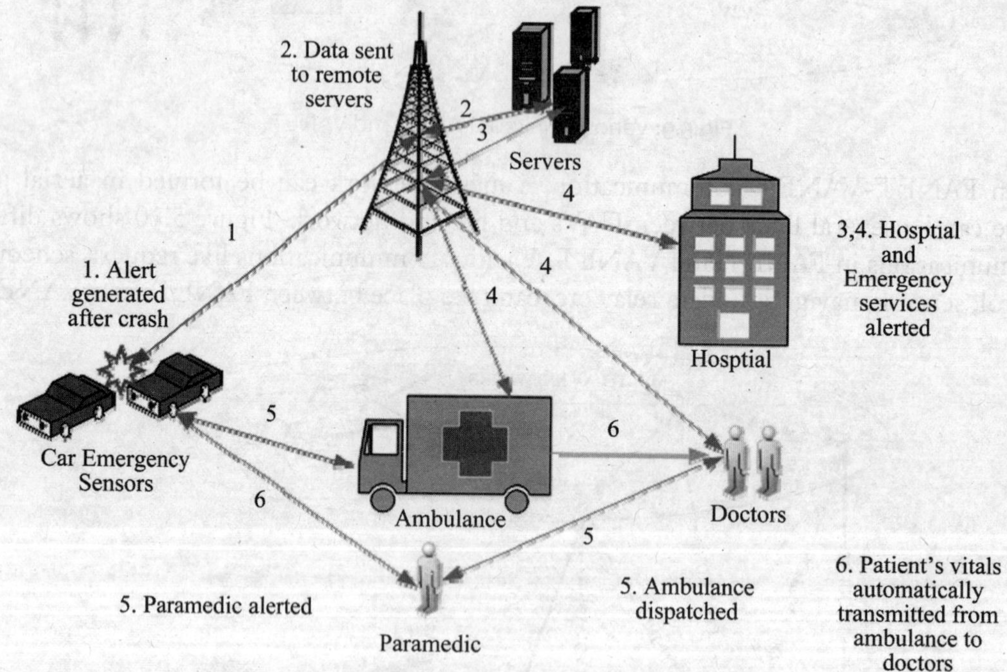

Fig.5.11: Example for M2M Communication

In the above example, when an accident occurs, from the emergency sensors in the car, information is sent to remote servers. The server alerts the hospital, emergency services, paramedics and the doctors. Ambulance and paramedics will be dispatched to the location where accident took place. Patient's vital information will be transmitted from the ambulance to the doctors automatically. This may help the doctors to get ready while the ambulance reaches the hospital. This is a typical example for M2M communication where there is no intervention of human beings.

M2M communication is similar to industrial Supervisory Control and Data Acquisition system (SCADA). SCADA is designed for isolated systems using proprietary solutions whereas M2M is designed for cross-platform integration. Figure 5.12 gives an overview of M2M communication.

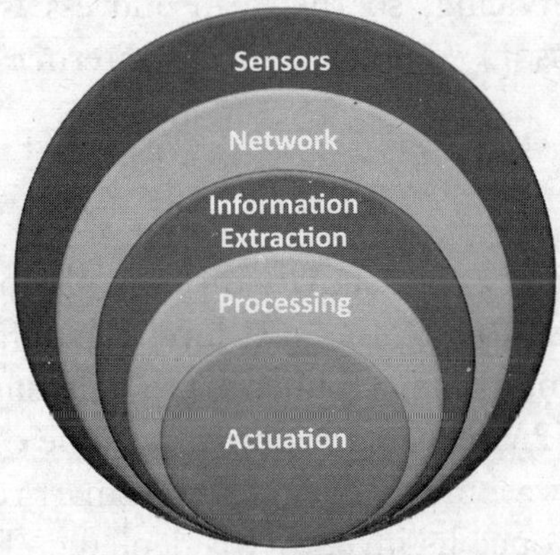

Fig.5.12: Overview of M2M Communication

At the outermost layer lie the sensors which sense the data. The sensed data is sent through a network to a server. At the server, information is extracted and processing is done. The action to be taken is sent to the actuators for appropriate action.

There are several features for M2M communication. Large number of nodes or devices can be involved in an M2M communication. Another feature of M2M is that it sends/receive small traffic per machine or device. Large quantity of collective data is generated which can be stored and queried later at any time. There is improved device connectivity because of the cloud data model. The cloud data model optimizes the device data communication aspect thereby reducing protocol overhead and easing device management. M2M communications are free from human intervention. Human intervention is required for operational stability and sustainability. In some situations, the device itself performs data analysis and correlation to trigger business decisions, with no programming skills required.

5.5.1 M2M Applications

Machine-to-Machine communications have diverse applications in many domains. With better sensors, wireless networks and increased computing capability, deploying an M2M makes sense for many sectors including environmental monitoring, civil protection & public safety, Supply Chain Management (SCM), energy & utility distribution industry (smart grid), intelligent transportation systems, healthcare, automation of building, military applications, agriculture, home networks etc. We will see some important applications in detail.

1. Manufacturing

Every manufacturing environment whether it is food processing or general product manufacturing relies on technology, to ensure costs are managed properly and processes are executed efficiently. Automating manufacturing processes within such a fast-paced environment is expected to improve processes even more. In the manufacturing world, this could involve highly automated equipment maintenance and safety procedures. For example, M2M tools allow business owners to be alerted on their smart phones when an important piece of equipment needs servicing, so they can address issues as quickly as they arise. Sophisticated networks of sensors connected to the Internet could even order replacement parts automatically.

2. Home Appliances

IoT already affects home appliance connectivity through platforms like Nest. However, M2M is expected to take home-based IoT to the next level. Manufacturers like LG and Samsung are already slowly unveiling smart home appliances to help ensure a higher quality of life for occupants. For example, an M2M-capable washing machine could send alerts to the owners' smart devices once it finishes washing or drying and a smart refrigerator could automatically order groceries from Amazon once its inventory is depleted. There are many more examples of home automation that can potentially improve quality of life for residents, including systems that allow members of the household to remotely control Heating Ventilation and Air Conditioning (HVAC) systems using their mobile devices. In situations where a homeowner decides to leave work early, he or she could contact the home heating system before leaving work to make sure the temperature at home will be comfortable upon arrival. He/she can contact the lighting system also so that the necessary lights will be on before he/she reaches home.

3. Healthcare Device Management

One of the biggest opportunities for M2M technology is in the realm of health care. With M2M technology, hospitals can automate processes to ensure the highest levels of treatment. Using devices that can react faster than a human healthcare professional in an emergency situation make this possible. For instance, when a patient's vital signs drop below normal, an M2M-connected life support device could automatically administer oxygen and additional care until a healthcare professional arrives on the scene. M2M also allows patients to be monitored in their own homes instead of in hospitals or care centers. For example, devices that track a frail or elderly person's normal movements can detect when he or she has had a fall and alert a healthcare worker to the situation.

Telemedicine offers another use. For instance, some heart patients wear special monitors that gather information about the way their heart is working. The data is sent to implanted devices that deliver a shock to correct an errant rhythm.

4. Smart Utility Management

In the new age of energy efficiency, automation will quickly become the new normal. As energy companies look for new ways to automate the metering process, M2M comes to the rescue, helping energy companies automatically gather energy consumption data, so they can accurately bill customers. Smart meters can track how much energy a household or business uses and automatically alert the energy company, which supplants sending out an employee to read the meter or requiring the customer to provide a reading. This is even more important as utilities move toward more dynamic pricing models, charging consumers more for energy usage during peak times.

5. Traffic Control

Traffic control is another dynamic environment that can benefit from M2M communications. In a typical system, sensors monitor variables such as traffic volume and speed. The sensors send this information to computers using specialized software that controls traffic-control devices, like lights and variable informational signs. Using the incoming data, the software manipulates the traffic control devices to maximize traffic flow. Researchers are studying ways to create M2M networks that monitor the status of infrastructure, such as bridges and highways.

Machine-to-machine communication appears to have a bright future. It's a flexible technology that uses common equipment in new ways. Every day, businesses, engineers, scientists, doctors and many others are finding new ways to use this new communications tool.

5.5.2 Types of Node in M2M

M2M has three types of sensor nodes. They are a) Low-end sensor nodes b) Mid-end sensor nodes c) High-end sensor nodes.

Low-end sensor nodes: These nodes are cheap and have low capabilities. They are static, energy efficient and simple. The deployment has high density in order to increase network lifetime and survivability. These nodes are resource constrained with no IP support. These nodes perform basic functionalities such as data aggregation, auto configuration and power saving. They are generally used for environment monitoring applications.

Mid-end sensor nodes: These nodes are more expensive than low-end sensor nodes. These nodes may have mobility. They have fewer constraints with respect to complexity and energy efficiency. They perform functionalities such as localization, Quality of Service (QoS) support, TCP/IP support, power control or traffic control and intelligence. These nodes are used in applications like home networks, Supply Chain Management (SCM), asset management and industrial automation.

High-end sensor nodes: These nodes are deployed in a low density manner. They are able to handle multimedia data (video) with QoS requirements. An essential feature of these nodes is mobility. Example for these types of nodes is smart phones. These nodes are applied in military or bio/medical application.

5.6 M2M Ecosystem

M2M ecosystem comprises of device providers, Internet service providers (ISPs), platform providers, service providers and service users. Figure 5.13 shows an M2M ecosystem. In this we have an M2M network which consists of various devices. The device provider is the one who owns the devices. The data from the M2M area network will be sent via a gateway to the Internet which is managed by Internet Service Provider (ISP). The RESTful architecture acts as the interface between device providers and ISP. RESTful architecture is used in low resource environment. From the ISP the data reaches the platform provider. The platform provider takes care of device management, user management, data analytics and user access. The data is then through a RESTful architecture which takes care of the business model to the service providers and users.

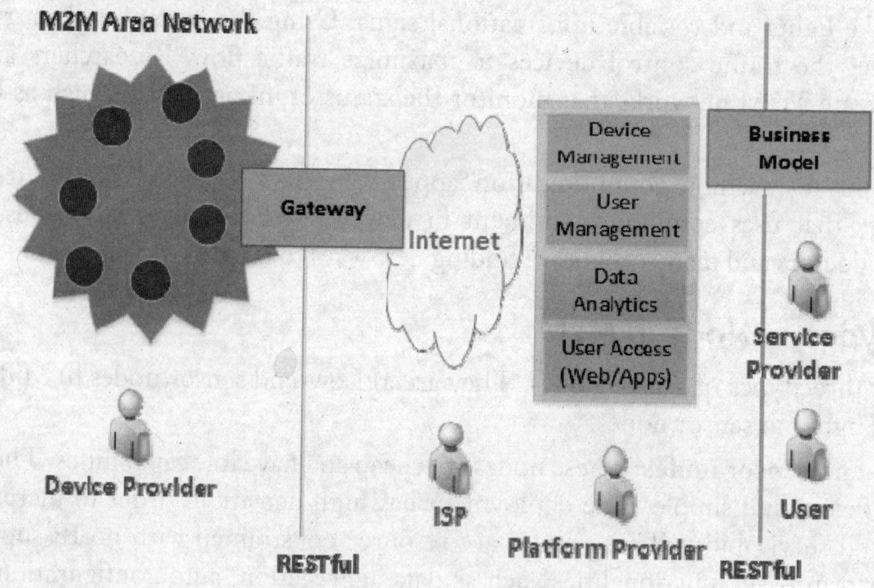

Fig.5.13: M2M Ecosystem

5.7 M2M Service Platform

In an M2M service platform, there are several functionalities for devices, users, applications and access. The data from these devices, users, applications and access passes through an access network like ZigBee, Wi-Fi etc. and are sent to M2M area network. Similarly the data from several M2M networks passes through the access network to the core network which supports all the platforms like devices, users, applications and access. Figure 5.14 depicts an M2M service platform. We will see each component in detail.

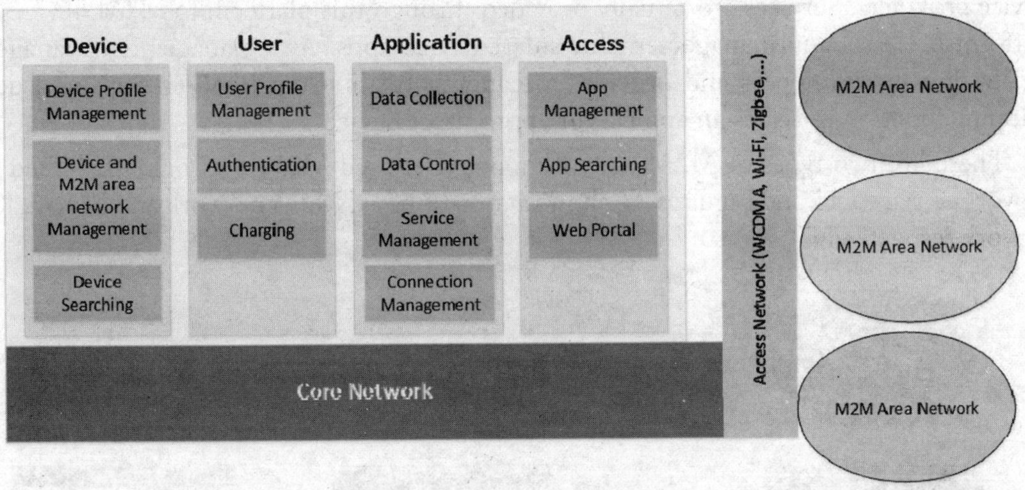

Fig.5.14: M2M Service Platform

M2M Device Platform

This platform enables access to objects or devices connected to the Internet anywhere and at any time. Registered devices create a database of objects from which managers, users and services can easily access information. This platform manages device profiles such as location of the devices, device type, address and description. M2M device platform provides authentication and authorization key management functionalities. It also monitors the status of devices and M2M area networks and controls them based on their status.

M2M User Platform

This platform manages M2M service user profiles and provides functionalities such as user registration, modification, charging and inquiry. M2M user platform interoperates with the M2M device platform and manages user access restrictions to devices, object networks or services. Service providers and device managers have administrative privileges on their devices or networks. Administrators can manage the devices through device monitoring and control.

M2M Application Platform

M2M application platform provides integrated services based on data sets collected by devices. Heterogeneous data merged from various devices are used for creating new devices. This platform collects control processing log data for the management of the devices by working with the device platform. This platform provides connection management with the appropriate network for seamless service.

M2M Access Platform

This platform provides app or Web access environment to users. Apps and links redirect to service providers. Services are actually provided through this platform to M2M devices. This platform provides app management for smart device apps. App management manages app registration by developers and provides a mapping relationship between apps and devices. Mapping function provides an app list for appropriate devices.

There are two types of M2M network a)non-IP based M2M network b)IP based M2M network. Figure 5.15 and Figure 5.16 shows a non-IP based M2M network and IP based M2M network respectively.

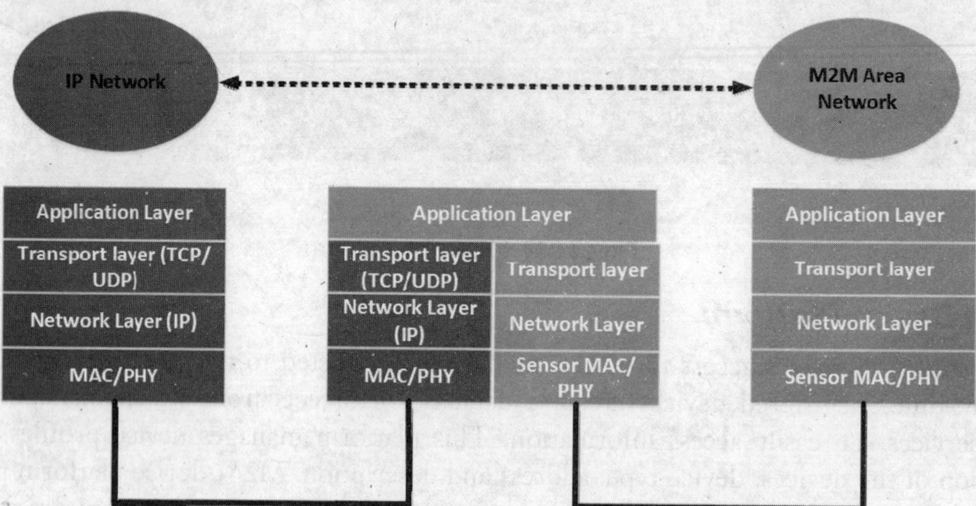

Fig.5.15: Non-IP based M2M Network

The application layer seamlessly integrates both the networks.

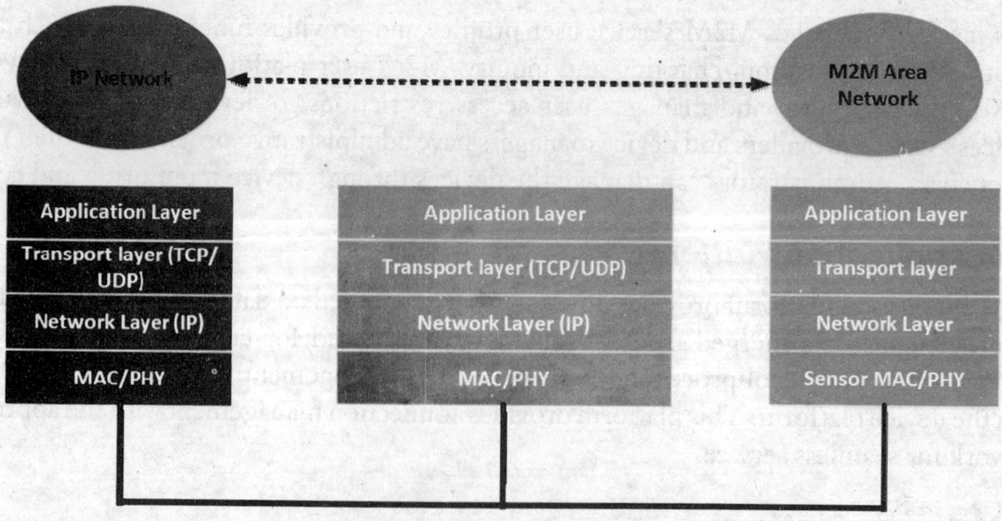

Fig.5.16: IP based M2M Network

In the above Figure 5.16, both M2M network and other network is IP based. Hence all the communication layers are the same for both the networks.

M2M area network management provides various features like fault-tolerance, scalability, low cost, low complexity, energy efficient, dynamic configuration capabilities, minimized management traffic and application dependence which includes data-centric application, emergency application and real-time application.

5.8 Interoperability

There are several challenges in IoT at present. Large scale cooperation and coordination of millions of nodes, heterogeneous IoT devices and their subnets, different configuration modes for IoT devices which come from unknown owners and different processing logics applied to same IoT networked devices or applications are to name a few.

Interoperability is the characteristic of a product or system, whose interfaces are completely understood to work with other products or systems, present or future, in either implementation or access, without any restrictions. Interoperability is the meaningful communication or exchange of data or services.

5.8.1 Need for Interoperability

a. Interoperability is required to fulfil the following IoT objectives.
   - Physical objects can interact with any other physical objects and can share their information.
   - Any device can communicate with any other devices anytime from anywhere.
   - Machine-to-Machine communication (M2M), Device-to-Device Communication (D2D) and Device-to-Machine Communication.
   - Seamless device integration with IoT network.

b. Heterogeneity
   - Different wireless communication protocols such as ZigBee (IEEE 802.15.4), Bluetooth (IEEE 802.15.1), GPRS, 6LoWPAN and Wi-Fi (802.11)
   - Different wired communication protocols like Ethernet (IEEE 802.3) and higher layer LAN protocols (IEEE 802.1)
   - Different programming languages used in computing systems and Websites such as JavaScript, Java, C, C++, Visual Basic, PHP and Python.
   - Different hardware platforms such as crossbow, NI etc.
   - Different operating systems. (For example the sensor nodes contain operating systems like TinyOS, SoS, MentisOS, RETOS and mostly vendor specific operating system while personal computers contain operating systems like Windows, Mac, Unix, Ubuntu etc.)

- Different databases like DB2, MySQL, Oracle, PostgreSQL, SQLite, SQL server, Sybase etc.
- Different data representations.
- Different control models.
- Different syntactic or semantic interpretations.

5.8.2 Types of Interoperability

Interoperability can be classified as a) user interoperability b) device interoperability. User interoperability is the interoperability problem between a user and a device whereas device interoperability is the interoperability problem between two different devices. Figure 5.17 which show the user and device interoperability issues.

Consider the following scenario where both devices A and B provide a real-time security service using IoT. Device A is placed at New Delhi, India while device B is placed at Tokyo, Japan. The devices A, B uses Hindi, Japanese languages respectively while user U uses English. The user U wants real-time service of CCTV camera from the devices A and B. The user does not understand the messages from devices A and B. Similarly devices A and B do not mutually understand each other. This is because devices A and B are different in terms of syntactic and semantic notions.

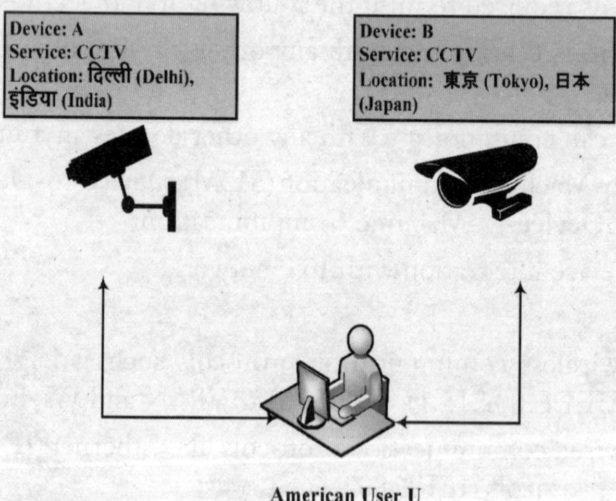

Fig.5.17: Issues in User and Device Interoperability

User Interoperability

In user interoperability, the following problem needs to be solved.

a. Device identification and categorization for discovery.
b. Syntactic interoperability for device interaction.
c. Semantic interoperability for device interaction.

In device identification and categorization for discovery, there are different solutions for generating unique address like Electronic Product Codes (EPC), Universal Product Code (UPC), Uniform Resource Identifier (URI) and IP addresses like IPv6. There are different device classification solutions like United Nations Standard Products and Services Code (UNSPSC)* and eCl@ss **. (UNSPSC)* is an open, global, multi-sector standard for efficient, accurate, flexible classification of products and services. eCl@ss ** is the standard for classification and clear description of cross-industry products.

In syntactic interoperability for device interaction, the interoperability between devices and device user is in terms of message formats. The message format from a device to a user should be understandable for the user's computer. On the other hand, the message format from the user to the device should be executable by the device. Some popular approaches in this regard are Service-Oriented Computing (SOC) based architecture, Web services, RESTful Web services, Open standard protocols such as IEEE 802.15.4, IEEE 802.15.1, Wireless Hart and closed protocols such as Z-wave. But Wireless Hart and Z-wave are incompatible with each other. There are middleware technologies like software middleware bridge which dynamically map physical devices with different domains. Based on the map, the devices can be discovered and controlled remotely. In cross-content syntactic interoperability, the exchange of messages takes place using XML syntax.

In semantic interoperability for device interaction, the interoperability between devices and device user is in terms of the meaning of messages. The device can understand the meaning of user's instruction that is sent from the user to the device. Similarly, the user can understand the meaning of device's response sent from the device. One of the approaches for semantic interoperability is ontology based approach which includes device ontology, physical domain ontology and estimation ontology. But ontology based solution is limited to the defined domain or context. Another approach is the collaborative conceptualization theory. In this the object is defined based on the collaborative concept, which is called cosign. The representation of a collaborative sign (cosign) is defined as follows.

Cosign of an object = (A, B, C, D), where A is a cosign internal identifier, B is a natural language, C is the context of A and D is a definition of the object. An example for CCTV cosign is given as cosign=(1234, English, CCTV, "Camera Type: Bullet, Communication: Network/IP, Horizontal Resolution: 2048 TVL"). This solution approach is applicable for different domains or contexts.

Device Interoperability

A solution approach for device interoperability is Universal Middleware Bridge (UMB). UMB solves seamless interoperability problems caused by the heterogeneity of several kinds of home network middleware. UMB creates virtual maps among the physical devices of all middleware home networks such as HAVI, Jini, LonWorks and UPnP. It creates compatibility among these middleware home networks. Figure 5.18 shows the architecture of Universal Middleware Bridge (UMB). UMB consists of UMB core (UMB-C) and UMB adaptor (UMB-A).

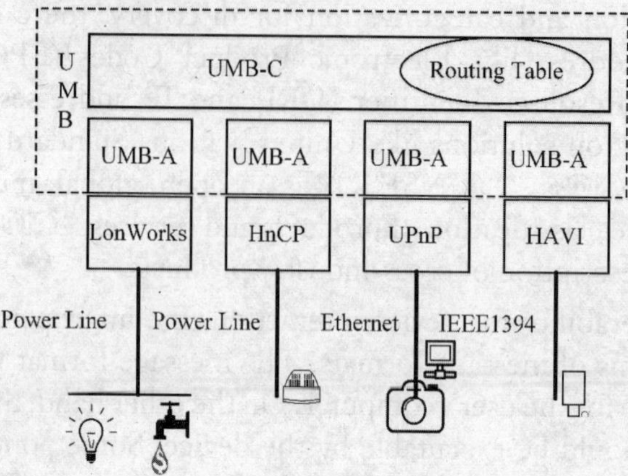

Fig.5.18: Architecture of Universal Middleware Bridge

The structure of UMB core and UMB adaptor is shown in Figure 5.19 and 5.20 respectively.

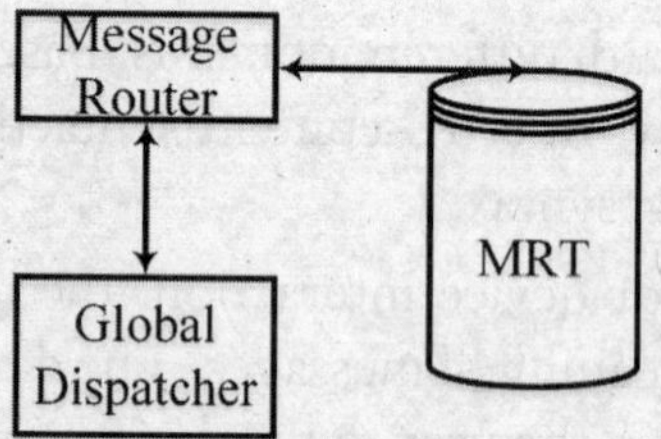

Fig.5.19: Structure of UMB Core (UMB-C)

The major role of the UMB core (UMB-C) is routing the universal metadata message to the destination or to any other UMB adaptor by the Middleware Routing Table (MRT).

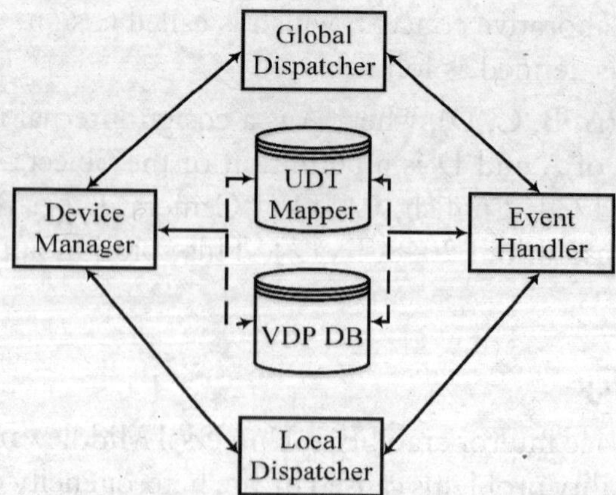

Fig.5.20: Structure of UMB Adaptor (UMB-A)

UMB-A converts physical devices into virtually abstracted one and store it in Virtual Device Proxy Database (VDP DB) as described by Universal Device Template (UDT). UDT consists of a global device id, global function id, global action id, global event id and global parameters. UMB adaptors translate the local middleware's message into global metadata's message. Figure 5.21 shows the flow when a new device is plugged in.

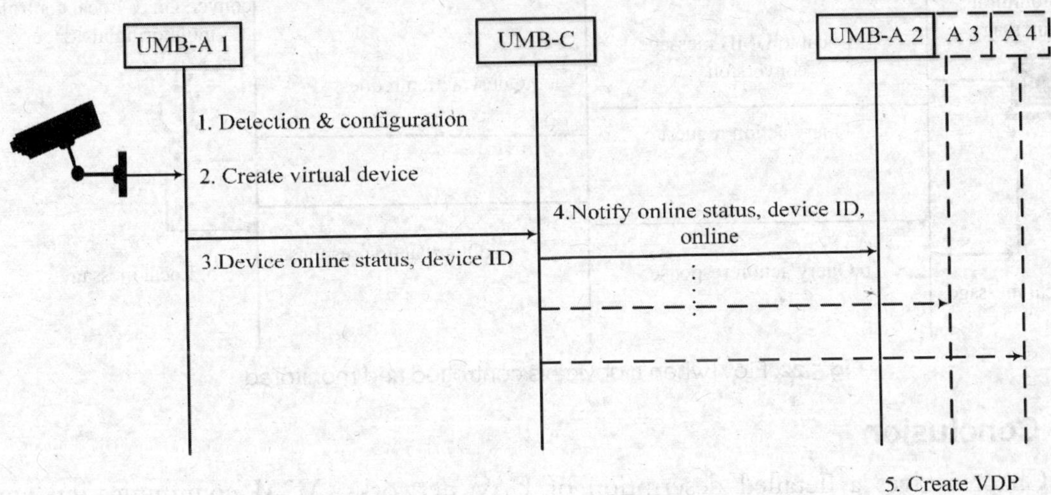

Fig.5.21: Flow when a new device is plugged in

When a new device is plugged in to the UMB-A1, the first step is to detect the device and configure the device. Then a virtual device is created. The information like device online status, device id etc. is sent from the UMB adaptor to the UMB core. From the UMB core, the online status of the device, device id etc. is sent to UMB adaptor of other devices namely UMB-A2, UMB-A3, UMB-A4 and so on. There Virtual Device Proxy Database (VDP DB) is created. This is how two heterogeneous devices following different configurations communicate with each other.

Consider the following scenario in which a device is controlled and monitored. The local control or monitoring message is sent from first device to UMB-A1.From UMB-A1, local to UMB message conversion takes place and a query/action request is sent to UMB-C. From UMB-C, this query/action request is sent to UMB-A2 of the second device. Here UMB to local message conversion and local control/monitoring message takes place. A local message is then sent to UMB-A2. From there a query/action response is sent to UMB-A1 through UMB-C. UMB-A1 sends back local message to first device. Figure 5.22 shows the flow when a device is controlled and monitored.

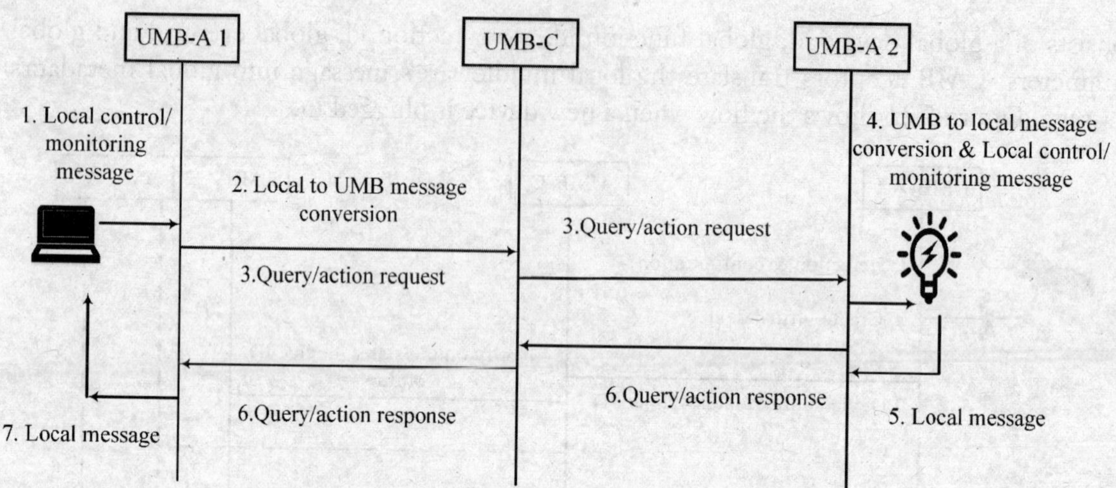

Fig.5.22: Flow when a device is controlled and monitored

5.9 Conclusion

This Chapter gives a detailed description of UAV networks, M2M communication and interoperability issues in IoT. The components of UAV network is illustrated in detail. The features, challenges and various topologies involved in UAV network are described. Another important concept called FANET, differences between FANET and the existing ad hoc networks, design considerations for FANET, communications in FANET, gateway selection in FANETs are elaborately explained. Another important topic known as M2M communication, its applications, different types of node in M2M, M2M ecosystem and M2M service platform are well explained. Finally, the interoperability in IoT, need for interoperability, types of interoperability are clearly illustrated.

6 PROGRAMMING WITH ARDUINO

6.1 Introduction

Arduino is a prototype platform (open-source) based on an easy-to-use hardware and software. It consists of a circuit board, which can be programmed referred to as a microcontroller and ready-made software called Arduino IDE (Integrated Development Environment), which is used to write and upload the computer code to the physical board. There are different types of Arduino boards. They are

- Arduino boards based on ATMEGA328 microcontroller.
- Arduino boards based on ATMEGA32U4 microcontroller.
- Arduino boards based on ATMEGA2560 microcontroller.
- Arduino boards based on AT91SAM3X8E microcontroller.

6.1.1 Features of Arduino

1. Arduino boards are able to read analog or digital input signals from different sensors and turn it into an output such as activating a motor, turning LED on/off, connect to the cloud and many other actions.
2. We can control our board functions by sending a set of instructions to the microcontroller on the board via Arduino IDE (referred to as uploading software).
3. Unlike most previous programmable circuit boards, Arduino does not need an extra piece of hardware (called a programmer) in order to load a new code onto the board. We can simply use a USB cable.
4. Arduino IDE uses a simplified version of C++, making it easier to learn to program.
5. Arduino provides a standard form factor that breaks the functions of the micro-controller into a more accessible package.

6.2 Components of Arduino Board

In this section, we will learn about the different components on the Arduino board. Here the

Arduino UNO board is used because it is the most popular board in the Arduino board family. In addition, it is the best board to get started with electronics and coding. Figure 6.1 shows an Arduino UNO board. Some boards look a bit different from the one given below, but most Arduinos have majority of these components in common.

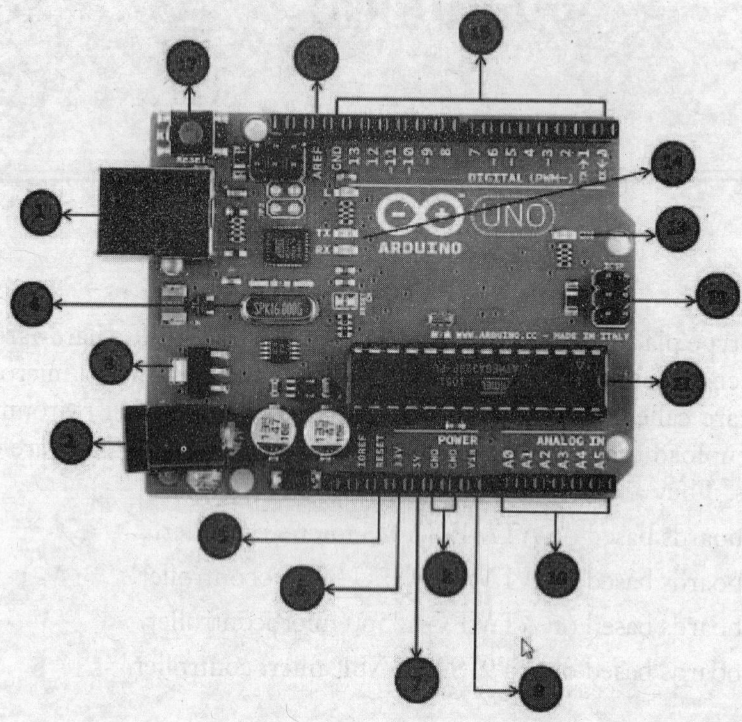

Fig.6.1: Arduino UNO Board

1. **Power USB**: Arduino board can be powered by using the USB cable from the computer. For this we need to connect the USB cable to the USB connection.
2. **Power (Barrel Jack)**: Arduino boards can be powered directly from the AC mains power supply by connecting it to the Barrel Jack.
3. **Voltage Regulator**: The function of the voltage regulator is to control the voltage given to the Arduino board and stabilize the DC voltages used by the processor and other elements.
4. **Crystal Oscillator:** The crystal oscillator helps Arduino in dealing with time issues. The number printed on top of the Arduino crystal is 16.000H9H. It tells us that the frequency is 16,000,000 Hertz or 16 MHz.
5. **Arduino Reset**: We can reset the UNO board in two ways. First, by using the reset button (17) on the board. Second, we can connect an external reset button to the Arduino pin labelled RESET (5).
6. **Pin (3.3)**: Supply 3.3 output volt

7. **Pin 5V:** Supply 5 output volt
8. **GND (Ground)**: There are several GND pins on the Arduino, any of which can be used to ground our circuit.
9. **Vin (9)**: This pin also can be used to power the Arduino board from an external power source, like AC mains power supply.
10. **Analog Pins**: The Arduino UNO board has five analog input pins A0 through A5. These pins can read the signal from an analog sensor like the humidity sensor or temperature sensor and convert it into a digital value that can be read by the microprocessor.
11. **Main Microcontroller**: Each Arduino board has its own microcontroller. We can consider it as the brain of our board. The main IC (integrated circuit) on the Arduino is slightly different from board to board. The microcontrollers are usually of the ATMEL Company. We must know what IC our board has before loading up a new program from the Arduino IDE. This information is available on the top of the IC. For more details about the IC construction and functions, we can refer to the data sheet.
12. **ICSP Pin**: ICSP is an AVR, a tiny programming header for the Arduino consisting of MOSI, MISO, SCK, RESET, VCC, and GND. It is often referred to as an SPI (Serial Peripheral Interface), which could be considered as an "expansion" of the output. We are making the output device a slave to the master of the SPI bus.
13. **Power LED indicator**: This LED should light up when you plug your Arduino into a power source to indicate that our board is powered up correctly. If this light does not turn on, then there is something wrong with the connection.
14. **TX and RX LEDs**: On the board, there will be two labels: TX (transmit) and RX (receive). They appear in two places on the Arduino UNO board. First at the digital pins 0 and 1. This indicates that the pins are responsible for serial communication. Second, the TX and RX led. The TX led flashes with different speed while sending the serial data. The speed of flashing depends on the baud rate used by the board. RX flashes during the receiving process.
15. **Digital I/O**:The Arduino UNO board has 14 digital I/O pins (15) (of which 6 provide PWM (Pulse Width Modulation) output. These pins can be configured to work as input digital pins to read logic values (0 or 1) or as digital output pins to drive different modules like LEDs, relays, etc. The pins labeled "~" can be used to generate PWM.
16. **AREF**: AREF stands for Analog Reference. It is sometimes, used to set an external reference voltage (between 0 and 5 Volts) as the upper limit for the analog input pins.

6.3 Arduino IDE

Arduino IDE is open source software that is used to program the Arduino controller board. It is based on variations of C and C++programming language. It can be downloaded from

Arduino's official Website and installed into PC. Following steps are required to set up an Arduino board.

1. Power the board by connecting it to a PC via USB cable: The power source is selected with a jumper, a small piece of plastic that fits onto two of the three pins between the USB and power jacks. Check that it is on the two pins closest to the USB port. The green power LED (labelled PWR) should glow.
2. Launch the Arduino IDE: After the Arduino IDE software is downloaded, we need to unzip the folder. Inside the folder, we can find the application icon with an infinity label (application.exe). Double-click the icon to start the IDE.
3. Open the first project: Once the software starts, we have two options – Create a new project or open an existing project example. To create a new project, select File → New. To open an existing project example, select File → Example.
4. Select the Arduino board -To avoid any error while uploading our program to the board, we must select the correct Arduino board name, which matches with the board connected to your computer. Go to Tools → Board and select your board. Here, we will be selecting Arduino Uno board, but we must select the name matching the board that we are using.
5. Select the serial port - Select the serial device of the Arduino board. Go to Tools → Serial Port menu. This is likely to be COM3 or higher (COM1 and COM2 are usually reserved for hardware serial ports). To find out, we can disconnect our Arduino board and re-open the menu, the entry that disappears should be of the Arduino board. Reconnect the board and select that serial port.
6. Upload the program to our board - Before explaining how we can upload our program to the board, we must demonstrate the function of each symbol appearing in the Arduino IDE toolbar. Figure 6.2 explains various symbols on Arduino IDE toolbar.

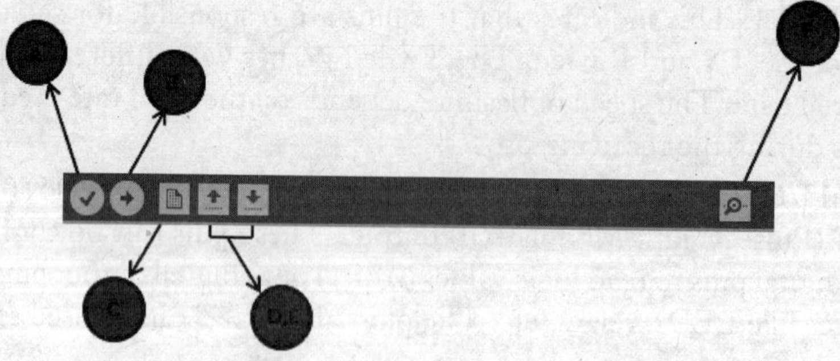

Fig.6.2: Symbols on Arduino IDE Toolbar

Program coded in Arduino IDE is called a SKETCH. Following are the explanation of various symbols used in the above diagram.

A – used to check if there is any compilation error.

B – used to upload a program to the Arduino board.

C – shortcut used to create a new sketch.

D – used to directly open one of the example sketch.

E – used to save our sketch.

F – Serial monitor used to receive serial data from the board and send the serial data to the board.

Now, simply click the "Upload" button in the environment. Wait a few seconds. We will see the RX and TX LEDs on the board, flashing. If the upload is successful, the message "Done uploading" will appear in the status bar. Following are the explanation of the various menus in Arduino IDE.

- To create a new sketch, select File → New. Creates a new blank sketch with basic structure.
- To open an existing sketch, select File → Open. Opens an existing sketch. There are some basic ready-to-use sketches available in the EXAMPLES section.
- Verify: Checks the code for compilation errors.
- Upload: Uploads the final code to the controller board.
- Save: Saves the current sketch.
- Serial Monitor: Opens the serial console. All the data printed to the console are displayed here.

6.4 Program Elements

This section explains various program elements or components like structure of an Arduino sketch, variables, data types, operators, decision making, loops, functions, string objects and arrays.

6.4.1 Program Structure

Arduino programs can be divided in three main parts: **Structure,Values (variables and constants) and Functions**. Let us start with the Structure. Values and Functions will be discussed in the coming sections. Structure consist of two main functions – setup () function and loop () function.

setup () function - The setup() function is called when a sketch starts. It is used to initialize the variables, pin modes, start using libraries, etc. The setup () function will only run once, after each power up or reset of the Arduino board.

loop () function - After creating a setup() function, which initializes and sets the initial values, the loop() function allows our program to iteratively do the specified task in the program. This is used to actively control the Arduino board.

6.4.2 Variables

A variable is a value that can change, depending on conditions or on information passed to the program. Arduino uses C programming language. Variables use a property called scope. A scope is a region of the program and there are three places where variables can be declared. They are

a. Variables declared inside a function or a block is called **local variables.**
b. Variables used in the definition of function parameters are called **formal parameters.**
c. Variables declared outside of all functions are called **global variables.**

Local Variables: Variables that are declared inside a function or block are local variables. They can be used only by the statements that are inside that function or block of code. Local variables are not known to function outside.

Global Variables: Global variables are defined outside of all the functions, usually at the top of the program. The global variables will hold their value throughout the life-time of the program. A global variable can be accessed by any function. A global variable is available for use throughout the entire program after its declaration. Following program uses global and local variables.

Program

```
float c = 0; Global variable declaration
void setup () {
              }

void loop () {
   int z; Local variable declaration
   z = 10;
}
```

6.4.3 Data Types

Data types in C refer to an extensive system used for declaring variables or functions of different types. The type of a variable determines how much space it occupies in the storage and how the bit pattern stored is interpreted. The following data types are supported by Arduino programming.

1. void - The void keyword is used only in function declarations. It indicates that the function is expected to return no information to the function from which it was called.
2. boolean - Boolean holds one of two values, true or false. Each boolean variable occupies one byte of memory.
3. char - A data type that takes up one byte of memory that stores a character value. Character literals are written in single quotes like ‘c’. For multiple characters called strings we use double quotes: “ABC”.
4. unsigned char - unsigned char is an unsigned data type that occupies one byte of memory. The unsigned char data type encodes numbers from 0 to 255.
5. byte - A byte stores an 8-bit unsigned number from 0 to 255.

6. int - Integers are the primary data-type for number storage. int stores a 16-bit (2-byte) value. This yields a range of -32,768 to 32,767 (minimum value of -2^15 and a maximum value of (2^15) - 1). The int size varies from board to board.
7. unsigned ints (unsigned integers) - They are the same as int in the way that they store a 2 byte value. Instead of storing negative numbers they only store positive values, yielding a useful range of 0 to 65,535 (2^16) - 1).
8. word - On the Uno and other ATMEGA based boards, a word stores a 16-bit unsigned number.
9. long - Long variables are extended size variables for number storage and store 32 bits (4 bytes) from -2,147,483,648 to 2,147,483,647.
10. unsigned long - unsigned long variables are extended size variables for number storage and store 32 bits (4 bytes). Unlike standard longs, unsigned longs will not store negative numbers, making their range from 0 to 4,294,967,295 (2^32 - 1).
11. short - A short is a 16-bit data-type. On all Arduinos a short stores a 16-bit (2-byte) value.
12. float - Data type for floating-point number is a number that has a decimal point. Floating-point numbers can be as large as 3.4028235E+38 and as low as 3.4028235E+38. They can store 32 bits (4 bytes) of information.
13. double - On the Uno and other ATMEGA based boards, double precision floating-point number occupies four bytes. That is, the double implementation is exactly the same as the float, with no gain in precision.

6.4.4 Operators

An operator is a symbol that tells the compiler to perform specific mathematical or logical functions. Arduino supports following types of operators.

Arithmetic Operators : addition (+), subtraction (-), multiplication (*), division (/), modulus(%) and assignment(=).

Comparison Operators: Logical equal to (==), not equal to (!=), less than (<), less than or equal to (<=), greater than (>) and greater than or equal to (>=).

Boolean Operators : Logical AND (&&), Logical OR (||) and Logical NOT(!)

Bitwise Operators : Bitwise AND (&), Bitwise OR (|), Bitwise Exclusive OR (^), Bitwise NOT (~), Bitwise Left Shift (<<) and Bitwise Right Shift (>>)

Compound Operators : Increment (++), Decrement (– –) and Shorthand (+=, –=, *=, /=, %=, |=, &=)

6.4.5 Decision Making

Decision making structures specify one or more conditions to be evaluated or tested by the program. It should be along with a statement or statements to be executed if the condition is determined is true and optionally other statements to be executed if the condition is false. Following are the decision making statements supported by Arduino.

a. ***if* statement**: It takes an expression in parenthesis and a statement or block of statements. If the expression is true then the statement or block of statements gets executed otherwise these statements are skipped. Following is the syntax of *if* statement.

```
if (expression) {
   block of statements;
}
```

Example Program

```
int a = 5;
void setup () {
}
void loop () {
   /* check the boolean condition */
   if (a>0) /* if condition is true then execute the following statement*/
   a++;
```

b. ***if ..else* statement**: An *if* statement can be followed by an optional **else** statement, which executes when the expression is false. Following is the syntax of *if..else* statement.

```
if (expression) {
   block of statements;
                    }
else {
   block of statements;
    }
```

Example Program

```
int a = 5;
void setup () {
}
void loop () {
   /* check the boolean condition */
   if (a>0) /* if condition is true then execute the following statement*/
   a++;
   else  /* else condition is true then execute the following statement*/
   a--;
```

c. ***if..else..if..else* statement**: The *if* statement can be followed by an optional *else if...else* statement, which is very useful to test various conditions using single *if...else if* statement. The syntax is as follows.

```
if (expression_1) {
   block of statements;
                   }
else if(expression_2) {
   block of statements;
                   }
else if(expression_n) {
   block of statements;
                   }
else {
   block of statements;
      }
```

Example Program

```
int a = 5;
void setup () {
}
void loop () {
   /* check the boolean condition */
  if (a>0) /* if condition is true then execute the following statement*/
   a++;
   else if(a<0)/* else if condition is true then execute the following
               statement*/
   a--;
   else /* else condition is true then execute the following statement*/
   a=0;
```

d. ***switch…case*** **statement** - *switch...case* controls the flow of programs by allowing the programmers to specify different codes that should be executed in various conditions. In particular, a switch statement compares the value of a variable to the values specified in the case statements. When a case statement is found whose value matches that of the variable, the code in that case statement is run. The ***break*** keyword makes the switch statement exit and is typically used at the end of each case. Without a break statement, the switch statement will continue executing the following expressions until a break or the end of the switch statement is reached. Following is the syntax of *switch* statement.

```
switch (variable) {
 case label:
   // statements
   break;
}
case label: {
```

```
    // statements
    break;
}
default: {
    // statements
    break;
}
```

Example Program

```
switch(phase) {
    case 0: Lo(); break;
    case 1: Mid(); break;
    case 2: Hi(); break;
    default: Message("Invalid state!");
}
```

e. **Conditional operator? :** This is the only ternary operator in C. Syntax of the conditional operator is as follows.

```
expression1? expression2: expression3
```

Here `expression1` is evaluated first. If its value is true, then `expression2` is evaluated and `expression3` is ignored. If `expression1` is evaluated as false, then `expression3` evaluates and `expression2` is ignored. The result will be a value of either `expression2` or `expression3` depending upon which of them evaluates as true. Conditional operator associates from right to left.

Example Program

```
/* Find max(a, b): */
max = ( a > b ) ? a : b;
```

6.4.6 Loops

A loop statement allows executing a statement or group of statements multiple times. Following are the loops supported by Arduino.

a. ***for* loop** - Following is the syntax of *for* loop.

```
for(initialization; termination condition; increment or decrement) {
   // statement block}
```

Example Program

```
for(i=1;i<=10;i++) {
   //statements block will executed 10 times}
```

b. ***while* loop** - *while* loops will iterate continuously and infinitely, until the expression inside the parenthesis () becomes false. The syntax of *while* loop is as follows.

```
while(expression) {
  block of statements;}
```

Example Program

```
n=10;
i=1;
while(i<=n) {
i++ //statements block will executed 10 times
}
```

c. ***do..while*** **loop** - The *do...while* loop is similar to the *while* loop. In the *while* loop, the loop-continuation condition is tested at the beginning of the loop before performed the body of the loop. The *do...while* statement tests the loop-continuation condition after performed the loop body. Therefore, the loop body will be executed at least once. Syntax of *do..while* is given below.

```
do {
    block of statements;
    }
while (expression);
```

Example Program

```
n=10;
i=1;
do{
i++ //statements block will executed 10 times
} while(i<=n);
```

d. **nested loop** – Arduino supports to use one loop inside another loop. The following shows the syntax of nested loop.

```
  for ( initialize ,control; increment or decrement) {
// statement block
for ( initialize ;control; increment or decrement) {
   // statement block
}
}
```

Example Program

```
for(i=1;i<=10;i++) {
//statements block will executed 10 times
for(j=0;j<=99;j++) {
   //statements block will executed 100 times
}
}
```

e. **infinite loop** - It is the loop having no terminating condition, so the loop becomes infinite. Following is the syntax for infinite loop used with *for*, *while* and *do…while* loops.

Using for loop

```
for (;;) {
   // statement block
}
```

Using while loop

```
while(1) {
   // statement block
}
```

Using do...while loop

```
do {
   block of statements;
}
while(1);
```

6.4.7 Functions

There are two required functions in an Arduino sketch or a program i.e. setup () and loop(). Other functions must be created outside the brackets of these two functions. The most common syntax to define a function is as follows.

```
return_type function_name (argument1, argument2….argumentn)
{
statements;
}
```

Function Declaration

A function is declared outside any other functions, above or below the loop function. We can declare the function in two different ways. The first method just declares the function above the loop function. The following example shows the demonstration of the function declaration using the first method.

Example Program

```
int sum(int x, int y) // function declaration {
   int z = 0;
   z = x+y ;
   return z; // return the value
}
```

```
void setup () {
  statements // group of statements
}
void loop () {
  int result = 0;
  result = sum(2,3); // function call
}
```

The second method is just writing the part of the function called a function prototype above the loop function. Function prototype must be followed by a semicolon (;). Function definition is done below the loop function. The function body consists of function return type, function name and function argument type.

Example Program

```
int sum(int,int ); // function prototype
void setup () {
  statements // group of statements
}
void loop () {
  int result = 0;
  result = sum(2,3); // function call
}

int sum(int x,int y) // function declaration {
  int z = 0;
  z = x+y ;
  return z; // return the value
}
```

6.4.8 Arrays

An array is a consecutive group of memory locations that are of the same type. To refer to a particular location or element in the array, we specify the name of the array and the position number of the particular element in the array. Arrays occupy space in memory. The index of an array starts from 0. An array can be declared of the form as given below.

```
type arrayName [arraySize];
```

The `arraySize` must be an integer constant greater than zero. For example, to tell the compiler to reserve 10 elements for integer array we use the following declaration.

```
int c[10]; // c is an array of 10 integers
```

We can declare an array as well as initialize it using the following forms.

```
int a[]={1,2,3,4,5}
int b[5]={1,2,3}
```

Multidimensional arrays are arrays with two dimensions (i.e., subscripts) often represent tables of values consisting of information arranged in rows and columns. To identify a particular array element, we must specify two subscripts. By convention, the first identifies the element's row and the second identifies the element's column. The basic syntax for declaring a multidimensional array is as follows.

```
type arrayName[rowSize][colSize];
```

The `rowSize` and `colSize` must be an integer constant greater than zero. For example, to tell the compiler to reserve 25 elements for integer two dimensional array, we use the following declaration.

```
int c[5][5]; // c is a two-dimensional array of 25 integers
```

A multidimensional array can be initialized in its declaration much like a one-dimensional array. For example, a two-dimensional array b with values 1 and 2 in its row 0 elements and values 3 and 4 in its row 1 elements could be declared and initialized as follows.

```
int b[2][2] = {{1,2},{3,4}};
```

The values are grouped by row in braces. Therefore, 1 and 2 initialize b[0][0] and b[0][1], respectively and 3 and 4 initialize b[1][0] and b[1][1] respectively.

6.4.9 String Objects

Strings are used to store text. There are two types of strings in Arduino programming.

a. Array of characters, which are the same as the strings used in C programming.
b. The Arduino String, which lets us use a string object in a sketch.

A string is a special array of characters that has one extra element at the end of the string, which always has the value of 0 (zero). This is known as a "null terminated string". Example for declaration of array of characters is given below. The declaration of array of objects is as given below.

```
char s[]="abcd";
```

It can also be declared as follows.

```
char s[4];
s[0]='a';
s[1]='b';
s[2]='c';
s[3]='d';
```

A string object can be declared as follows. Here s is an object of class String.

```
String s="abc";
```

There are several built-in functions for String object. Some of them are given below.

`s.toUpperCase()`: Changes all the characters of string s to uppercase.

`s.toLowerCase()`: Changes all the characters of string s to lowercase.

`s.length()`: Returns the length of the string.

`s.replace(s1,s2)`: If s1 is the substring of s, it will be replaced by s2.

6.4.10 Time

Arduino provides four different time manipulation functions. They are given below.

1. **delay ()** function - It accepts a single integer (or number) argument. This number represents the time (measured in milliseconds).
2. **delayMicroseconds ()** function - The delayMicroseconds() function accepts a single integer (or number) argument. There are a thousand microseconds in a millisecond, and a million microseconds in a second.
3. **millis ()** function- This function is used to return the number of milliseconds at the time the Arduino board begins running the current program.
4. **micros ()** function - The micros() function returns the number of microseconds from the time the Arduino board begins running the current program. This number overflows i.e. goes back to zero after approximately 70 minutes.

6.5 Function Libraries

There are several function libraries in Arduino that contains Input-Output functions, character functions, math library and trigonometric functions. We will see one by one.

6.5.1 Input-Output Functions

The pins on the Arduino board can be configured as either inputs or outputs using the `pinMode()` function. Arduino pins are by default configured as inputs, so they do not need to be explicitly declared as inputs with `pinMode()` when we are using them as inputs. Pins configured as INPUT are said to be in a high-impedance state. Pins configured as OUTPUT with pinMode() are said to be in a low-impedance state. The syntax of `pinMode()` function is as follows.

```
void setup () {
  pinMode(pin,mode);
}
```

where `pin` is the pin number on the Arduino board that we wish to set to a mode and `mode` can be either INPUT or OUTPUT.

digitalWrite() - Writes a HIGH or LOW value to a digital pin.

analogRead() - Reads from the analog input pin i.e., voltage applied across the pin.

Example Program for Blinking LED

Requirement

- Arduino controller board, USB connector, bread board, LED, 1.4 Kohm resistor, connecting wires, Arduino IDE.

Connection

- Connect the LED to the Arduino using the bread board and the connecting wires.

- Connect the Arduino board to the PC using the USB connector.
- Select the board type and port.
- Write the sketch in the editor, verify and upload.
- Connect the positive terminal of the LED to digital pin 12 and the negative terminal to the ground pin (GND) of Arduino board.

Sketch

```
void setup(){
pinMode(12,OUTPUT); //Set the pin mode
}
void loop(){
digitalWrite(12, HIGH); // Turn on the LED
delay(1000);
digitalWrite(12, LOW); //Turn of the LED
delay(1000);
}
```

Explanation

Initially the pin mode is set as OUTPUT which is connected to the LED, pin 12 in this case. The digitalWrite() function is used to set the output as HIGH and LOW. The function delay() is used to specify the delay between HIGH-LOW transition of the output. The next procedure is to connect the board to the PC. Select the port and board type from Arduino IDE. Verify the code and upload. We can notice the TX-RV LED in the board starts flashing as the code is uploaded.

6.5.2 Character Functions

All data is entered into computers as characters, which includes letters, digits and various special symbols. The character-handling library includes several functions that perform useful tests and manipulations of character data. The following are the functions of the character-handling library. When using functions from the character-handling library, it is necessary to include the <cctype> header.

1. int isdigit(int c) - Returns 1 if c is a digit and 0 otherwise.
2. int isalpha(int c) - Returns 1 if c is a letter and 0 otherwise.
3. int isalnum(int c) - Returns 1 if c is a digit or a letter and 0 otherwise.
4. int isxdigit(int c) - Returns 1 if c is a hexadecimal digit character and 0 otherwise.
5. int islower(int c) - Returns 1 if c is a lowercase letter and 0 otherwise.
6. int isupper(int c) - Returns 1 if c is an uppercase letter, 0 otherwise.
7. int isspace(int c) - Returns 1 if c is a white-space character—newline ('\n'), space

(' '), form feed ('\f'), carriage return ('\r'), horizontal tab ('\t'), or vertical tab ('\v') and 0 otherwise.

1. int iscntrl(int c) - Returns 1 if c is a control character, such as newline ('\n'), form feed ('\f'), carriage return ('\r'), horizontal tab ('\t'), vertical tab ('\v'), alert ('\a'), or backspace ('\b')—and 0 otherwise.
2. int ispunct(int c) - Returns 1 if c is a printing character other than a space, a digit, or a letter and 0 otherwise.
3. int isprint(int c) - Returns 1 if c is a printing character including space (' ') and 0 otherwise.
4. int isgraph(int c) - Returns 1 if c is a printing character other than space (' ') and 0 otherwise.

6.5.3 Math Library

We need to include the **math.h** header file for using mathematical functions. Following are the mathematical functions included in math library.

- cos(double radian);
- sin(double radian);
- tan(double radian);
- fabs(double val);
- fmod(double val1, double val2);
- exp(double val);
- log(double val);
- log10(double val);
- square(double val);
- pow(double base, double power);

6.6 Random Numbers

To generate random numbers, we can use Arduino random number functions. We have two functions **(a) randomSeed(seed) (b) random().**

randomSeed (seed): The function randomSeed(seed) resets Arduino's pseudorandom number generator. Although the distribution of the numbers returned by random() is essentially random, the sequence is predictable. We should reset the generator to some random value. If we have an unconnected analog pin, it might pick up random noise from the surrounding environment. These may be radio waves, cosmic rays, electromagnetic interference from cell phones, fluorescent lights and so on.

Example

```
randomSeed(analogRead(5)); // randomize using noise from analog pin 5
```

random( ): The random function generates pseudo-random numbers. Following is the syntax.

```
long random(max) // it generate random numbers from 0 to max
long random(min,max) // it generate random numbers from min to max
```

6.7 Interrupts

An external signal for which system blocks the current running process to process that signal is called an interrupt. There are two types of interrupts.

Hardware Interrupts – They occur in response to an external event, such as an external interrupt pin going high or low.

Software Interrupts – They occur in response to an instruction sent in software.

Interrupts are very useful in Arduino programs as it helps in solving timing problems. A good application of an interrupt is reading a rotary encoder or observing a user input. Generally, an Interrupt Service Routine (ISR) should be as short and fast as possible. If our sketch uses multiple ISRs, only one can run at a time. Other interrupts will be executed after the current one finishes in an order that depends on the priority they have. Typically, global variables are used to pass data between an ISR and the main program. To make sure variables shared between an ISR and the main program is updated correctly, declare them as volatile. The only type of interrupt that the "Arduino language" supports is the `attachInterrupt()` function. The format of `attachInterrupt()` function is as follows.

```
attachInterrupt(digitalPinToInterrupt(pin),ISR,mode);
digitalPinToInterrupt(pin): change the actual digital pin to the specific
interrupt number.
pin: the pin number
ISR: the ISR to call when the interrupt occurs
mode: defines when the interrupt should be triggered.
```

The following three constants are predefined as valid values for the mode of the pin.

d. LOW to trigger the interrupt whenever the pin is low.
e. CHANGE to trigger the interrupt whenever the pin changes value.
f. FALLING whenever the pin goes from high to low.

Following program illustrates this.

```
int pin = 2; //define interrupt pin to 2
volatile int state = LOW; // To make sure variables shared between an ISR
//the main program are updated correctly,declare them as volatile.
void setup() {
  pinMode(13, OUTPUT); //set pin 13 as output
  attachInterrupt(digitalPinToInterrupt(pin), blink, CHANGE);
  //interrupt at pin 2 blink ISR when pin to change the value
}
```

```
void loop() {
   digitalWrite(13, state); //pin 13 equal the state value
}
void blink() {
   //ISR function
   state = !state; //toggle the state when the interrupt occurs
}
```

6.8 Case Studies

In this section, we will discuss some practical applications where Arduino board is used. Three case studies are explained – traffic control system, Digital Humidity and Temperature sensor used with Arduino and servo motor interfaced with Arduino.

6.8.1 Traffic Control System

Requirement

Arduino board, 3 different color LEDs, 330 ohm resistors and jumper wires.

Connection

- Connect the positive terminals of the LEDs to the respective digital Output pins in the board assigned in the code.
- Connect the negative terminals of the LED to the ground.

Sketch

```
// LED pins
int r=2;
int g=3;
int y=4;
void setup()
{ Serial.begin(9600);
  pinMode(r,OUTPUT);
  pinMode(g,OUTPUT);
  pinMode(y,OUTPUT);
  digitalWrite(r,LOW);
  digitalWrite(g,LOW);
  digitalWrite(y,LOW);
}
void traffic()
{
digitalWrite(g,HIGH);
Serial.println("Green LED:ON,GO");
```

```
//delay of 5 seconds
delay(5000);
digitalWrite(g,LOW);
digitalWrite(y,HIGH);
Serial.println("Green LED:OFF,Yellow LED:ON,WAIT)
delay(5000);
digitalWrite(y,LOW);
digitalWrite(r,HIGH);
Serial.println("Yellow LED:OFF, Red LED ON,STOP");
delay(5000);
digitalWrite(r,LOW);
Serial.println("ALL OFF");
}
void loop()
{
 traffic();
 delay(10000);
}
```

Explanation

Initially all the LEDs are turned off. The LEDs are turned on one at a time with a delay of 5 seconds. The message is displayed accordingly to the serial port using the function `Serial.println()`.

6.8.2 DHT Sensor with Arduino

In this example, we will see the integration of sensors with Arduino board. Sensors as we know are electronic elements which sense the data. It converts physical quantity/measurements into electrical signals. They can be analog or digital. In this example, we have used Digital Humidity and Temperature sensor (DHT). This sensor has four pins PIN 1, 2, 3, 4 (from left to right). Following are the pin descriptions.

PIN 1 – 3.3 v to 5v power supply

PIN 2 - data

PIN 3 – null

PIN 4 – Ground

Arduino supports a special library DHT for DHT11 and DHT22 sensors. This provides function to read the temperature (`dht.readTemperature()`) and humidity (`dht.readHumidity()`) values from the data pin.

Connection

- Connect Pin 1 of the DHT to the 3.3v supply pin on the board.

- Data pin (Pin 2) can be connected to any digital pin. Here it is 12.
- Connect Pin 4 to the ground (GND) pin of the board.

Sketch

We need to install the DHT sensor library. Go to Sketch □Include Library□ Manage Library. Search for DHT sensor. Select the "DHT sensor library" and install it.

```
#include<DHT.h>
DHT dht(8,DHT22);//Initialize DHT sensor
float humidity;//Stores humidity value.
float temperature;//Stores temperature.
void setup()
{Serial.begin(9600);
 dht.begin();
}
void loop(){
//Read data from the sensor and store it to variables humidity and //
temperature
humidity=dht.readHumidity();
temperature=dht.readTemperature;
//Print temperature and humidity values to serial monitor.
Serial.print("Humidity: ");
Serial.print(humidity);
Serial.print("%, Temperature: ");
Serial.print(temperature);
Serial.println("Celsius");
delay(2000);//Delay of 2 seconds
```

Connect the board to the PC. Select the port and board type. Verify and upload the code.

Output

The readings are printed at a delay of 2 seconds as specified by the `delay()` function.

6.8.3 Servo Motor Interfaced with Arduino

In this section, we discuss the integration of actuators with Arduino board. In this example, we use a servo motor interfaced with Arduino. Actuators are mechanical or electromechanical device that converts energy into motion. It is mainly used to provide controlled motion to other components. The basic working principle of a motor is that it uses different combination of various mechanical structures like screws, ball bearings and gears to produce motion. There are various types of motor actuators like servo motor, stepper motor, hydraulic motor, solenoid, relays, AC motor etc.

Servo motor is a high precision motor which provides rotary motion 0 to 180 degree. There are 3 wires in the servo motor: black or darkest is the Ground, red is the power supply and yellow is for signal pin. Arduino provides different library for different actuators. Servo library is the library containing functions to operate the servo motor. Following are some of the functions available with servo library.

1. Knob() - Control the position of a RC (hobby) servo motor with Arduino and a potentiometer.
2. Sweep() - Sweeps the shaft of a RC servo motor back and forth across 180 degrees.
3. write() - Writes a value to the servo, controlling the shaft accordingly. On a standard servo, this will set the angle of the shaft (in degrees), moving the shaft to that orientation. On a continuous rotation servo, this will set the speed of the servo (with 0 being full-speed in one direction, 180 being full speed in the other, and a value near 90 being no movement). Below is the syntax of write().

   ```
   servo.write(angle)
   ```

   where `servo` is a variable of type Servo and `angle` is the value to write to the servo, from 0 to 180.
4. writeMicroseconds() - Writes a value in microseconds (uS) to the servo, controlling the shaft accordingly. On a standard servo, this will set the angle of the shaft. On standard servos a parameter value of 1000 is fully counter-clockwise, 2000 is fully clockwise, and 1500 is in the middle. Following is the syntax.

   ```
   servo.writeMicroseconds(uS)
   ```

   where `servo` is a variable of type Servo and `uS` is the value of the parameter in microseconds (int)
5. read() - Read the current angle of the servo (the value passed to the last call to write()). Below is the syntax.

   ```
   servo.read()
   ```

   where `servo` is a variable of type Servo. The function returns the angle of the servo, from 0 to 180 degrees.
6. attach() - Attach the servo variable to a pin. Following is the syntax.

   servo.attach(pin)

   servo.attach(pin, min, max)

   where `servo` is a variable of type Servo, `pin` is the number of the pin that the servo is attached to and min (optional) is the pulse width, in microseconds, corresponding to the minimum (0-degree) angle on the servo (defaults to 544) and max (optional) is the pulse width in microseconds corresponding to the maximum (180-degree) angle on the servo (defaults to 2400)
7. detach() - Detach the servo variable from its pin. Following is the syntax.

   servo.detach()

   where `servo` is a variable of type Servo.

Connection

Connect the ground of the servo to the Ground of the Arduino board. Connect the power supply wire to the 5v pin of the board. Connect the signal wire to any digital output pin. Here we have used pin 8.

Sketch

```
#include<Servo.h>
//Including the servo library for the program
int servoPin=12;
Servo ServoDemo;//Creating a servo object
void setup(){
//The servo pin must be attached to the servo before it can be used.
ServoDemo.attach(servoPin);
}
void loop(){
//servo moves to 0 degrees
ServoDemo.Write(0);
delay(1000);
//servo moves to 90 degrees
ServoDemo.Write(90);
delay(1000);
//servo moves to 180 degrees
ServoDemo.Write(180);
delay(1000);
}
```

We have created an instance of the class Servo to use it in the sketch. The instance must be attached to the pin before being used in the code. `Write()` function takes the degree value and rotates the motor accordingly. Connect the board to the PC. Select the port and board type. Verify and upload the code.

Output

The motor turns 0, 90 and 180 degrees with a delay of 1 second each.

6.9 Conclusion

This Chapter explains the programming with Arduino. The features of Arduino, components of Arduino board, Arduino IDE are illustrated in detail with diagrams. Various program elements like structure of an Arduino programs, variables, data types, operators, decision making statements, loops, functions, arrays, String objects and time functions. Function libraries supported by Arduino including Input-Output functions, character functions and math library are explained. Random numbers and interrupts in Arduino are illustrated. Case studies of Arduino for Traffic Control System, integration of DHT sensor with Arduino and Servo motor interfaced with Arduino are explained with Arduino sketch.

7 INTRODUCTION TO PYTHON PROGRAMMING

7.1 Introduction

Python is a general-purpose interpreted, interactive, object-oriented, and high-level programming language. Python source code is available under the GNU General Public License (GPL) and it is now maintained by a core development team at the National Research Institute. Python is a versatile language which is easy to script and easy to read. It doesn't have strict rules for syntax. Python is open source and it forms a strong backbone to build large applications. We can run Python from a Graphical User Interface (GUI) environment if we have a GUI application on our system that supports Python. IDLE is the Integrated Development Environment (IDE) for Python. Its installation comes with integrated development environment for programming. Other examples for Python IDE are Spyder, PyCharm etc. All the programs in this book follow Python 3.4.3 for Windows.

7.2 Input-Output Statements

The function used to print output on a screen is the *print* statement where we can pass zero or more expressions separated by commas. The *print* function converts the expressions we pass into a string and writes the result to standard output.

Example 1

```
>>>print("Learning Python is fun and enjoy it.")
```

This will produce the following output on the screen.

```
Learning Python is fun and enjoy it.
```

In Python, we need not declare the type of the variable as in C or C++ The type of the variable depends on the value assigned to it. Hence we can simply assign a value to a variable.

Example 2

```
>>>a=2
>>>print("The value of a is",a)
```

This will produce the following output on the screen. `The value of a is 2`

The input([prompt]) function assumes the input is a valid Python expression and returns the evaluated result to us.

Example

```
n = input("Enter a number ")
print("The number is: ", n)
```

Output

```
Enter a number: 5
The number is: 5
```

7.3 Operators

Python supports various operators in like arithmetic operators, comparison (relational) operators, assignment operators, logical operators, bitwise operators, membership operators and identity operators. Table 7.1 shows the arithmetic operators in Python.

Table 7.1: Arithmetic Operators in Python

Operator	Operation	Description
+	Addition	Adds values on either side of the operator.
-	Subtraction	Subtracts right hand operand from left hand operand.
*	Multiplication	Multiplies values on either side of the operator.
/	Division	Divides left hand operand by right hand operand.
%	Modulus	Divides left hand operand by right hand operand and returns remainder.
**	Exponent	Performs exponential (power) calculation on operators.
//	Floor Division	The division of operands where the result is the quotient in which the digits after the decimal point are removed.

Comparison operators compare the values on either sides of them and decide the relation among them. They are also called relational operators. Python supports the following relational operators. Table 7.2 shows the comparison or relational operators in Python.

Table 7.2: Comparison Operators in Python

Operator	Description
==	If the values of two operands are equal, then the condition becomes true.
!=	If values of two operands are not equal, then condition becomes true.
>	If the value of left operand is greater than the value of right operand, then condition becomes true.

<	If the value of left operand is less than the value of right operand, then condition becomes true.
>=	If the value of left operand is greater than or equal to the value of right operand, then condition becomes true.
<=	If the value of left operand is less than or equal to the value of right operand, then condition becomes true.

Python provides various assignment operators. Various shorthand operators for addition, subtraction, multiplication, division, modulus, exponent and floor division are also supported by Python. Table 7.3 provides the various assignment operators.

Table 7.3: Assignment Operators in Python

Operator	Description
=	Assigns values from right side operands to left side operand.
+=	It adds right operand to the left operand and assign the result to left operand.
-=	It subtracts right operand from the left operand and assign the result to left operand.
*=	It multiplies right operand with the left operand and assign the result to left operand.
/=	It divides left operand with the right operand and assign the result to left operand.
%=	It takes modulus using two operands and assign the result to left operand.
**=	Performs exponential (power) calculation on operators and assign value to the left operand.
//=	It performs floor division on operators and assign value to the left operand.

Bitwise operator works on bits and performs bit by bit operation. The following are the bitwise operators supported by Python. Table 7.4 gives a description of bitwise operators in Python.

Table 7.4: Bitwise Operators in Python

Operator	Operation	Description
&	Binary AND	Operator copies a bit to the result if it exists in both operands.
|	Binary OR	It copies a bit if it exists in either operand.
^	Binary XOR	It copies the bit if it is set in one operand but not both.
~	Binary Ones Complement	It is unary and has the effect of 'flipping' bits.
<<	Binary Left Shift	The left operands value is moved left by the number of bits specified by the right operand.
>>	Binary Right Shift	The left operands value is moved right by the number of bits specified by the right operand.

Table 7.5 shows the various logical operators supported by Python language.

Table 7.5: Logical Operators in Python

Operator	Operation	Description
and	Logical AND	If both the operands are true then condition becomes true.
or	Logical OR	If any of the operands are true then condition becomes true.
not	Logical NOT	Used to reverse the logical state of its operand.

Python's membership operators test for membership in a sequence, such as strings, lists, or tuples. There are two membership operators as explained below in Table 7.6. Strings, lists and tuples will be covered in the next section.

Table 7.6: Membership Operators in Python

Operator	Description
in	Evaluates to true if the variables on either side of the operator point to the same object and false otherwise.
not in	Evaluates to true if it does not finds a variable in the specified sequence and false otherwise.

Identity operators compare whether two elements points to the same memory locations. There are two Identity operators as shown in below Table 7.7.

Table 7.7: Identity Operators in Python

Operator	Description
is	Evaluates to true if the variables on either side of the operator point to the same object and false otherwise.
is not	Evaluates to false if the variables on either side of the operator point to the same object and true otherwise.

7.4 Data Types

There are 6 data types in Python. They are numbers, string, list, tuple, set and dictionary.

Numbers

Number data types store numeric values. Number objects are created when you assign a value to them. For example `a = 1, b = 20`. Python supports four different numerical types.

- int (signed integers)
- long (long integers, they can also be represented in octal and hexadecimal)

- float (floating point real values)
- complex (complex numbers)

String

Strings in Python are identified as a contiguous set of characters represented in the quotation marks. Python allows for either pairs of single or double quotes. Subsets of strings can be taken using the slice operator ([ ] and [:]) with indexes starting at 0 in the beginning of the string and ending at -1.

Example Program

```
str = 'Welcome to Python Programming '
print(str)             # Prints complete string
print(str[0])          # Prints first character of the string
print(str[11:17])      # Prints characters starting from 11th to 17th
print(str[11:])        # Prints string starting from 11th character
```

Output

```
Welcome to Python Programming
W
Python
Python Programming
```

There are several built-in functions for string. Here we will see one of the commonly used built-in function `split()`.

split(str="", num=string.count(str)) - Returns a list of all the words in the string, using `str` as the separator (splits on all whitespace if left unspecified), optionally limiting the number of splits to `num`.

Example Program

```
#Demo of split(str="",num=string.count(str))
s="Python programming is fun"
print(s.split(' '))
s="Python*programming*is*fun"
print(s.split('*'))
s="Python*programming*is*fun"
print(s.split('*',2))
```

Output

```
['Python', 'programming', 'is', 'fun']
['Python', 'programming', 'is', 'fun']
['Python', 'programming', 'is*fun']
```

List

List is an ordered sequence of items. It is one of the most used data type in Python and is very flexible. All the items in a list do not need to be of the same type. Items separated by commas are enclosed within brackets [ ]. The values stored in a list can be accessed using the slice operator ([ ] and [:]) with indexes starting at 0 in the beginning of the list and ending with -1.

Example Program

```
first_list = ['abcd', 147, 2.43, 'Tom', 74.9]
print(first_list)              # Prints complete list
print(first_list[0])           # Prints first element of the list
print(first_list[1:3])         # Prints elements starting from 2nd till 3rd
print(first_list[2:])          # Prints elements starting from 3rd element
```

Output

```
['abcd', 147, 2.43, 'Tom', 74.9]
abcd
[147, 2.43]
[2.43, ‹Tom›, 74.9]
```

Tuple

A tuple is another sequence data type that is similar to the list. A tuple consists of a number of values separated by commas. The main differences between lists and tuples are lists are enclosed in square brackets ([ ]) and their elements and size can be changed, while tuples are enclosed in parentheses (( )) and cannot be updated. Tuples can be considered as read-only lists.

Example Program

```
first_tuple = ('abcd', 147, 2.43, 'Tom', 74.9)
print(first_tuple)          # Prints complete tuple
print(first_tuple[0])       # Prints first element of the tuple
print(first_tuple[1:3])     # Prints elements starting from 2nd till 3rd
print(first_tuple[2:])      # Prints elements starting from 3rd element
```

Output

```
('abcd', 147, 2.43, 'Tom', 74.9)
abcd
(147, 2.43)
(2.43, 'Tom', 74.9)
```

Set

Set is an unordered collection of unique items. Set is defined by values separated by comma inside braces { }. It can have any number of items and they may be of different types (integer, float, tuple, string etc.). Items in a set are not ordered. Since they are unordered we cannot access or change an element of set using indexing or slicing. We can perform set operations like union, intersection, difference on two sets. Set have unique values. They eliminate duplicates. The slicing operator [] does not work with sets. An empty set is created by the function set().

Example Program

```
# Demo of Set Creation
s1={1,2,3} #set of integer numbers
print(s1)
s2={1,2,3,2,1,2}#output contains only unique values
print(s2)
s3={1, 2.4, 'apple', 'Tom', 3}#set of mixed data types
print(s3)
```

Output

```
{1, 2, 3}
{1, 2, 3}
{1, 3, 2.4, 'apple', 'Tom'}
```

Dictionary

Dictionary is an unordered collection of key-value pairs. It is generally used when we have a huge amount of data. We must know the key to retrieve the value. In Python, dictionaries are defined within braces {} with each item being a pair in the form key:value. Key and value can be of any type. Keys are usually numbers or strings. Values, on the other hand, can be any arbitrary Python object. Dictionaries are enclosed by curly braces ({ }) and values can be assigned and accessed using square braces ([]).

Example Program

```
dict={1:"one",2:"two"}
print(dict)
```

Output

```
{1:"one",2:"two"}
```

7.5 Decision Making

Decision making is required when we want to execute a code only if a certain condition is satisfied. The `if…elif…else` statement is used in Python for decision making.

***if* statement**

Syntax

```
if test expression:
    statement(s)
```

Here, the program evaluates the `test expression` and will execute statement(s) only if the text expression is `True`. If the text expression is `False`, the statement(s) is not executed. In Python, the body of the `if` statement is indicated by the indentation. Body starts with an indentation and ends with the first unindented line. Python interprets non-zero values as `True`. `None` and `0` are interpreted as `False`.

Example Program

```
num =int(input("Enter a number: "))
if num == 0:
    print("Zero")
print("This is always printed")
```

Output

```
Enter a number: 0
Zero
This is always printed
```

***if....else* statement**

Syntax

```
if test expression:
    Body of if
else:
    Body of else
```

Example Program

```
num =int(input("Enter a number: "))
if num >= 0:
    print("Positive Number or Zero")
else:
    print("Negative Number")
```

Output

```
Enter a number: 5
Positive Number or Zero
```

***if...elif...else* statement**

Syntax

```
if test expression:
    Body of if
elif test expression:
    Body of elif
else:
    Body of else
```

The `elif` is short for else if. It allows us to check for multiple expressions. If the condition for `if` is `False`, it checks the condition of the next `elif` block and so on. If all the conditions are `False`, body of else is executed. Only one block among the several `if...elif...else` blocks is executed according to the condition.

Example Program

```
num =int(input("Enter a number: "))
if num > 0:
    print("Positive number")
elif num == 0:
    print("Zero")
else:
    print("Negative number")
```

Output

```
Enter a number: 5
Positive Number
```

7.6 Loops

Python provides various control structures that allow for repeated execution. A loop statement allows us to execute a statement or group of statements multiple times.

for loop

The `for` loop in Python is used to iterate over a sequence (list, tuple, string) or other objects that can be iterated.

Syntax

```
for item in sequence:
    Body of for
```

Here, `item` is the variable that takes the value of the item inside the sequence of each iteration. The sequence can be list, tuple, string, set etc. Loop continues until we reach the last item in the sequence. The body of `for` loop is separated from the rest of the code using indentation.

Example Program 1

```
#Program to find the sum of all numbers stored in a list
# List of numbers
numbers = [2,4,6,8,10]
# variable to store the sum
sum = 0
# iterate over the list
for item in numbers:
```

```
    sum = sum+item
# print the sum
print("The sum is",sum)
```

Output 1

```
The sum is 30
```

Example Program 2

```
flowers = ['rose', 'lotus',  'jasmine']
for flower in flowers:
   print('Current flower:', flower)
```

Output 2

```
Current flower: rose
Current flower: lotus
Current flower: jasmine
```

for loop with *else* statement

Python supports to have an else statement associated with a loop statement. If the *else* statement is used with a *for* loop, the **else** statement is executed when the loop has finished iterating the list. A `break` statement can be used to stop a *`for`* loop. In this case, the `else` part is ignored. Hence, a *`for`* loop's *`else`* part runs if no break occurs. Break statement will be discussed in the next section.

Example Program

```
#Program to find whether an item is present in the list
list=[10,12,13,34,27,98]
num = int(input("Enter the number to be searched in the list: "))
for item in range(len(list)):
 if list[item] == num:
   print("Item found at: ",(item+1))
   break
else:
   print("Item not found in the list")
```

Output

```
Enter the number to be searched in the list:34
Item found at:4
```

while loop

The `while` loop in Python is used to iterate over a block of code as long as the test expression (condition) is true. We generally use this loop when we don't know the number of times to iterate in advance.

Syntax

```
while test_expression:
    Body of while
```

In `while` loop, `test_ expression` is checked first. The body of the loop is entered only if the `test_expression` evaluates to `True`. After one iteration, the test expression is checked again. This process is continued until the `test_expression` evaluates to `False`. In Python, the body of the `while` loop is determined through indentation. Body starts with indentation and the first unindented line shows the end. When the condition is tested and the result is false, the loop body will be skipped and the first statement after the while loop will be executed.

Example Program

```
# Program to find the sum of first N natural numbers
n =int(input("Enter the limit: "))
sum=0
i=1
while i<=n:
    sum=sum+i
    i=i+1
print("Sum of first", n, "natural numbers is ", sum)
```

Output

```
Enter the limit: 5
Sum of first 5 natural numbers is 15
```

***while* loop with *else* statement**

If the `else` statement is used with a `while` loop, the `else` statement is executed when the condition becomes false. `while` loop can be terminated with a `break` statement. In such case, the `else` part is ignored. Hence, a `while` loop's `else` part runs if no break occurs and the condition is false.

Example Program

```
# Domo of While with else
count-1
while count<=3:
    print("Python Programming")
    count=count+1
else:
    print("Exit")
print("End of Program")
```

Output

```
Python Programming
```

```
Python Programming
Python Programming
Exit
End of Program
```

7.7 Control Statements

Control statements change the execution from normal sequence. Loops iterate over a block of code until test expression is false, but sometimes we wish to terminate the current iteration or even the whole loop without checking test expression. The `break` and `continue` statements are used in these cases. Python supports the following three control statements.

1. `break`
2. `continue`
3. `pass`

break statement

The `break` statement terminates the loop containing it. Control of the program flows to the statement immediately after the body of the loop. If it is inside a nested loop (loop inside another loop), `break` will terminate the innermost loop. It can be used with both `for` and `while` loops.

Example Program

```
#Demo of break statement in Python
for i in range(2,10,2):
 if i==6: break
 print(i)
print("End of Program")
```

Output

```
2
4
End of Program
```

The `continue` statement is used to skip the rest of the code inside a loop for the current iteration only. Loop does not terminate but continues on with the next iteration. Continue returns the control to the beginning of the loop. The `continue` statement rejects all the remaining statements in the current iteration of the loop and moves the control back to the top of the loop. The **continue** statement can be used in both *while* and *for* loops.

Example Program

```
# Demo of continue in Python
for letter in 'abcd':
 if letter =='c': continue;
 print(letter)
```

Output

```
a
b
d
```

pass statement

In Python programming, `pass` is a null statement. The difference between a comment and `pass` statement in Python is that, while the interpreter ignores a comment entirely, `pass` is not ignored. But nothing happens when it is executed. It results in no operation.

It is used as a placeholder. Suppose we have a loop or a function that is not implemented yet, but we want to implement it in the future. The function or loop cannot have an empty body. The interpreter will not allow this. So, we use the `pass` statement to construct a body that does nothing.

Example

```
for val in sequence:
    pass
```

7.8 Functions

The following specifies simple rules for defining a function.

- Function block or Function header begins with the keyword `def` followed by the function name and parentheses (( )).
- Any input parameters or arguments should be placed within these parentheses. We can also define parameters inside these parentheses.
- The first string after the function header is called the `docstring` and is short for documentation string. It is used to explain in brief, what a function does. Although optional, documentation is a good programming practice.
- The code block within every function starts with a colon (:) and is indented.
- The `return` statement [expression] exits a function, optionally passing back an expression to the caller. A `return` statement with no arguments is the same as `return None.` We can also write a function without `return` statement.

Syntax

```
def functionname( parameters ):
    "function_docstring"
    function_suite
    return [expression]
```

Example Program with Return Statement

```
def sum_of_two_numbers(a,b): #Function Header with 2 parameters a and b
```

```
 "This Function is to find the sum of two numbers" #Docstring
 sum=a+b
 return sum
```

Example Program without Return Statement

```
def sum_of_two_numbers(a,b): #Function Header with 2 parameters a and b
 "This Function is to find the sum of two numbers" #Docstring
 sum=a+b
 print("sum=",sum)
```

After defining a function, we can call the function from another function or directly from the Python prompt. The order of the parameters specified in the function definition should be preserved in function call also.

Example Program for Function Calling with Return Statement

```
#Main Program Code
a = int(input("Enter the first number:"))
b = int(input("Enter the second number:"))
s = sum_of_two_numbers(a,b)#Function calling
print("Sum of",a,"and",b,"is", s)
```

Output

```
Enter the first number:4
Enter the second number:3
Sum of 4 and 3 is 7
```

Example Program for Function Calling without Return Statement

```
#Main Program Code
a = int(input("Enter the first number:"))
b = int(input("Enter the second number:"))
s = sum_of_two_numbers(a,b)#Function calling
```

Output

```
Enter the first number:4
Enter the second number:3
Sum of 4 and 3 is 7
```

Variable Scope in Python

Global variables are those variables declared out of any function, but can be accessed inside as well as outside the function. Parameters and variables defined inside a function is not visible from outside. Hence, they have a local scope. Lifetime of a variable is the period throughout which the variable exists in the memory. The lifetime of variables inside a function is as long as the function executes. All variables in a program may not be accessible at all locations in that program. This depends on where we have declared a variable. The scope of a variable determines the portion of the program where we can access a particular identifier. They are destroyed once we return from the function. Hence, a function does not remember the value of a variable from its previous calls.

Example Program

```
a=10
def value_change(a): #Function Header
 a=100
 print("Value inside function=",a) #prints the value of a inside function
 return
#Main Program Code
value_change(a)#Function calling
print("Value outside function=",a) #prints value of a outside function
```

Output

```
Value inside function= 100
Value outside function= 10
```

Function with more than one return value

Python has a strong mechanism of returning more than one value at a time. This is very flexible when the function needs to return more than one value. Instead of writing separate functions for returning individual values, we can return all the values within same function. The following shows an example for function returning more than one value.

Example Program

```
#Python Function Returning more than One value
def calc(a,b):
    sum=a+b
    diff-a-b
    prod-a*b
    quotient=a/b
    return sum, diff, prod, quotient
a=int(input("Enter first number:"))
b=int(input("Enter second number:"))
s,d,p,q=calc(a,b)
print("Sum=",s)
print("Difference=",d)
print("Product=",p)
print("Quotient=",q)
```

Output

```
Enter first number:10
Enter second number:5
Sum= 15
Difference= 5
Product= 50
Quotient= 2
```

7.9 Modules

Modules refer to a file containing Python statements and definitions. We use modules to break down large programs into small manageable and organized files. Further, modules provide reusability of code. A module can define functions, classes and variables. A module can also include runnable code. Python has a lot of standard modules (built-in modules) available.

Creating Modules

We can define our most used functions in a module and import it, instead of copying their definitions into different programs. A file containing Python code, for e.g.: `prime.py`, is called a module and its module name would be `prime`. Let us create a module for finding the sum of two numbers. The following code creates a module in Python. Type the code and save it as `test.py`.

Example

```
# Python Module example
"""This program adds two
   numbers and return the result"""
def sum(a, b):
   result = a + b
   return result
```

Here we have a function `sum()` inside a module named `test`. The function takes in two numbers and returns their sum.

import Statement

We can use any Python source file as a module by executing an import statement in some other Python source file. User-defined modules can be imported the same way as we import built-in modules.

We use the `import` keyword to do this. The import has the following syntax.

```
import module1[, module2[,... moduleN]
```

When the interpreter encounters an import statement, it imports the module if the module is present in the search path. A search path is a list of directories that the interpreter searches before importing a module. For example, to import the module `test.py`, you need to put the following command at the top of the script.

Example

```
import test
print(test.sum(2,3))
```

Output

```
5
```

A module is loaded only once, regardless of the number of times it is imported. This prevents the module execution from happening over and over again if multiple imports occur.

import with renaming

We can import built-in or user-defined modules with an alias name. The following code shows how the built-in module `math` can be imported using an alias name.

Example Program

```
import math as m
print("The value of pi is", m.pi)
```

Output

```
The value of pi is 3.141592653589793
```

We have renamed the `math` module as `m`. This can save typing time in some cases. It is important to note that the name `math` is not recognized in our scope. Hence, `math.pi` is invalid, `m.pi` is the correct implementation.

from...import statement

We can import specific names form a module without importing the module as a whole. The module math contains a lot of built-in functions. But if we want to import only the `pi` function, the `from...import` statement can be used. The following example illustrates importing `pi` from `math` module.

Example Program

```
from math import pi
print("The value of pi is :", pi)
```

Output

```
The value of pi is : 3.14159265359
```

We have imported only the `pi` function from the `math` module. Hence no need to use the dot operator. We can also import multiple attributes from the module using `from...import` statement. The following example illustrates the import of `pi` as well as `sqrt()` from the `math` module using `from...import` statement.

Example Program

```
from math import pi,sqrt
print("The value of pi is :", pi)
print("The square root of 4 is:",sqrt(4))
```

Output

```
The value of pi is: 3.14159265359
The square root of 4 is: 2.0
```

import all names

We can import all names (definitions) from a module using the following construct. The following example shows how all the definitions from the `math` module can be imported. This makes all names except those beginning with an underscore, visible in our scope.

Example Program

```
from math import *
print("The value of pi is :", pi )
print("The square root of 4 is:",sqrt(4))
```

Output

```
The value of pi is: 3.14159265359
The square root of 4 is: 2.0
```

Here all functions in the module `math` are imported. But we have used only `pi` and `sqrt`. Importing everything with the asterisk (*) symbol is not a good programming practice. This can lead to duplicate definitions for an identifier.

7.10 Exception Handling

An exception is an abnormal condition that is caused by a runtime error in the program. It disturbs the normal flow of the program. An example for an exception is division by 0. When a Python script encounters a situation that it cannot deal with, it raises an exception. An exception is a Python object that represents an error.

If the exception object is not caught and handled properly, the interpreter will display an error message. If we want the program to continue with the execution of the remaining code, then we should try to catch the exception object thrown by the error condition and then display appropriate messages for taking corrective actions. This task is known as exception handling.

Python has a collection of built-in Exception classes. If the runtime error belongs to any of the pre-defined built-in exception, it will throw the object of the appropriate exception. Python uses a keyword `try` to prepare a block of code that is likely to cause an error and throw an exception. An `except` block is defined which catches the exception thrown by the `try` block and handles it. The `try` block can have one or more statements that could generate an exception. If anyone statement generates an exception, then the remaining statements in the block are skipped and execution jumps to the `except` block that is placed next to the `try` block.

The `except` block can have more than one statement and if the except parameter matches with the type of the Exception object, then the exception is caught and statements in the `except` block will be executed. Every `try` block should be followed by atleast one `except` statement.

try....except

The following gives the syntax of try....except statement.

Syntax

```
try:
   suite
except Exception1:
   Exception1_suite#Executes when Exception1 occurs.
except Exception2:
   Exception2_suite#Executes when Exception2 occurs.
else:
   else_suite #Executes if there is no exception in the try block.
```

When an exception occurs inside a try block, it will go to the corresponding except block. If no exception is raised inside a try block then after the try block, the statements in the else block is executed. The else block can also be considered a place to put the code that does not raise any exception.

Example Program

```
#Exception Handling
try:
    a=int(input("First Number:"))
    b=int(input("Second Number:"))
    result=a/b
    print("Result=",result)
except ZeroDivisionError:
    print("Division by Zero")
else:
    print("Successful Division")
```

Output

```
First Number:10
Second Number:0
Division by Zero
```

In the above example, the second number is 0. Since division by zero is not possible, an exception is thrown and the execution goes to the `except` block. All the rest of the statements is bypassed in the `try` block. Hence the output is displayed as `Division by Zero.`

7.11 File Handling

File is a named location on disk to store related information. When we want to read from or write to a file we need to open it first. When we are done, it needs to be closed, so that resources that are tied with the file are freed. Hence, in Python, a file operation takes place in the following order.

a. Open a file
b. Read or write (perform operation)
c. Close the file

Opening a File

Before we can read or write a file, we have to open it using Python's built-in open() function. This function returns a file object, also called a handle, as it is used to read or modify the file accordingly.

We can specify the mode while opening a file. In mode, we specify whether we want to read 'r', write 'w' or append 'a' to the file. We also specify if we want to open the file in text mode or binary mode.

The following shows the syntax for opening a file.

Syntax

```
file object = open(filename,accessmode)
```

`filename`: The `filename` argument is a string value that contains the name of the file that we want to access.

`accessmode`: The `accessmode` determines the mode in which the file has to be opened, i.e., read, write, append, etc. A complete list of possible values is given below. This is optional parameter and the default file access mode is read (r).

Modes for Opening a File

1. `'r'` - Opens a file for reading only. The file pointer is placed at the beginning of the file. This is the default mode.
2. `'r+'` - Opens a file for both reading and writing. The file pointer placed at the beginning of the file.
3. `'w'` - Opens a file for writing only. Overwrites the file if the file exists. If the file does not exist, creates a new file for writing.
4. `'w+'` - Opens a file for both writing and reading. Overwrites the existing file if the file exists. If the file does not exist, creates a new file for reading and writing.

5. 'wb+' - Opens a file for both writing and reading in binary format. Overwrites the existing file if the file exists. If the file does not exist, creates a new file for reading and writing.
6. 'a' - Opens a file for appending. The file pointer is at the end of the file if the file exists. That is, the file is in the append mode. If the file does not exist, it creates a new file for writing.
7. 'a+' - Opens a file for both appending and reading. The file pointer is at the end of the file if the file exists. The file opens in the append mode. If the file does not exist, it creates a new file for reading and writing.

Reading from a File

To read the content of a file, we must open the file in reading mode. The `read()` method reads a string from an open file. It is important to note that Python strings can have binary data, apart from text data. The following gives the syntax for reading from a file.

Example Program

```
#Open a file in read mode
fo = open("test.txt", "r")
str = fo.read(11)     #Reads first 11 characters from the file
print("String Read is : ", str)
# Close opened file
fo.close()
```

1. file.read() – Here, the passed parameter `size` is the number of bytes to be read from the opened file. This method starts reading from the beginning of the file and if `size` is missing, then it tries to read as much as possible, maybe until the end of file.
2. file.readline()-The method readline()reads one entire line from the file. A trailing newline character is kept in the string. An empty string is returned only when EOF is encountered immediately
3. file.readlines([sizeint]) - The method readlines() reads until EOF and returns a list containing the lines. sizeint is an optional argument and if it is present, instead of reading up to EOF, whole lines approximate to sizeint bytes are read. An empty string is returned only when EOF is encountered immediately.

Writing to a File

In order to write into a file we need to open it in write 'w', append 'a' or exclusive creation 'x' mode. We need to be careful with the 'w' mode as it will overwrite into the file if it already exists. All previous data will be erased.

Writing a string or sequence of bytes (for binary files) is done using `write()` method. This method returns the number of characters written to the file. The `write()` method does not add a newline character ('\n') to the end of the string. The following shows the syntax of `write()` method.

Syntax

```
fileObject.write(string);
```

Here, passed parameter `string` is the content to be written into the opened file.

Example Program

```
# Open a file in writing mode
fo = open("test.txt", "w")
fo.write("Programming with Python is Fun.\nLet's try Python!\n");
# Close opened file
fo.close()
print("File", fo.name, "closed.")
```

with Statement to Open a File

Python's *with* statement is handy when we have two related operations which we would like to execute as a pair, with a block of code in between. The classic example is opening a file, manipulating the file, then closing it.

Example Program

```
with open('output.txt', 'w') as f:
    f.write('Hello Python!')
```

The above with statement will automatically close the file after the nested block of code. The advantage of using a *with* statement is that it is guaranteed to close the file no matter how the nested block exits. If an exception occurs before the end of the block, it will close the file before the exception is caught by an outer exception handler.

CSV Files

Python has a Comma Separated Values (CSV) module for supporting CSV files. Following example illustrates how to write to a CSV file.

Example Program

```
import csv
data=["1,2,3,4,5,6,7,8,9".split(",")]
file="output.csv"
with open(file,"w")as csv_file:
    writer=csv.writer(csv_file,delimiter=",")
    for line in data:
        writer.writerow(line)
csv_file.close()
```

Output

A CSV file named "output.csv" with contents 1,2,3,4,5,6,7,8,9 is created.

Below example shows how to read from a CSV file.

Example Program

```
import csv
file="output.csv"
with open(file,"r")as csv_file:
    reader=csv.reader(csv_file)
    for row in reader:
        print(" ".join(row))
csv_file.close()
```

Output

```
1 2 3 4 5 6 7 8 9
```

7.12 Reading Images

Python supports Pillow library for image related operations. For this we need to install PIL through PIP. Python Image library is used to work with image files.

```
from PIL import Image
```

- Open an image file
  `image=Image.open(image_name)`
- Display the image
  `image.show()`
- resize(): Resizes the image to a specified size.
  `image.resize(255,255)`
- `rotate()`: Rotates the image to the specified degrees counter clockwise.
  `image.rotate(90)`
- `format` – Gives the format of the image.
- `size`- Gives a tuple with 2 values as width and height of the image in pixels.
- `mode`-Gives the band of the image, "L" for grey scale, "RGB" for true color image.
- `print(image.format,image.size, image.mode)`
- Converting image to different mode Any image can be converted from one mode to "L" or "RGB" mode. Conversion between modes other than "L" and "RGB" needs conversion into any of these 2 intermediate modes.
  `conv_image=image.convert("L")`

Following program converts a sample image into grey scale.

```
from PIL import Image
im=Image.open("C:/Python34/Lib/Jeeva.jpg")
```

```
im.show()
grey_image=im.convert("L")
grey_image.show()
grey_image.save("Greyscale.jpg")
```

7.13 Networking

Python supports network services for client-server model. Socket support in the operating system allows implementing clients and servers for both connection-oriented and connectionless protocols. Python has libraries that provide higher-level access to specific application level network protocols.

To create a socket, we must import the socket module. The socket.socket() function available in the socket module, helps to create a socket. It has the following syntax.

```
s = socket.socket(socket_family,socket_type,protocol = 0)
```

`socket_family` - The family of protocols that is used as the transport mechanism. These values are constants such as AF_INET, PF_INET, PF_UNIX, PF_X25, and so on.

`socket_type`- The type of communications between the two endpoints. The values are SOCK_STREAM for connection-oriented protocols and SOCK_DGRAM for connectionless protocols.

Example

```
import socket
s=socket.socket(socket.AF_INET,socket.SOCK_STREAM)
```

Here we made a socket instance and passed it two parameters. The first parameter is AF_INET and the second one is SOCK_STREAM. AF_INET refers to the address family ipv4. Secondly the SOCK_STREAM means connection oriented TCP protocol. Now we could connect to a server using this socket.

Making a Server

A server has a `bind() method` which binds it to a specific IP and port so that it can listen to incoming requests on that IP and port. Next a server has a `listen()` method which puts the server into listen mode. This allows the server to listen to incoming connections. And lastly a server has an `accept()` and `close()` method. The `accept` method initiates a connection with the client and the `close` method closes the connection with the client. Now let's begin making our simple server.

Example Program

```
# first of all import the socket library
import socket
# next create a socket object
```

```
s = socket.socket()
print("Socket successfully created")
# reserve a port on your computer in our
# case it is 12345 but it can be anything
port = 12345
# Next bind to the port
# we have not typed any ip in the ip field
# instead we have inputted an empty string
# this makes the server listen to requests
# coming from other computers on the network
s.bind(('', port))
print("socket binded to %s" %(port))
# put the socket into listening mode
s.listen(5)
print("socket is listening")
# a forever loop until we interrupt it or
# an error occurs
while True:
   # Establish connection with client.
   c, addr = s.accept()
   print('Got connection from', addr)
   # send a thank you message to the client.
   c.send('Thank you for connecting')
   # Close the connection with the client
   c.close()
```

Output

```
Socket successfully created
socket binded to 12345
socket is listening
```

First of all we import socket which is necessary. Then we made a socket object and reserved a port on our personal computer. After that we binded our server to the specified port. Passing an empty string means that the server can listen to incoming connections from other computers as well. If we would have passed 127.0.0.1 then it would have listened to only those calls made within the local computer. After that we put the server into listen mode with parameter 5. It means that 5 connections are kept waiting if the server is busy and if a 6th socket tries to connect then the connection is refused. Lastly we make a while loop and start to accept all incoming connections and close those connections after a thank you message to all connected sockets. Now we have to program a client.

Making a Client

Let us write a very simple client program which opens a connection to a given port 12345 and a given host. It is very simple to create a socket client using the Python's socket module function. The `socket.connect(hosname,port)` opens a TCP connection to hostname on the port. Once we have a socket open, you can read from it like any IO object. When done, remember to close it, as we would close a file. Type these commands in the terminal.

```
# start the server
$ python server.py
# keep the above terminal open
# now open another terminal and type:
$ telnet localhost 12345
```

After typing these commands we will get the following output in our terminal.

```
# in the server.py terminal you will see
# this output:
Socket successfully created
socket binded to 12345
socket is listening
Got connection from ('127.0.0.1', 52617)
# In the telnet terminal you will get this:
Trying ::1...
Trying 127.0.0.1...
Connected to localhost.
Escape character is '^]'.
Thank you for connectingConnection closed by foreign host.
```

This output shows that our server is working. Now let's make our client.

Example Program

```
# Import socket module
import socket
# Create a socket object
s = socket.socket()
# Define the port on which you want to connect
port = 12345
# connect to the server on local computer
s.connect(('127.0.0.1', port))
# receive data from the server
print(s.recv(1024))
# close the connection
s.close()
```

Output

```
# start the server:
$ python server.py
```

```
Socket successfully created
socket binded to 12345
socket is listening
Got connection from ('127.0.0.1', 52617)
$ python client.py
Thank you for connecting
```

7.14 Conclusion

This Chapter explains about Python programming. Various components of Python like input-output statements, operators are explained. Data types of Python namely numbers, string, list, tuple, set and dictionary are explained with example programs. Decision making statements, for loop, for loop with else statement, while loop, while loop with else statement and control statements are explained with illustrations. Function definition, function calling, global and local variables, functions returning more than one value are explained with example programs. Modules, different types of importing a module, exception handling techniques, file handling methods, reading images and networking or socket programming is illustrated.

8 IoT IMPLEMENTATION WITH RASPBERRY Pi

8.1 Introduction

Raspberry Pi is a low cost, **credit-card sized computer** that plugs into a computer monitor or TV and uses a standard keyboard and mouse. It is a little device that enables people of all ages to explore computing. Programs are written in languages like Scratch and Python. It's capable of doing everything we expect from a desktop computer. We can browse the Internet, play high-definition video, to make spreadsheets, word-processing and playing games. There are several generations of Raspberry Pi like Raspberry Pi 3 model B, Raspberry Pi 2 model B, Raspberry Pi zero.

8.2 Architecture

Figure 8.1 shows the basic architecture of Raspberry Pi. It is a low cost single-board computer which is easy to access. Table 8.1 gives a comparison of the specifications of most commonly used versions of Raspberry Pi.

Table 8.1: Comparison of the Specifications of Commonly Used Versions of Raspberry Pi

Key Features	Raspberry Pi 3 Model B	Raspberry Pi 2 Model B	Raspberry Pi Zero
RAM	1 GB SDRAM	1 GB SDRAM	512 MB SDRAM
CPU	Quad Cortex A53 @1.2 GHz	Quad Cortex A53 @900 MHz	ARM11 @ 1 GHz
GPU	400 MHz Video Core IV	250 MHz Video Core IV	250 MHz Video Core IV
Ethernet	10/100	10/100	None
Wireless	802.11/Bluetooth 4.0	None	None
Video Output	HDMI/Composite	HDMI/Composite	HDMI/Composite
GPIO	40	40	40

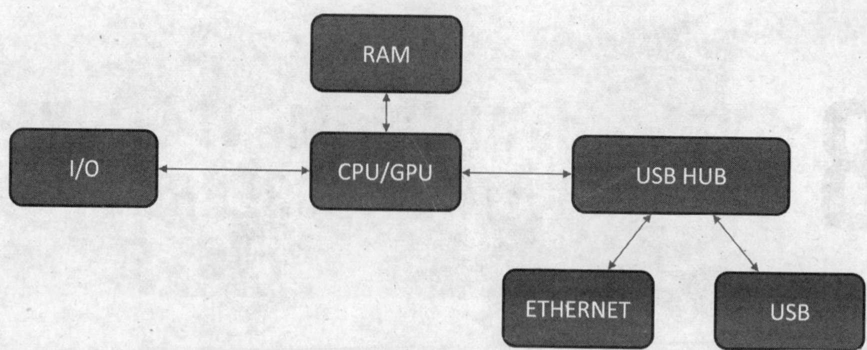

Fig.8.1: Basic Architecture of Raspberry Pi

The basic set up for Raspberry Pi includes HDMI cable, monitor, keyboard, mouse, 5 volt power adapter for Raspberry Pi, LAN cable, 2 GB micro SD card (minimum). The official operating systems supported are Raspbian and NOOBS. Other third party operating systems like Ubuntu mate, Snappy Ubuntu Core, Windows 10 Core, Pinet and Risc OS are also supported by Raspberry Pi.

For downloading Raspbian, following steps are required.

1. Download latest Raspbian image from Raspberry Pi official Website https://www.raspberrypi.org/downloads
2. Unzip the file and end up with a .img file.
3. Next step is to write Raspbian OS in SD card. For that install "Win32 Disk Imager" software in Windows machine.
4. Run Win32 Disk Imager.
5. Plug SD Card into our PC.
6. Select the "Device".
7. Browse the "Image File" (Raspbian Image).

Secure Shell (SSH) is a feature of Linux that allows you to effectively open a terminal session on your Raspberry Pi from the command line of your host computer. Recent versions of Rasbpian do not enable SSH access by default. For enabling SSH, following steps are required.

1. Open command prompt and type `sudo raspi-config` and press enter key.
2. Navigate to SSH in advanced option.
3. Enable SSH.

For expanding the file system, perform the following operations.

1. Open command prompt and type `sudo raspi-config` and press enter.
2. Navigate to Expand File System.
3. Press enter key to expand it.

Most commonly used programming languages in Raspberry Pi are Python, C, C++, Java, Scratch and Ruby. Any language that will compile for ARMV6 can be used with Raspberry Pi. The popular applications developed using Raspberry Pi are media streamer, home automation, controlling robot, Virtual Private Network (VPN), light weight Web server with IoT etc.

8.3 PIN Configuration

GPIO pins in Raspberry Pi are the general purpose Input-Output pins. These pins are to communicate with other circuitry such as extension boards, custom circuits and much more. For getting an output, we can turn a GPIO pin HIGH or LOW. Similarly for an input, it can detect a GPIO pin as HIGH or LOW. Figure 8.2 shows the pin configuration of Raspberry Pi.

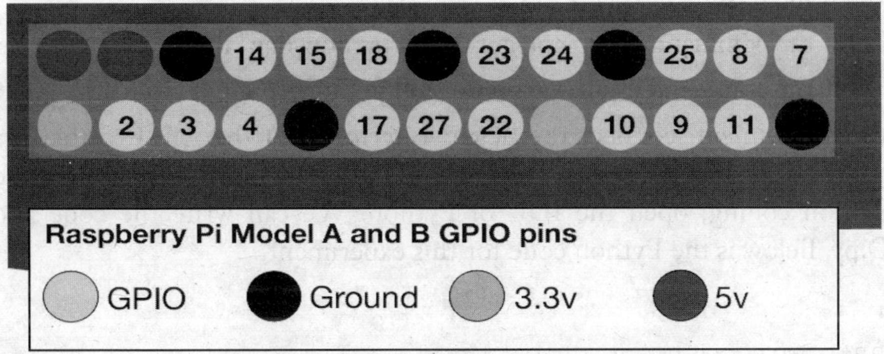

Fig.8.2: Pin Configuration of Raspberry Pi

These pins are a physical interface between the Pi and the outside world. At the simplest level, you can think of them as switches that you can turn on or off (input) or that the Pi can turn on or off (output). Seventeen of the 26 pins are GPIO pins. Others are power or ground pins. Each pin can turn on or off, or go HIGH or LOW in computing terms. When the pin is HIGH it outputs 3.3 volts (3v3) and when the pin is LOW, it is off.

We can program the pins to interact in amazing ways with the real world. Inputs don't have to come from a physical switch. It could be input from a sensor or a signal from another computer or device. The output can also do anything, from turning on an LED to sending a signal or data to another device. If the Raspberry Pi is on a network, we can control devices that are attached to it from anywhere and those devices can send data back. Connectivity and control of physical devices over the Internet is a powerful and exciting thing and the Raspberry Pi is ideal for this.

8.4 Case Studies

In this section, we will discuss about 2 example projects using Raspberry Pi. The first one is blinking an LED and the second one is taking a picture using PiCam. The codes for both the examples are written in Python.

8.4.1 Blinking LED

Following are the requirements for this experiment.

- Raspberry Pi
- LED
- 100 ohm resistor
- Bread board
- Jumper cables

We need to install the GPIO library. Following are the steps for installing the GPIO library.

1. Open the terminal
2. Enter the command “sudo apt-get install python-dev” to install python development.
3. Enter the command “sudo apt-get install python-rpi.gpio” to install GPIO library.

For this experiment, connect the negative terminal of the LED to the ground pin of Raspberry Pi and connect the positive terminal of the LED to the output pin of the Raspberry Pi. For Python coding, open the IDE of Python. We can write the code and save it as BlinkLED.py. Below is the Python code for this experiment.

Program

```
import RPi.GPIO as GPIO # GPIO Library
import time
# Set the board for pin numbering
GPIO.setmode(GPIO.BOARD)
# Set GPIO pin as output pin
GPIO.setup(11,GPIO.OUT)
for i in range(0,5):
    GPIO.output(11,True)#Turn on GPIO pin 11
    time.sleep(1)
    GPIO.output(11,False)
    time.sleep(2)
    GPIO.output(11,True)
GPIO.cleanup()
```

The LED blinks in a loop with delay of 1 and 2 seconds for 5 times.

8.4.2 Taking Pictures using PiCam

For this we need Raspberry Pi and a Raspberry Pi camera. There is a specific camera module which needs to be imported while writing the Python code. There is a dedicated CSI slot in Raspberry Pi for connecting the camera. The cable slot is placed between Ethernet port and

HDMI port. Boot the Raspberry Pi once the camera is connected to Raspberry Pi. Following are the steps needed to configure Raspberry Pi for camera.

- In the terminal, run the command "sudo raspi-config" and press enter key.
- Navigate to "Interfacing Options" and press enter key.
- Navigate to "camera" option.
- Enable the camera.
- Reboot Raspberry Pi.

Next step is to capture image. For this, open the terminal and enter the following command.

```
raspistill-o image.jpg
```

This will store the image as "image.jpg".

PiCam can also be processed using Python camera module python-picamera. For that we need to install the module using the following command.

```
sudo apt-get install python-picamera
```

Below is the python code for capturing the image.

```
import picamera
camera=picamera.PiCamera()
camera.capture("Image.jpg")
```

8.5 Implementation of IoT with Raspberry Pi

In this section, we will see the implementation of Raspberry Pi with Internet of Things. For this we need to integrate sensors and actuators interfaced with Raspberry Pi. The data will be read from the sensor. The actuator will be controlled according to the reading from the sensor. We will see an example of a Temperature Dependent Auto Cooling System.

8.5.1 Temperature Dependent Auto Cooling System

In this experiment a DHT sensor senses the temperature and when the temperature goes above 30^0 C, a fan needs to be automatically turned on.

Requirements

- DHT sensor
- 4.7 K ohm resistor
- Relay
- Jumper Wires
- Raspberry Pi
- Mini fan

DHT Sensor

We have already seen the Digital Humidity and Temperature (DHT) sensor in the previous chapter. There are four pins PIN 1, 2, 3, 4 (left to right).

PIN 1 – 3.3 v to 5v power supply

PIN 2 - data

PIN 3 – null

PIN 4 – Ground

Relay

This is a mechanical or electromechanical switch. There are 3 output terminals from left to right.

No – Normal Open

Common

NC – Normal Close

Connection

1. **Sensor Interface with Raspberry Pi**
    - Connect pin 1 of DHT sensor to the 3.3v pin of Raspberry Pi.
    - Connect pin 2 of DHT sensor to any input pins of Raspberry Pi. Here we have used pin 11.
    - Connect pin 4 of DHT sensor to the GND (ground) pin of Raspberry Pi.
2. **Relay Interface with Raspberry Pi**
    - Connect the Vcc pin of relay to the 5v supply pin of Raspberry Pi.
    - Connect the GND (ground) pin of relay to the GND (ground) pin of Raspberry Pi.
    - Connect the input or signal pin of relay to the assigned output pin of Raspberry Pi. Here we have used pin 7.
3. **Fan interface with Raspberry Pi**
    - Connect the Li-Po battery in series with the fan.
    - NO terminal of the relay is connected to the positive terminal of the fan.
    - Common terminal of the relay is connected to positive terminal of the battery.
    - Negative terminal of the battery is connected to the negative terminal of the fan.

Adafruit provides a library to work with the DHT22 sensor. Install the library in our Raspberry Pi. Get the clone from GIT as follows.

```
git clone https://github.com/adafruit/Adafruit_Python_DHT
```

Go to the folder Adafruit_Python_DHT

```
cd Adafruit_Python_DHT
```

Install the library

```
sudo python setup.py install
```

Following is the Python code for interfacing DHT22, Relay and Fan with Raspberry Pi.

Program

```
import RPi.GPIO as GPIO # GPIO Library
from time import sleep
import Adafruit_DHT # importing the Adafruit Library
# Set the board for pin numbering
GPIO.setmode(GPIO.BOARD)
GPIO.setwarnings(False)
#Create an instance of the sensor type
sensor=Adafruit_DHT.AM2302
print("Getting data from the sensor")
#humidity and temperature are 2 variables that store
#the values received from the sensor
humidity,temperature=Adafruit_DHT.read_retry(sensor,17)
print("Temp={0:0.1f}*c humidity={1:0.1f%".format(temperature,humidity))
# Set GPIO pin as output pin
GPIO.setup(13,GPIO.OUT)
if temperature>30:
    GPIO.output(13,0)#Relay is active low
    print("Relay is on")
    sleep(5)
    GPIO.output(13,1)#Relay is turned off after delay of 5 seconds
```

The result is the fan is switched on whenever the temperature is above the threshold value set in the code. Here we have set the threshold value as 30.

8.5.2 Remote Data Logging

In this a DHT sensor senses the data and this data is send to a remote server. The data will be stored in the server. The intention is to collect data from the devices in the network. Send the data to a server or remote machine and control the network remotely. The connection of DHT sensor with Raspberry Pi and installation of the library is same as those explained in the previous section. Our next step is to send data to the server using network protocols. For this, we need to create a server and a client and establish the connection between the server and the client. Once the connection is established, the data need to be sent from the client to the server.

In this case, socket programming is needed. First we need to create a two-way communication between two nodes in a network. The nodes are termed as server and client. The server performs the task or service requested by the client. Following code creates a server object.

```
s=socket.socket()#creating a socket object
host=socket.gethostname()# gets the local machine name/address
port=12321 #port number for the server
s.bind((host,port))#binds to the port
s.listen(5)#waiting for the client to connect
while True:
    c,addr=s.accept()#accept the connection request from the client
    print("connected to",addr)
    c.send("connection successful")
c.close()#close the socket
```

Below is the code for creating a client object.

```
s=socket.socket()#creating a socket object
host=socket.gethostname()# gets the local machine name/address
port=12345 # assigning a port
s.connect((host,port))#binds to the port
print(s.recv(1024))
s.close()#close the socket
```

The code given below is the code for the client to obtain readings from the DHT sensor. This function `sensordata()` returns the values from the DHT sensor.

```
def sensordata():
    GPIO.setmode(GPIO.BOARD)
    GPIO.setwarnings(False)
    sensor=Adafruit_DHT.AM2302
    humidity,temperature=Adafruit_DHT.read_retry(sensor,17)
    return(humidity,temperature)
```

Following code connects the client to the server and sends data to the server.

```
sock=socket.socket(socket.AF_INET, socket.sock_DGRAM)#Create UDP socket
server_address=("10.14.3.194",10001)
try:
    while(1):
        h,t=sensordata()
        message=str(h)+","+str(t)
    #send data
        print(sys.stderr,"sending "%s""%message)
        sent=sock.sento(message,server_address)
```

```
finally:
    print(sys.stderr,"closing socket")
    sock.close()
```

Below is the code for the server to receive data from the client and save it in the server.

```
sock=socket.socket(socket.AF_INET, socket.sock_DGRAM)#Create UDP socket
server_address=("10.14.3.194",10001)
sock.bind(server_address)
while True:
        data,address = sock.recvfrom(4096)
        with open("Datalog.txt","a")as f:
            mess=str(data)
            f.write(mess)
            print(mess)
        f.close()
```

The result of the codes given above is that client takes reading from the sensor and sends it to the server. The server receives the data from the client and saves it in a text file "Datalog.txt".

8.5.2 Data Plotting

After receiving the data from the client, the data needs to be processed before it can be used further. It includes two steps (a) data splitting or filtering (b) data plotting. Data from the client is saved in the text file "Datalog.txt". The values in this file (humidity and temperature) are separated by a comma.

```
message=str(h)+','+str(t)
```

The function split() is used to split the string and return as a list. This function is already discussed in Chapter 7. After splitting the data, we need to plot it. For plotting we need the matplotlib module of Python. The matplotlib module in Python will be explained here.

Matplotlib is a Python library used to plot graphs in 2D. Following are the commonly used functions to plot a graph in matplotlib.

- `plot(x, y)`: plots the values x and y.
- `xlabel("X axis")`: labels the x-axis.
- `ylabel("Y-axis")`: labels the y-axis.
- `title("Simple Plot")`: adds title to the plot.
- `figure()`: creates a new figure.
- `grid()`: enables oe disables axis grids in the plot.
- `ion()`: turns on the interactive mode.
- `subplot()`: adds subplot in a figure.
- `close()`: close the current figure window.
- `scatter()`: make a scatter plot of the given points.

Example Program

```
import matplotlib.pyplot as myplot
myplot.plot([1,2,3,4])
myplot.ylabel("Y-axis")
myplot.show()
```

Figure 8.3 shows the output of the basic plot explained in the above program. By default, the values are taken for y-axis and the values for x-axis are generated automatically staring from 0.

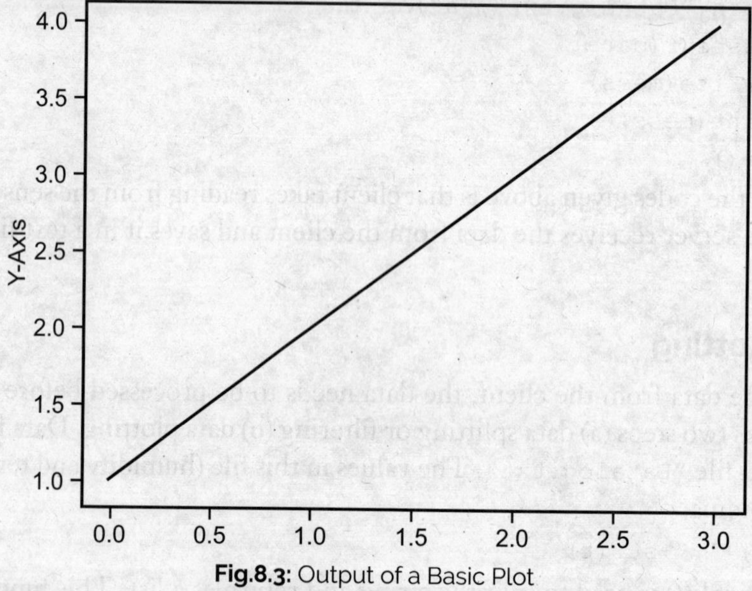

Fig.8.3: Output of a Basic Plot

Once the data is received in the server, we can plot the data. Following is the code for plotting the data.

Program

```
import matplotlib.pyplot as plt
def coverage_plot(data,i):
    hum=data.split(",")[0]
    tem=dat.split(",")[1]
    print("temp= "+str(tem)+"iter="+str(i))
    plt.ion()
    fig=plt.figure(num=1,figsize=(6,6))
    plt.title("IoT Temperature and Humidity Monitor")
    ax=fig.add_subplot(121)
    ax.plot(tem,i,c='r',marker=r'$Theta$')
    plt.xlabel("Temp($^0C$)")
```

```
    ax.grid()
    ax=fig.add_subplot(122)
    ax.plot(hum,i,c='b',marker=r'$\Phi$')
    plt.xlabel("Humidity($\%$)")
    ax.grid()
    fig.show()
    fig.canvas.draw()
sock=socket.socket(socket.AF_INET,socket.SOCK_DGRAM)
server_address("10.14.3.194",10001)
sock.bind(server_address)
i=0
while True:
    data,address=sock.recvfrom(4096)
    with open("Datalog.txt","a") as f:
        mess=str(data)
        f.write(mess)
        coverage_plot(mess,i)
        print(mess)
        i+=1
    f.close()
```

Two different plots for temperature and humidity are drawn as shown Figure 8.4.

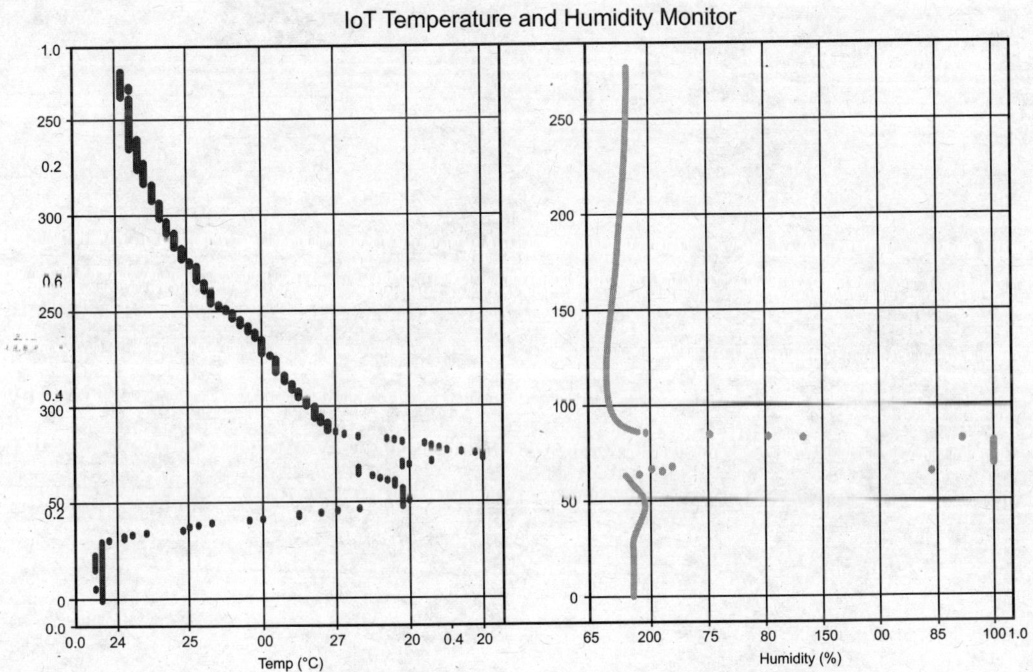

Fig.8.4: Plots for Temperature and Humidity

8.6 Conclusion

This Chapter explains the IoT implementation with Rasbperry Pi. The architecture of Raspberry Pi and its PIN configuration is explained with necessary diagrams. Two case studies namely blinking LED and taking pictures using PiCam is explained with Python code. Finally implementation of IoT with Raspberry Pi is shown using temperature dependent auto cooling system. Various steps involved like how to create a client, how to create server and how to send data from the client to the server using socket programming is explained. The received data in the server is plotted using matplotlib module in Python.

9 SOFTWARE DEFINED NETWORKING

9.1 Introduction

Software Defined Networking (SDN) is for restructuring the current network infrastructure. SDN is an umbrella term encompassing several kinds of network technology aimed at making the network as agile and flexible as the virtualized server and storage infrastructure of the modern data center. The goal of SDN is to allow network engineers and administrators to respond quickly to changing business requirements. In an SDN, a network administrator can shape traffic from a centralized control console without having to touch individual switches, and can deliver services to wherever they are needed in the network, without regard to what specific devices a server or other hardware components are connected to. The key technologies for SDN implementation are functional separation, network virtualization and automation through programmability.

9.2 Limitations of Current Network

Consider the scenario of current day networks. For this we are taking the example of a wired network with L3 switches. Figure 9.1 shows the network topology of current network.

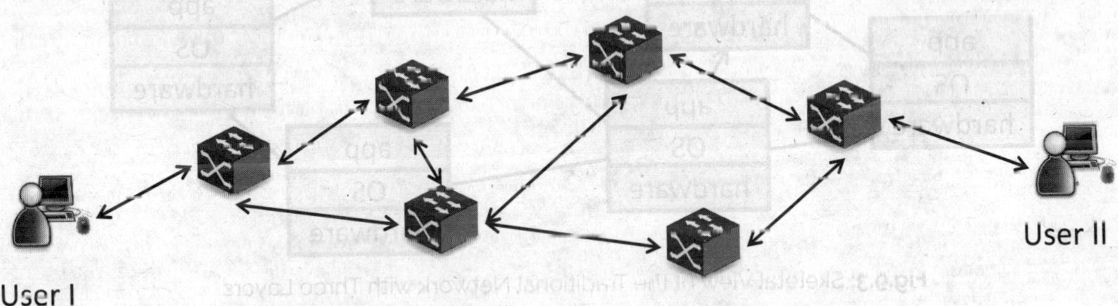

Fig.9.1: Network Topology of Current Network

The data needs to be send from user 1 to user 2 and vice versa as shown in Figure 9.1. The data can be sent through several routes. The packet traverses through multiple L3 switches before it reaches its destination. The protocol used for switching is the Open Shortest Path First (OSPF) protocol. Open Shortest Path First (OSPF) is a routing protocol for Internet Protocol (IP) networks. Each router knows to which router the packet needs to be sent based on the routing table it has. Each router doesn't have a global view of the network as a whole.

Consider the situation where one of the routers or switches has been attacked as shown in Figure 9.2. The attacked switch will be down for one reason or another.

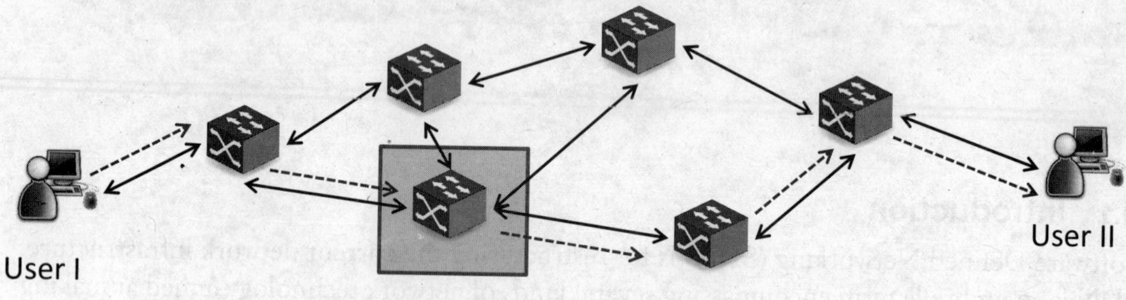

Fig.9.2: One of the Switches is Attacked

In a traditional network, when a router is down, another route needs to be identified to transfer the packets. Since there is no centralized control over the routers this becomes a difficult task. So in a traditional network, when a switch is down, it can affect other switches also. Each router in a network has three layers comprising of hardware at the bottom layer, operating system running on top of the hardware and applications on the top most layer. The skeletal view of the traditional network with these layers is shown in Figure 9.3.

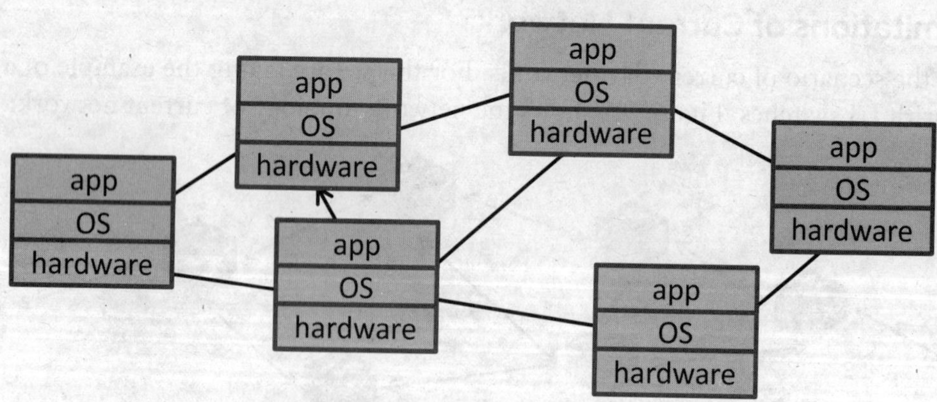

Fig.9.3: Skeletal View of the Traditional Network with Three Layers

There are several limitations in current network which is given below.

- Centralized control of the network is not feasible in traditional networks.
- Vendor-specific architecture of switches limits dynamic configuration according to application-specific requirements.

- Each switch may have different operating system. Switches are required to configure according to the installed operating system.

In a traditional network, each router or switch will be running thousands of lines of code. Each router may comprise of millions of logic gates contributing to 10 GB RAM approximately, cost expensive and running various kinds of application programs such as routing, mobility management etc. Each of the routers in traditional network has specialized packet forwarding hardware, different operating system and different applications for routing, mobility management etc. The goal of the Software Defined Networking is to overcome the limitations or challenges of traditional network.

9.3 Origin of SDN

The concept of SDN is to separate the hardware from the operating system and application programs as shown in Figure 9.4.

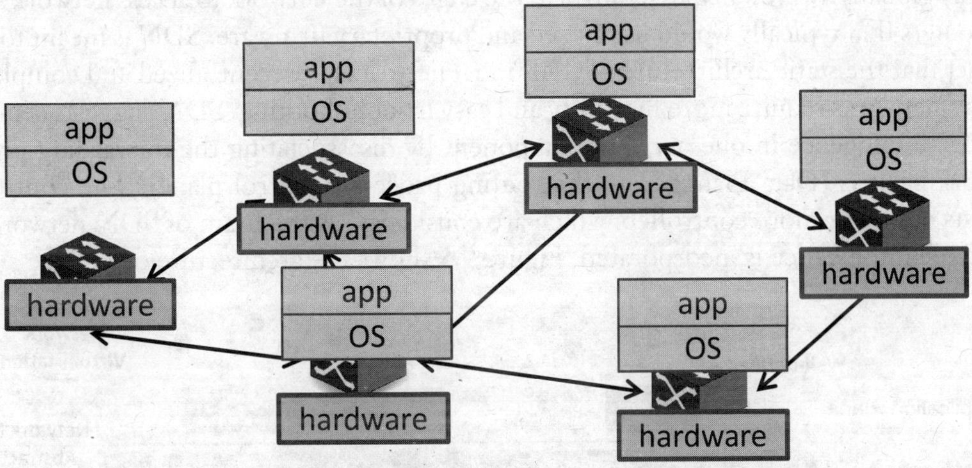

Fig.9.4: Concept of SDN

The history of SDN principles can be traced back to the separation of the control and data plane first used in the public switched telephone network as a way to simplify provisioning and management well before this architecture began to be used in data networks. The Internet Engineering Task Force (IETF) began considering various ways to decouple the control and forwarding functions in a proposed interface standard published in 2004 appropriately named "Forwarding and Control Element Separation" (ForCES). The ForCES Working Group also proposed a companion SoftRouter Architecture. Additional early standards from the IETF that pursued separating control from data include the Linux Netlink as an IP Services Protocol and A Path Computation Element (PCE)-Based Architecture.

These early attempts failed to gain traction for two reasons. One is that many in the Internet community viewed separating control from data to be risky, especially owing to the potential for a failure in the control plane. The second is that vendors were concerned that creating standard application programming interfaces (APIs) between the control and data planes would result in increased competition. The use of open source software in split control/data plane architectures traces its roots to the Ethane project at Stanford's computer sciences department. Ethane's simple switch design led to the creation of OpenFlow. An API for OpenFlow was first created in 2008. That same year witnessed the creation of NOX—an operating system for networks. Work on OpenFlow continued at Stanford, including with the creation of testbeds evaluating use of the protocol in a single campus network, as well as across the WAN as a backbone for connecting multiple campuses.

Beyond academia, the first deployments were by Nicira in 2010. The Open Networking Foundation was founded in 2011 to promote SDN and OpenFlow.

9.4 SDN Architecture

Software Defined networking (SDN) is an approach to using open protocols, such as OpenFlow, to apply globally aware software control at the edges of the network to access network switches and routers that typically would use closed and proprietary firmware. SDN is meant to address the fact that the static architecture of traditional networks is decentralized and complex while current networks require more flexibility and easy troubleshooting. SDN suggests centralizing network intelligence in one network component by disassociating the forwarding process of network packets (Data Plane) from the routing process (Control plane). The control plane consists of one or more controllers which are considered as the brain of SDN network where the whole intelligence is incorporated. Figure 9.5 shows the architecture of SDN.

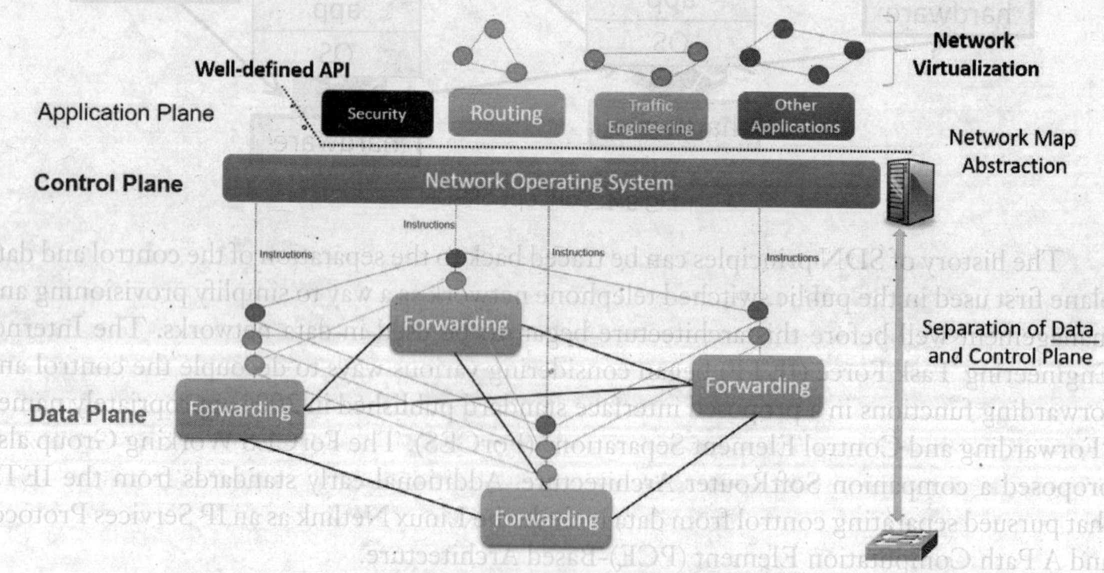

Fig.9.5: Architecture of SDN

The components or attributes of SDN are hardware switches, controller, applications, flow-rules and Application Programming Interfaces (API). The basic concept of SDN is to separate control logic from hardware switches. The control logic is defined in a centralized manner and controls the entire network including the switches. Communication between the application, control and data planes are done through APIs.

The Data plane contains various switches for forwarding. The Control plane contains the network operating system. At the top is the application plane which performs various functionalities like security, routing, traffic engineering and other applications. The concept of SDN is made possible through Network Function Virtualization. The interface between Application plane and Control plane is known as Northbound API whereas the interface between Control plane and Data plane is known as Southbound API. The protocol that supports Southbound API is the OpenFlow protocol. East-Westbound APIs are used to communicate among multiple controllers in the control layer.

The current status of SDN shows that companies such as Google have started to implement SDN at their data center networks. The current networks could be replaced with SDN in a phased manner. With SDN, operational cost and delay caused due to link failure can be significantly minimized. The two main challenges in the implementation of SDN are (a) rule placement (b) controller placement.

9.5 Rule Placement

Switches forward traffic based on a rule called "Flow Rule". This is defined by the centralized controller. In the traditional network, there will be a routing table at every switch or router. Here in SDN, a Flow Table is maintained at every switch. Each entry in the Flow Table is the Flow Rule. Each Rule has a specific format, which is defined by a protocol. In SDN, it is OpenFlow protocol. Figure 9.6 shows an example for Flow Rules based on OpenFlow protocol.

Match SDN Applications First and Use Normal for Unmatched Packets (Hybrid Default Forwarding)

Priority	Ingress Port	MAC Source Address	MAC Destination	Protocol	Vlan ID	IP Source Address	IP Destination	Source Port	Destination Port	Instruction
10000	–	–	–	TCP	–	–	10.1.1.20/32		80	Forward to Port 1
5000	–	–	–	–	–	–	10.1.1.0/24	–	–	Forward to Port 2
300	–	–	–	–	2600	–	–	–	–	Send to Controller
0				–	–	–	–	–	–	OF Normal

Fig.9.6: Example for Flow Rules based on OpenFlow Protocol

Consider the first row of the Flow Table. When a packet arrives at a router, it will check for the priority. If the priority matches, the values for Ingress port, MAC source address, MAC destination can be anything because it is a wildcard. If the protocol is TCP, IP destination is 10.1.1.20/32 and destination port is 60, then the instruction is "Forward to port 1". Likewise other rows (Flow Rules) of the Flow Tables are used for routing.

The Flow Tables are stored at the switches. Flow Tables are stored in a specialized memory known as Ternary Content Addressable (TCAM) memory. The size of TCAM memory is limited and hence only a limited number of rules can be inserted. TCAM memories can do the processing very faster and that is why this memory is used at the switches. TCAM is very expensive also.

When a request is received for which no Flow Rule is present in the Flow Table, the switch send a PACKET-IN message to the controller. The controller then decides a suitable Flow Rule for the request and sends back to the switch. It is then inserted into the Flow Table. Whenever there is a new rule insertion, there will be a delay of 3-5 ms delay.

It is a challenging task to define or place the rules at switches while considering available TCAM. This is because TCAM is small and expensive and not easy to scale. Another challenge is how to define rules, so that less number of PACKET_IN messages is sent to the controller.

9.6 OpenFlow Protocol

OpenFlow protocol is the only one protocol that is available for rule placement. It has different versions like 1.0, 1.1, 1.2, 1.3 etc. to have different number of match fields. Different match fields include source IP, destination IP, source port, priority etc. One of the issues with OpenFlow protocol is how long a Flow Rule is to be kept at the switch. For addressing this issue, two strategies are used. The first one is the hard timeout and the other one is the soft timeout. In hard timeout, all the Flow Rules are deleted from the switch. This can be used to reset the switch. In a soft timeout, if no Flow is received associated with a Rule, then the Rule is deleted. This is used to empty the Rule space by deleting an unused Rule.

SDN and OpenFlow is not the same. SDN is a technology or concept while OpenFlow is a protocol used to communicate between data plane and control plane. We may have other protocols for this purpose. However, OpenFlow is the only protocol present today. There are various softwares associated with OpenFlow implementation. Some of them are given below.

- Indigo – Indigo is an open source project aimed at enabling support for OpenFlow on physical and hypervisor switches.
- LINC – LINC is a pure OpenFlow software switch. It gives a lot of flexibility and allows quick development and testing of new OpenFlow features. It supports OpenFlow protocol 1.2, OpenFlow protocol 1.3 and OpenFlow protocol 1.4. It has a modular architecture which is easily extensible.
- Pantou – Pantou turns a commercial wireless router or access point to an OpenFlow-enabled switch. OpenFlow is implemented as an application on top of OpenWrt. Pantou is based on the BackFire OpenWrt release (Linux 2.6.32).
- Of13softswitch – This is an OpenFlow 1.3 compatible user-space software switch implementation. The code is based on the Ericsson TrafficLab 1.1 softswitch implementation, with changes in the forwarding plane to support OpenFlow 1.3.

- Open vSwitch – This is an open source software which is the most popular one which is present today for SDN implementation.

9.7 Controller Placement

Controllers define Flow Rules according to the application specific requirements. Control logic is taken care by the Control plane. The controller knows what has to be done with a particular Flow. The controllers must be able to handle all the incoming requests from the switches. Rules should be placed without incurring much delay. Typically, a controller can handle 200 requests in a second through a single thread. Currently multi-threaded applications are also possible in controllers.

The controllers are logically connected to the switches in one-hop distance. The switch thinks that controller is just a hop away from it. Physically, they are connected to the switches in multi-hop distance. If we have a very small number of controllers for a large network, the network might be congested with control packets i.e. PACKET-IN messages. Various architectures for Controller Placement are Flat architecture, Hierarchical (Tree) architecture, Ring architecture and Mesh architecture. Figure 9.7 shows a Flat architecture for Controller Placement.

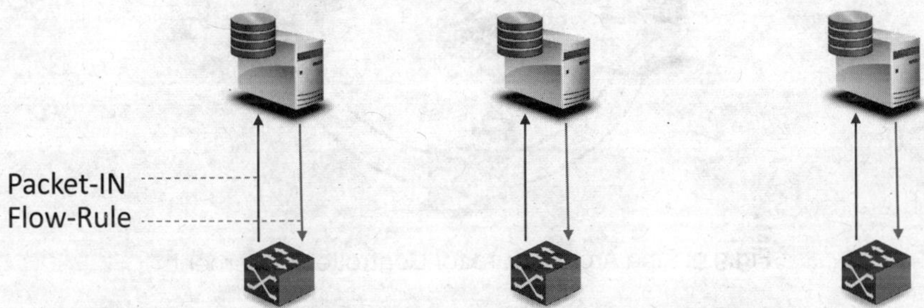

Fig.9.7: Flat architecture for Controller Placement

In Flat architecture, the Controller is logically one hop away from the switch. The switch sends the PACKET-IN message to the controller, if the Flow Rule for the particular Flow that it has received is not in the Flow Table. The Controller sends back the new Flow Rule to the switch. Figure 9.8 shows the Hierarchical (Tree) architecture for Controller Placement.

In a Hierarchical architecture, the controllers and switches are arranged like a tree structure. Figure 9.9 shows the Ring architecture for Controller Placement. In a Ring architecture, multiple controllers are arranged in a ring fashion. But a particular switch is connected to only one controller. A PACKET-IN message will be sent to a single Controller only and the Controller sends back the Flow Rule to that particular switch.

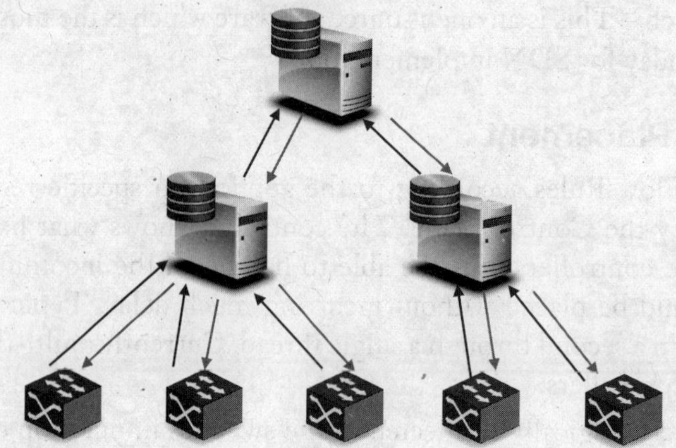

Fig.9.8: Hierarchical (Tree) Architecture for Controller Placement

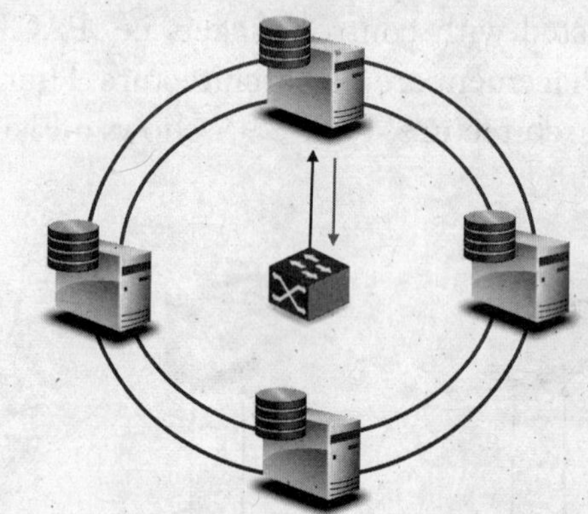

Fig.9.9: Ring Architecture for Controller Placement

Figure 9.10 shows the Mesh architecture for Controller Placement. Mesh architecture increases reliability and fault-tolerance. For example we can see two switches connected to the same controller. Even if a switch goes down, the other switch can take care of it.

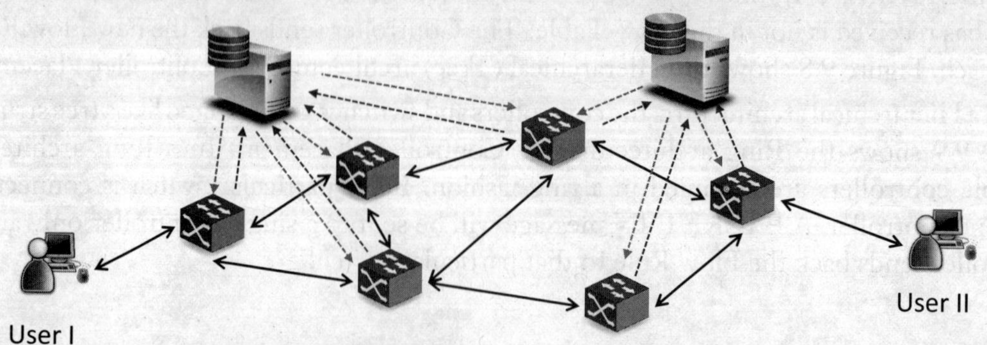

Fig.9.10: Mesh Architecture for Controller Placement

The control mechanisms can be either distributed or centralized. In a distributed control mechanism, the control decisions can be taken in a distributed manner. For example, each sub-network is controlled by a different controller. In a centralized control mechanism, the control decisions are taken in a centralized manner. For example, a network is controlled by a single controller. If the primary controller is down, a backup controller takes up the duties of the primary controller to have uninterrupted network service.

For experimenting with SDN, we need simulators or emulators. The emulators can be connected to the real network and can analyze the data. Simulators on the other hand, simulate the entire network including nodes and packet flows. The simulator or emulator takes care of infrastructure deployment and Controller Placement. Both must be supported with OpenFlow protocol. In Controller Placement, the controllers can be either remote or local. In a remote Controller, the Controller can be situated in a remote place and communicated using IP address and port number.

For switch deployment, Mininet software based on Python language can be used. This software can be used to create a virtual network with OpenFlow enabled switches. It supports both remote and local controllers. Various softwares are available for Controller configuration like Pox, Nox, FloodLight, OpenDayLight and ONOS. Among these OpenDayLight and ONOS are two popularly used softwares for Controller configuration.

Performance of SDN depends on Rule Placement and Controller Placement in the network. Control message overhead may be increased due to additional number of packets (PACKET-IN) messages. Unified network management is possible using SDN, while leveraging the global view of the network.

9.8 Security in SDN

There is enhanced security while using SDN. The security is implemented using firewall, proxy, HTTP and Intrusion Detection System (IDS). Figure 9.11 shows a topology to implement security in SDN.

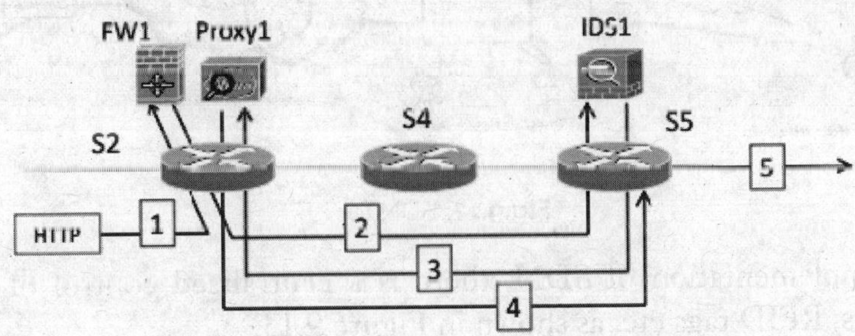

Fig.9.11: A Topology to Implement SDN

1. When an HTTP request comes, it is first forwarded to Firewall 1 (FW1).
2. From the Firewall 1, it is sent to Intrusion Detection System 1 (IDS1).

3. From (IDS1), it is sent to Proxy 1
4. Finally, it is sent from Proxy1 to the outside network.

9.9 Integrating SDN in IoT

In this section we will see how SDN can be used with IoT. There are several benefits of integrating SDN with IoT.

1. With SDN, intelligent routing decisions can be deployed.
2. Simplification of information collection, analysis and decision making.
3. Visibility of network resources which includes network management simplification based on user, device and application specific requirements.
4. Intelligent traffic pattern analysis and coordinated decisions.

Consider the use of SDN for IoT as shown in Figure 9.12. In this there are several IoT devices in different sub-networks. The data from these devices through mobile access channels or fixed access channels are collected and transmitted to the data aggregator. The data aggregation from various IoT devices takes place at the data aggregator and then it passes through a transport network. From there it goes to different gateways and the packet segregation is done at the packet gateways. When we integrate SDN with IoT, we are going to integrate SDN controller with various devices, performs better orchestration of various devices and protocols that are running. Overall it will improve the service logic.

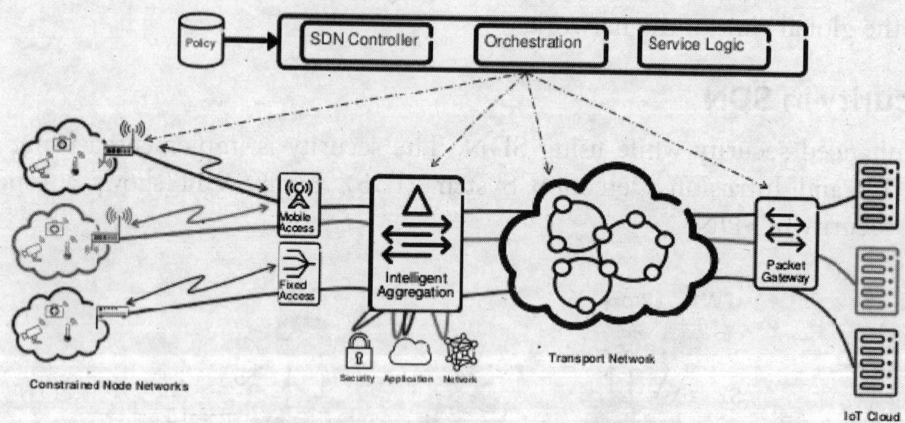

Fig.9.12: SDN for IoT

With the implementation of SDN, there is a centralized control of IoT devices like sensors, actuators, RFID tags etc. as shown in Figure 9.13.

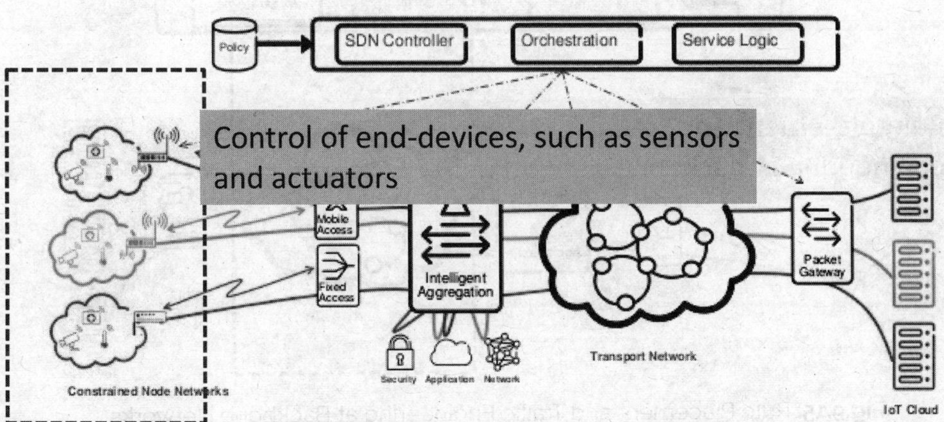

Fig.9.13: Centralized Control of IoT Devices

The Rule-placement at access devices, while considering mobility and heterogeneity of end-users can be taken care by the fixed access channels, mobile access channels and intelligent aggregation as shown in Figure 9.14.

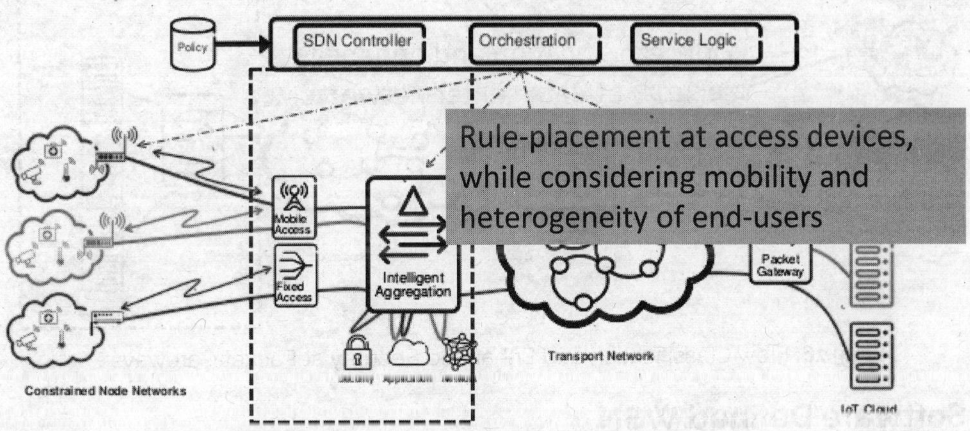

Fig.9.14: Rule Placement at Access Devices

Rule Placement and traffic engineering at backbone networks is implemented by the Transport Network as shown in Figure 9.15.

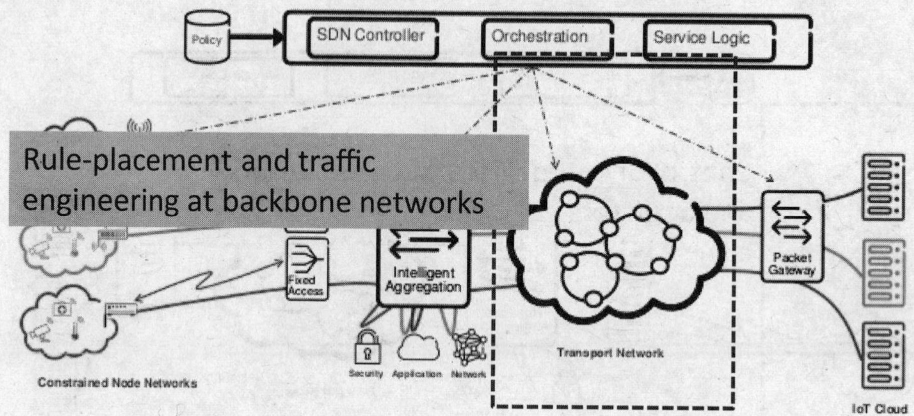

Fig.9.15: Rule Placement and Traffic Engineering at Backbone Networks

Finally Flow classification and enhanced security at data center networks is done at packet gateways or data center networks as shown in Figure 9.16.

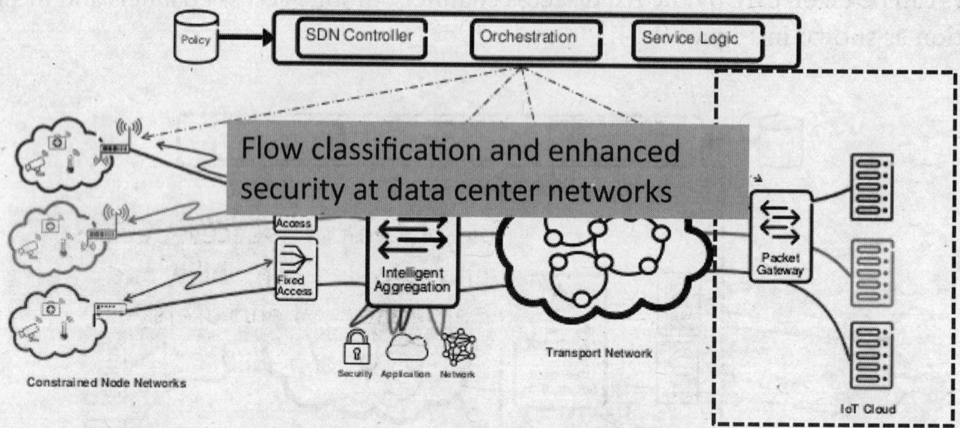

Fig.9.16: Flow Classification and Enhanced Security at Packet Gateways

9.10 Software Defined WSN

There are several challenges in WSNs. Real-time programming of sensor nodes is difficult. The sensor nodes and corresponding network follow vendor specific architecture. Each nodes made by different vendors have their own architecture and different layers implemented in them. Sensor nodes are resource-constrained i.e. heavy computations cannot be performed at the nodes. In addition, memory is also limited so that we cannot insert too many control programs. These challenges give the opportunity for the following.

- Can we program the sensor nodes in real-time?
- Can we change the forwarding path in real-time
- Can we integrate different sensor nodes in a WSN?

There are different solutions proposed for the above opportunities.

Sensor OpenFlow

One solution is the Sensor OpenFlow protocol. This protocol takes care of data forwarding in two different ways. One is the value-centric data forwarding which forwards the sensed data, if it exceeds a certain value. The other one is the in-centric data forwarding which forwards the sensed data based on the ID of the source node. Real life implementation of such a method is not available. It still exists in its infant stage.

Soft-WSN

Soft-WSN is another protocol for sensor device management and topology management. The sensor device management comprises of a) sensor management b) delay management and c) active-sleep management. In sensor management, multiple sensors can be implemented in a single board and sensors can be used depending on application-specific requirements. In delay management, delay for sensing can be changed dynamically in real-time. In active-sleep management, the status of active and sleep mode can be changed dynamically.

Topology management comprises of (a) node-specific management and (b) network-specific management. In node-specific management, forwarding logic of a particular sensor can be modified. Network-specific management decides whether to forward all traffic of a node in the network or to drop all traffic of a node in the network.

The network performance can be improved using software defined WSN over traditional WSN. Packet delivery ratio in the network increases and number of replicated data packets is reduced using Soft-WSN compared to the traditional WSN. The number of control messages in the network is higher using Soft-WSN over the traditional WSN. This is due to the PACKET-IN message in the network. Each time a node receives a new packet, it asks the Controller for getting adequate forwarding logic.

SDN-WISE

A third protocol is SDN-WISE. SDN-WISE proposes a Software Defined Networking platform for WSN. Flow-Table for the Rule Placement is available at sensor nodes. Any programming language can be used through API to program the nodes in real-time. In SDN-WISE, the sensor node includes IEEE 802.15.4 protocol, Micro Control Unit (MCU) and IEEE 802.15.4 stack over which the SDN-WISE really functions. Forwarding layer consists of Flow Rules and In Network Packet Processing (INPP) process the packets in SDN-WISE.

9.11 SDN for Mobile Networking

Meeting current market requirements is virtually impossible with traditional network architectures. Faced with flat or reduced budgets, enterprise IT departments are trying to squeeze the most from their networks using device-level management tools and manual processes. Carriers face similar challenges as demand for mobility and bandwidth explodes. Profits are being reduced by escalating capital equipment costs and flat or declining revenue.

Existing network architectures were not designed to meet the requirements of today's users, enterprises and carriers. Network designers are constrained by the limitations of current networks, which include the following.

a. **Complexity:** Networking technology to date has consisted largely of discrete sets of protocols designed to connect hosts reliably over arbitrary distances, link speeds and topologies. To meet business and technical needs over the last few decades, the industry has evolved networking protocols to deliver higher performance and reliability, broader connectivity and more stringent security. Protocols tend to be defined in isolation, however, with each solving a specific problem and without the benefit of any fundamental abstractions. This has resulted in one of the primary limitations of today's network complexity. For example, to add or move any device, IT must touch multiple switches, routers, firewalls, Web authentication portals, etc. and update Access Control Lists (ACLs), Virtual LANs (VLANs), Quality of Services (QoS) and other protocol-based mechanisms using device-level management tools. In addition, network topology, vendor switch model and software version all must be taken into account. Due to this complexity, today's networks are relatively static as IT seeks to minimize the risk of service disruption. The static nature of networks is in stark contrast to the dynamic nature of today's server environment, where server virtualization has greatly increased the number of hosts requiring network connectivity and fundamentally altered assumptions about the physical location of hosts.

   Prior to virtualization, applications resided on a single server and primarily exchanged traffic with select clients. Today, applications are distributed across multiple virtual machines (VMs), which exchange traffic flows with each other. VMs migrate to optimize and rebalance server workloads, causing the physical end points of existing flows to change (sometimes rapidly) over time. VM migration challenges many aspects of traditional networking, from addressing schemes and namespaces to the basic notion of a segmented, routing-based design. In addition to adopting virtualization technologies, many enterprises today operate an IP converged network for voice, data and video traffic. While existing networks can provide differentiated QoS levels for different applications, the provisioning of those resources is highly manual. IT must configure each vendor's equipment separately and adjust parameters such as network bandwidth and QoS on a per-session, per-application basis. Because of its static nature, the network cannot dynamically adapt to changing traffic, application and user demands.

b. **Inconsistent policies**: To implement a network-wide policy, IT may have to configure thousands of devices and mechanisms. For example, every time a new virtual machine is brought up, it can take hours, in some cases days, for IT to reconfigure ACLs across the entire network. The complexity of today's networks makes it very difficult for IT to apply a consistent set of access, security, QoS and other policies to increasingly mobile users, which leaves the enterprise vulnerable to security breaches, non-compliance with regulations and other negative consequences.

c. **Inability to scale**: The network becomes vastly more complex with the addition of hundreds or thousands of network devices that must be configured and managed. IT has also relied on over subscription to scale the network, based on predictable traffic patterns. However, in today's virtualized data centers, traffic patterns are incredibly dynamic and therefore unpredictable.

d. **Vendor dependence**: Carriers and enterprises seek to deploy new capabilities and services in rapid response to changing business needs or user demands. However, their ability to respond is hindered by vendors' equipment product cycles, which can range to three years or more. Lack of standard and open interfaces limits the ability of network operators to tailor the network to their individual environments. This mismatch between market requirements and network capabilities has brought the industry to a tipping point. In response, the industry has created the Software-Defined Networking (SDN) architecture and is developing associated standards.

The important aspects of SDN for mobile networking are

- Flow Table paradigm of SDN which is well suited for end –to-end communication over multiple technologies such as WiFi, 3G, 4G etc.
- Logically centralized control which is particularly useful for efficient base station coordination for addressing inter-cell reference.
- Path management in which data can be routed based on service requirements without depending on core routing policies.
- Network virtualization which abstracts the physical resources from the network services. This helps in providing seamless connectivity and service differentiation among users.

Figure 9.17 shows the diagram for interference management in Software Defined Wireless Mobile Network (SDWMN).

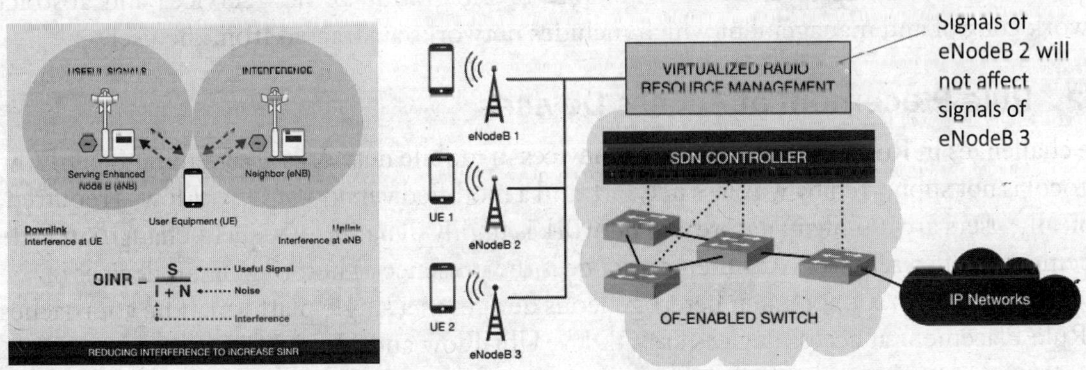

Fig.9.17: Interference Management in SDWMN

Consider a traditional mobile network. When mobile equipment operates, it connects with a base station or access point for sending data back and forth. At the same time, the equipment may get affected by another access point which is known as interference. SDWMN tries to address the problem of interference with the help of SDN. In the above Figure, we can see an SDN controller and Virtualized Radio Resource Management Unit which takes care of interference. For example, the signals from eNodeB2 will not affect the signals eNodeB3 as shown in the Figure 9.17.

Mobile traffic management in Software Defined Wireless Mobile Network (SDWMN) is shown in Figure 9.18.

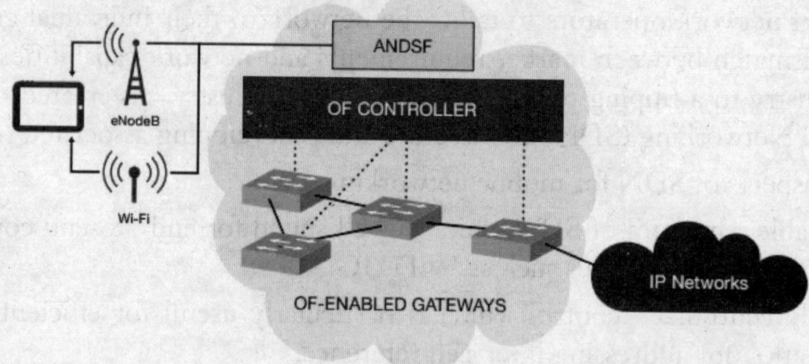

Fig.9.18: Mobile Traffic Management in SDWMN

In Figure 9.18, the Access Network Discovery and Service Function (ANDSF) takes care of the mobile traffic management in SDWMN. When a user moves, he can be first connected to WiFi and then to the cellular network 3G, 4G and so on the SDN enabled wireless networks takes care of the traffic management and connectivity.

The key benefits of SDN in mobile networks are centralized control of devices manufactured by multiple vendors, higher rate of integration of new services and abstract network control and management which includes networks abstracted from the user.

9.12 Rule Placement at Access Devices

The challenges in Rule Placement at access devices in mobile networks are General OpenFlow protocol is not supported by wireless network and a modified version of OpenFlow is required. Typically, users are mobile in nature and network is highly dynamic. Frequent changes in Rule Placement are also required. Another challenge is the presence of heterogeneous devices in the network and how to support such heterogeneous devices in a single platform. The approaches for Rule Placement at access devices are ODIN, Ubi-Flow and Mobi-Flow.

9.12.1 ODIN

In Open Data centre with Interoperable Network (ODIN), an agent is placed at access points to communicate with controller. ODIN is an SDN framework programmable enterprise WLANs. It provides a platform for developing typical enterprise WLAN services such as mobility managers, and load balancers as "network applications". Two components are present – an ODIN agent and ODIN master. ODIN agent is placed with the physical devices and ODIN master is placed at the Controller end. Figure 9.19 shows the architecture of ODIN.

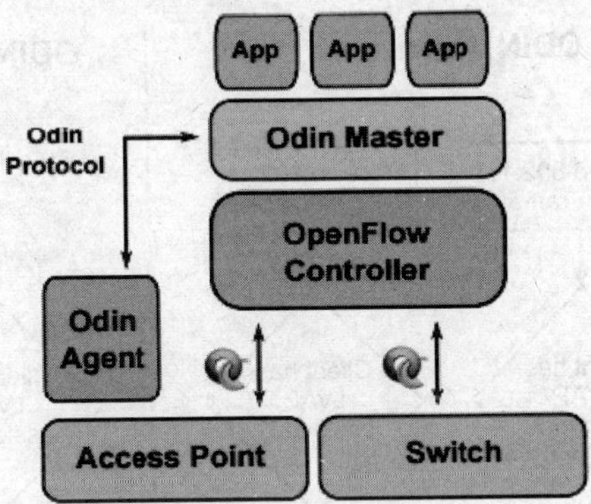

Fig.9.19: Architecture of ODIN

Odin's architecture comprises of a single master and a set of agents that run on the (Access Points) APs. The master is implemented as an OpenFlow application on top of the Controller. The agents are implemented and run on the APs. The APs run Open vSwitch so that OpenFlow rules can be installed at each AP as well. Every Light Virtual Access Point (LVAP) has a set of OpenFlow rules attached to it, which enable faster mobility and can potentially be used to do access control as well.

An LVAP is basically a per-client, virtual AP. Every time a client performs a probe scan, a central controller spawns an LVAP on a physical AP close to the client. The LVAP is what responds to the client's probe scan with a probe response. The client can then continue the regular 802.11 association handshake with the LVAP. Once this is done, an association is formed between a client device capable of mobility and an LVAP. At this point, the client is only concerned with getting ACKs for the data frames it generates and receiving beacons from its LVAP in a timely fashion. Just like virtual machines in a data center can be migrated to a different physical server, an LVAP can be migrated to another physical AP. If an LVAP is migrated to another physical AP fast enough such that it retains all the necessary state to maintain its associations and the client continues to receive ACKs and beacon frames, then the client can continue transmitting data frames without having to perform a re-association. Thus, an LVAP migration gives the effect of a handoff, without actually inducing a state machine change at the client and if this is done fast enough, the client won't even notice any period of disconnectivity.

Odin applications run atop the master, and control the placement of LVAPs. For instance, a mobility manager would attempt to place the LVAPs as close to the client as possible, and a load balancer would move LVAPs between physical APs such that the APs have an even processing load. Applications written on top of Odin can be both reactive, and proactive. Reactive applications use a pub-sub mechanism to receive notifications for specific MAC layer events that they can subscribe to. Proactive applications merely run within a loop, cycling between sleeping and doing some work. The flow diagram for the communication between ODIN master and ODIN agent is shown below in Figure 9.20.

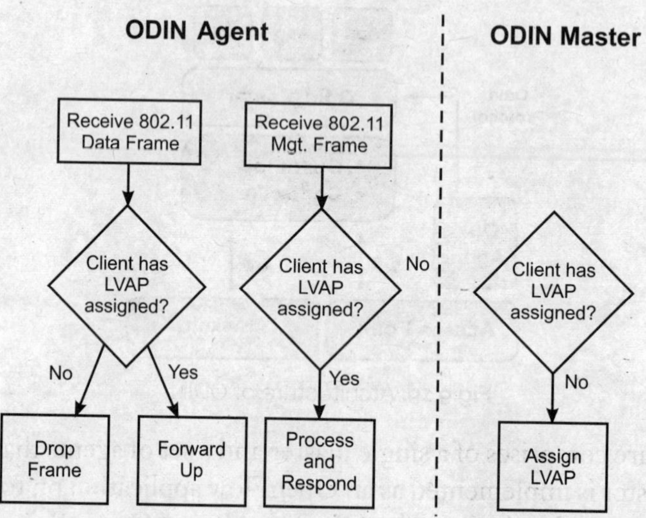

Fig.9.20: Flow Diagram for Communication between ODIN Master and ODIN Agent

9.12.2 Ubi-Flow

Ubi-Flow is the first software-defined IoT system for ubiquitous flow control and mobility management in urban heterogeneous networks. To achieve light-weight processing in IoT devices, in UbiFlow all jobs related to mobility management, handover optimization, access point selection and flow scheduling are executed by the coordination of distributed controllers. Specifically, UbiFlow adopts multiple controllers to divide an urban-scale SDN into different geographic partitions to achieve distributed control of IoT flows. A distributed hashing based overlay structure is proposed to maintain network scalability and consistency. Based on this UbiFlow overlay structure, relevant issues in mobility management such as scalable control, fault tolerance and load balancing have been carefully taken care of. The UbiFlow controller differentiates flow scheduling based on per-device requirements as well as whole-partition capabilities. Flow scheduling comprises of network partition, network matching and load balancing. Therefore, it can present a network status view for the optimized selection of access points in multi networks to satisfy flow requests, while guaranteeing the network performance in each partition. Figure 9.21 shows the architecture of Ubi-Flow.

The key contributions of UbiFlow are:

- A novel overlay structure to achieve mobility management and fault tolerance in software-defined IoT.

- An optimal assignment algorithm for the controller to match the best available access points to IoT devices, with network status analysis and flow requests as inputs.
- A load balancing scheme for distributed controllers by analyzing the variations in flow traffic characteristics.

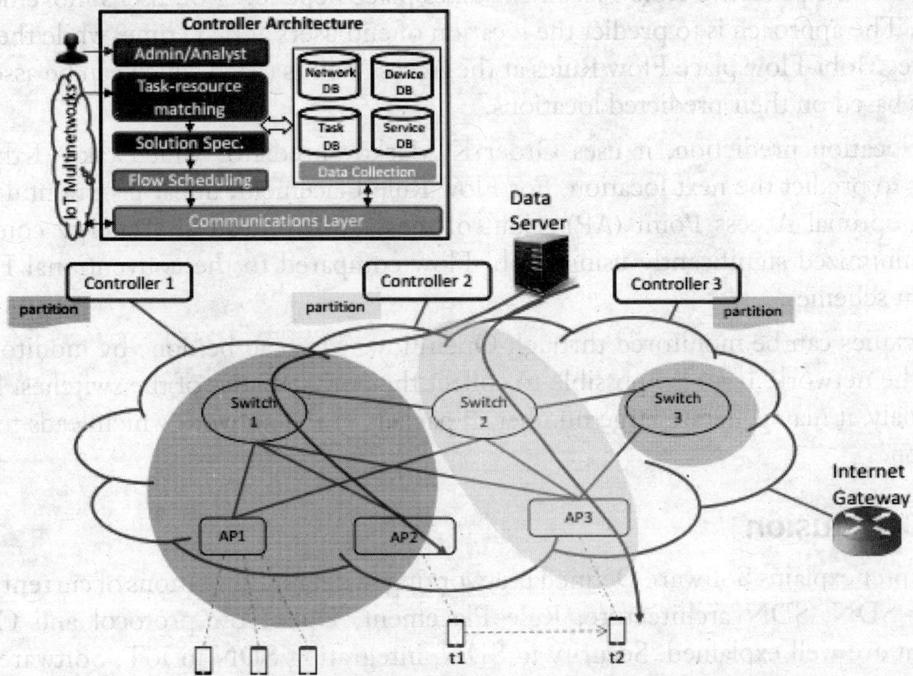

Fig.9.21: Architecture of Ubi-Flow

9.12.3 Mobi-Flow

Figure 9.22 shows the Mobi-Flow Rule Placement in Software Defined Internet of Things (SDIoT).

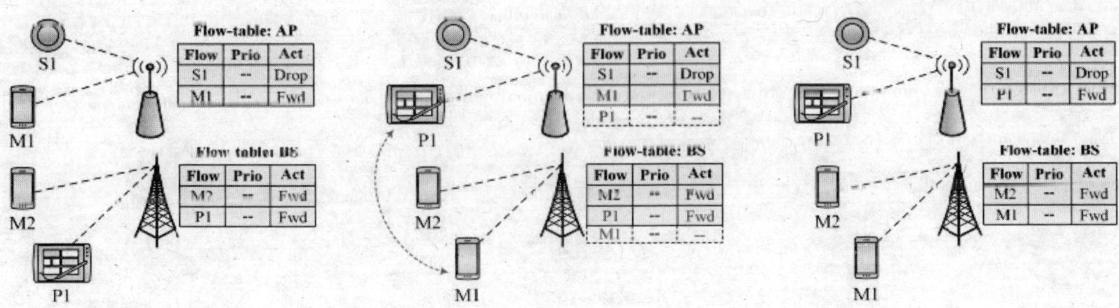

Fig.9.22: Mobi-Flow Rule Placement in SDIoT

There are devices S1 and M1 connected to one Access Point (AP) and another two devices P1 and M2 connected to another Base Station (BS). The corresponding Flow Tables are also available. Imagine that the device P1 and M1 has interchanged its position. So a new Flow Rules need to be added in the respective Flow Tables. But the memory of Flow Tables is restricted. In Mobi-Flow, a proactive Rule Placement takes place depending on user's movement in the network. The approach is to predict the location of end users at (t+1) time, while the users are at (t) time. Mobi-Flow place Flow Rules at the Access Points (APs) which can be associated to the users based on their predicted locations.

For location prediction, it uses Order-K Markov predictor which takes Kth location instances to predict the next location. For Flow Rule Placement, linear programming is used to select optimal Access Point (AP). Control message overhead and energy consumption can be minimized significantly using Mobi-Flow compared to the conventional Flow Rule placement schemes.

Anomalies can be monitored through OpenFlow. This can be done by monitoring each Flow in the network. It is also possible to collect the port statistics of the switches. If there is any anomaly, it may generate large number of packets in the network which leads to network congestion.

9.13 Conclusion

This Chapter explains Software Defined Networking in detail. Limitations of current network, origin of SDN, SDN architecture, Rule Placement, OpenFlow protocol and Controller Placement are well explained. Security in SDN, integrating SDN in IoT, Software Defined WSN and SDN for mobile networking is described. Finally Rule Placement approaches at access devices including ODIN, Ubi-Flow and Mobi-Flow are clearly illustrated.

10 CLOUD COMPUTING

10.1 Introduction

The roots of cloud computing begins from Cluster computing where homogeneous computing nodes which are connected loosely or lightly works together. Then came the Grid computing where heterogeneous computing nodes are distributed over a wide area to perform very large tasks. Ubiquity computing was the successor of Grid computing in which packaged resources are available for computing and storage. Finally the computing model Cloud computing emerged which has shared pool of configurable computing resources which is ubiquitous, dynamic and provides on-demand access.

The history of cloud computing trace back to year 1950 when time shared mainframe computers came into existence. ARPANET was introduced in 1969 which added to the enhancement of technology. In 1970, virtual machines were introduced by IBM and in 1990 the expansion of Virtual Private Network (VPNs) accelerated the advancements in Internet. It was in 1996-97 the cloud computing technology was first introduced. Later in 1999, salesforce.com, Amazon Web Services (AWS) in 2002, Amazon EC2 in 2006 and finally in 2008 Google App Engine and Microsoft Azure released its cloud. Several other clouds also came into existence during these years.

10.2 Architecture

Cloud computing is a model for enabling convenient, on-demand network access to a shared pool of configurable computing resources such as network infrastructure, servers, storage, applications etc. This computing model is advancement in Utility computing. Cloud computing provides high level generalization or abstraction of computation and storage models. The resources can be allocated rapidly and released with low management effort. Cloud computing has some essential characteristics, service models and deployment models. It provides on-demand services that can be accessed from any place and at any time. Figure 10.1 shows the National Institute of Standards and Technology (NIST) model of Cloud computing.

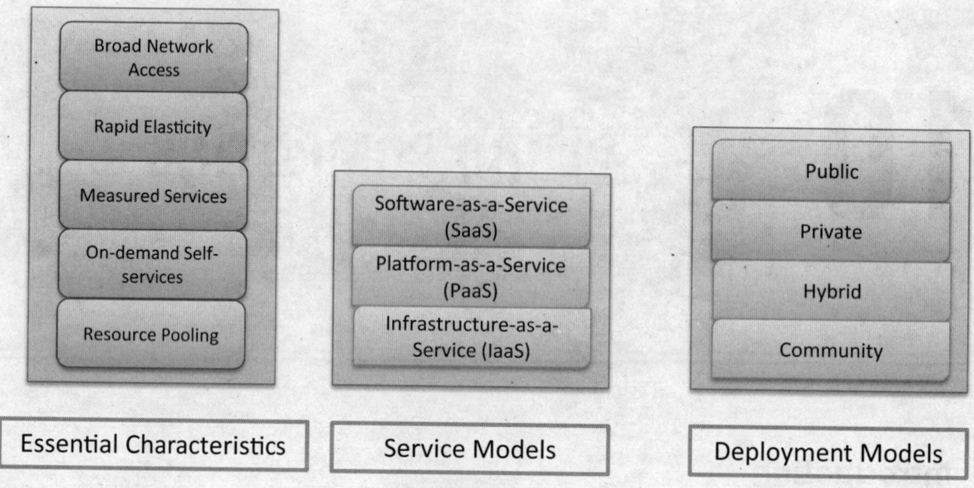

Fig.10.1: NIST Model of Cloud Computing

This computing model contains three components: essential characteristics, service models and deployment models. We will see each component in detail in the coming sections. There are several business advantages for Cloud computing. Businesses require nearly zero cost for upfront infrastructure investment. Real time infrastructure availability, more efficient resource utilization, usage based costing and reduced time to market are other business potentials of Cloud computing. Following are the components of Cloud computing.

- Clients or end users: The clients or end users can be thick or thin clients. (e.g., mobile phones, tablets, laptops, and workstations).
- Services: This includes products and solutions.
- Applications: Web Apps, Software-as-a-Service (SaaS).
- Platform: Apps or Web Hosting using PaaS.
- Storage: Database, Data-Storage-as-a-Service (DSaaS).
- Infrastructure: Virtualization, EC2, Infrastructure-as-a-Service (IaaS).

10.3 Characteristics

The characteristics of Cloud computing can be classified as general characteristics and essential characteristics. The **general characteristics** of cloud computing are as follows.

a. Improved agility in resource planning - Agility for organizations may be improved, as cloud computing may increase user's flexibility with re-provisioning, adding, or expanding technological infrastructure resources.

b. Cost reduction - Cost reductions are claimed by cloud providers. A public-cloud delivery model converts capital expenditures (e.g., buying servers) to operational expenditure. Less in-house IT skills are required for implementation of projects that use cloud computing.

c. Device or location independence – Cloud computing enable users to access systems using a web browser regardless of their location or what device they use (e.g., PC, mobile phone). As infrastructure is off-site (typically provided by a third-party) and accessed via the Internet, users can connect to it from anywhere.

d. Less maintenance – Maintenance of cloud computing applications is easier, because they do not need to be installed on each user's computer and can be accessed from different places (e.g., different work locations, while travelling, etc.).

e. Multitenancy – This enables sharing of resources and costs across a large pool of users thus allowing for centralization of infrastructure in locations with lower costs (such as real estate, electricity, etc.), peak-load capacity increases (users need not engineer and pay for the resources and equipment to meet their highest possible load-levels) and utilisation and efficiency improvements for systems that are often only 10–20% utilised.

f. Productivity – This may be increased when multiple users can work on the same data simultaneously, rather than waiting for it to be saved and emailed. Time may be saved, as information does not need to be re-entered when fields are matched, nor do users need to install application software upgrades to their computer.

g. Reliability – This improves with the use of multiple redundant sites, which makes well-designed cloud computing suitable for business continuity and disaster recovery.

h. Scalability and elasticity - Dynamic or "on-demand" provisioning of resources on a fine-grained, self-service basis in near real-time is possible in Cloud computing. This gives the ability to scale up when the usage need increases or down if resources are not being used.

i. Security – This can improve due to centralization of data, increased security-focused resources, etc. But concerns can persist about loss of control over certain sensitive data and the lack of security for stored kernels. Security is often as good as or better than other traditional systems because service providers are able to devote resources to solving security issues that many customers cannot afford to tackle or which they lack the technical skills to address. However, the complexity of security is greatly increased when data is distributed over a wider area or over a greater number of devices, as well as in multi-tenant systems shared by unrelated users. In addition, user access to security audit logs may be difficult or impossible. Private cloud installations are motivated by user's desire to retain control over the infrastructure and avoid losing control of information security.

Essential characteristics are one of the components in NIST model of Cloud computing. They are given below.

- Broad network access – Cloud resources are available over the network and accessed through standard mechanisms that promote use by heterogeneous thin or thick client platforms (e.g., mobile phones, tablets, laptops, and workstations).

- Rapid elasticity – Cloud resources should be rapid, elastic and automatic. Dynamic allocation or release facility to scale rapidly outward and inward with demand. Consumers should feel that the resources are infinite. Facility for adding or removing resources in any quantity at any time.
- Measured service – Resource usage needs to be recorded and monitored. Cloud systems automatically control and optimize resource use by leveraging a metering capability at some level of abstraction appropriate to the type of service (e.g., storage, processing, bandwidth, and active user accounts). Resource usage can be monitored, controlled and reported, providing transparency for both the provider and consumer of the utilized service.
- On-demand self-service – A consumer can unilaterally provision computing capabilities, such as server time and network storage, as needed automatically without requiring human interaction with each service provider.
- Resource pooling – The provider's computing resources are pooled to serve multiple consumers using a multi-tenant model, with different physical and virtual resources dynamically assigned and reassigned according to consumer demand.

10.4 Deployment Models

A cloud deployment model represents a specific type of cloud environment, primarily distinguished by ownership, size and access. Each deployment model has specific trade-offs for agencies that are migrating services and operations to cloud-based environments. Because of the different characteristics and trade-offs of the various cloud computing deployment models, it is important that the agency or IT professionals have a clear understanding of their agency's specific needs as well as how the various systems can help them their business needs. There are 4 important deployment models like public cloud, private cloud, hybrid cloud and community cloud. Other deployment models include multi-cloud, distributed cloud, inter-cloud, Big data cloud, High Performance Computing (HPC) cloud etc. We will see each one in detail.

10.4.1 Public Cloud

A public cloud is a publicly accessible cloud environment owned by a third-party cloud provider. Examples of public cloud are Amazon Web Services (AWS), Google Compute Engine, Microsoft Azure etc. The IT resources on public clouds are usually provisioned via the previously described cloud delivery models and are generally offered to cloud consumers at a cost or are commercialized via other avenues such as advertisement. The cloud provider is responsible for the creation and on-going maintenance of the public cloud and its IT resources. Figure 10.2 shows a partial view of the public cloud landscape, highlighting some of the primary vendors in the marketplace.

The advantages of this model are easy to set up at low cost as provider covers the hardware, application and bandwidth cost. This model is scalable to meet growing needs. No resources are wasted from the user's perspective as the payment is done on a pay-per-use basis.

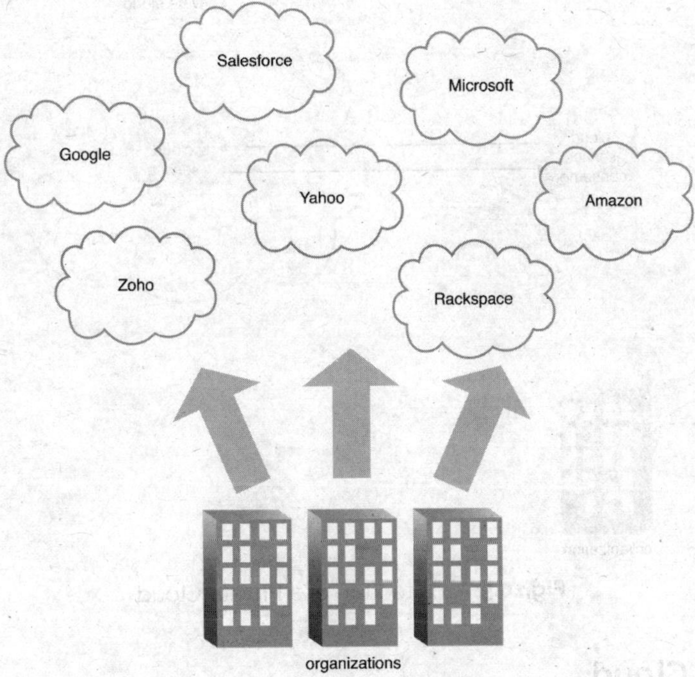

Fig.10.2: Public Cloud

10.4.2 Private Cloud

A private cloud is owned by a single organization. Private clouds enable an organization to use cloud computing technology as a means of centralized access to IT resources by different parts, locations, or departments of the organization. When a private cloud exists as a controlled environment, the risks and challenges are less compared to public cloud. The disadvantage is that regular maintenance is required for this deployment model. The use of a private cloud can change how organizational and trust boundaries are defined and applied. The actual administration of a private cloud environment may be carried out by internal or outsourced staff.

A cloud service consumer in the organization's on-premise environment accesses a cloud service hosted on the same organization's private cloud via a virtual private network. With a private cloud, the same organization is technically both the cloud consumer and cloud provider. In order to differentiate these roles a separate organizational department typically assumes the responsibility for provisioning the cloud and therefore assumes the cloud provider role. The departments requiring access to the private cloud assume the cloud consumer role.

Even though the private cloud may physically reside on the organization's premises, IT resources it hosts are still considered "cloud-based" as long as they are made remotely accessible to cloud consumers. IT resources hosted outside of the private cloud by the departments acting as cloud consumers are therefore considered "on-premise" in relation to the private cloud-based IT resources. Figure 10.3 shows the architecture of a private cloud.

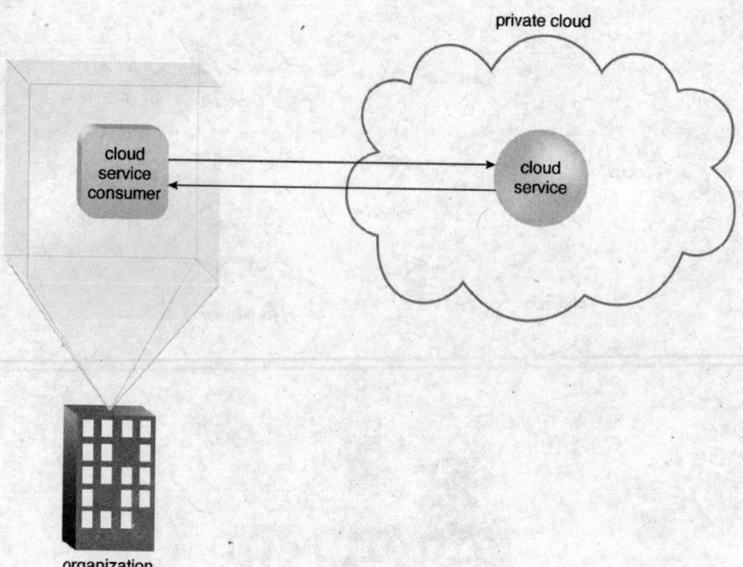

Fig.10.3: Architecture of a Private Cloud

10.4.3 Hybrid Cloud

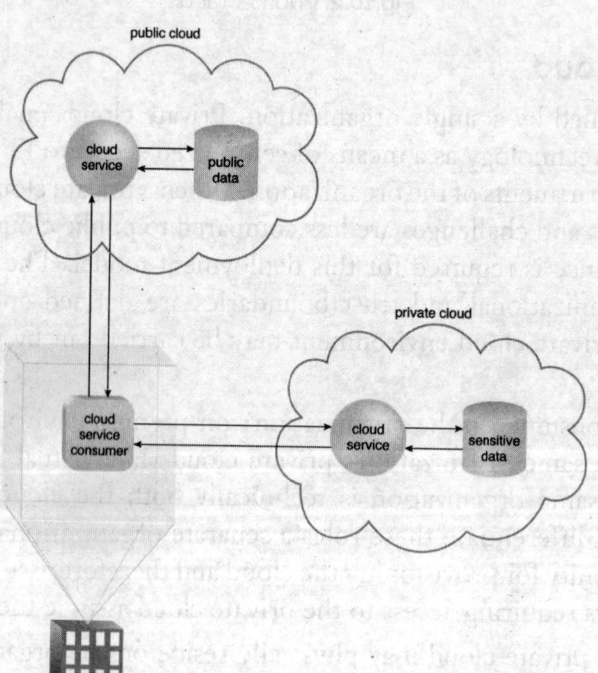

Fig.10.4: Architecture of a Hybrid Cloud

A hybrid cloud is a cloud environment comprised of two or more different cloud deployment models. These different deployment models are pooled together by standardized tools.For example, a cloud consumer may choose to deploy cloud services processing sensitive data to a private cloud and other less sensitive cloud services to a public cloud. The result of this combination is a hybrid deployment model. Hybrid deployment architectures can be complex, challenging to create and maintain due to the potential disparity in cloud environments. The management responsibilities are typically split between the private cloud provider organization and the public cloud provider.

This deployment model supports data and application portability. For example, it supports the facility for load-balancing between clouds. Figure 10.4 shows the architecture of a hybrid cloud.

10.4.4 Community Cloud

A community cloud is similar to a public cloud except that its access is limited to a specific community of cloud consumers. The community cloud may be jointly owned by the community members or by a third-party cloud provider that provisions a public cloud with limited access. The member cloud consumers of the community typically share the responsibility for defining and evolving the community cloud. Membership in the community does not necessarily guarantee access to or control of all the cloud's IT resources. Parties outside the community are generally not granted access unless allowed by the community. Figure 10.5 shows the architecture of community cloud.

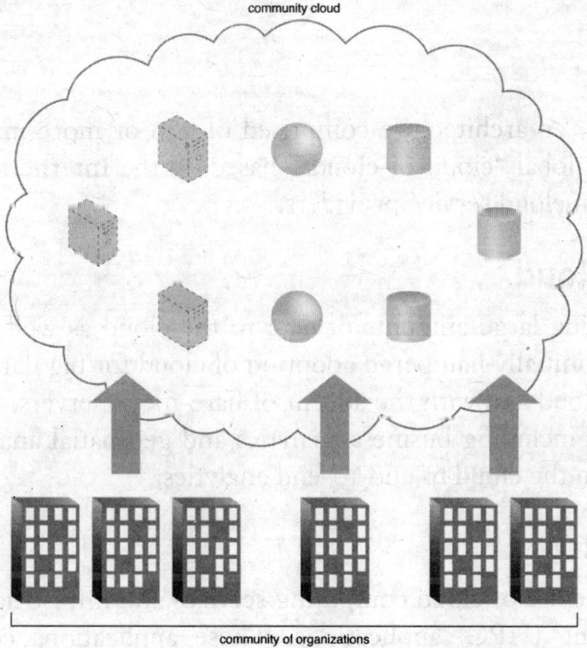

Fig.10.5: Architecture of Community Cloud

10.4.5 Multi-Cloud

Multi-cloud is the use of multiple cloud computing services in a single heterogeneous architecture to reduce reliance on single vendors, increase flexibility through choice, mitigate against disasters, etc. It differs from hybrid cloud in that it refers to multiple cloud services, rather than multiple deployment modes (public, private, legacy). It increases fault tolerance and flexibility.

10.4.6 Distributed Cloud

A cloud computing platform can be assembled from a distributed set of machines in different locations, connected to a single network or hub service. It is possible to distinguish between two types of distributed clouds: public-resource computing and volunteer cloud.

Public-resource computing — This type of distributed cloud results from an expansive definition of cloud computing, because they are more akin to distributed computing than cloud computing. Nonetheless, it is considered a sub-class of cloud computing and some examples include distributed computing platforms such as BOINC and Folding@Home.

Volunteer cloud — Volunteer cloud computing is characterized as the intersection of public-resource computing and cloud computing, where a cloud computing infrastructure is built using volunteered resources. Many challenges arise from this type of infrastructure, because of the volatility of the resources used to build it and the dynamic environment it operates in. It can also be called peer-to-peer clouds, or ad-hoc clouds. An example for such model is Cloud@Home, which is aimed to implement a cloud computing infrastructure using volunteered resources.

10.4.7 Inter-Cloud

This model is based on an architecture comprised of two or more inter-connected clouds. It is considered as the global "cloud-of-clouds" based on the Internet. This model supports interoperability between cloud service providers.

10.4.8 Big Data Cloud

The issues of transferring large amounts of data to the cloud as well as data security once the data is in the cloud initially hampered adoption of cloud for big data. But now that much data originates in the cloud and with the advent of bare-metal servers, the cloud has become a solution for use cases including business analytics and geospatial analysis. Solutions range from Hadoop hosting in the cloud to end-to-end analytics.

10.4.9 HPC Cloud

HPC cloud refers to the use of cloud computing services and infrastructure to execute High Performance Computing (HPC) applications. These applications consume considerable amount of computing power and memory and are traditionally executed on clusters of computers. Various vendors offer servers that can support the execution of these applications. In HPC cloud, the deployment model allows all HPC resources to be inside the cloud provider infrastructure or different portions of HPC resources to be shared between cloud provider and client on-premise infrastructure. The adoption of cloud to run HPC applications started mostly for applications composed of independent tasks with no inter-process communication. As cloud providers began to offer high-speed network technologies such as InfiniBand, multiprocessing tightly coupled applications started to benefit from cloud as well.

10.5 Service Models

A cloud delivery model represents a specific, pre-packaged combination of IT resources offered by a cloud provider. Three common cloud delivery models have become widely established and formalized. Figure 10.6 shows the Cloud computing service models arranged as layers in a stack.

1. Infrastructure-as-a-Service (IaaS)
2. Platform-as-a-Service (PaaS)
3. Software-as-a-Service (SaaS)

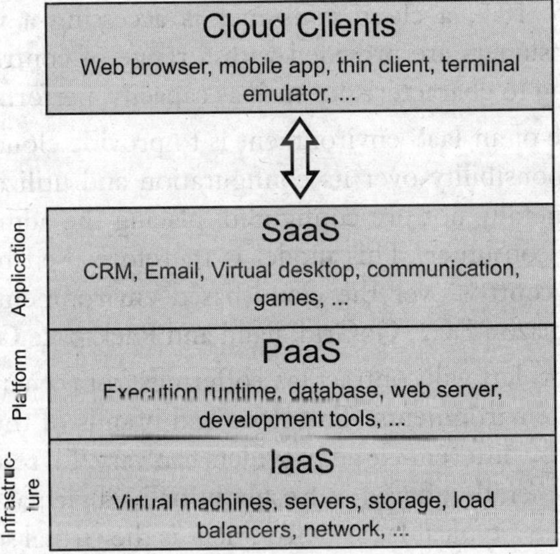

Fig.10.6: Cloud Computing Service Models Arranged as Different Layers

10.5.1 Infrastructure-as-a-Service (IaaS)

The Infrastructure-as-a-Service (IaaS) delivery model represents a self-contained IT environment comprised of infrastructure-centric IT resources that can be accessed and managed via cloud service-based interfaces and tools. This environment can include hardware, network, connectivity, operating systems and other "raw" IT resources. In contrast to traditional hosting or outsourcing environments, with IaaS, IT resources are typically virtualized and packaged into bundles that simplify up-front runtime scaling and customization of the infrastructure. Figure 10.7 shows the architecture of IaaS.

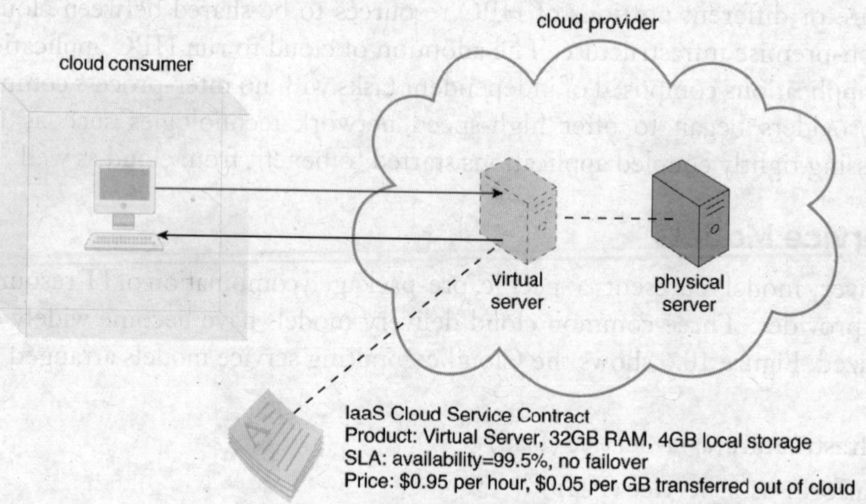

Fig.10.7: Architecture of IaaS

In the above Figure 10.7, a cloud consumer is accessing a virtual server from IaaS environment. Cloud consumers are provided with a range of contractual guarantees by the Cloud provider pertaining to characteristics such as capacity, performance and availability.

The general purpose of an IaaS environment is to provide cloud consumers with a high level of control and responsibility over its configuration and utilization. The IT resources provided by IaaS are generally not pre-configured, placing the administrative responsibility directly upon the cloud consumer. This model is therefore used by cloud consumers that require a high level of control over the cloud-based environment they intend to create. Examples for IaaS are Amazon EC2, GoGrid, iland and Rackspace Cloud servers.

Sometimes cloud providers will contract IaaS offerings from other cloud providers in order to scale their own cloud environments. The types and brands of the IT resources provided by IaaS products offered by different cloud providers can vary. IT resources available through IaaS environments are generally offered as freshly initialized virtual instances. A central and primary IT resource within a typical IaaS environment is the virtual server. Virtual servers are leased by specifying server hardware requirements, such as processor capacity, memory and local storage space.

IaaS contains the basic building blocks for Cloud IT and typically provides access to network features, computers (virtual or dedicated hardware) and data storage space. It provides on-demand delivery of computing infrastructure.

Why IaaS?

New businesses can operate without investing on computer hardware. IaaS is scalable for rapidly growing businesses or organizations that experience huge success immediately. IaaS is suitable for serving fluctuating computing demands. For example, during festival seasons, online stores like Amazon and Flipkart experience huge computational requirements due to heavy shopping that takes place in these Websites. IaaS is suitable for new business model trials as there is no need for investment. It also helps in minimizing the capital expenses especially for those entrepreneurs who starts business on a low budget.

Working Methodology

The cloud service provider offers resource management. The user rents servers, software, data center space or network equipment and an outsourced service on-demand model is made available. There is a physical server and a virtualized server as shown in Figure 10.8. In this, the physical server contains the hardware, operation system and applications. In the virtualized server, there are virtual machines VMs. These VMs contain operating system and applications. On top of hardware, there will be multiple VMs executing and the hypervisor is situated between hardware layer and VM layer. This hypervisor coordinates the operations between hardware layer and VM layer.

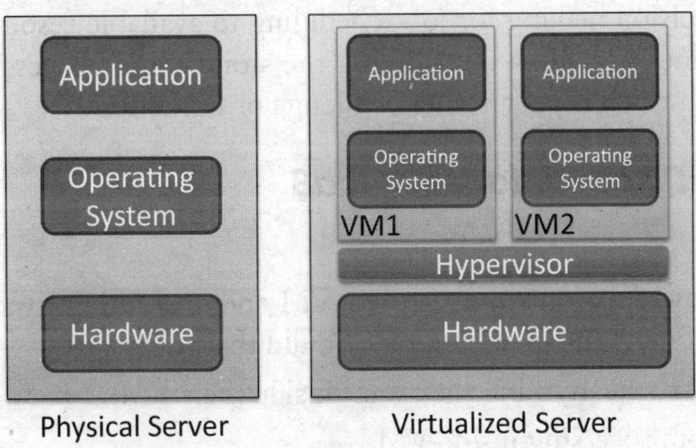

Fig.10.8. Physical Server and Virtualized Server

Essential Characteristics

- Scalability and elasticity – Dynamic scaling of required infrastructure resources is possible in IaaS. Large amount of resource allocation or release or resources can be done in a short span of time. There is no variation in system performance while scale-in and scale-out.
- Manageability and interoperability – Clients have total control of the virtualized infrastructure resources. There is pre-configured facility for allocation of virtualized resources. The virtualized resources are to be monitored for their running status. The usage and billing system records the use of infrastructure resources and calculate payment accordingly.

- Availability and reliability - The clients should be able to access the computational resources without failure and here stored data can be retrieved at any time without failure. Uninterrupted facility for computation and communication is yet another feature of IaaS.
- Performance and optimization – There may be high utilization of physical resources among different clients. To enable high computing power with large pool of physical resources, parallel processing is used.
- Accessibility and portability – There is facility for the client to ease various tasks such as control, manage and access infrastructure resources. IaaS also facilitates easy reallocation and duplication of allocated infrastructure resources.

Challenges and Limitations

There are several challenges or limitations for IaaS. Seamless scaling of services independent of traffic variation should be made possible with Iaas. But this could not be practically achieved always. Network latency is yet another challenging issue. The network latency may degrade the level of expected performance in Cloud computing. Another challenge is that users may require automated decision making for job scheduling to available resources. Sometimes the regulatory approval does not allow outsourcing the storage and processing of sensitive data (e.g. medical records), which is yet another challenge or limitation.

Advantages and Disadvantages of IaaS

IaaS (Advantages)

- Customers have full control over their VM and everything inside it; customers can choose to automate the provisioning or build their own VM.
- A customer can run anything they want inside their VM.
- Full control of processing inside VM.
- Simplifies Integration with enterprise infrastructure.
- The customer in essence can run and control its own virtual infrastructure without the over heads of cost and maintenance from running its own hardware.

IaaS (Disadvantages)

- Most expensive, since the customer is now leasing a tangible resource, the provider can charge for every cycle, bit of RAM or disk space used.
- Customer is responsible for backups and all aspects of VM management.
- No control over which server or the physical (geographical) location of the VM.

10.5.2 Platform-as-a-Service (PaaS)

The PaaS delivery model represents a pre-defined "ready-to-use" environment typically comprised of already deployed and configured IT resources. Specifically, PaaS relies on (and is primarily defined by) the usage of a ready-made environment that establishes a set of pre-packaged products and tools used to support the entire delivery lifecycle of custom applications. PaaS remove the need for organizations to manage the underlying infrastructure usually hardware and operating system. It helps to focus on the deployment and management of our applications.

Common reasons a cloud consumer would use and invest in a PaaS environment include:

- The cloud consumer wants to extend on-premise environments into the cloud for scalability and economic purposes.
- The cloud consumer uses the ready-made environment to entirely substitute an on-premise environment.
- The cloud consumer wants to become a cloud provider and deploy it's own cloud services to be made available to other external cloud consumers.

By working within a ready-made platform, the cloud consumer is spared the administrative burden of setting up and maintaining the bare infrastructure IT resources provided via the IaaS model. Conversely, the cloud consumer is granted a lower level of control over the underlying IT resources that host and provision the platform in PaaS. Figure 10.9 shows the architecture of PaaS.

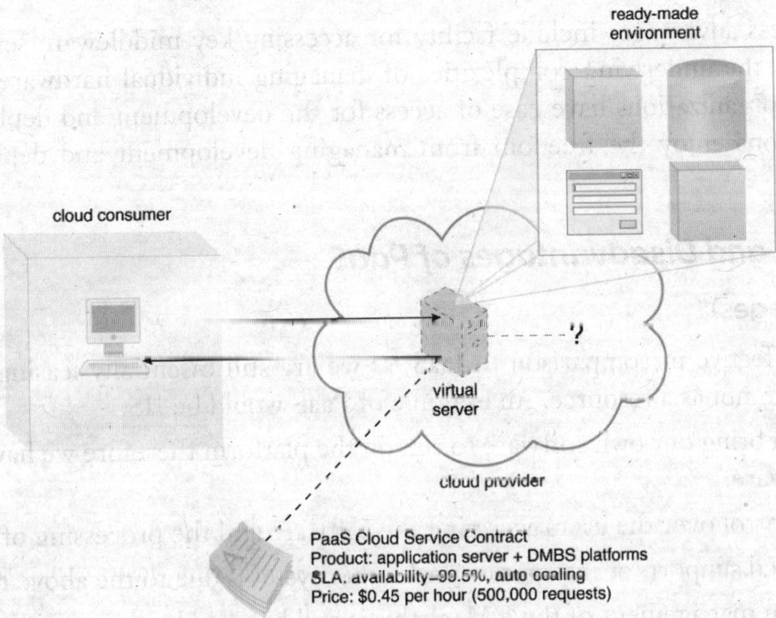

Fig.10.9: Architecture of PaaS

In Figure 10.9, a cloud consumer is accessing a ready-made PaaS environment. The question mark indicates that the cloud consumer is intentionally shielded from the implementation details of the platform.

PaaS products are available with different development stacks. For example, Microsoft Azure provides a .NET-based environment, while Google App Engine offers a Java and Python-based environment.

Why PaaS?

- PaaS provides the platform which allows developers to create applications which can be offered as services via Internet.
- Simplifies the application development and deploy the cloud-aware feature.
- PaaS is an application middlewarc offered as a service to developers.
- Provides abstraction and security for deployed applications.
- Facilitates development and managing applications without the complexity of maintaining the underlying infrastructure.
- Allows customers to rent virtualized servers and associated services.
- Provides elastic scaling of the user's deployed application.

PaaS working model allows users to create software applications using offered tools. This model provides pre-configured features that customers can subscribe. PaaS support is available for managing the infrastructure and applications for customers. Services are regularly updated with new features.

The business advantages include facility for accessing key middleware services without worrying about the underlying complexities of managing individual hardware and software elements. The organizations have ease of access for the development and deployment tools. The organizations enjoy the freedom from managing development and deployment tools individually.

Advantages and Disadvantages of PaaS

PaaS (Advantages)

- Cost effective in comparison to IaaS, as we are still essentially leasing the software platform not as a resource. An example of PaaS would be IIS.
- We can bring our own software to run on the platform therefore we have full control of software.
- Full control over the users accessing the software and the processing of data.
- Improved support for integration with other systems due to the above reasons.
- Minimal management of the VM, as this is still handled by the provider.

PaaS (Disadvantages)

- No control over the VM or processing of data, this is a big security risk as we don't know what's happening with our data.

- Possibly no control over platform depending on Cloud provider.
- Platform is most likely a shared platform, for example there could be other customers running different websites on the same IIS platform.
- Management task can become time consuming and tedious as we are responsible for updates and upgrades of application.
- Not as cost effective as SaaS and not as much control over VM as IaaS.

10.5.3 Software-as-a-Service (SaaS)

A software program positioned as a shared cloud service and made available as a "product" or generic utility represents the typical profile of a SaaS offering. The SaaS delivery model is typically used to make a reusable cloud service widely available (often commercially) to a range of cloud consumers. An entire marketplace exists around SaaS products that can be leased and used for different purposes and via different terms. Figure 10.10 shows the architecture of SaaS.

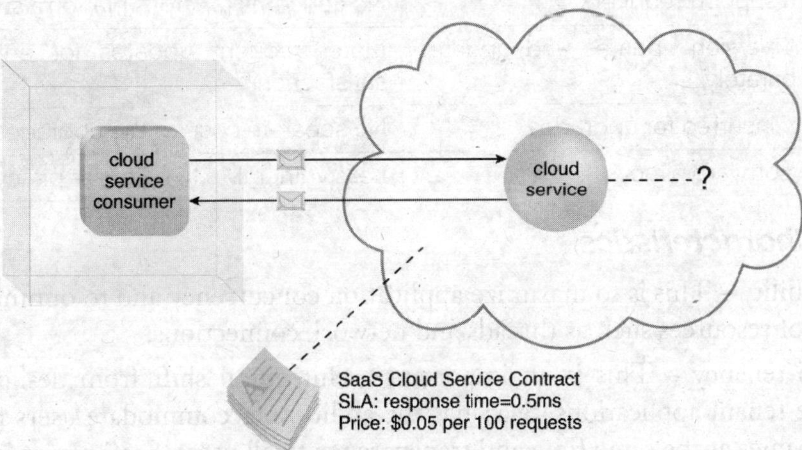

Fig.10.10: Architecture of SaaS

In the above architecture, the cloud service consumer is given access the cloud service contract, but not to any underlying IT resources or implementation details. A cloud consumer is generally granted very limited administrative control over a SaaS implementation. It is most often provisioned by the cloud provider, but it can be legally owned by whichever entity assumes the cloud service owner role. For example, an organization acting as a cloud consumer while using and working with a PaaS environment can build a cloud service that it decides to deploy in that same environment as a SaaS offering. The same organization then effectively assumes the cloud provider role as the SaaS-based cloud service is made available to other organizations that act as cloud consumers when using that cloud service.

SaaS provides with a completed product that is run and managed by the service provider. In most cases, people referring to SaaS are referring to end-user applications. SaaS is a simplified model of software delivery over Internet. Here, operation, maintenance and technical support is provided by the service provider. In other words, SaaS provides facility to execute service provider's application at user's end. Applications are available as services. The service is typically offered via Web browser working as a thin client. End users do not possess the control of the cloud infrastructure. This model supports a fully pay-as-you-go model. SaaS provides facility for access and control of commercial software via Internet. Examples of SaaS are Google Apps, SalesForce, Learn.com etc. Table 10.1 shows the advantages of traditional software with SaaS.

Table 10.1: Comparison of Traditional Software with SaaS

Traditional Software	SaaS
Customers install, manage and maintain.	Customers use over the Internet.
Runs on individual organization on dedicated instantiation.	Runs on multiple customers simultaneously.
Cross platform support required.	No concerns for cross platform support.
Less frequent version updates and updates purchased separately.	More frequent updates for enhanced user satisfaction.
Separate costs incurred for upgrades.	No separate cost for the upgrades.
Vulnerable to software piracy.	Less vulnerable to software piracy.

Essential Characteristics

- Scalability – This is to maximize application concurrency and to optimize the shared pool of resources such as threads and network connections.
- Multi-tenancy – This is an important architectural shift from designing isolated, single tenant applications. SaaS has the ability to accommodate users from multiple companies at the same time and transparency to all users. SaaS maximize the sharing of resources across tenants while distinguishing user's individual data.
- Configurability – This is to facilitate parallel allocation of a single application on a single server to several users. To customize the application for one customer will change the application for other customers as well. Separate data space is allocated for different users.

Advantages and Disadvantages of SaaS

SaaS (Advantages)

- The most cost effective Cloud service as we only lease the software and not the resource.
- SaaS requires minimal planning and is easy to setup, as applications are usually simple in usage and readymade.

- Rapid deployment as the software is fully provisioned on demand.
- The customer does not need to worry about the management of applications, as this is all handled by the provider.
- Software is usually very stable, as it is supported by the Cloud provider's large infrastructure and IT team.

SaaS (Disadvantages)

- The customer has no control over the system processing its data.
- There is no control over which customers use the software. The software is used by a large amount of users. An example of SaaS would be Dropbox.
- Little or no control over the parameters of software.
- Little control over deployment, upgrade and testing methodology (e.g. Dev, UAT, Live systems availability)
- Currently only a limited number of software solutions are offered in the form of SaaS.
- Integration with other software on any other systems is either difficult or unsupported (e.g. single sign-on)
- Cloud provider has full access to customers' data, unless cryptography is used. But this would mean no processing could be done on the Cloud thus reducing the usefulness of the Cloud.

Figure 10.11 shows a comparison of different service models and traditional software.

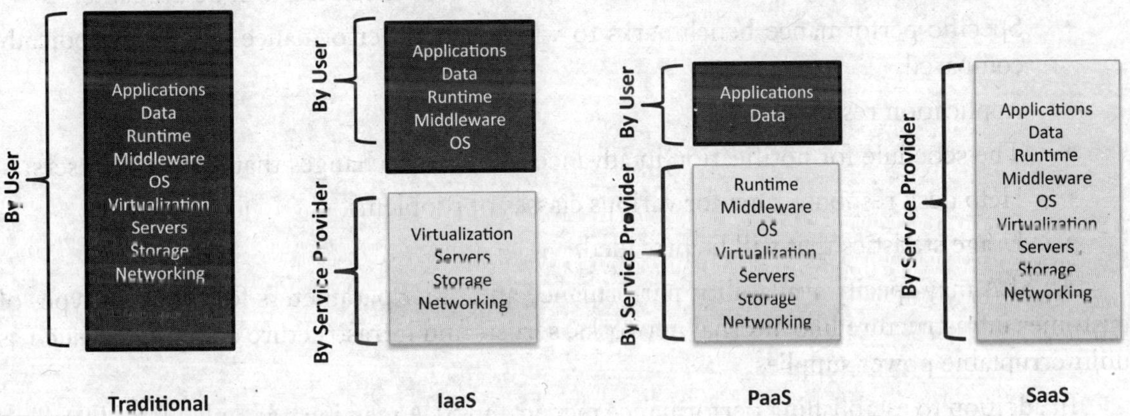

Fig.10.11: Comparison of Traditional Software and Service Models

10.6 Service Management

For effective administration of all the elements associated with cloud service delivery, cloud service management and cloud monitoring tools enable providers to keep up with the continually shifting capacity demands of a highly elastic environment.

Cloud monitoring and cloud service management tools allow cloud providers to ensure optimal performance, continuity and efficiency in virtualized, on-demand environments. These tools or software that manages and monitors networks, systems and applications enable cloud providers not just to guarantee performance, but also to better orchestrate and automate provisioning of resources.

Cloud monitoring tools specifically enable cloud providers to track the performance, continuity and security of all of the components that support service delivery: the hardware, software and services in the data center and throughout the network infrastructure. Through successful cloud service management and monitoring, cloud providers can use service quality to differentiate themselves. Effective cloud service management also helps lower the risk of frequent cloud outages that can jeopardize security systems. Using these tools also supports greater operational efficiency, helping cloud providers minimize costs and maximize profit margins. However, achieving these goals can be difficult in a complex virtual delivery environment where visibility and control are limited.

10.6.1 Service Level Agreement

A service-level agreement (SLA) is a contract between a service provider and its internal or external customers that documents what services the provider will furnish and defines the performance standards the provider is obligated to meet. SLAs establish customer expectations with regard to the service provider's performance and quality in a number of ways. Some metrics that SLAs may specify include:

- Availability and uptime -- the percentage of the time services will be available.
- Specific performance benchmarks to which actual performance will be periodically compared.
- Application response time.
- The schedule for notification in advance of network changes that may affect users.
- Help desk response time for various classes of problems.
- Usage statistics that will be provided.

An SLA may specify availability, performance and other parameters for different types of customer infrastructure like internal networks, servers and infrastructure components such as uninterruptable power supplies.

In addition to establishing performance metrics, an SLA may include a plan for addressing downtime and documentation for how the service provider will compensate customers in the event of a contract breach. Service credits are a typical remedy. Here, the service provider issues credits to the customer based on an SLA-specified calculation. Service providers, for example, might provide credits commensurate with the amount of time it exceeded the SLA's performance guarantee. The SLA will also include a section detailing exclusions, that is, situations in which an SLA's guarantees and penalties for failing to meet them don't apply. The list might include events such as natural disasters or terrorist acts.

10.6.2 Accounting and Billing

Service accounting aims to obtain resource usage information typically in the form of records. It depends on infrastructure and service monitoring as usage information is obtained from metric measurements. Service provider calculates billing information using accounting records, resource prices and billing rules.

IaaS Billing and Metering Services

The primary concept of IaaS includes the following.

- Servers per hour serving an on-demand model.
- Reserved servers for better planning.
- Higher and lower compute resource units based on application performance.
- Volume-based metering on the number of instances consumed.
- Prepaid and reserved infrastructure resources.
- Clustered server resources.

The billing for most of these elements is on a per-month basis, where each server is decommissioned and returned within a few minutes as initially provisioned. Billing charges accrued over the whole month include instances of servers running for the complete 30 days as well as servers running only up to one minute. Each compute cycle is charged a complete hour regardless of whether it ran for one minute or one hour.

The advanced billing and planning with reserved instances enables lower monthly as well as hourly costs to make compute resource models with known usage patterns and established baselines available as needed. In a model where servers are reserved in advance, an initial investment is required to secure specific servers in certain areas to minimize the hourly usage of virtual machines (VMs). In some cases, the initial investment can reduce the hourly price by up to 50 percent.

In most cases, scaling back instances during non-peak hours and scaling up during peak hours or seasons help to improve availability and response times. In general, if applications are tuned correctly, we would achieve a transaction per second rate that can scale horizontally with the number of servers added to the cloud computing infrastructure. The only concern is third-party resources that are not scaled with the infrastructure exponentially—for example, the database, authentication services and other services that the scalable infrastructure accesses.

At a certain number of started servers, a discount occurs because of the large volume of virtual servers running—for example, when we reserve 100 VMs. This bulk discount helps the cloud computing provider plan for capacity demands and therefore minimizes the cost and risk of on-demand instances. Similarly, prepaid instances help the cloud computing provider estimate capacity and minimize the on-demand risk of running out of resources or sitting on too many unused instances. Discounts and usage often expire if the resources are not consumed within a certain amount of time. For instance, prepaid instances could be used for the baseline computing resource (a web server for the corporate intranet that is outward facing).

In larger deployments, starting and stopping instances and being billed by cluster utilization consolidates cost and management of IaaS. Because the management of single servers and resource utilization increase with enterprise applications, billing by cluster possibly including custom resources such as routers and other devices and services helps to reduce cost for management.

PaaS Billing and Metering Services

Platform as a Service (PaaS) billing and metering are determined by actual usage, as platforms differ in aggregate and instance-level usage measures. Actual usage billing enables PaaS providers to run application code from multiple tenants across the same set of hardware depending on the granularity of usage monitoring. For example, the network bandwidth, CPU utilization, and disk usage per transaction or application can determine PaaS cost.

The primary concepts for PaaS metering and billing include:

- Incoming and outgoing network bandwidth.
- CPU time per hour.
- Stored data.
- High availability.
- Monthly service charge.

The bandwidth of incoming and outgoing network traffic determines the usage per user and creates a metric for billing and metering. The bandwidth metric is helpful, because web applications can be larger depending on their content. For instance, for most web services that return RESTful payloads, the number of rows may not be significant compared to transactions that include pictures, video and audio media.

Transaction and HTTP request metering based on CPU time per hour, minute, or second is the most accurate billing and metering model, as each transaction can be measured for total cost. Because you can't pin-point which transaction user is consuming a given amount of CPU resources per request, it's difficult to allocate resources at the user level. Therefore, a simple and effective measure for billing and metering is to determine the amount of stored data the user is consuming. Doing so helps in capacity planning, billing, and metering for services such as storage as a service, where data is stored in larger amounts on servers across the infrastructure. In such a case, a billing model based on gigabytes used determines what the costs of the service per month will be.

As in any enterprise application, the quality of service doubles (in most cases) the investment and price of implementation—sometimes more than double, because the infrastructure is replicated and includes additional infrastructure items to support high availability. High-availability billing and metering enables improved quality of service based on actual demand in cases where demand can be anticipated.

Advanced platforms that have a limited instance-level ability to provide metering and billing often opt to provide generalized billing models in which there is a flat fee to run application code. Such platforms typically include requirements for secure code that doesn't have long-running, CPU-consuming transactions as well as other, built-in security measures to curb utilization on the infrastructure. For example, a platform in which application code is deployed as a file and the underlining run time is provided with enhanced security measures and scalability by the platform as a service provider.

SaaS billing and Metering Services

The traditional concept for billing and metering SaaS applications is a monthly fixed cost. In some cases, depending on the amount of data, the billing and pricing are optimized. The number of users is determined by the number of users the organization allows to access the SaaS applications, which increases the price of the monthly fee. In some cases, if certain volumes are met, there is a discount. For instance, sales software provided as a service would cost US$50 per month per sales agent for a company using the application.

The primary concepts for SaaS billing and metering include:

- Monthly subscription fees.
- Per-user monthly fees.

The monthly subscription fee is a fixed cost billed per month, often for a minimum contracted length of agreement of one year. The billing model per month changes the high initial investment from a software capital cost to a monthly operational expense. This model is especially appealing to small and medium-sized organizations to help them get started with the software required for their business initiatives. Scalability, or pay-as-you-grow models, are helpful for organizations that start with a small initial investment and a few users and grow as demand grows. In some cases, these organizations can scale down while providing access to the same data.

10.6.3 Benefits of Scaling

Traditional data centers have heterogeneous hardware, networked computing and a remote server whereas Cloud computing has a virtual hosting solution involving heterogeneous hardware, software and networks on the Cloud. Cloud computing economics depends on four customer population metrics.

1. Number of Unique Customer Sets (n)
2. Customer Set Duty Cycles (λ,f)
3. Relative Duty Cycle Displacement (t)
4. Customer Set Load (L)

These metrics drive the cloud provider's ability to use the minimum amount of physical IT resources to service a maximum level of IT resource demand. Properly balancing these factors across a well characterized user group can lead to approximately 30-percent savings in IT resources and enables the near real-time modification of the underlying physical infrastructure required for the delivery of the desired illusion of infinite resources synonymous with a cloud computing user's experience.

Cloud computing provides some strong benefits and economic incentives. Selecting a public, private, hybrid or community cloud implementation will depend on a customer's specific application, performance, security and compliance requirements. Proper deployment can provide significant savings, better IT services and a higher level of reliability. Following are some economic incentives.

- Lower cost.
- Capital expenditure free computing.
- Deploy projects faster, foster innovation.
- Scale as needed.
- Lower maintenance costs.
- Resiliency and redundancy.

10.7 Cloud Security

Public cloud computing requires a security model that coordinates scalability and multi-tenancy with the requirement for trust. As enterprises move their computing environments with their identities, information and infrastructure to the cloud, they must be willing to give up some level of control. In order to do so they must be able to trust cloud systems and providers, as well as to verify cloud processes and events. Important building blocks of trust and verification relationships include access control, data security, compliance and event management - all security elements well understood by IT departments today, implemented with existing products and technologies and extendable into the cloud. The cloud security principles comprise three categories: identity, information and infrastructure.

The security concerns are loss of data, account seizing, service traffic hindrance and vulnerable APIs. The solution for cloud security is the protection from theft, leakage and deletion by providing secure policies.

The foundational infrastructure for a cloud must be inherently secure whether it is a private or public cloud or whether the service is SaaS, PaaS or IaaS. The infrastructure security can be viewed, assessed and implemented according to its building levels - the network, host and application levels.

10.7.1 Network Level Security

When looking at the network level of infrastructure security, it is important to distinguish between public clouds and private clouds. With private clouds, there are no new attacks, vulnerabilities or changes in risk specific to this topology that information security personnel need to consider. If public cloud services are chosen, changing security requirements will require changes to the network topology and the manner in which the existing network topology interacts with the cloud provider's network topology should be taken into account. There are four significant risk factors in this use case:

- Ensuring confidentiality and integrity of organization's data-in-transit to and from a public cloud provider.
- Ensuring proper access control (authentication, authorization, and auditing) to whatever resources are used at the public cloud provider.
- Ensuring the availability of Internet-facing resources in a public cloud that are being used by an organization or have been assigned to an organization by public cloud providers.
- Replacing the established model of network zones and tiers with domains.

10.7.2 Host Level Security

When reviewing host security and assessing risks, the context of cloud services delivery models (SaaS, PaaS, and IaaS) and deployment models public, private and hybrid) should be considered. Host security at PaaS and SaaS involves hiding the operating system from end-users. The host security responsibilities in SaaS and PaaS services are transferred to the provider of cloud services. IaaS customers are primarily responsible for securing the hosts provisioned in the cloud (virtualization software security, customer guest OS or virtual server security). Example of threat for IaaS customers is the attack on hypervisors.

10.7.3 Application Level Security

Application or software security should be a critical element of a security program. Most enterprises with information security programs have yet to institute an application security program to address this realm. Designing and implementing applications aims at deployment on a cloud platform will require existing application security programs to reevaluate current practices and standards. The application security spectrum ranges from standalone single-user applications to sophisticated multiuser e-commerce applications used by many users. The level is responsible for managing

- Application-level security threats.
- End user security.
- SaaS application security.
- PaaS application security.
- Customer-deployed application security.
- IaaS application security.

10.7.4 Data Security

In cloud, data security includes data privacy, data protection, data availability, data location, and secure transmission. The security challenges in the cloud include threats, data loss, service disruption and outside malicious attacks. Data security issues are primarily at SaaS, PaaS and IaaS level and the major challenge in cloud computing is data sharing. The objective of data security is to achieve confidentiality, integrity and availability. This can be achieved through identity management, encryption and access control.

Identity and Access Management (IAM) is a branch of cloud security that allows the legitimate persons to retrieve the legitimate resources at the legitimate time for the legitimate reasons. User identities and access permissions are instigated, caught, administered and recorded by IAM. Authentication, authorization and evaluation of all users are done according to the role, terms and conditions for the users. Features of IAM includes single access control interface, increased security, access control over resource level, improvement of operational efficiency and improvement of regulatory compliance management.

Access control layers in cloud include cloud access, server access, service access, database access, VM access and access to objects within a VM. Management of these layers depends on provider or consumer based on the deployment model.

Trust and reputation are needed by the customer to select appropriate cloud provider. Trust is the independent expectancy between two entities for any specific context at a given time. Reputation is the belief of an entity's standing by the community. Different modes of trust establishment include accomplishment of service level agreement, application of audit standards, measuring and ratings and questionnaires for self-assessment.

User authentication process is done between new users and service providers. During authentication, the properties and safety of process can be invaded by attack causing severe damages. User authentication is done at PaaS layer. Threat to authentication process can lead to divulge of confidential data to a fake user.

10.8 Conclusion

This Chapter gives a detailed description of Cloud computing. The architecture of Cloud computing and the characteristics of Cloud computing are well explained. Different Cloud deployment models like public cloud, private cloud, hybrid cloud, community cloud, multi-cloud, distributed cloud, inter-cloud, big data cloud and HPC Cloud are described in detail. The Cloud service models like Infrastructure-as-a-Service (IaaS), Platform-as-a-Service (PaaS) and Software-as-a-Service (SaaS) is well explained. Service management which includes service level agreement, accounting and billing and benefits of scaling is also covered in this Chapter. Finally the Cloud security which includes network level security, host level security, application level security and data security is also explained.

11 SENSOR CLOUD

11.1 Introduction

The advancement and application of Wireless Sensor Networks become an invincible trend into the various industrial, environmental and commercial fields. A typical sensor network may consist of a number of sensor nodes acting upon together to monitor a region and fetch data about the surroundings. A WSN contains spatially distributed self-regulated sensors that can cooperatively monitor the environmental conditions like sound, temperature, pressure, motion, vibration, pollution and so forth. Each node in a sensor network is loaded with a radio transceiver or some other wireless communication device, a small microcontroller and an energy source most often cells or battery. The nodes of sensor network have cooperative capabilities, which are usually deployed in a random manner. These sensor nodes basically consist of three parts: sensing, processing and communication. Some of the most common sensor devices deployed in sensor network as sensor nodes are camera sensor, accelerometer sensor, thermal sensor, microphone sensor and so forth.

Currently, WSNs are being utilized in several areas like healthcare, defense such as military target tracking and surveillance, government and environmental services like natural disaster relief, hazardous environment exploration, seismic sensing and so forth. These sensors may provide various useful data when they are closely attached to each of their respective applications and services directly. However, sensor networks have to face many issues and challenges regarding their communications like short communication range, security and privacy, reliability, mobility, etc. and resources like power considerations, storage capacity, processing capabilities, bandwidth availability, etc. Besides, WSN has its own resource and design constraints. Design constraints are application specific and dependent on monitored environment. Based on the monitored environment, network size in WSN varies. For monitoring a small area, fewer nodes are required to form a network whereas the coverage of a very large area requires a huge number of sensor nodes. For monitoring large environment, there is limited communication between nodes due to obstructions into the environment, which in turn affects the overall network topology or connectivity. All these limitations on sensor networks would probably impede the service performance and quality. In the midst of these issues, the emergence of cloud computing is seen as a remedy.

In a sensor network, the sensors are utilized by their specific application for a special purpose, and this application handles both the sensor data and the sensor itself such that other applications cannot use this. This makes wastage of valuable sensor resources that may be effectively utilized when integrating with other application's infrastructure. To realize this scenario, Sensor-Cloud infrastructure is used that enables the sensors to be utilized on an IT infrastructure by virtualizing the physical sensor on a cloud computing platform. These virtualized sensors on a cloud computing platform are dynamic in nature and hence facilitate automatic provisioning of its services as and when required by users. Furthermore, users need not worry about the physical locations of multiple physical sensors and the gapping between physical sensors. Instead, they can supervise these virtual sensors using some standard functions.

Within the Sensor-Cloud infrastructure, to obtain QoS, the virtual sensors are monitored regularly so users can destroy their virtual sensors when they become meaningless. A user interface is provisioned by this Sensor-Cloud infrastructure for administering, that is, for controlling or monitoring the virtual sensors, provisioning and destroying virtual sensors, registering and deleting of physical sensors and for admitting the deleting users. For example, in a health monitoring environment, a patient may use a wearable computing system that may include wearable accelerometer sensors, proximity sensors, temperature sensors, etc. like Life Shirt and Smart Shirt or may use a handheld device loaded with sensors and consequently the data captured by the sensors may be made accessible to the doctors. But out of these computing systems, active continuous monitoring is most demanding, and it involves the patient wearing monitoring devices to obtain pervasive coverage without being inputted or intervened.

Sensor modeling language (SML) can be used to represent any physical sensor's metadata like their type, accuracy, physical location and so forth. It also uses Extensible Markup Language (XML) encoding for the measurement and description processes of physical sensors. This XML encoding for physical sensors enabled these to be implemented across several different hardware, platforms (OS), applications and so forth with relatively less human intervention. To transliterate the commands coming from users to virtual sensors and in turn to the commands for their pertinent physical sensors, a mapping is done between the physical and virtual sensors.

11.2 Comparison with WSN

In a traditional WSN, there is only one single user. Data is aggregated and sent to the WSN user. At the device level, the device is dedicated to a single user. But in a sensor cloud, the benefits can be reaped by multiple users or applications. Data aggregation in sensor cloud is taken care by the sensor-cloud infrastructure. Nodes in sensor cloud can serve multiple applications. Figure 11.1 shows the comparison of WSN with sensor cloud.

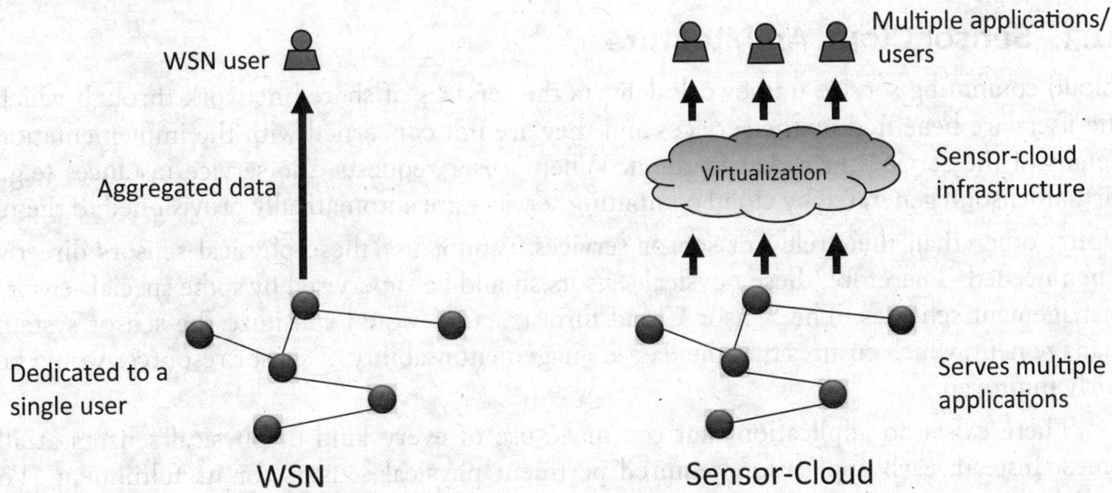

Fig.11.1: Comparison of WSN with Sensor Cloud

In a sensor cloud there is more than one actor and multiple roles. Various actors in Sensor Cloud are end users, sensor owner and Sensor Cloud Service Provider (SCSP). End users enjoy Sensor-as-a-Service (Se-aaS) through applications as per the requirements. The end users are unknown about what and which physical sensor is allocated to serve the application. Sensor owner plays a role from business perspective. They purchase physical sensor devices deployed over different geographical locations and lend these devices to the sensor cloud. Sensor Cloud Sensor Provider (SCSP) is a business actor. SCSP charges from the end users as per their usage of Se-aaS.

In traditional WSN, all attributes like ownership, deployment, redeployment, maintenances, overhead and usage are managed by the WSN users. In Sensor Cloud, the redeployment, maintenances and overhead are managed by SCSP while ownership and deployment are managed by sensor owner and usage by end users. Figure 11.2 shows a comparison of attributes in WSN with Sensor Cloud.

Actors and Roles		
Attributes	**WSN**	**Sensor Cloud**
Ownership	WSN-user	Sensor-owner
Deployment	WSN-user	Sensor-owner
Redeployment	WSN-user	SCSP
Maintenances	WSN-user	SCSP
Overhead	WSN-user	SCSP
Usage	WSN-user	End-user

Fig.11.2: Comparison of WSN and Sensor Cloud

11.3 Sensor Cloud Architecture

Cloud computing service framework delivers the services of shared network through which the users are benefited by the services and they are not concerned with the implementation details of the services provided to them. When a user requests, the service instances (e.g., virtual sensors) generated by cloud computing services are automatically provisioned to them. Users, other than their relevant sensor services, cannot use these physical sensors directly when needed. Therefore, these physical sensors should be supervised by some special sensor-management schemes. The Sensor Cloud infrastructure would subsidize the sensor system management, which ensures that the data-management usability of sensor resources would be fairly improved.

There exists no application that can make use of every kind of physical sensors at all times. Instead, each application required pertinent physical sensors for its fulfillment. To realize this concept, publish/subscription mechanism is being employed for choosing the appropriate physical sensor. In multiple sensor networks, every sensor network publishes its sensor data and metadata. The metadata comprises of the types, locations and so forth for the physical sensors. Application either subscribes to one or maybe to more sensor networks to retrieve real-time data from the physical sensors by allowing each application to opt for the appropriate physical sensors' type. The Sensor Cloud infrastructure procreates virtual sensors from multiple physical sensors, which can then be utilized by users. However, prior to availing the virtual sensor facility, users should probe first for the physical sensor's availability and might also inspect the physical sensor's faults to maintain the data quality emerging from these physical sensors. Also on every sensor node, application program senses the application and sends the sensor data back to the gateway in the cloud directly through the base station or in multihop manner through other nodes.

Sensor Cloud infrastructure provides service instances (virtual sensors) automatically to the end users as and when requested, in such a way that these virtual sensors are part of their IT resources (like disk storage, CPU, memory, etc.). These service instances and their associated appropriate sensor data can be used by the end users via a user interface through the web crawlers. Figure 11.3 shows the architecture of Sensor Cloud.

For the service instance generation, the IT resources (like CPU, storage devices, etc.), sensor capable devices and service templates (which is used to create virtual sensors) should be prepared first in Sensor Cloud infrastructure. Users make the request for service instances according to their needs by selecting an appropriate service template of Sensor Cloud, which will then provide the needed service instances freely and automatically because of cloud computing services integration. Once service instances become useless, they can then be deleted quickly by users to avoid the utilization charges for these resources. Sensor service provider will manage the service templates (ST) and it can add or delete the new service template when the required template is no longer needed by applications and services. Automation of services plays a vital role in provisioning of cloud computing services and automation can cause the delivery time of services to be better. Before the emergence of cloud computing, services were provided by human influence and the performance metrics like efficiency, flexibility, delivery times and so forth would have experienced an adverse effect on the system. However, the cloud computing service model has reduced the cost expenses and delivery time and has also improved the efficiency and flexibility.

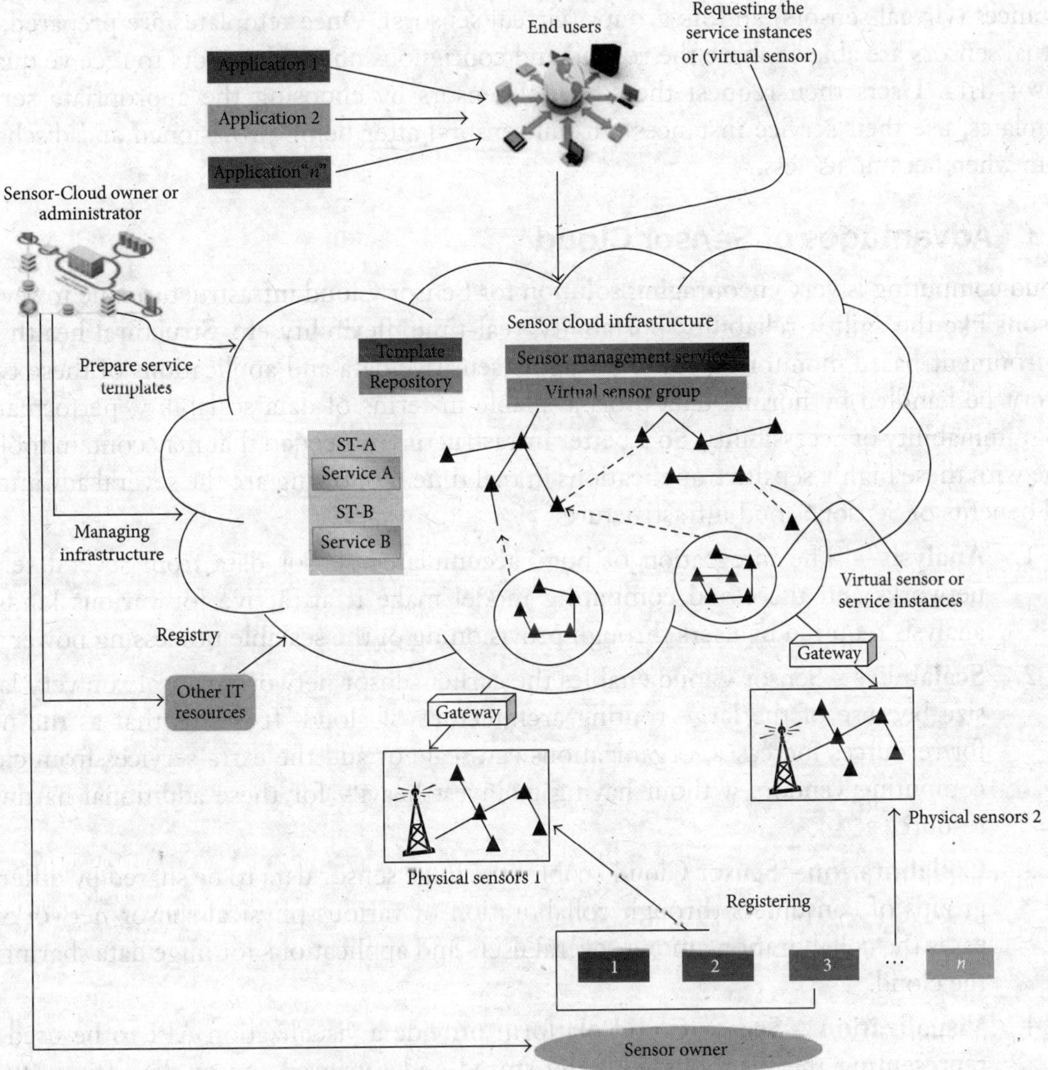

Fig.11.3: Architecture of Sensor Cloud

The physical sensors are ranked on a basis of their sensor readings as well as on their actual distance from an event. Since the cloud computing enables the physical sensors to be virtualized, the users of the Sensor Cloud infrastructure need not worry about the status of their connected physical sensors (i.e., whether a fault free or not). However, they should concern only with the status of their virtual sensors provided only when the users are not concerned with the accurate results. To achieve accurate results, users must be concerned about the status of physical sensors too. In a Sensor Cloud infrastructure, sensor owners are free to register or unregister their physical sensors and can join this infrastructure. These IT resources (physical sensors, database servers, processors, etc.) and sensor devices are then prepared to become operational. After that, templates are created for generating the service instances (virtual sensors) and its groups (virtual sensors). Once templates are prepared, the virtual sensors are able to share the related and contiguous physical sensors to receive quality sensor data. Users then request these virtual sensors by choosing the appropriate service templates, use their service instances (virtual sensors) after being provisioned and discharge them when became useless.

11.4 Advantages of Sensor Cloud

Cloud computing is very encouraging solution for Sensor Cloud infrastructure due to several reasons like the agility, reliability, portability, real-time, flexibility etc. Structural health and environment-based monitoring contains highly sensitive data and applications of these types cannot be handled by normal data tools available in terms of data scalability, performance, programmability or accessibility. So a better infrastructure is needed that may contain tools to cope with these highly sensitive applications in real time. Following are the several advantages and benefits of Sensor Cloud infrastructure.

1. **Analysis** – The integration of huge accumulated sensor data from several sensor networks and the cloud computing model make it attractive for various kinds of analysis required by users through provisioning of the scalable processing power.
2. **Scalability** – Sensor Cloud enables the earlier sensor networks to scale on very large size because of the large routing architecture of cloud. It means that as the need for resources increases, organizations can scale or add the extra services from cloud computing vendors without having to invest heavily for these additional hardware resources.
3. **Collaboration** – Sensor Cloud enables the huge sensor data to be shared by different groups of consumers through collaboration of various physical sensor networks. It eases the collaboration among several users and applications for huge data sharing on the cloud.
4. **Visualization** – Sensor Cloud platform provide a visualization API to be used for representing the diagrams with the stored and retrieved sensor data from several device assets. Through the visualization tools, users can predict the possible future trends that have to be incurred.
5. **Free Provisioning of Increased Data storage and Processing Power** - It provides free data storage and organizations may put their data rather than putting onto private computer systems without hassle. It provides enormous processing facility and storage resources to handle data of large-scale applications.

6. **Dynamic Provisioning of Services** – Users of Sensor Cloud can access their relevant information from wherever they want and whenever they need rather than being stick to their desks.
7. **Multitenancy** – The number of services from several service providers can be integrated easily through cloud and Internet for numerous service innovations to meet user's demand. Sensor Cloud allows the accessibility to several numbers of data centers placed anywhere on the network world.
8. **Automation** – Automation played a vital role in provisioning of Sensor Cloud computing services. Automation of services improved the delivery time to a great extent.
9. **Flexibility** – Sensor Cloud provides more flexibility to its users than the past computing methods. It provides flexibility to use random applications in any number of times and allows sharing of sensor resources under flexible usage environment.
10. **Agility of Services** – Sensor Cloud provides agile services and the users can provision the expensive technological infrastructure resources with less cost. The integration of Wireless Sensor Networks with cloud allows the high-speed processing of data using immense processing capability of cloud.
11. **Resource Optimization** – Sensor Cloud infrastructure enables the resource optimization by allowing the sharing of resources for several number of applications. The integration of sensors with cloud enables gradual reduction of resource cost and achieves higher gains of services. With Sensor-Cloud, both the small and midsized organizations can benefit from an enormous resource infrastructure without having to involve and administer it directly.
12. **Quick Response Time** – The integration of WSN with cloud provides a very quick response to the user, that is, in real-time due to the large routing architecture of cloud. The quick response time of data feeds from several sensor networks or devices allows users to make critical decisions in near real time.

11.5 Sensor Cloud Service Life Cycle Model

The Sensor Cloud service life-cycle model is illustrated in this section. Figure 11.4 depicts the Sensor-Cloud service life cycle. The users of the sensors can select the appropriate service template and request the required service instances. These service instances are provided automatically and freely to the users, which can then be deleted quickly when they become useless. From a single service template, multiple numbers of service instances can be created. Service provider regulates the service templates and can add new service templates as and when required by a different number of users.

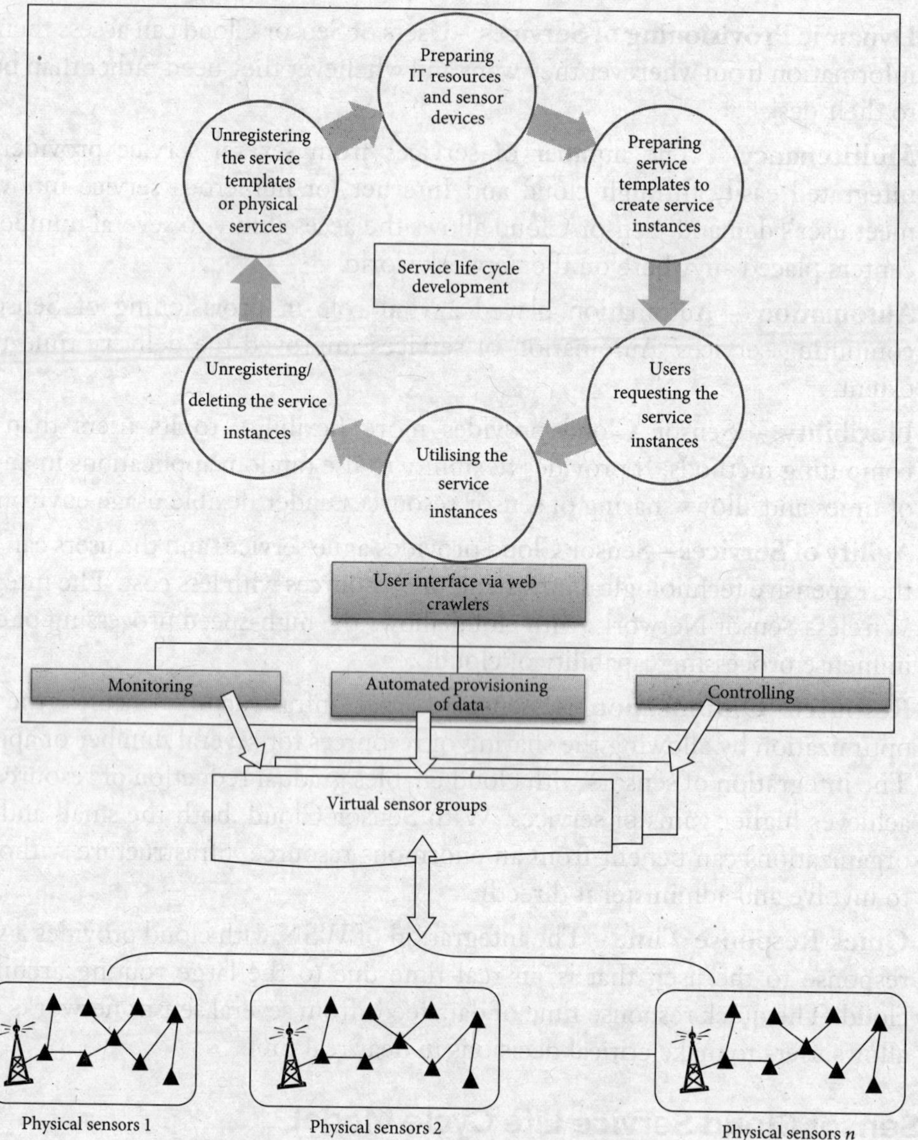

Fig.11.4: Sensor Cloud Service Life Cycle

Before creating the service instances within Sensor Cloud infrastructure, preparation phase is needed which includes (1) Preparing the IT resources (processors, storage, disk, memory etc.) (2) Preparing the physical sensor devices (3) Preparing the service templates.

11.6 Sensor Cloud Layered Structure

Figure 11.5 depicts the layered architecture of the Sensor Cloud platform, which is divided mainly into three layers: (1) User and application layers (2) Sensor Cloud and virtualization layers (3) Template creation and tangible sensor layers.

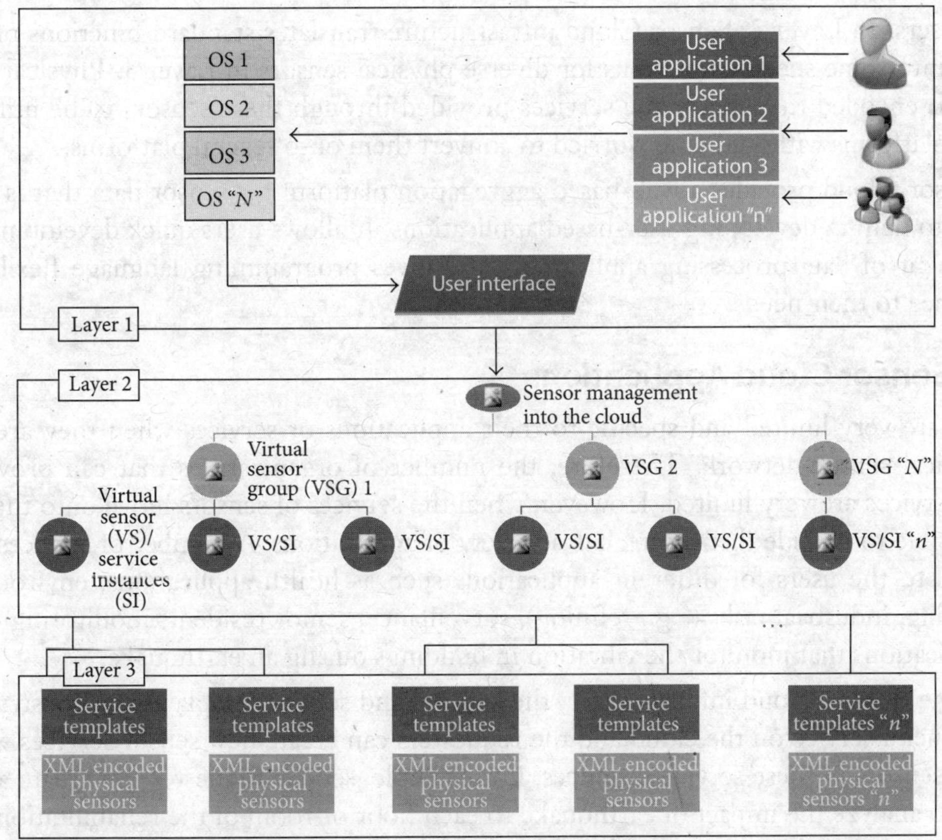

Fig.11.5: Layered Architecture of Sensor Cloud Platform

Layer 1 - This layer deals with the users and their relevant applications. Several users want to access the valuable sensor data from different OS platforms, such as mobile phones OS, Windows OS, or Mac OS for a variety of applications. This structure allows users of different platforms to access and utilize the sensor data without facing any problem because of the high availability of cloud infrastructure and storage.

Layer 2 - This layer deals with virtualization of the physical sensors and resources in the cloud. The virtualization enables the provisioning of cloud-based sensor services and other IT resources remotely to the end-user without being worried about the sensor's exact locations. The virtualized sensors are created by using the service templates automatically. Service templates are prepared by the service providers as service catalog and this catalog enables the creation of service instances automatically that are accessed by multiple users.

Layer 3 - This is the last layer which deals with the service template creation and service catalog definition layers in forming catalog menu. Physical sensors are located and retrieved from this layer. Since each physical sensor has its own control and data collection mechanism, standard mechanisms are defined and used to access sensors without concerning the differences among various physical sensors. Standard functions are defined to access the virtual sensors by the users. In Layer 2, Sensor Cloud infrastructure translates standard functions of virtual sensors into some specific functions for diverse physical sensors in Layer 3. Physical sensors are XML encoded that enable the services provided through these sensors to be utilized on various platforms without being worried to convert them onto several platforms.

Sensor Cloud provides a web-based aggregation platform for sensor data that is flexible enough to help in developing user-based applications. It allows users quick development and deployment of data processing applications and gives programming language flexibility in accordance to their needs.

11.7 Sensor Cloud Applications

Sensors are very limited and specific to their applications or services when they are linked to a typical sensor network. Therefore, the number of organizations that can provide the sensor services are very limited. However, when the services of sensors move onto the cloud, it is possible to include them to realize a variety of applications. A number of services can be provided to the users for different applications such as health applications, environmental monitoring, industrial tasks (e.g., refining), surveillance, senior residents monitoring or even the applications that monitor the vibration in buildings during an earthquake.

In the Sensor Cloud infrastructure, the sensors and service templates are constructed as catalog menu service on the cloud and the requesters can create new sensor services with the existing sensors in these service instances. For example, service requester can create a sensor service to analyze the impact of earthquake to each floor or room of the rehabilitation center or hospital, and at the same time it can also create sensor services to support older residents with the same set of sensors (virtualized sensors). This service will then help the caregiver to shift the older adults one by one into a safe place. Using the identical sensor services for healthcare, another service requester can create dissimilar sensor service to track the patient's medicine intake and then to analyze the effectiveness of pills through the use of some selected healthcare sensors. Thus, the service requesters can be provided with new services using the same set of sensors on cloud service platforms. This will reduce the cost for resource usage and could have numerous elastic merits to it. Various Sensor Cloud applications that exist are given below.

1. **Nimbits** - Nimbits is a free and social service that is used to record and share sensor data on cloud. It is a cloud-based data processing service and is an open-source platform for the IoT (Internet of Things). We can feed the versatile numeric, text-based, JSON, GPS, or XML values by creating a data point in the cloud. The data points can be connected to Scalable Vector Graphic (SVG) process control, spreadsheets, diagrams, websites and more. Data points can also be configured to generate alerts data-relay to social networks and to perform calculations. Nimbits also provide an alert management mechanism, data compression mechanism and data calculation on received sensor data by employing some simple mathematical formulas.

2. **Pachube Platform** - Pachube is one of the first online database service providers, which allows us to connect sensor data to the web. It is a real-time cloud-based platform for IoT with a scalable infrastructure that enables us to configure IoT products and services, store, share and discover real-time energy, environment and healthcare sensor data from devices and buildings around us. Pachube has a very interactive website for managing the sensor data and an open easily-accessible API. Pachube system provides free usage and has several number of interfaces for producing a sensor or mobile-based application for managing the sensor data within a cloud framework anytime.
3. **IDigi** - IDigi is a machine-to-machine (M2M) Platform as a Service (PaaS) that minimizes the barriers to build scalable, secure and cost-effective solutions, which can bind the enterprise applications and device assets together. IDigi eases the connectivity of remote assets devices and provides all the tools to manage, store, connect and move the information across the enterprise irrespective of its reach. To simplify the remote device connectivity and integration, it uses connector software called IDigi Dia. Regardless of the network location, IDigi platform manages communication between remote device assets and enterprise applications.
4. **ThingSpeak** - ThingSpeak is another open source IoT application and has an open API to store and retrieve data from device assets or things via LAN or using HTTP over the Internet. With this platform, location tracking applications, sensor logging applications and social network of device assets with proper update of its status can be created. ThingSpeak allows numeric data processing like averaging, time-scaling, rounding, median, summing and so forth to store and retrieve the numeric and alphanumeric data. ThingSpeak application features a JavaScript-based chart, read/write API key management and a time-zone management.

Although the above services are able to visualize the sensor data and sensor-driven information, they are lacking secure access to data and interface availability for linking the external or mobile applications for further processing. It means that most of these aforementioned projects do not address the issues of data management and interoperability issues caused by heterogeneous data resources found in the present modern environmental tracking or electronic healthcare systems. But introducing these aforementioned works with Cloud computing infrastructure may overcome the issues related to heterogeneous data access and data management functionality. There are many other applications that are emerging based on the Sensor-Cloud infrastructure, which can be summarized as follows.

1. **Ubiquitous Healthcare Monitoring** - Sensor Clouds can be used for health monitoring by using a number of easily available and most often wearable sensors like accelerometer sensors, proximity, ambient light and temperature sensors and so forth to collect patient's health-related data for tracking sleep activity pattern, blood sugar, body temperature and other respiratory conditions. These wearable sensor devices must have support of BWI (Bluetooth's Wireless Interface), UWB (Ultra Wide Band)

and so forth interface for streaming of data and are connected wirelessly to any smart phone through this interface. These smart phone devices pretend to function like a gateway between the remote server and sensor through the Internet, maybe GPRS/ Wi-Fi or other sort of gateways.

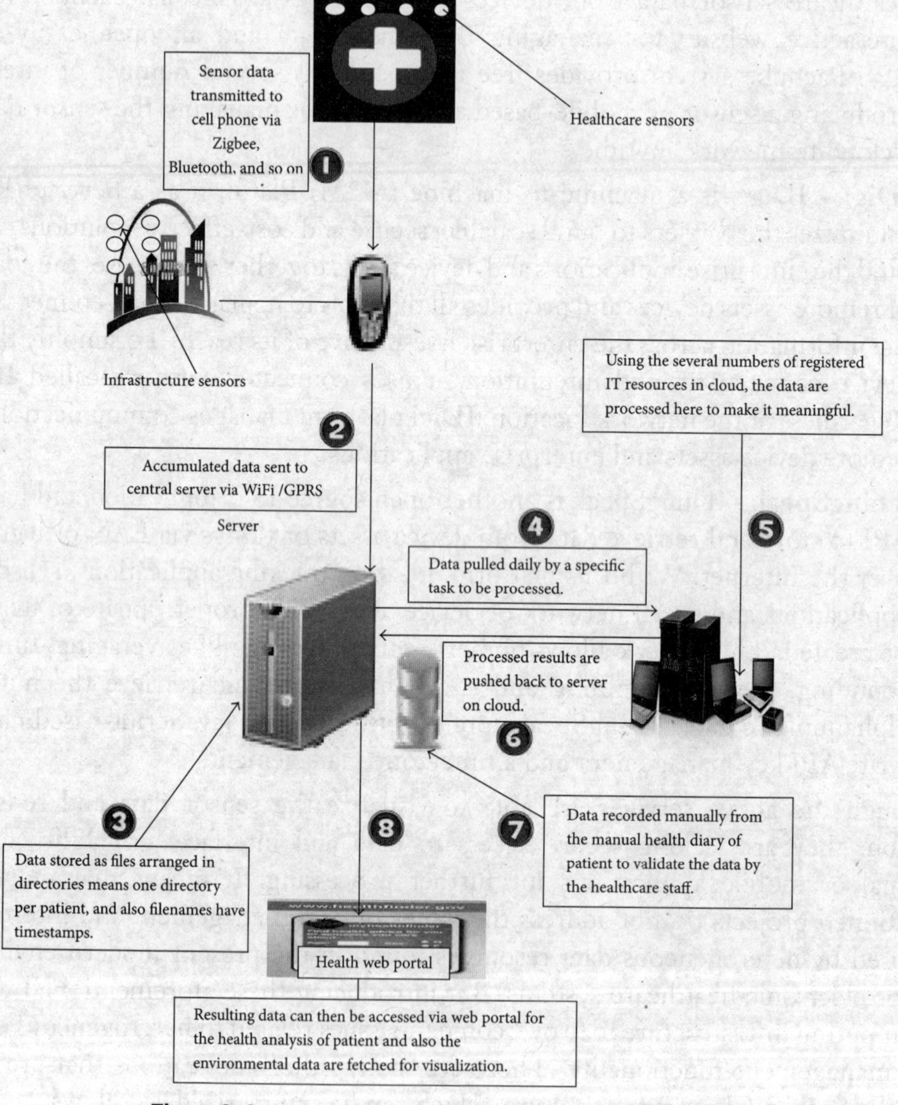

Fig.11.6: Sensor-Cloud Implementation in Healthcare

To transform this system into services-based structure, web-services-based interfaces are used by smart phone device to connect to the server. The system prototype should have made to be robust, mobile and scalable. Robust in the sense means that it should recover itself from circumstances which may lack connectivity issues due to power (i.e., battery), failure, or gateway cutoff to patient's wearable devices. Mobile in the sense means that it should be capable of tracking signals into heterogeneous environments. It must catch the signals irrespective of whether the patient went outside or still resided into the hospital or building. It should be scalable so that it could be deployed easily for several users concurrently without affecting the performance metrics.

Finally, such prototype system should be re-targetable and extensible in nature. Re-targetable refers to the fact that it can handle various displays with distinct form factors and screen resolution. It means that the same health applications can be displayed to any smart phone display like PDA (Personal Digital Assistant) or to a bigger console device in a hospital where doctors, helpers or nurses may track the acquired data or processed information from distance. The extensibility aspect requires that if any newer sensing devices are introduced into the system for acquiring the patient's health-based information, the system should function efficiently and conveniently without affecting backend server of the services. In this platform, context awareness can be achieved that can direct us to derive a better level of emergency services to the patient. The information regarding recent operational laboratories, missing doses of pills, number of handicaps and other situations would be helpful in health monitoring. The system should not adhere to any changes made into the operating system or intermediate components of sensing devices and is designed in such a way that it would cause minimal disturbance to services provided to existing end users of the system. Sensor Cloud implementation is shown in Figure 11.6.

In this scenario, several numbers of sensors pick up the patient data and these accumulated data are uploaded to a server on cloud. If any noise data is found, they are filtered using some filtering mechanism on a server. The doctors or health employees, nurses and others can then access the patient's data on cloud through a web service portal after being authenticated or permitted by the patient.

2. **Environmental Monitoring for Emergency or Disaster Detection** - In environmental applications, it is possible to detect the earthquake and volcano explosion before its eruption by continuously monitoring them through the use of several numbers of different sensors like strain, temperature, light, image, sound, acceleration, barometer sensors and so forth through the use of Wireless Sensor Networks. Through the Sensor Cloud infrastructure, the sensor instances engaged in environmental monitoring can be used in parallel with several other sensor instances. For example the healthcare department can avoid any future casualty, or with crop harvesting application services they can avoid the damage caused by bad weather condition.
3. **Telematics** – Sensor Clouds can be used for telematics, meant to deploy the long distance transmission of our computerized or information to a system in continuum. It enables the smooth communication between system and devices without any intervention.

4. **Google Health** - It is a centralization service of Google that provides personal health information and serves as cloud health data storages. Google users are allowed to monitor their health records by logging into their accounts at collaborated cloud health service providers into the Google health system. However, in a recent declaration Google has announced the discontinuation of this health service.
5. **Microsoft HealthVault** - This cloud platform is developed by Microsoft to store and maintain health and fitness-related information. HealthVault helps users to store, gather and share their health relevant information and its data can be acquired from several pharmacies, cloud providers, health employees, health labs, equipment and from the users itself.
6. **Agriculture and Irrigation Control (Field Server Sensors)** – Sensor Cloud can be used in the field of agriculture to monitor the crop fields in order to upkeep it. For this, a field server is developed that comprises of a camera sensors, air sensor, temperature sensor, concentration sensor, soil moisture and temperature sensors and so forth. These sensors continuously upload the field data via Wi-Fi access point to the field owner to track the health of their crops. This can also be used for harvesting.
7. **Earth Observation** - A sensor grid is developed for data gathering from several GPS stations, to process, analyze, manage and visualize the GPS data. This GPS data would then be uploaded onto the cloud for efficient monitoring, early warning and decision-making capability for critical situations like the volcanic eruptions, earthquakes, tsunamis, cyclones and so forth to the users all around the world.
8. **Transportation and Vehicular Traffic Applications** – Sensor Cloud can be used to provide an efficient, stable, equilibrium and sustainable tracking system. Earlier existing technologies like GPS navigation can only track the status and current location of vehicle. On the other hand, when vehicle monitoring is implemented using cloud computing, it is possible to incorporate centralized web service, GPS and GSM enabled devices and embedded device with sensors which will provide the following benefits:
   i. To identify the current name of the location.
   ii. To predict the time of arrival.
   iii. To find status of driver via alcohol breath sensor.
   iv. To find the total distance covered.
   v. To track the level of fuel.

   All the data fetched are stored onto some centralized server that will be resided into the cloud. The vehicle owner can access this data on cloud via web portal and can retrieve all data on cloud in real time to visualize the vehicle information.
9. **Tunnel Monitoring** - WSN can be used to implement the distributed sensing of light levels inside the tunnel and under-bridges to provide necessary input information for adapting light functionality. This tunnel information can be put onto the cloud and is

used to monitor the light intensity in real time to avoid the automobile users (drivers) casualty and to save the energy spent unnecessarily for lightening throughout the day.

10. **Wildlife Monitoring** – Sensor Cloud can also be used for tracking the wildlife sanctuaries, forests and so forth to regularly monitor the endangered species in real time.

11.8 Multiservice Provisioning on Multiple Platforms

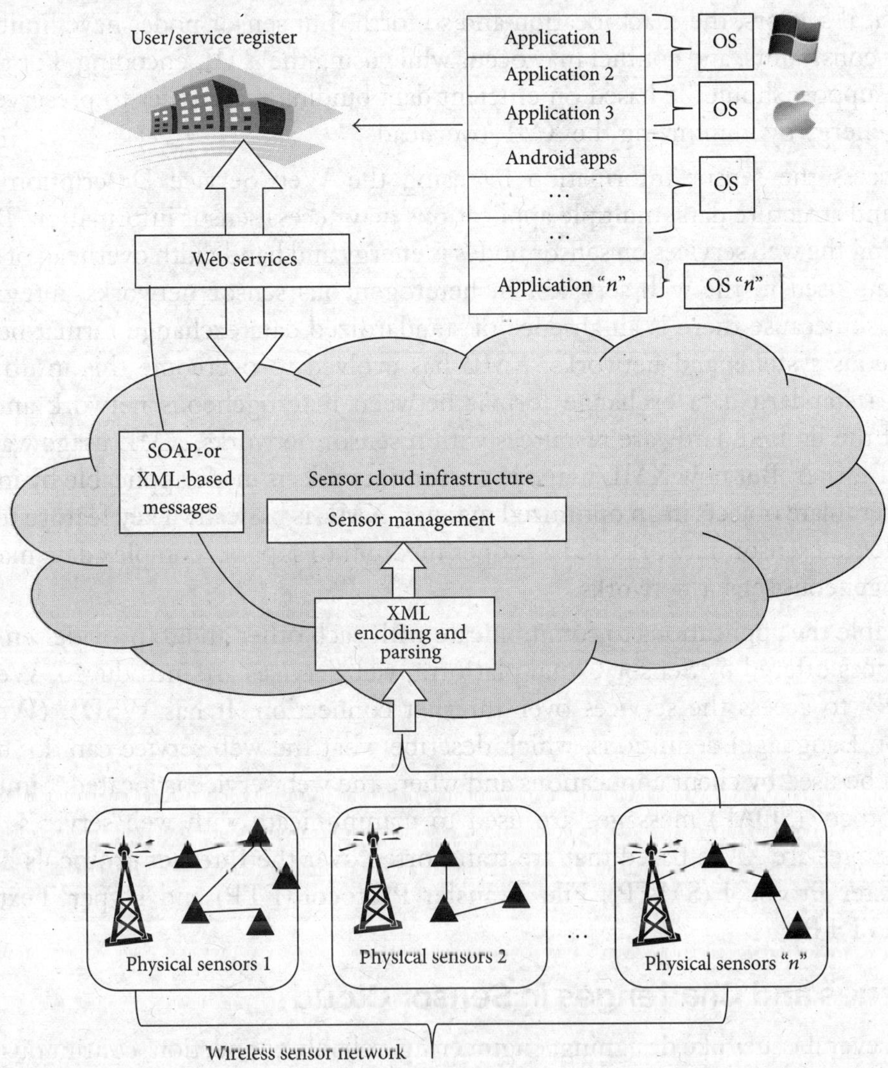

Fig.11.7: XML Encoded Physical Sensors into the Sensor Cloud

Integrating the WSN into heterogeneous networks is a complex task. The reason behind this is the absence of standardized data exchange functions, which may support the participating sub-networks of heterogeneous network. Using XML in sensor networks encourages the interchangeability of different types of sensors and systems. Figure 11.7 shows XML encoded physical sensors into the Sensor Cloud.

The lower part of Figure 11.7 deals with the XML encoded physical sensors. The XML encoding defines some set of rules for these physical sensors such that it will be both human readable and machine readable with less intervention and will enable these to be implemented on several number of different platforms. XML enables documents to give physical sensor's metadata, that is, the type of the physical sensors, its specifications, the accuracy or intensity of these physical sensors, the exact location and so forth. But sensor nodes have limited storage and power constraints, and conflict may occur while using the XML encoding. For this reason, the XML support should be based on efficient data binding techniques to preserve the time, space and energy by minimizing the XML overhead.

To access the sensor information by using the Web Service Description Language (WSDL) and structure data, multiple applications may access sensor information. But the key issue in using the web services on sensor nodes is energy and bandwidth overhead of structured data formats used in the web services. In heterogeneous sensor networks, integration is a complex task because there is an absence of standardized data exchange format between the heterogeneous systems and networks. XML has evolved to overcome this insufficiency by providing a standard data exchange format between heterogeneous network and systems. Because of the limited hardware resources within sensor networks, XML usage was not fully introduced earlier. But now XML usage in sensor networks is made applicable by introducing the XML template objects in an optimized manner. XML is basically a key feature towards the service-oriented sensor networks and a proper medium to support complex data management and heterogeneous sensor networks.

To enable the applications to communicate with each other and to provide remote access to the services offered by Sensor Cloud platform, web services are introduced. Web services mainly refer to access the services over Internet connection. It has WSDL (Web Service Description Language) definitions, which describe what the web service can do, how a web service can be used by client applications and where the web service is located. Simple Object Access Protocol (SOAP) messages are used to communicate with web services, and these SOAP messages are XML based that are transported over the Internet protocols like Simple Mail Transfer Protocol (SMTP), File Transfer Protocol (FTP) and Hyper Text Transfer Protocol (HTTP).

11.9 Issues and Challenges in Sensor Cloud

There are several issues like designing, engineering, reliable connection, continuous data flow, power issues and so forth that need to be handled while proposing Sensor Cloud infrastructure for health care and other different applications. Some of the main issues are as follows.

11.9.1 Design Issues

There are several issues while designing the system in real scenario like nursing home, health care, hospitals and so forth which require fault-tolerant and reliable continuous transfer of data from sensor devices to the server. For example, in a private health care, the patient may be out of coverage area from the smart phone gateway because of patients coming in and out frequently. This scenario would be more prone to connection failure between the server and smart phone (or any other display device, like PDA) and thus this scenario must be considered while designing such system in order to avoid accumulation of errors.

11.9.2 Storage Issues

Some engineering issues like storage of data at server side and transferring data from phone to server must have to be considered. To tackle this, timestamps are sent with each data packet to assist in reconstruction of data on the server side. Most of the data processing is done at server end so the system must be designed to avoid the bursty processing due to multiple users connected simultaneously to the system. The system must be designed to accommodate multiple users to connect at the same time.

Storage issues can be tackled with the introduction of predictive storage concept. This concept of storage keeps it easily fit to the correlated behavior of the physical environment and builds an architecture that focuses the sensor data archival at some remote sensors of Sensor Cloud infrastructure. It also uses predictive caching at proxies.

11.9.3 Authorization Issues

A web-based user interface is used for doctors, patients, helpers, care-givers and so forth to inspect and analyze the patient's health-related results remotely. Therefore, the system should offer different authorization roles for different types of users and authenticated via this web interface. This will enable the privacy to some extent by allowing the care givers to restrict them to the patients that he or she will take care of.

11.9.4 Power (Battery) Issues

While using smart phone as a gateway, power (battery) is the main issue that has to be taken care of because the continuous processing and wireless transmission would drain out the mobile battery within few hours or days. Thus, it is important to tackle power issues while connecting mobile phone gateway with the Sensor Cloud infrastructure.

11.9.5 Event Processing and Management

Sensor Cloud has to cope with very complex event processing and management issues such as the following.

i. How the events have to be synchronized that may come from different sources in different time because of delays in network?

ii. How the event processing rules have to be changed without affecting the system?

iii. How the messages and events of varying types are supported?

iv. How to support the enormous numbers of events and its conditions in an optimal way?
v. How can we recognize the context (*i.e.*, spatial, temporal, semantic) to its relevant situation detection?

11.9.6 Service Level Agreement (SLA) Violation

Consumer's dependency on cloud providers for their application's computing needs (i.e. their processing, storage, and analysis of enormous sensor data) on demand may require a specific Quality of Service (QoS) to be maintained. But if cloud providers are unable to provide QoS on user's demand even in the case of processing huge sensor data in critical environmental situations, it would result in SLA violation and cloud provider must be responsible for that. So, we need a reliable dynamic collaboration among cloud providers. But opting for the best combination of cloud providers in dynamic collaboration is a big challenge in terms of cost, time and discrepancy between providers and QoS.

11.9.7 Need for Efficient Information Dissemination

In Sensor Cloud, an efficient information dissemination mechanism is needed that can match the published events or sensor data to appropriate user's applications. But there are some issues like maintaining flexibility in providing a powerful subscription schema, which may capture information about events, guaranteeing the scalability with respect to a number of subscribers and published events or sensor data. Since the data sets and their relevant access services are distributed geographically, the allocation of data storage and dissemination becomes critical challenges.

11.9.8 Security and Privacy Support Issues

There are fewer standards available to ensure the integrity of the data in response to change due to authorized transactions. The consumers need to know whether his/her data at cloud center is well encrypted or who supervises the encryption/decryption keys (i.e., the cloud vendor or customer himself). Private health data may become public due to fallacy or inaccuracy. A consumer's privacy may be lost into cloud and sensor data or information uploaded into clouds may not be supervised correctly by user. The US WellPoint disclosed that 130,000 records of its consumers had leaked out and become available publicly over the Internet. So better privacy policies are demand of the time which can offer services themselves while maintaining the privacy.

11.9.9 Real-Time Multimedia Content Processing and Massive Scaling

Usage of large amount of multimedia data and information in real time and its mining is a big challenge in the integration of heterogeneous and massive data sources with cloud. To classify this real-time multimedia information and contents such that it may trigger the relevant services and assist the user in his current location is also a big challenge to be handled.

11.9.10 Collective Intelligence Harvesting

The heterogeneous real-time sensor data feed enhances the decision-making capability by using the appropriate data and decision level fusion mechanisms. But maximization of intelligence developed from the massively collected information in cloud is still a very big challenge.

11.9.11 Energy Efficiency Issues

The basic disadvantages of a WSN and cloud computing are almost the same and energy efficiency of sensor nodes is lost due to the limited storage and processing capacity of nodes. For example, a health monitoring using the textile sensors can work much better and give more accurate results. These textile sensors can be easily sewed and are even washable. Although the proposed system of textile sensors is performing well in the majority of aspects, the battery can last only 24 hours after continuous monitoring and data transmitting regarding user's heartbeat rate, movement, respiratory conditions and so forth. The gathered accumulated data can then be visualized in charts using some web applications and the results are received at user end through an alert message remotely on user's smart phone. But in order to extend system independency, energy efficiency of such systems (textile sensors and microcontroller based) is a primary issue that has to be handled.

Data caching mechanism can be used to reuse bygone sensor data for applications that are tolerant to time. For example, an application related to variant room temperature. If this bygone sensor data is used to satisfy the various requests for a common sensor data, the energy consumption will be reduced. Still more work is needed to overcome the energy consumption.

To improve the energy efficiency and memory usage in a Sensor Cloud infrastructure, there should be a middleware which can tackle the adverse situation in case of continuous and long duration monitoring of data. This can be done through the gateway that is acting as a middleware and collects the huge sensor data from sensor nodes. This middleware should be able to compress the sensor data to avoid the transmission load and then transmits it back to the gateway acting as a middleware on cloud side which in turn decompresses and stores it there. When the transmission overload reduces, the energy consumption of sensor nodes improves automatically due to less processing.

11.9.12 Bandwidth Limitation

Bandwidth limitation is one of the current big challenges that have to be handled in Sensor Cloud system when the number of sensor devices and their cloud users increases dramatically. However, there is a number of optimal and efficient bandwidth allocation methods proposed, but to manage the bandwidth allocation with such a gigantic infrastructure consisting of huge device assets and cloud users, the task of allocating bandwidth to every devices and users becomes very difficult.

11.9.13 Network Access Management

There are various numbers of networks to deal with in Sensor Cloud architecture applications.

So a proper and efficient access management scheme for these networks is needed because this will optimize the bandwidth usage and improve link performance.

11.9.14 Pricing Issues

Access to the services of Sensor Cloud involves both the Sensor Service Provider (SSP) and Cloud Service Provider (CSP). However, both SSPs and CSPs have different customer's management, services management and modes and methods of payments and pricing. So all this together will lead to a number of issues such as

i. How to set the price?
ii. How the payment is to be made?
iii. How the price is be distributed among different entities?

The growing demand for controlling and monitoring the environment and its applications results in the growth of a large number of devices while the cost of deployment and connecting them to heterogeneous network continues to drop. However, the interfaces, protocols, connections and so forth increase at exponential rate, thereby making it difficult and expensive for information technology (IT) people to integrate the devices (sensor devices) into the cloud world. To eradicate the complexity and cost associated with integrating the sensors into cloud or any highly distributed system, there exists emerging and existing standards from both domains. For example, embedded sensor and IT domains within a service-oriented sensor architecture (SOSA).

The service oriented paradigm can be extended to a sensor network and use the service oriented process parameter (like profiling sensors for web services), which helps in intelligence integration into the Internet. This solution when extended to Sensor Cloud would result in high availability and reliability. It was found that the energy consumption of sensor nodes reduced drastically when the data exchange is done among sensors into a heterogeneous network with gateway through the SPWS (Sensor Profiles for Web Services) as compared to traditional SOAP messages. It has been observed also that the cost of memory usage in sensor nodes remains constant with SPWS whereas it is increased with SOAP messages.

The entity which is most responsible for the cost of Sensor Cloud service model is the message exchanged among sensors into a heterogeneous network environment. Using SPWS, power consumption of sensor nodes as well as the memory usages in sensor nodes is reduced drastically. In the Sensor Cloud infrastructure, the cost of communication among sensors is more than the processing cost. Hence the reduction in power consumption and memory usage leads to less communication cost which also enables an energy efficient model of Sensor Cloud.

11.9.15 Interface Standardization Issues

Web interfaces currently provide the interface among Sensor Cloud users (may be smart phone users) and cloud. But web interface may cause overhead because the web interfaces are not specifically designed for smart phones or mobile devices. Also, there would be compatibility issues for web interface among devices and in this case signaling, standard protocol, and interface for interacting between Sensor Cloud users and the cloud would require seamless services for implementation. Thus, interoperability would be a big issue when the Sensor Cloud users need to access the services with cloud.

11.9.16 Maintenance Issues

In order to keep the end user's loyalty, the cloud should cope with the service failure. For this a regular maintenance is needed and redundancy techniques should be implemented to ensure the smooth and continuous flow of services. This can be done by backing up the data regularly and by distributing their multiple data centers geographically across the world.

11.9.17 Resource and Hardware Compatibility Issues

Hardware compatibility as well as software compatibility both can be solved in cloud computing environment by allowing the sharing of hardware or software resources or services. But there may be the case when sensor or some other resources being used are lost due to some calamity or severe weather condition. To handle these issues, there is an architecture called PRESTO architecture that enables users or clients to view the data in a single logical view which is distributed across several sensor proxies and remote sensors. This enables the users to view variability at several lossy levels and unreliable remote sensor network resources. The PRESTO also supports archival queries on data resources that enable the historical data query to prevent any unusual events to better understand them for future application scenarios.

11.10 Conclusion

This Chapter gives a detailed explanation of the Sensor Cloud. The comparison with WSN, Sensor Cloud architecture, advantages of Sensor Cloud, Sensor Cloud service life cycle model and Sensor Cloud layered structure are well explained. Various Sensor Cloud applications and multiservice provisioning on multiple platforms are illustrated in detail. Finally issues and challenges in Sensor Cloud like design issues, storage issues, authorization issues, power (battery) issues, event processing and management, service level agreement (SLA) violation, need for efficient information dissemination, security and privacy support issues, real-time multimedia content processing and massive scaling, collective intelligence harvesting, energy efficiency issues, bandwidth limitation, network access management, pricing issues, interface standardization issues, maintenance issues and resource and hardware compatibility issues are lucidly explained.

12 FOG COMPUTING

12.1 Introduction

Fog computing is a term created by Cisco that refers to extending Cloud computing to the edge of an enterprise's network. It is also known as Edge computing or fogging. Fog computing facilitates the operation of compute, storage and networking services between end devices and cloud computing data centers. Cisco introduced its fog computing vision in January 2014 as a way of bringing cloud computing capabilities to the edge of the network and as a result, closer to the rapidly growing number of connected devices and applications that consume cloud services and generate increasingly massive amounts of data. By handling these services that make up the Internet of Things (IoT) at the network edge, data can in many cases be processed more efficiently than if it needed to be sent to the cloud for processing.

Fog computing is the concept of a network fabric that stretches from the outer edges of where data is created to where it will eventually be stored, whether that's in the cloud or in a customer's data center.

Fog is another layer of a distributed network environment and is closely associated with cloud computing and the Internet of Things (IoT). Public infrastructure as a service (IaaS) cloud vendors can be thought of as a high-level, global endpoint for data. The edge of the network is where data from IoT devices is created. Fog is an intermediate layer between cloud and devices that generate data as shown Figure 12.1.

Fig.12.1: Fog Layer between Cloud and Device

According to a survey report, 40% of the whole world's data will come from sensors by 2020. The amazing fact is that 90% of the world's data were generated only during the period of last 2 years. 2.5 quintillion bytes of data is generated per day and total expenditure on IoT devices will be $1.7 trillion by 2020. The total number of connected vehicles worldwide will be 250 million by 2020 and there will be more than 30 billion IoT devices. The amount of data generated by IoT devices is simply huge that the Cloud computing model is insufficient to handle the requirements of IoT.

12.2 Why Fog Computing?

There are several issues in Cloud computing of which the major ones are volume, latency and bandwidth. Figure 12.2 shows the present day Cloud model. In present day Cloud model, devices generate data and send this data for analysis and storage in the Cloud. After analysis or upon the request, the data is send back to the devices or to execute an action.

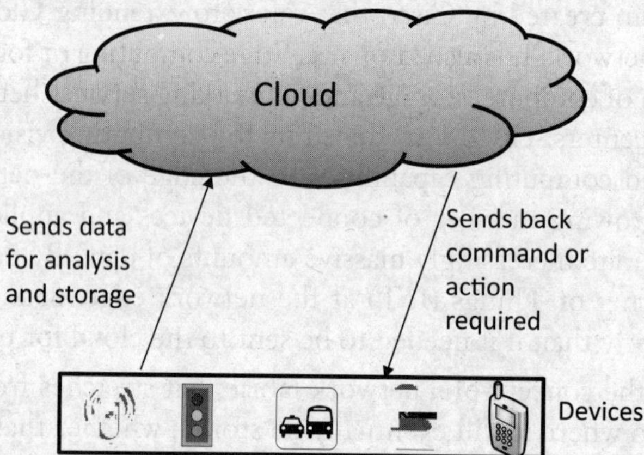

Fig.12.2: Present Day Cloud Model

Data Volume

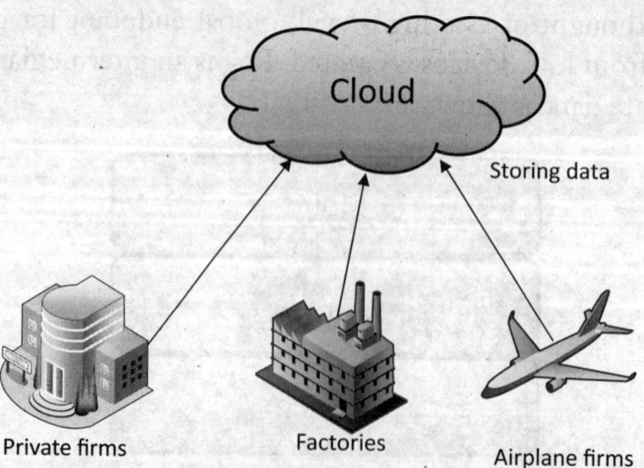

Fig.12.3: Huge Volume of Data Generation

The volume of data is exploding and it is estimated that by 2020, about 50 billion devices will be online. Presently billions of devices produce exa bytes of data every day. The device density is also increasing every day. Current cloud model is unable to process this huge volume of data. Private firms, factories, airplane companies, healthcare sectors produces enormous amount of data every day. In some cases, the data generated need to be filtered before storing. Figure 12.3 shows the huge volume of data generation.

Latency

The desire to slash latency is perhaps the most important reason to embrace fog computing. Fog services have small and deterministic latency that enables real time systems such as Artificial Intelligence, Virtual Reality, real time control loops, streaming data analytics and more. Latency is defined as the time taken by a data packet for a round trip. This means the time taken by the data to travel from the devices to the Cloud and back to the devices. Latency is an important aspect for handling time sensitive data.

If edge devices send time sensitive data to Cloud for analysis and wait for the Cloud to give a proper action, then it can lead to many unwanted results. While handling time sensitive data, a millisecond can make a huge difference. When time sensitive data is send to the cloud for analysis, latency will be increased. Latency can be calculated as follows.

$$\text{Latency} = T_{\text{from device to cloud}} + T_{\text{data analysis}} + T_{\text{from cloud to device}}$$

Where T = time

When the action reaches the device, it may not be meaningful or in situations like connected vehicles, accidents may occur.

Bandwidth

If all the data generated by IoT devices are sent to Cloud for storage and analysis, then the traffic generated by these devices will be simply gigantic. This will consume almost all the bandwidth. Handling this kind of traffic is really challenging. If all the devices become online, even IPv6 will not be able to provide facility to all the devices. There are certain situations in which data may be confidential where the firms do not want to share online. In such situations, Fog computing is a solution.

12.3 Requirements of IoT

For successfully implementing IoT, following requirements are to be satisfied.

a. **Reduce Latency of Data**: The most important requirement of IoT is the latency reduction. Latency can be reduced by analyzing the data close to the data source. Appropriate actions in real-time are needed in several applications. Delay in taking decisions make huge differences or sometimes results in major accidents or machine failure.

b. **Data Security**: IoT data must be secured and protected from the intruders. Data are required to be monitored on a 24 X 7 basis in IoT. Appropriate actions need to be taken before the attack causes major harm to the network.

c. **Operation Reliability**: The data generated from IoT devices are used to solve real-time problem. Integrity and availability of the data must be guaranteed in IoT. Unavailability and tampering of data can be hazardous.

d. **Processing of Data at Respective Suitable Place**: Data can be divided into 3 types based on sensitivity. They are time sensitive data, less time sensitive data and data which are not time sensitive. Extremely time sensitive data must be analyzed very near to the data source. Data which are not time sensitive will be analyzed in the cloud.

e. **Monitor Data Across Large Geographical Area**: The location of connected IoT devices can be spread across a large geographical region. For example, monitoring the railway track of a country or a state. Sometimes the devices are exposed to harsh environment conditions like heavy winds, rain, snowfall etc.

The Fog computing is used mainly in four situations.

- If the data need to be analyzed within a fraction of a second.
- If there are huge number of devices.
- If the devices are separated by a large geographical distance.
- If the devices are subjected to extreme conditions.

12.4 Architecture of Fog

Fog computing architecture is the arrangement of physical and logical network elements, hardware and software to implement a useful IoT network. Key architectural decisions involve the physical and geographical positioning of fog nodes, their arrangement in a hierarchy, the numbers, types, topology, protocols and data bandwidth capacities of the links between fog nodes, things and the cloud, the hardware and software design of individual fog nodes and how a complete IoT network is orchestrated and managed. In order to optimize the architecture of a fog network, one must first understand the critical requirements of the general use cases that will take advantage of fog and specific software applications that will run on them. Then these requirements must be mapped onto a partitioned network of appropriately designed fog nodes.

From a systematic perspective, fog networks provide a distributed computing system with a hierarchical topology. Fog networks aim at meeting stringent latency requirements, reducing power consumption of end devices, providing real-time data processing and control with localized computing resources and decreasing the burden of backhaul traffic to centralized data centers. Figure 12.4 shows the architecture of Fog computing.

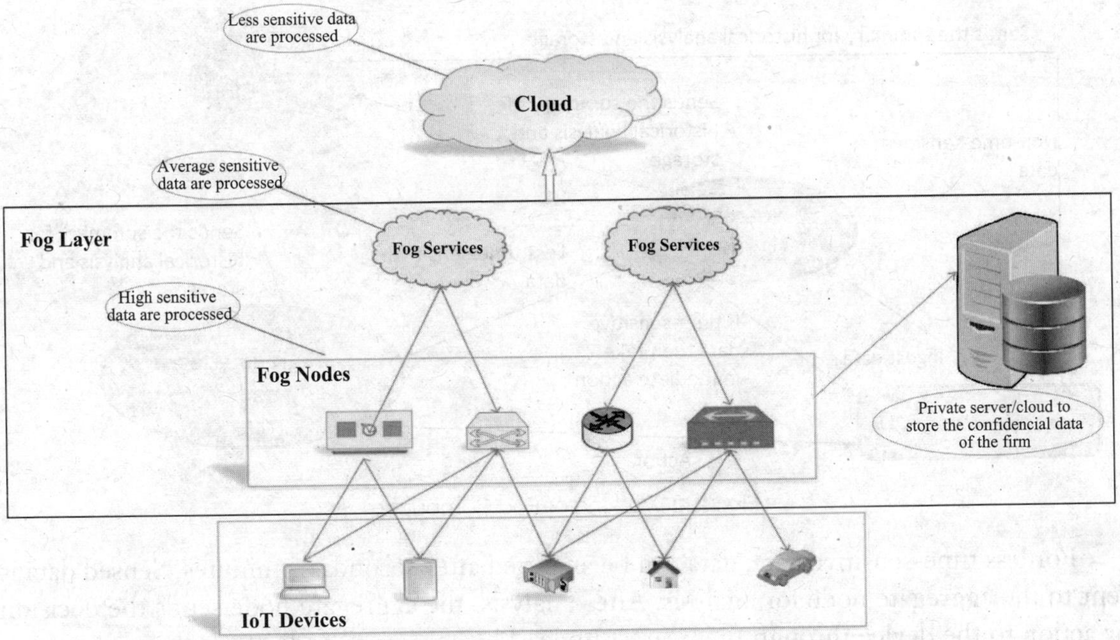

Fig.12.4: Architecture of Fog Computing

Fog nodes posses several characteristics. The characteristic for a Fog node is as follows.

- Storage to provide transient storage.
- Computing facility to process the data before it is sent to the cloud and to take quick decisions.
- Network connectivity to connect with IoT devices, other Fog nodes and Cloud.
- Deployable anywhere inside the network.
- Each fog nodes have their aggregate fog node.

12.5 Working of Fog

As we have already discussed, there are three types of data: most time-sensitive data, less time-sensitive data and data which are not time-sensitive. Fog nodes work according to the type of data they receive. An IoT application should be installed to each Fog node. The nearest Fog node ingests data from the devices. Figure 12.5 shows the working of Fog computing.

In the case of most time-sensitive data, data need to be analyzed within fraction of a second. If possible data should be analyzed at the nearest node itself. After analyzing the data, the decision or action is sent to the devices. After that it sends and stores the summary to cloud for future analysis.

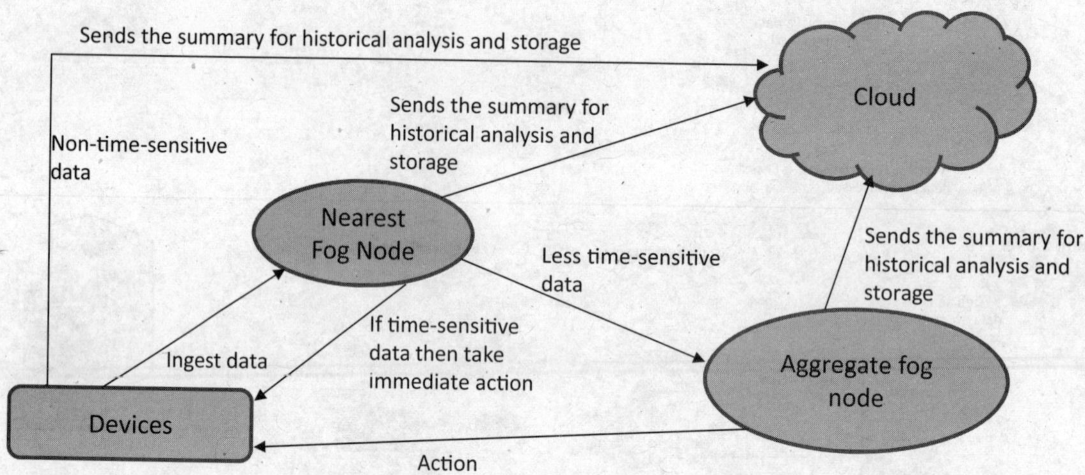

Fig.12.5: Working of Fog Computing

For less time-sensitive data, data can be analyzed after seconds or minutes. Sensed data is sent to the aggregate node for analysis. After analysis, the aggregate node sends the decision or action to the device through the nearest node. The aggregate node sends the summary to cloud for storage and future analysis.

The data which are not time sensitive can wait for hours, days or weeks. In this case, data is sent to cloud for storage and future analysis. Those summaries from fog nodes can be considered as less-time sensitive data. Table 12.1 shows a comparison of various attributes for three types of data.

Table 12.1: Comparison of Various Attributes for Three Types of Data

	Fog nodes closest to devices	Fog aggregate nodes	Cloud
Analysis Duration	Fraction of a second	Seconds to minutes	Hours to weeks
IoT Data Storage Duration	Transient	Hours to days	Months to years
Geographical Coverage	Very local	Wider	Global

12.6 Advantages of Fog

- **Security** – Fog computing provides better security. Fog nodes can be protected using the same controls, procedures and policy you use in other areas of IT environment.
- **Low operation costs** - Fog computing can save network bandwidth by processing selected data locally, instead of sending it to the cloud for analysis.
- **Reduces unwanted accidents** – With fog computing, latency can be reduced which results in quick decision making. This may avoid unwanted accidents.

- **Better privacy** - The sensitive data can be analyzed locally instead of sending it to the cloud for analysis. The IT team can keep track and control the devices that collect, analyze and store data.
- **Greater business agility** - By utilizing the right set of tools, developers can seamlessly develop fog applications and deploy them whenever needed. Fog applications drive the machine to function in a way according to customers need.
- **Supports mobility** – In Fog computing, nodes can be mobile. This means nodes can join and leave the network at any time.
- **Deployable in remote places** – Fog nodes can be deployed in remote places. The nodes can be subjected to harsh environmental conditions or in places such as under sea, railway tracks, vehicles, factory floors etc.
- **Better data handling** – Fog nodes can operate with less bandwidth since data can be analyzed locally. Hence it reduces the risk of latency.

12.7 Applications of Fog

Fog Computing works best in a cloud-based control environment to offer control and deeper insight across a range of nodes. These include wind energy, transportation, smart cities, surveillance and smart buildings. Let's have a look at some of the real-life examples where and how fog computing can be helpful.

Smart Homes

With the rapid development of the Internet of Things, more and more smart devices and sensors are connected at home. However, products from different vendors are hard to work together. Some tasks, which require large amount of computation and storage for e.g. real-time video analytics, are infeasible due to the limited capability of hardware. To solve these problems, Fog computing is utilized to integrate all debris into a single platform and empower those Smart Home applications with elastic resources. To use home security application as an example, widely deployed secure sensors consist of smart lock, video or audio recorder, various sensor monitors (*e.g.* light sensor, occupancy sensor, and motion sensor etc). If not products of same vendor, those secure devices are hard to combine.

Fog computing can provide home security applications: (1) unified interface to integrate all kinds of independent devices, (2) flexible resources to support computation and storage, (3) real-time processing and low-latency response. Once the Fog platform is set up, each secure sensor is connected as a client. The corresponding server application can be installed in independent VMs. Advanced processing logic can also be implemented on VMs in which it can process data shared by those secure monitor applications. For example, a motion sensor detects a suspicious motion in a certain room and then a cleaning robot with video camera will be commanded to check out the exact location. Real-time video analytics will process those video and confirm whether it is a false alarm. Notification and report will be sent to house owner and the system will call police if applicable.

Smart Grid

The smart grid is an electricity distribution network, with smart meters deployed at various locations to measure the real-time status information. A centralized server called SCADA system gathers and analyzes the status information and sends commands to respond to any demand change or emergency to stabilize the power grid. Fog computing can benefit the smart grid greatly. With Fog computing, SCADA can be complemented by a decentralized model with micro-grids, which can not only improve scalability, cost efficiency, security and rapid response of the power system but also integrate distributed power generators (wind farms, solar panels and PHEVs) with the main power grid. With Fog computing, the smart grid will turn into a multi-tier hierarchical system with the interplay between the Fog and SCADA. In such system, a Fog is in charge of a micro-grid and communicates with neighboring fogs and higher tiers. The higher the tier, the larger will be the latency and the wider will be the geographical coverage. The final global coverage is provided by SCADA, which is responsible for long-time repository and economic analytics.

Smart Vehicle

Fog computing can be integrated into vehicular networks. Depending on whether extra infrastructure is needed, vehicular Fog computing can be categorized into two types, infrastructure-based and autonomous. The former, such as VTube, relies on Fog nodes deployed along the roadside. Fog nodes are responsible to send or retrieve information to or from the driving-by vehicles. In autonomous vehicular Fog computing, it utilizes vehicles on-the-fly to form Fog and/or cloud to support ad-hoc events. In this each Fog can communicate its client within and other Fogs. There are various applications for vehicular Fog computing, no matter the first type or the second type. Popular applications are: traffic light scheduling, congestion mitigation, precaution sharing, parking facility management, traffic information sharing, etc.

Smart Cities

Large cities face a number of challenges including public safety, sanitation, traffic congestion, high-energy utilization and municipal services. The solution to these challenges lies in a single IoT network by installing a network of Fog nodes. The major issues in establishing smart cities are the shortage of broadband bandwidth and connectivity. Modern cities have multiple cellular networks and ample coverage. These networks have the capacity and peak bandwidth limits that is not enough to meet the needs of the existing customers. However, deploying fog computing architecture, allows Fog nodes to offer local storage and processing and hence, optimizing the network usage.

Smart cities also strive hard with safety and security issues. To address this issue, time-critical performance requires advanced real-time analytics. The network may transmit traffic and data along with life-critical systems. Fog computing resolves security issues, data encryption and distributed analytics requirements.

Smart Buildings

Commercial buildings are equipped with several sensors to inspect various building operations such as parking space occupancy, temperature and keycard readers. Data from these sensors must be watched to find what actions are required like triggering a fire alarm if smoke is sensed.

Fog computing permits free local operations for optimized control function. Not only a single floor but also individual room can have its own Fog node, allowing emergency monitoring and response functions, climate control, lighting control and supplementing the limited capacity of computers and smart devices.

Health Data Management

Health data management has been a sensitive issue since health data contains valuable and private information. With Fog computing, it is able to realize the goal that patient will take possession of their own health data locally. Those health data will be stored in Fog node such as smart phone or smart vehicle. The computation will be outsourced in a private-preserving manner when patient is seeking help from a medical lab or a physician's office. Modification of data happens directly in patient-owned Fog node.

Real-time health analysis can be done for patients with chronic illness or stroke patients. The data is analyzed in real-time and during emergency situations, the doctors and ambulance systems will be alerted automatically. Also historical data analysis of these patients can predict future dangers of the patient.

Visual Security

Video cameras are used in public places, parking lots and residential areas to enhance safety and security. The bandwidth of visual data collected over a large-scale network makes it impossible to carry the data to the cloud and collect real-time insights. Consider for example, a busy shopping mall with thousands of people moving around simultaneously. Real-time monitoring and discovery of irregularities carry strict low latency requirements on surveillance systems. However, Fog computing helps in real time, latency sensitive distributed surveillance systems that uphold privacy. With the help of fog architecture, video processing is logically divided between Fog nodes located with the cloud and the cameras. It helps in real time tracking, anomaly detection and collection of results from data captured over time.

Rail Monitoring

Fog nodes can be deployed in railway tracks for the real-time monitoring of the track conditions. Similarly sending data from a high speed train to the cloud for analysis is inefficient. Fog nodes provide faster data analysis in this case which in turn improves safety and reliability.

Pipeline Optimization

Gas and petroleum products transported through pipelines can be monitored in real-time.

In this case real-time monitoring of pressure, flow and compression is necessary. This can be done with the Fog computing architecture. In case of any leakage or fire, it can be monitored in real-time and fire and rescue services may be alerted or fire fighting equipments may be turned on.

12.8 Challenges in Fog

a. **Data security**: Fog computing and IoT have significant privacy and security concerns. Due to the heterogeneous nature of both, security and privacy are usually cast aside in order to achieve general functionality and interoperability. In other words, encryption and strict privacy policies make it more difficult for arbitrary devices to exchange data. Therefore, many manufacturers today simply do away with these features. Moreover, encryption algorithms and security protocols, which are complex, are often implemented or configured with mistakes, leaving sensitive user data exposed to attackers. This problem is further worsened by the dispersed ownership of fog nodes. Fog nodes are usually owned by different parties, such as universities, corporations, commonwealth organizations and personal households. Some fog nodes may even be jointly owned by two or more parties. Users approaching a fog node may be weary of the services provided by these parties, due to their vastly differing motivations. As we have seen with online social networking, collection and resale of private user data is highly valuable to corporations. Meanwhile, these parties also need authentication protocols to protect themselves against distributed denial of service (DDoS) attacks and other malicious activities. It will be important in the future to make fog computing applications preserve user privacy, provide rigorous security guarantees and address the needs of all the parties involved.

b. **Data consistency**: Data consistency can be achieved by coordinating the cloud servers in the data centers where the cloud is deployed. In Fog computing, however, things become complicated. When writing data objects in a Fog environment, it is necessary to not only coordinate the back-end cloud servers, but also invalidate the cached data on the fog nodes as well as on the client devices if strong data consistency is needed. This may result in deteriorated write performance, which weakens the benefits of using fog nodes as the write cache servers. On the other hand, Fog computing also provides opportunities of achieving data consistency more efficiently than cloud computing. For example, if the write requests on a data object are sent to only one fog node during a certain time period, which we envision is a common case in Fog computing, the system may temporarily transfer the ownership of the data object from the cloud to the Fog node. By doing this, data consistency can be achieved on the Fog node, which promises better write performance than cloud computing, as the Fog node resides at the edge of network. Nevertheless, to fully exploit the opportunities of achieving data consistency in Fog computing is still challenging and requires plenty of research efforts.

c. **Data management**: Data management for Fog computing applications also introduces new challenges. Perhaps the ideal abstraction for both users and developers is a "global storage," which can always be accessed, has an infinite size and yet performs with the speed of information stored locally. With Fog computing, this dream may finally be realized. However, how to implement such a storage system is still an open question. What efficient algorithms can be used to shuffle data among devices? How can pre-fetching be best implemented to achieve the lowest latency? What namespace scheme should be used? How can sensitive and encrypted data be cached privately and effectively? Furthermore, energy consumption and network usage must be conserved on mobile devices, as they typically have energy limits enforced by limited battery technology and data limits enforced by mobile carriers.

d. **Scheduling**: Fog computing introduces a variety of new and interesting scheduling challenges. Since tasks can now be moved between different physical devices (i.e., client devices, Fog nodes and back-end cloud servers), scheduling is much more complex. Some of the research questions are listed as follows. For Fog nodes with heterogeneous hardware, is it acceptable to trade energy for reduced latency? Should a process running on a Fog node be interrupted when the user moves toward another Fog node? How should tasks be scheduled considering a) latency b) energy consumption c) mobility and d) existing workload? Where the scheduling program should be executed? What are the benefits of jointly scheduling tasks? Beside these questions, some other concerns must also be taken into account. For example, security and privacy considerations are complex in Fog computing and tasks from sensitive applications should be scheduled on more trustworthy nodes. Furthermore, on traditional desktop and server machines, completely fair scheduling (CFS) dominates the landscape. For Fog computing, however, this algorithm may not be ideal, as different Fog nodes may have different hardware resources and some tasks (e.g., those making the user wait) may be more important than others (e.g., background services such as the backup/snapshot functionality). What other scheduling algorithms can be used to optimize the factors that are important for highly mobile computing, such as low latency?

e. **Programming architecture:** Fog computing is a novel computing paradigm, which demands a new programming model. We need to design intuitive and effective tools and frameworks for developers, helping them orchestrate dynamic, hierarchical and heterogeneous resources to build compatible applications on diverse platforms. To take task scheduling and migration for example, various questions may arise. How can we provide a simple abstraction for developers to mark tasks that can be migrated? What choices and preferences should be left to users? How can we allow developers to specify migration rules on various devices? Furthermore, we should avoid forcing developers to re-implement functionalities that will likely be common, such as distributed caching, workload balancing, system monitoring and so on.

f. **Service discovery protocols**: An attractive aspect of cloud computing is the automatic discovery of services. As Fog nodes differ from location to location, users can arrive at a new location and take advantage of the various services provided by the Fog nodes in that particular location. Given that this feature relies on the prudent deployment accomplished by service developers, implementing service discovery protocols in Fog computing can be quite challenging. Moreover, service provisioning is usually done dynamically in Fog computing, i.e., new virtual machines (VMs) are orchestrated on the spot when a particular service is needed. This raises many questions. When should services be started and stopped? What is the best way to balance workload? Should VM-based or container-based virtualization be used? It may even be possible to predict what services will be needed and provisions them in advance, before users even arrive. What methodologies should be used to efficiently provision services for hundreds, thousands and millions of users? Some services are deployed on fog nodes to aggregate information from nearby client devices. What is the best way to split workload for these services, with regard to the energy efficiency on the client side?

g. **Latency**: There are many factors introducing high latency of application or service performance on Fog computing platforms. High latency will ruin the user experience and satisfaction, since fog computing is targeting at delay-sensitive applications and services. There are several possibilities to bring in latency in Fog computing:
   - Data aggregation: The geo-distributed nature of Fog computing paradigm determines that there will be delay if data aggregation is not finished before data processing. However, there are many ways to mitigate this problem, such as applying data partitioning/filtering and utilizing locality in hierarchy to reduce computation volume on higher layer.
   - Resource provisioning: There will be delay in provisioning resources for certain tasks, especially for resource-limited Fog nodes. We may need carefully designed scheduling by using priority and mobility model.
   - Node mobility, churn and failure: Fog computing needs to be resilient to node mobility, churn and failure. Both system monitor and location service will work together to provide information to help on choosing mitigation strategies such as check-pointing, rescheduling and replication.

h. **Power consumption**: Power consumption is high in Fog nodes. Fog use addition nodes and hence power consumption is higher than centralized Cloud.

12.9 Conclusion

This Chapter describes Fog Computing in a detailed manner. The need for Fog Computing, requirements of IoT, architecture of Fog and working of Fog is clearly illustrated. Finally the advantages of Fog, applications of Fog in various fields of IoT and challenges that exits in Fog which needs to be mitigated are well explained.

13 SMART HOMES

13.1 Introduction

In this Chapter we will discuss about Smart Homes. Smart home technology, also known as home automation, provides homeowners security, comfort, convenience and energy efficiency by allowing them to control smart devices, often by a smart home app on their smart phone or other networked device. A part of the Internet of Things (IoT), smart home systems and devices often operate together, sharing consumer usage data among themselves and automating actions based on the homeowner's preferences.

13.2 Origin of Smart Home

With the 1975 release of X10, a communication protocol for home automation, the smart home, came to life. X10 sends 120 kHz radio frequency (RF) bursts of digital information onto a home's existing electric wiring to programmable outlets or switches. These signals convey commands to corresponding devices, controlling how and when the devices operate. A transmitter could, for example, send a signal along the house's electric wiring, telling a device to turn on at a specific time.

However, as electrical wiring isn't designed to be particularly free from radio-band "noise," X10 was not always fully reliable. Signals would be lost and in some cases signals wouldn't cross circuits that were wired on different polarities, created when 220-volt service is split into a pair of 100-volt feeds, as is common in the U.S. Additionally, X10 was initially a one-way technology, so while smart devices can take commands, they cannot send data back to a central network. Later two-way X10 devices became available at a higher cost.

When home automation company Insteon came on the scene in 2005, it introduced technology that combined electric wiring with wireless signals. Other protocols, including ZigBee and Z-Wave, have since emerged to counter the problems prone to X10, though X10 remains a widely installed communications protocol to this day.

Nest Labs was founded in 2010 and released its first smart product, the Nest Learning Thermostat, in 2011. The company also created smart smoke/carbon monoxide detectors and security cameras. After being acquired by Google in 2015, it became a subsidiary of Alphabet Inc. in the same year.

In 2012, SmartThings Inc. launched a Kickstarter campaign, raising $1.2 million to fund its smart home system. Following additional funding, the company came on the market in August 2013 and was acquired by Samsung in 2014.

More recently, companies including Amazon, Apple and Google have released their own smart home products and smart home platforms, including Amazon Echo, Apple HomeKit and Google Home.

13.3 Examples of Smart Home Technologies

Nearly every aspect of life where technology has entered the domestic space (lightbulbs, dishwashers and so on) has seen the introduction of a smart home alternative. Some examples of smart home technologies are given below.

- Smart TVs connect to the Internet to access content through applications, such as on-demand video and music. Some smart TVs also include voice or gesture recognition. In addition to being able to be controlled remotely and customized, smart lighting systems, such as Hue from Philips Lighting Holding B.V., can detect when occupants are in the room and adjust lighting as needed. Smart lightbulbs can also regulate themselves based on daylight availability.
- Smart thermostats, such as Nest from Nest Labs Inc., come with integrated Wi-Fi, allowing users to schedule monitor and remotely control home temperatures. These devices also learn homeowners' behaviors and automatically modify settings to provide residents with maximum comfort and efficiency. Smart thermostats can also report energy use and remind users to change filters, among other things.
- Using smart locks and garage-door openers, users can grant or deny access to visitors. Smart locks can also detect when residents are near and unlock the doors for them.
- With smart security cameras, residents can monitor their homes when they are away or on vacation. Smart motion sensors are also able to identify the difference between residents, visitors, pets and burglars and can notify authorities if suspicious behavior is detected. Pet care can be automated with connected feeders. Houseplants and lawns can be watered by way of connected timers.
- Kitchen appliances of all sorts are available, including smart coffee makers that can brew you a fresh cup as soon as your alarm goes off. Smart refrigerators that keep track of expiration dates make shopping lists or even create recipes based on ingredients currently on hand.
- Household system monitors may, for example, sense an electric surge and turn off appliances or sense water failures or freezing pipes and turn off the water so there isn't a flood in our basement.

13.4 Smart Home Implementation

While many smart home systems still run on X10 or Insteon, Bluetooth and Wi-Fi have grown in popularity. ZigBee and Z-Wave are two of the most common home automation communication protocols in use today. In both mesh network technologies, they use short-range, low-power radio signals to connect smart home systems. Though both target the same smart home applications, Z-Wave has a range of 30 meters to ZigBee's 10 meters, with ZigBee often perceived as the more complex of the two. ZigBee chips are available from multiple companies, while Z-Wave chips are only available from Sigma Designs.

All devices in a smart home are controlled by a master home automation controller, often called a smart home hub. The smart home hub is a hardware device that acts as the central point of the smart home system and is able to sense, process data and communicate wirelessly. It combines all of the separate apps into a single smart home app that can be controlled remotely by homeowners. Examples of smart home hubs include Amazon Echo, Google Home, Insteon Hub Pro, Samsung SmartThings and Wink Hub etc.

Some smart home systems can be created from scratch, for example, using a Raspberry Pi or other prototyping board. Others can be purchased as a bundled smart home kit which is also known as a smart home platform. It contains the pieces needed to start a home automation project.

In simple smart home scenarios, events can be timed or triggered. Timed events are based on a clock, for example, lowering the blinds at 6:00 p.m., while triggered events depend on actions in the automated system. For example, when the owner's smart phone approaches the door, the smart lock unlocks and the smart lights go on.

Machine learning and Artificial Intelligence (AI) are becoming increasingly popular in smart home systems, allowing home automation applications to adapt to their environments. For example, voice-activated systems, such as Amazon Echo or Google Home, contain virtual assistants that learn and personalize the smart home to the resident's preferences and patterns.

13.5 Home Area Networks (HANs)

For implementing smart homes, we need to have an idea about Home Area Networks (HAN). A home area network (HAN) is a network that is deployed and operated within a small boundary, typically a house or small office/home office (SOHO). It enables the communication and sharing of resources like the Internet between computers, mobile and other devices over a network connection. As a type of IP-based Local Area Network (LAN), a HAN may be wired or wireless. In a typical implementation, a HAN consists of a broadband Internet connection that is shared between multiple users through a vendor/third party wired or wireless modem.

User host devices may be standard computers, laptops, mobiles and tablets. The modem generally has network switch capabilities that provide wired LAN ports or wireless connectivity to host users. A HAN also may include other devices, such as a fax, printer, scanner or small network attached storage that is shared by all host devices. Figure 13.1 shows the components of a Home Area Network (HAN).

Fig.13.1: Components of a HAN

13.5.1 HAN Elements

HAN elements comprises of Internet Protocol, Wired HAN and Wireless HAN. A multi-protocol gateway bridges non-IP network to IP network. Bridging between new technologies is limited. For new technologies or networks, a new mapping is required for bridging to perform satisfactorily. Wired HAN helps for the easy integration with pre-existing house infrastructure which is cost effective. Wired HAN uses power lines, coaxial cables, telephone lines, optical fibers and other such technologies for communication. Wireless HAN uses popular home Wi-Fi, ZigBee and even new standards such as 6LoWPAN. Wireless HAN makes implementation easy.

Figure 13.2 shows the HAN medium classification.

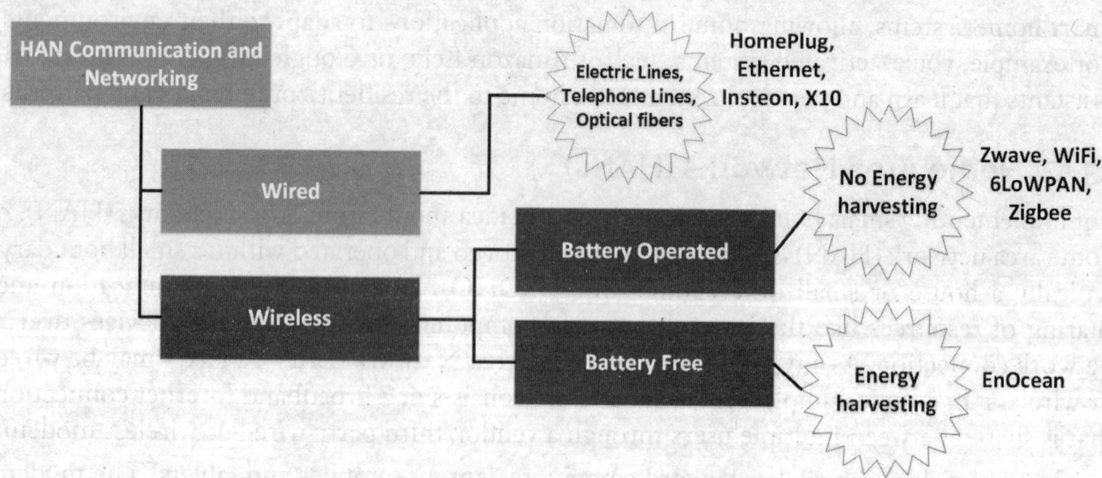

Fig.13.2: HAN Medium Classification

13.5.2 HAN Standards

There are various HAN standards which are explained below.

Universal Plug and Play (UPnP): Universal Plug and Play (UPnP) is a set of networking protocols that permits networked devices, such as personal computers, printers, Internet gateways, Wi-Fi access points and mobile devices to seamlessly discover each other's presence on the network and establish functional network services for data sharing, communications, and entertainment. UPnP is intended primarily for residential networks without enterprise-class devices. It is an application layer technology, mainly web-based. TCP/IP protocol stack provides support for the lower layers and enables seamless integration of various technologies. It provides transparent networking with support for zero-configuration networking and automatic discovery of devices.

Digital Living Network Alliance (DLNA): Digital Living Network Alliance (DLNA) (originally named Digital Home Working Group [DHWG]) was founded by a group of consumer electronics companies in June 2003 (with Sony in the lead role) to develop and promote a set of interoperability guidelines for sharing digital media among multimedia devices under the auspices of a certification standard. DLNA certified devices include smart phones, tablets, PCs, TV sets and storage servers. In a typical use case, a user sends videos, pictures or music from their smart phone or storage server through their home WLAN to a TV set or tablet for display. DLNA connects cable-based networks with wireless networks for increased sharing of media, control and access. It domestically shares network media resources.

Konnex (KNX): This is an open important standard for home and building networks. KNX is a standardised (EN 50090, ISO/IEC 14543), OSI-based network communications protocol for building automation. KNX is the successor to, and convergence of, three previous standards: the European Home Systems Protocol (EHS), BatiBUS and the European Installation Bus (EIB or Instabus). It utilizes the full range of home communication infrastructure like power lines, coaxial cables, twisted pair, RF, etc. It must be setup and configured via software before its proper usage.

Local Operation Networks (LonWorks): LonWorks is a networking platform specifically created to address the needs of control applications. The platform is built on a protocol created by Echelon Corporation for networking devices over media such as twisted pair, power lines, fiber optics and RF. It is used for the automation of various functions within buildings such as lighting and heating, Ventilation and Air Conditioning (HVAC). Every device includes a Neuron Chip, a transceiver and the application electronics. Neuron chip is a System on a Chip (SOC) with multiple microprocessors, RAM, ROM and IO interface ports. LonWorks splits device groups into intelligent elements, which can communicate through a physical communication medium.

ZigBee: We have already discussed about this standard in Chapter 3. ZigBee consists of four layers namely physical layer, Medium Access Control layer, network layer and application layer. Physical and MAC layers are defined by IEEE 802.15.4, whereas network and application layers are defined by ZigBee. ZigBeee aims at low-cost, low-energy devices. ZigBee Alliance is composed of Mitsubishi, Honeywell, Invensys, Motorola and Philips.

X-10: X-10 is a protocol for communication among electronic devices used for home automation. It primarily uses power line wiring for signaling and control, where the signals involve brief radio frequency bursts representing digital information. A wireless radio based protocol transport is also defined. X-10 enables remote control of compliant transmitters and receivers over power lines and electrical wirings present in the house. It is adopted by GE and Philips. This standard defines procedures for transmission of bits over AC carrier signals. It posses low speed and low data rate. This standard is mainly used for control of lighting, appliance networks and security sensors.

13.5.3 HAN Architectures

HAN has two architectures namely DomoNet and Jini.

DomoNet: DomoNet architecture uses XML for description and web-services for control. It follows a Service Oriented Architecture (SOA). This is not tied to any software, language or architecture. In this a central gateway connects different technologies and a tech manager for each technology provides web services for control and access.

Jini: Jini is a network architecture concept that Sun Microsystems calls "spontaneous networking." Using Jini, users will be able to plug printers, storage devices, speakers and any kind of device directly into a network and every other computer, device and user on the network will know that the new device has been added and is available. Each pluggable device will define itself immediately to a network device registry. When someone wants to use or access the resource, their computer will be able to download the necessary programming from it to communicate with it. The special device support software known as a device driver need not be present in an operating system. The operating system will know about all accessible devices through the network registry. Jini architecture connects various devices sharing their resources with auto-configuration and auto-installation. It is based on JAVA environment and pursued by Sun Microsystems. It constructs an organized distribution system without a central node (federation). Jini apps use bytecode to run JVM and are portable. It follows Object Oriented Paradigm.

13.5.4 HAN Initiatives

Project HYDRA and Amigo are two HAN initiatives. Project HYDRA is a middleware for embedded intelligent systems. It connects a Service Oriented Architecture Network. Connected devices may have limited resources, low processing power, memory and energy consumption. Each device has an embedded HYDRA client which acts as a proxy between the device and the middleware. Figure 13.3 shows the protocol stack for Project HYDRA.

The initiative Amigo is aimed at ambient intelligent systems for networked home systems. It has user-friendly interfaces, interoperability and automatic discovery of devices and services.

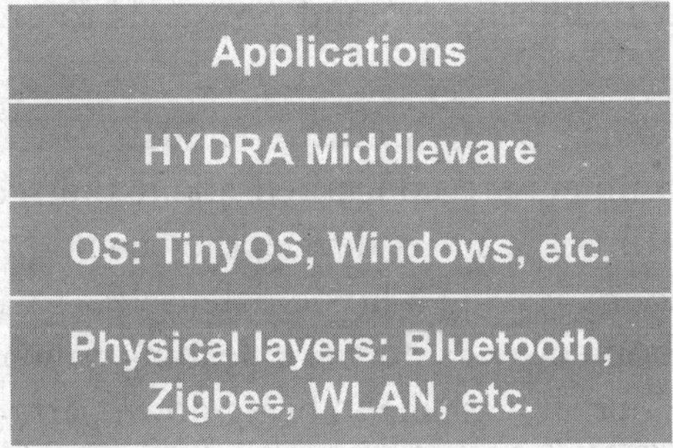

Fig.13.3: Protocol Stack for Project HYDRA

13.6 Smart Home Benefits and Issues

Benefits

One of the most important benefits of home automation is providing peace of mind to homeowners, allowing them to monitor their homes remotely, countering dangers such as a forgotten coffee maker left on or a front door left unlocked.

Smart homes are also beneficial for the elderly, providing monitoring that can help seniors to remain at home comfortably and safely, rather than moving to a nursing home or requiring 24/7 home care.

Smart homes can accommodate user preferences. For example, as soon as we arrive home, our garage door will open, the lights will go on, the fireplace will roar and our favorite tunes will start playing on our smart speakers.

Home automation also help consumers improve efficiency. Instead of leaving the air conditioning on all day, a smart home system can learn your behaviors and make sure the house is cooled down by the time you arrive home from work. The same goes for appliances. And with a smart irrigation system, our lawn will only be watered when needed and with the exact amount of water necessary. With home automation, energy, water and other resources are used more efficiently, which helps save both natural resources and money for the consumer.

Issues

Home automation systems have struggled to become mainstream due to their technical nature. A drawback of smart homes is their perceived complexity. Some people have difficulty with technology or will give up on it with the first annoyance. Smart home manufacturers and alliances are working on reducing complexity and improving the user experience to make it enjoyable and beneficial for users of all types and technical levels.

For home automation systems to be truly effective, devices must be interoperable regardless of who manufactured them, using the same protocol or, at least, complementary ones. As it is such a nascent market, there is no gold standard for home automation yet. However, standard alliances are partnering with manufacturers and protocols to ensure interoperability and a seamless user experience.

Another major issue is smart home security. A 2016 NTT Data Corporation report found that 80% of U.S. consumers are concerned about the security of their smart home data. If hackers are able to infiltrate a smart device, they could potentially turn off the lights and alarms and unlock the doors, leaving a home defenseless to a break-in. Further, hackers could potentially access the homeowner's network, leading to worse attacks or data theft. In October 2016, the Mirai IoT botnet was able to bring down parts of the Internet in a series of distributed denial-of-service (DDoS) attacks using badly secured cameras, DVRs and routers as entry points.

In addition to security, many smart home opponents worry about data privacy. The NTT Data report found 73% of consumers are concerned about the privacy of the data shared by their smart home devices. While smart home device and platform manufacturers may collect consumer data to better tailor their products or offer new and improved services to customers, trust and transparency are critical to manufacturers building trust with the users of their smart products.

13.7 Conclusion

In this Chapter a detailed explanation of smart homes is given. The origin of smart home, examples of smart home technologies and smart home implementation is described. Home Area Networks (HANs) including HAN elements, HAN standards, HAN architectures and HAN initiatives are discussed. Finally smart home benefits and issues are explained in this Chapter.

14 SMART GRIDS

14.1 Introduction

A smart grid is an electricity network based on digital technology that is used to supply electricity to consumers via two-way digital communication. This system allows for monitoring, analysis, control and communication within the supply chain to help improve efficiency, reduce energy consumption and cost and maximize the transparency and reliability of the energy supply chain. In traditional electric grid, energy generation is done in centralized power plants. Energy distribution is one directional from the power plant to the homes or industries. The monitoring and restoration of grid is done manually. The communication is uni-directional. The smart grid was introduced with the aim of overcoming the weaknesses of conventional electrical grids by using smart net meters. Many government institutions around the world have been encouraging the use of smart grids for their potential to control and deal with global warming, emergency resilience and energy independence scenarios.

Smart grids achieve high reliability in power streams. It is a cyber-physical system equipped with sustainable models of energy production, distribution and usage. Smart grid is conceptualized as a planned nationwide network that uses information technology to deliver electricity efficiently, reliably and securely. Smart grid is also named as electricity with a brain or the energy Internet or electronet. Smart grid is a modernized grid that enables bidirectional flow of energy and uses two-way communication and control capabilities that will lead to an array of new functionalities and applications.

14.2 Characteristics of Smart Grid

Enables active participation by consumers— Consumer choices and increased interaction with the grid bring tangible benefits to both the grid and the environment, while reducing the cost of delivered electricity. The real-time monitoring of consumption, control of smart appliances, building automation and real-time pricing are some important characteristics of smart grid.

Accommodates all generation and storage options— Diverse resources with "plug-and-play" connections multiply the options for electrical generation and storage, including new opportunities for more efficient, cleaner power production. Integration of renewable energy sources and micro-grid is possible in smart grid.

Enables new products, services and markets — The grid's open-access market reveals waste and inefficiency and helps drive them out of the system while offering new consumer choices such as green power products and a new generation of electric vehicles. Reduced transmission congestion also leads to more efficient electricity markets.

Provides power quality for the digital economy — Digital-grade power quality for those who need it avoids production and productivity losses, especially in digital-device environments. Load forecasting is also possible with smart grids.

Optimizes asset utilization and operates efficiently — Desired functionality at minimum cost guides operations and allows fuller utilization of assets. More targeted and efficient grid maintenance programs result in fewer equipment failures and safer operations.

Anticipates and responds to system disturbances (self-heals) — The smart grid will perform continuous self-assessments to detect, analyze, respond to and as needed, restore grid components or network sections.

Operates resiliently against attack and natural disaster — The grid deters or withstands physical or cyber attack and improves public safety.

14.3 Benefits of Smart Grid

Smart Grids are equally beneficial for consumers as well as the stakeholders. Benefits to consumers are the following.

- Reduced operations and management costs for utilities and ultimately lower power costs for consumers.
- Reduced peak demand which will also help lower electricity rates.
- Better integration of customer-owner power generation systems including renewable energy systems.
- Quicker restoration of electricity after power disturbances.
- Improved security.
- Updated information on their energy usage in real-time.
- Enabling electric cars, smart appliances and other smart devices to be charged.
- The smart devices can be programmed to run during off-peak hours to lower energy bills.
- Different pricing options.

Benefits to stakeholders are as follows.

- Increases grid reliability.
- Reduces the frequency of power blackouts and brownouts.
- Provide infrastructure for monitoring analysis and decision making.

- Increases grid resiliency by providing detailed information.
- Reduce inefficiencies in energy delivery.
- Integrate the sustainable resources of wind and solar alongside the main grid.
- Improved management of distributed energy sources, including micro-grid operations and storage management.

14.4 Smart Grid Architecture

Figure 14.1 shows the basic architecture of a smart grid. There is a source of power generation which can be from renewable and non-renewable sources.. From the source of power generation, the electricity is transmitted through power transmission and distribution lines and is fed to a Neighborhood Area Network (NAN) comprising of various homes and offices. Each of the homes have smart appliances with smart meters. The power generation systems have various sensors and actuators connected to IP networks. IP networks are connected to Meter Data Management System (MDMS). MDMS can be connected to power transmission and distribution lines. At the same time MDMS can be connected to data aggregator unit which collects data from smart meters. In this there is a hand shaking between traditional electric grid and information flow.

Figure 14.2 shows the conceptual model of smart grid domains. Various components of conceptual model are customers, service providers, markets, generation systems, transmission systems and distribution systems. The dotted lines show electrical flow between various components and solid lines show the secure communication flow between various components.

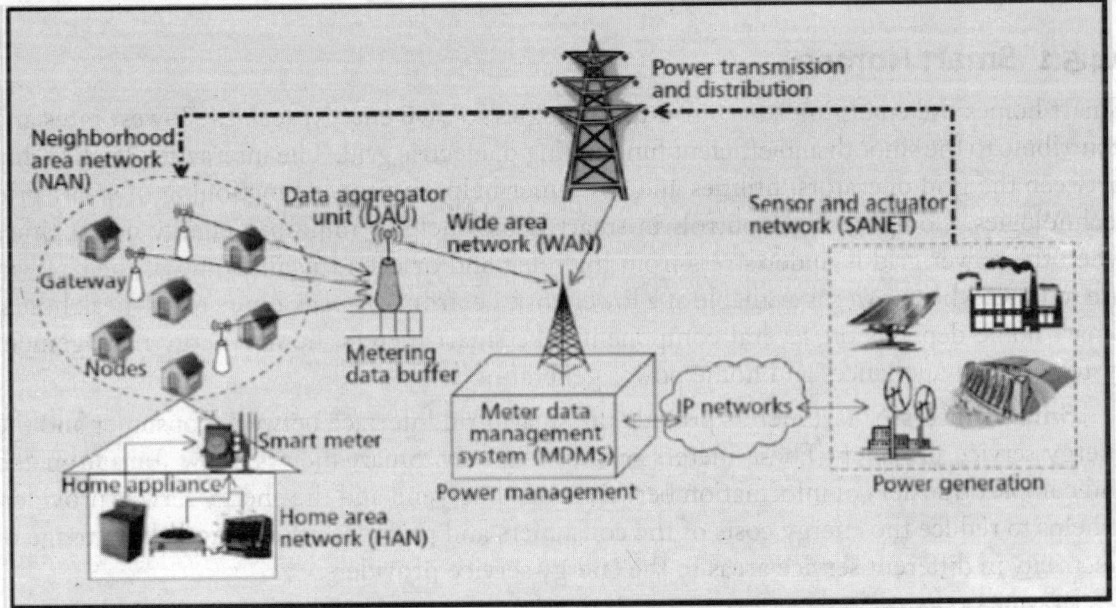

Fig.14.1: Architecture of a Smart Grid

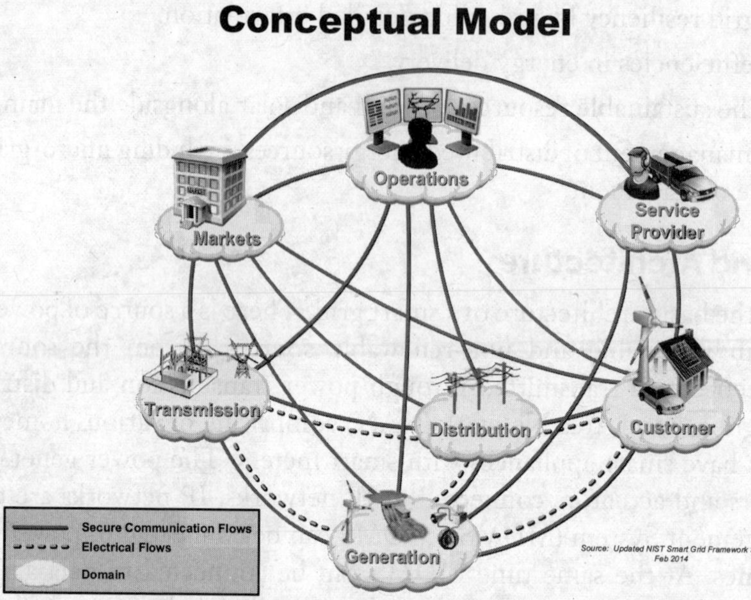

Fig.14.2: Conceptual Model of Smart Grid Domains

14.5 Components of Smart Grid

The components of a smart grid are smart homes, renewable energy, consumer engagement, operation centers, distribution intelligence and plug-in electric vehicle. We will see each one in detail.

14.5.1 Smart Homes

Smart homes use emerging smart grid technologies to save energy, seek the lowest rates and contribute to the smooth and efficient functioning of electric grid. The interactive relationship between the grid operators, utilities and consumer helps in proper functioning of smart grid technologies. Computerized controls in smart homes help to minimize energy use at times when the power grid is under stress from high demand or even to shift some of their power use to times when power is available at a lower cost, i.e. from on-peak hours to off-peak hours. Smart home depends on several components like smart meters, home energy management systems, smart appliances and home power generation.

Smart meters: Smart meters provide the smart grid interface between consumer and the energy service provider. These meters operate digitally. Smart meters allow for automated and complex transfers of information between consumer-end and the energy service provider. It helps to reduce the energy costs of the consumers and provides information about usage of electricity in different service areas to the energy service providers.

Home energy management systems: It allows consumers to track energy usage in detail to better save energy. Energy management systems allow consumers to monitor real-time information and price from the energy service provider. It provides settings to automatically use power when prices are lowest. The peak demand rates can be avoided using home energy management system. Further, it helps to balance the energy load in different area and also prevents blackouts. In return, the service provider may chose to provide financial incentives.

Smart appliances: These appliances are automated and robust in nature. It responds to signals from the energy service provider to avoid energy usage during times of peak-demand. For example an appliance may turn off automatically for few hours during peak hours to save energy. It can include consumer controls to override the automated controls. By overriding, the consumer can consume energy as per their requirements, while paying minimum is not ensured.

Home power generation: Power generation system at consumer end is one of the features of smart homes. Smart homes can have rooftop solar electric systems, small wind turbines or small hydropower systems. Home fuel cell systems that produce heat and power from natural gas can also be included in smart homes. Surplus energy generated by the home power generation systems can be fed back into the grid.

14.5.2 Renewable Energy

According to the International Energy Agency, renewable energy is derived from natural processes that are replenished constantly. In its various forms, it derives directly from the sun or from heat generated deep within the earth. Electricity and heat generated from solar, wind, ocean, hydropower, biomass, geo-thermal resources and bio-fuels are termed renewable energy. It reduces environmental pollution.

Consumers capable of generating energy from renewable energy sources are less dependent on the micro-grid or main grid. In addition, they can supply surplus amount of energy from the renewable resources and can make profit out of it.

14.5.3 Consumer Engagement

Consumers can save energy with proper scheduling of smart home appliances. Consumers need to pay less for energy consumed during off-peak hours. Energy service provider gives incentives based on the energy consumption of the consumer and they can save money. Consumer's engagement can be in following ways.

a. **Time-of-use pricing**: The consumers are encouraged to consume energy during off-peak hours when the energy load is less. Throughout the day, the energy load on the grids is dynamic. During on-peak hours, if the requested amount of energy is higher, it leads to less efficient energy distribution and more pollution as the grid depends on non-renewable energy resource to meet the peak requirements. Home energy management system tries to schedule the smart appliances in off-peak hours to ensure efficient services and to pay less.

b. **Net metering**: This is feasible with the installation of smart meters. Consumers are paid high, if they were supplying excess amount of generated energy to the grid during on-peak hours. The price is less in during off-peak hours. Final bills to be paid by the consumers depends on the in-flow of energy (from the grid to the consumers-end) and the out-flow of energy (from the consumers-end to the grid).

c. **Financial incentives**: Energy service provider offers some financial incentives for the consumer's participation. The consumer may get incentives from the energy service provider at the end of the year based on the net metering value. The incentives may include for shifting operation of the appliances to the off-peak hours and for using the stored energy at the battery installed at the consumer's end or at the plug-in hybrid electric vehicles (PHEVs).

14.5.4 Operation Centers

There are several drawbacks for the traditional operation centers. Some of them are given below.

a. Traditional grid tries to make sure that the amount of generated energy is getting used.
b. The grid is unstable, if the grid voltage drops due to excess energy generation.
c. There are limited control capabilities in traditional grid.
d. There are no means to detect oscillation which leads to blackout.
e. Limited information about the energy flow through the grid.

Smart grids on the other hand have the following advantages.

- Smart grids provide information and control on the transmission system.
- Makes the energy grid more reliable.
- Minimize the possibility of widespread blackouts.

For monitoring and controlling the transmission system in smart grid, Phasor Measurement Unit (PMU) is used. PMU samples voltage and current with a fixed sample rate at the installed location. It provides a snapshot of the active power system at that location. By increasing the sampling rate, PMU provides the dynamic scenario of the energy distribution system. PMU helps to identify the possibility of blackout in advance. Multiple PMUs form a phasor network. The information collected by the phasor network is analyzed at centralized system which is known as Supervisory Control and Data Acquisition (SCADA) system.

Self-healing of the grid is another advantage of smart grids. The smart grids dampen unwanted power oscillations. It avoids unwanted flows of current through the grid. The smart grids reroute power flows in order to avoid overloading in a transmission line. Demand side energy distribution is possible in smart grids. In this energy supply is done based on the requirement of consumers. The consumers pay according to the energy consumed and price is decided by the energy service provider at that time. In smart grids, the energy distributors can form coalition and serve the energy requirement in a specific geographic location.

14.5.5 Distribution Intelligence

Distribution intelligence means the energy distribution systems that are equipped with smart IoT devices. Smart meter is an example for distribution intelligence. Other features of distribution intelligence are the identification of the source of a power outage and ensure power flow automatically by combining automated switching. Distribution intelligence can optimize the balance between real and reactive power. There are devices that store and release energy. This may cause increased electrical currents without consuming real power. Intelligent distribution system maintains the proper level of reactive power in the system. In addition, it protects and controls the feeder lines.

14.5.6 Plug-in Electric Vehicles

Smart grids have the infrastructure needed to enable the efficient use of Plug-in Electric Vehicle (PEVs). PEVs reduce dependency on oil and further there is no pollution when running on electricity. PEVs rely on power plants to charge their batteries. Energy service provider encourages the consumer to charge batteries of PEVs during off-peak hours. PEVs can also be used as an energy source during on-peak hours. PEVs get incentives from energy service providers for providing energy to the grid through discharging.

14.6 Smart Grid Communication

Various components for smart grid communication are smart home appliances, smart meters, gateways, data aggregator units (DAUs) and Meter Data Management Systems (MDMSs). All these components are shown in the architecture of smart grid in Figure 14.1. There are different networks associated with smart grid communication like Home Area Networks (HANs), Neighborhood Area Networks (NANs), Wide Area Networks (WANs), IP networks and Sensors and Actuators networks (SANETs).

Smart meters and gateways: Smart meters forward the energy consumption information from the home appliances to gateways. The smart meters also forward the billing amount and the control information from the gateways to the home appliances. Gateways act as link between the smart meters and the Data Aggregator Units (DAUs). Each gateway connects few closely located smart meters. Gateways helps in two-way communication and the communications are mostly based on WiFi.

Data Aggregator Units (DAUs): They aggregate the energy consumption or energy request of certain geographical area. DAUs forward the energy consumption information to the centralized coordinator known as Meter Data Management System (MDMS). DAUs maintain a buffer to queue the energy consumption information of the consumers.

Meter Data Management Systems (MDMSs): They act as the centralized coordinator for smart grid communication. MDMSs are handled by energy service providers. It is a part of the operation center. MDMS decides the price per unit energy to be paid by the consumers.

For smart home communication, there are several protocols available. The protocols, data rate transmission and operational frequency are given below.

- C-BUS – The data rate is 3500 bits/sec and is able to handle lengths up to 1000m.
- DECT – The data rate is 64000 bits/sec and operates in 1880-1930 MHz.
- EnOcean – The data rate is 9600 bits/sec and operates in 902 MHz in North America.
- Universal Power Line Bus – The data rate is 480 bits/sec. It is a two-way communication protocol.
- Thread – The data rate is between 20 to 250 Kbits/sec. The IPv6 addressing based 6LoWPAN networking protocol is used.
- ZigBee – The data rate is between 20 to 250 Kbits/sec. It operates in 2.4 GHz band. Communication range is nearly 100m.
- Simplified Cable Solution (SCS) – The data rate is 9.6 Kbits/sec. It works on twisted pair and is developed based on OpenWebNet.

14.7 Smart Grid Security

Smart grid is a cyber physical system. There are several vulnerabilities in a smart grid. They are mainly integrity, availability, dynamic system attacks, physical threats and coordinated attacks.

Integrity

Integrity refers to the credibility of the data collected and transferred over the grid. The threats to integrity are Data Injection Attacks (DIAs) and system damage. DIA is the manipulation of exchanged data such as sensor readings, feedback control signals and electricity price signals. It is performed by compromising the hardware components or interrupting the communication links.

In system damage, an attacker can manipulate the system measurements so that a congested transmission line falsely seems to not have reached its thermal transmission limit. System damage may arise due to large fluctuations in system dynamics that can lead to tripping additional lines, disconnecting generators, load shedding or even a system blackout. The financial benefit for the intruders is the manipulation of electricity prices. One can buy energy with lesser price from a service provider and make high profit.

Another threat to integrity is the time synchronization attacks. The attacks that target PMU time synchronization are known as time synchronization attacks. An adversary can manipulate the time reference of the time stamped measured phasors to create a false visualization of the actual system conditions thus yielding inaccurate control and protection actions.

Availability

Availability is the accessibility to every grid component as well as to the information transmitted and collected. Attacks that compromise the availability are known as Denial-of-Service (DoS).

Intruders block key signals to compromise the stability of the grid and observation of its states. They can also manipulate generation-load balance.

Dynamic System Attacks

Dynamic system attacks include Replay Attacks (RAs), Dynamic Data Injection Attacks (DDIAs) and covert attack. In RAs, the intruders inject input data in the system without causing changes to the measurable outputs. RAs compromise sensors by monitoring their outputs, learns the outputs and repeats them while injecting its attack signal. DDIAs use knowledge of the grid's dynamic model to inject data which can lead to system collapse. Covert attack is the closed loop version of replay attacks.

Physical Threats

This involves the attack of a physical component such as a generator, substation or transmission line. These types of attacks are very prominent. Another type of physical threat is the physical manipulation of smart meters for energy theft purposes.

Coordinated Attacks

Usually power system typically incorporates robustness measures. Coordinated attack is an attack that leads to the failure of one or few components. Coordinated attacks exploit the dense interconnections between grid components to launch simultaneous attacks of different types targeting various components.

14.8 Smart Grid and Cloud

In smart grids, cloud applications take a lead in several aspects like energy management, information management and security. Figure 14.3 shows the integration of Cloud and smart grid.

Various components are substation, micro-grid, customer etc. The two important aspects of cloud is that the electricity is stored in cloud energy storage and information is stored in cloud data storage. The cloud integrated smart grids have made possible the integration of two different cloud approaches like energy storage and data storage.

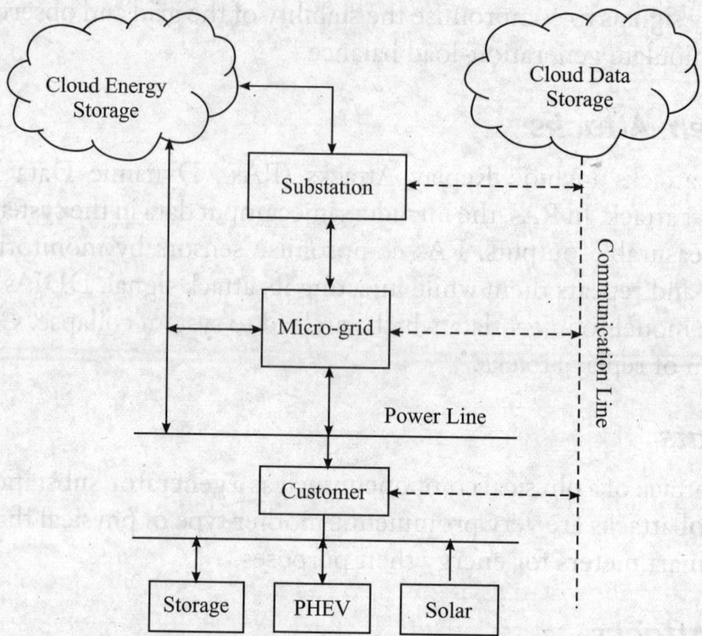

Fig.14.3: Integration of Cloud and Smart Grid

14.8.1 Energy Management

The energy management in smart grid can be more efficient by using cloud applications. With the integration of cloud with smart grid, the requests from customers are scheduled which are to be executed depending on the available resources, priority and other applicable constraints. Integrating cloud computing applications for micro-grid management is in the form of different modules such as infrastructure, power management and service. With this integration, the number of customers that can be supported increases. With this model, information streaming from multiple smart meters can be integrated and analyzed simultaneously in order to balance the real-time demand and supply curves.

Another advantage is that real-time energy usage and pricing information can be shared. Mobile agents can be used to monitor power system using cloud computing platform due to the smart grid's heterogeneous architecture.

14.8.2 Information Management

Information processing in smart grid fits well with the computing and storage mechanisms available for cloud applications. Information from different components and the supply and demand state conditions can be shared with the help of cloud computing. Real-time distributed data management and parallel processing of information can be utilized using smart grid data cloud application. With the flexibility of cloud computing, information is retrieved from the data cloud more conveniently in smart grid. Cloud computing services are used as a dynamic data center to store the real-time information from the smart meters.

Dynamic pricing mechanism in smart grid is feasible with the use of cloud application. Multi-mobile agent can be combined with cloud computing for profitable smart grid operation. Interactive cooperation using cloud services are used to support multiple customers and multiple energy sources. This will help for the large-scale development of smart grid for energy management. Figure 14.4 shows the information management in cloud.

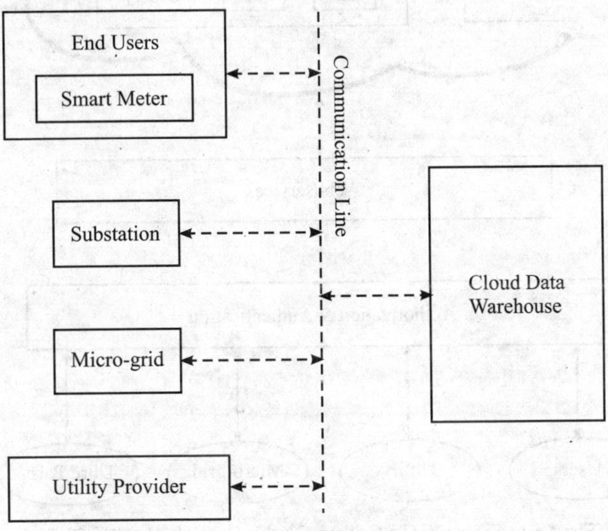

Fig.14.4: Information Management in Cloud

14.8.3 Security

An electric power information security and protection system can be developed based on cloud security. There are private cloud platforms that are suitable for scaling out and processing millions of data from users. Using the cloud computing platform, the electrical utilities can quickly and effectively deal with malicious software. In security and protection system for electrical power, servers act as cloud and take decision according to the client's data.

Cloud computing applications can quickly and effectively deal with malicious software. Data storage security for distributed verification in smart grid can be done using cloud application. Real-time data can be analyzed and estimated using cloud in smart grid. Cloud-based information privacy scheme can be used for smart grid data privacy. Figure 14.5 shows the security in smart grid integrated with cloud.

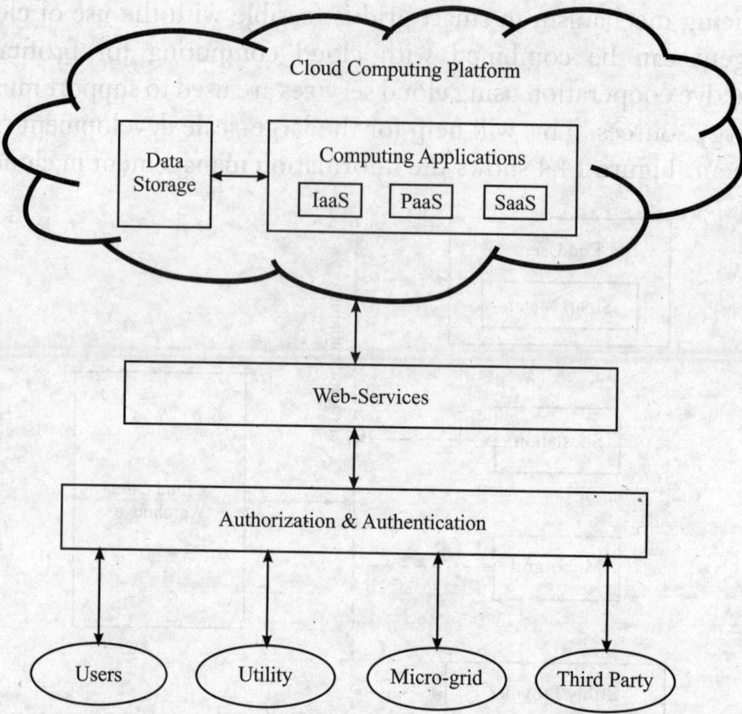

Fig.14.5: Security in Smart Grid Integrated with Cloud

14.9 Conclusion

This Chapter gives an overview about smart grids, one of the applications of Internet of Things. The characteristics of smart grid, benefits of smart grid and smart grid architecture are explained in detail. The components of smart grid namely smart homes, renewable energy, consumer engagement, operation centers, distribution intelligence and plug-in electric vehicles are well explained. Other aspects of smart grid like smart grid communication and smart grid security are clearly illustrated. Finally integration of smart grid with cloud applications for energy management, information management and security is also covered in this Chapter.

15 SMART CITIES

15.1 Introduction

In this Chapter, we will see an important application of Internet of Things namely smart cities. Smart cities are gaining momentum now-a-days with the explosion of Internet of Things.

A smart city is an urban area that uses different types of electronic data collection sensors to supply information which is used to manage assets and resources efficiently. This includes data collected from citizens, devices and assets that is processed and analyzed to monitor and manage traffic and transportation systems, power plants, water supply networks, waste management, law enforcement, information systems, schools, libraries, hospitals and other community services. The smart city concept integrates information and communication technology (ICT), and various physical devices connected to the network to optimize the efficiency of city operations and services and connect to citizens. Smart city technology allows city officials to interact directly with both community and city infrastructure and to monitor what is happening in the city and how the city is evolving.

ICT is used to enhance quality, performance and interactivity of urban services, to reduce costs and resource consumption and to increase contact between citizens and government. Smart city applications are developed to manage urban flows and allow for real-time responses. A smart city may therefore be more prepared to respond to challenges than one with a simple "transactional" relationship with its citizens. Major technological, economic and environmental changes have generated interest in smart cities, including climate change, economic restructuring, the move to online retail and entertainment, ageing populations, urban population growth and pressures on public finances. The European Union (EU) has devoted constant efforts to devising a strategy for achieving 'smart' urban growth for its metropolitan city-regions. The EU has developed a range of programmes under 'Europe's Digital Agenda". In 2010, it highlighted its focus on strengthening innovation and investment in ICT services for the purpose of improving public services and quality of life.

15.2 Characteristics of Smart Cities

It has been suggested that a smart city also known as smart community, business cluster, urban agglomeration or region uses information technologies for the following.

a. Make more efficient use of physical infrastructure (roads, built environment and other physical assets) through artificial intelligence and data analytics to support a strong and healthy economic, social, cultural development.

b. Engage effectively with local people in local governance and decision by use of open innovation processes and e-participation, improving the collective intelligence of the city's institutions through e-governance, with emphasis placed on citizen participation and co-design.

c. Learn, adapt and innovate and thereby respond more effectively and promptly to changing circumstances by improving the intelligence of the city. They evolve towards a strong integration of all dimensions of human intelligence, collective intelligence and also artificial intelligence within the city. The intelligence of cities "resides in the increasingly effective combination of digital telecommunication networks (the nerves), ubiquitously embedded intelligence (the brains), sensors and tags (the sensory organs) and software (the knowledge and cognitive competence)".

These forms of intelligence in smart cities have been demonstrated in three ways. They are as follows.

Orchestration intelligence: Orchestration intelligence means cities establish institutions and community-based problem solving and collaborations.

Empowerment intelligence: Cities provide open platforms, experimental facilities and smart city infrastructure in order to cluster innovation in certain districts.

Instrumentation intelligence: Here city infrastructure is made smart through real-time data collection, with analysis and predictive modeling across city districts. There is much controversy surrounding this, particularly with regard to surveillance issues in smart cities. Examples of instrumentation intelligence have been implemented in Amsterdam. This is implemented through a common IP infrastructure that is open to researchers to develop applications, wireless meters and devices that transmit information at the point in time, a number of homes being provided with smart energy meters to become aware of energy consumption and reduce energy usage and solar power garbage compactors, car recharging stations and energy saving lamps.

15.3 Smart City Frameworks

In order to achieve an accurate description and explanation of the concept of smart city it is needed to first analyze the topic through a specific framework. The framework is divided into 4 main dimensions: Technology framework, Human framework, Institutional framework and Energy framework. We will see each framework in detail.

1. Technology Framework

Several concepts of the smart city rely heavily on the use of technology. A technological smart city is not just one concept but there are different combinations of technological infrastructure that build a concept of smart city.

Digital city: It combines service oriented infrastructure, innovation services and communication infrastructure. A digital city is a connected community that combines broadband communications infrastructure, flexible, service-oriented computing infrastructure based on open industry standards. It has innovative services to meet the needs of governments and their employees, citizens and businesses. The main purpose is to create an environment in which citizens are interconnected and easily share information anywhere in the city.

Virtual city: In these kinds of cities, functions are implemented in a cyberspace. It includes the notion of hybrid city, which consists of a reality with real citizens and entities and a parallel virtual city of real entities and people. Having a smart city that is virtual means that in some cities it is possible the coexistence between these two reality. However the issue of physical distance and location is still not easy to manage. The vision of the world without distance still remains unmet in many ways. In practice this idea is hold up through physical IT infrastructure of cables, data centers and exchanges.

Information city: It collects local information and delivered them to the public portal. In that city, many inhabitants are able to live and even work on the Internet because they could obtain each information through IT infrastructures. Using this approach, an information city could be an urban centre both economically and socially. The most important thing is the linkage among civic services, people interactions and government institutions.

Intelligent city: It involves function as research or technological innovation to support learning and innovation procedure. The notion emerges in a social context in which knowledge, learning process and creativity have great importance and the human capital is considered the most precious resource within this type of technological city. In particular, one of the most significant features of an intelligent city is that every infrastructure is up to date which means this city has the latest technology in telecommunications, electronic and mechanical technology.

Ubiquitous city (U-city): It creates an environment that connects citizens to any services through any device. U-city is a further extension of digital city concept because of the facility in terms of accessibility to every infrastructure. This makes easier to the citizen the use of any available devices to interconnect them. Its goal is to create a city where any citizen can get any services anywhere and anytime through any kind of devices. It is important to highlight that the ubiquitous city is different from the above virtual city. While the virtual city creates another space by visualizing the real urban elements within the virtual space, U-city is given by the computer chips inserted to those urban elements.

Cognitive Smart City: Cognitive smart city expands the concept of the smart city by referring to the convergence of the emerging Internet of Things (IoT) and smart city technologies, their generated big data and artificial intelligence techniques. Continuous learning through human interactions and consequently performing a dynamic, flexible behavior and actions based on the dynamic environment of the city are the core components of such framework.

2. Human framework

Human infrastructure like creative occupations and workforce, knowledge networks and voluntary organizations is a crucial axis for city development.

Creative city: Creativity is recognized as a key driver to smart city and it represents also a version of it. Social infrastructures, like for instance intellectual and social capital are indispensable factors to build a city that is smart according to the human framework. These infrastructures concern people and their relationship. Smart city benefits from social capital and it could be possible and easier to create a smart city concept if there are mix of education and training, culture and arts, business and commerce.

Learning city: A learning city is involved in building skilled workforce. This type of city in the human context improves the competitiveness in the global knowledge economy. Cities that are learning to be smart are individually proactive city, city cluster, one-to-one link between cities and city network.

Human city: It exploits human potential, in particular the knowledge workforce. With this approach, it is possible to focus on education and builds a center of higher education thereby obtaining better-educated individuals. This view moves a smart city concept in a city full of skilled workforces. The same reasoning could be made for those high tech knowledge-sensitive industries which want to migrate in a so dynamic and proactive community.

Knowledge city: It is related to knowledge economy and innovation process. This type of smart city is very similar to a learning city. The concept of knowledge city is linked with similar evolving concepts of smart city such as intelligent city and educating city. The most important feature of this city is the fundamental concept of knowledge-based urban development, which has become an important and widespread mechanism for the development of knowledge cities.

3. Institutional framework

Members of these frameworks are people that share their interest and work in a partnership with government and other institutional organizations to push the use of IT to improve the quality of daily life as a consequence of different worsening in daily actions. A smart community makes a conscious and agreed-upon decision to deploy technology as a catalyst to solving its social and business needs. It is very important to understand that this use of IT and the consequent improvement could be more demanding without the institutional help. A city is smart when investments in human/social capital and IT infrastructure fuel sustainable growth and enhance quality of life, through participatory governance.

4. Energy framework

Smart cities use data and technology to create efficiencies, improve sustainability, create economic development and enhance quality of life factors for people living and working in the city. It also means that the city has a smarter energy infrastructure. A smart city is powered by "smart connections" for various items such as street lighting, smart buildings, distributed energy resources (DER), data analytics and smart transportation. Amongst these things, energy is paramount. This is why utility companies play a key role in smart cities. Electric companies, working partnership with city officials, technology companies and a number of other institutions, are among the major players that helped accelerate the growth of America's smart cities.

5. Data Management framework

Smart city employs a combination of data collection, processing and disseminating technologies in conjunction with networking and computing technologies. Data security and privacy measures encouraging application innovation to promote the overall quality of life for its citizens. The dimensions include utilities, health, transportation, entertainment and government services.

15.4 Challenges in Smart Cities

There are several challenges that exist in the implementation of smart cities. The development of smart city confronts several challenges from the technological perspective.

Security and privacy: Preserving privacy of citizens and end users is a big concern since most of the frameworks require collecting data from the citizens. The data collected can be exposed to attacks, vulnerabilities and multi-tenancy which include the risk of data leakage.

Heterogeneity: It involves the integration of varying hardware platforms and specifications. Various radio specifications and software platforms need to be integrated. Accommodating varying user requirements is another challenging task in smart ciy.

Reliability: There can be unreliable communication in smart cities due to vehicle mobility. Delivery failures are still significant in smart cities. There can be delay in receiving data due to mobility of deployed nodes. Distribution of devices can affect monitoring tasks also.

Legal and social aspects: The legal aspects of smart cities include services based on user provided information which is subject to local or international laws. Social issue is that individual and informed consent is required for using humans as data sources.

Big data: Challenges related to Big data include storage, management, fusion, consistency, trustworthiness and 3V's (Volume, Velocity and Variety). In a smart city context, this becomes more significant. Transfer, storage and maintenance of huge volumes of data are expensive. Data cleaning and purification of data is time consuming. Analytics on gigantic data volumes is process intensive. On-device and embedded intelligence to support light-weight artificial intelligence on IoT and resource-constrained devices that build the smart city infrastructure is yet another challenge.

Sensor networks: Choice of appropriate sensors for individual sensing tasks and energy planning is crucial. Device placement and network architecture is important for reliable end-to-end IoT implementation. Communication medium and means play an important role in seamless function of IoT in smart cities.

15.5 Data Fusion

IoT is expected to be a major producer of big data. This data would be produced by various vendors giving rise to data as a service. Sharing and collaboration of data and other resources would be the key for enabling sustainable ubiquitous environments such as smart cities and societies. The fusion of various types and forms of data, i.e. data fusion, to enhance data quality and decision making therefore would be of prime importance in ubiquitous environments. Data fusion is defined as 'the theory, techniques and tools which are used for combining sensor data or data derived from sensory data, into a common representational format. A timely fusion and analysis of big data (volume, velocity, variety and veracity), acquired from IoT and other sources, to enable highly efficient, reliable and accurate decision making and management of ubiquitous environments would be a grand future challenge. Computational intelligence would play a key role in this challenge.

Enormous amount of data is produced periodically in a smart city environment. Challenges include making the available or incoming large data volume precise and accurate. The quality of data precision and accuracy affects the quality of decision making in IoT enabled smart cities. Data fusion enables optimum utilization of massive data gathered from multiple sources and across multiple platforms.

In a multi-sensor data fusion, it combines information from multiple sensor sources. Multi-sensor data fusion enhances the ability of decision making systems to include a multitude of variables prior to arriving at a decision. Inferences drawn from multiple sensor data type is qualitatively superior to single sensor type data. Information generated from multiple heterogeneous sensors provides for better understanding of the operational surroundings. Multi-sensor data fusion helps for the optimal amalgamation of data. It also enables hiding of critical data sources and semantics which is useful in military applications, medical cases etc. Figure 15.1 shows the single-hop and multi-hop sensor data fusion. With respect to Figure 15.1, IoT data fusion can also be seen with two different perspectives. First, it can be viewed as a single hop where every sensor transmits data to the data fusion center directly. Second, it can occur by a multi-hop process, where data passes across adjacent sensors.

There are various stages of data fusion include decision level, feature level, pixel level and signal level. In signal level data fusion, fusion of information takes place at the sensor node or within the local network itself. In pixel level data fusion, fusion of information takes place at the imaging device level itself. In feature level data fusion, fusion of information takes place prior to decision making. Data fusion at decision level is an ensemble of decisions.

Mathematical models of data fusion include probability based, Artificial Intelligence (AI) based or Theory of Evidence based. Probability based methods include Bayesian analysis, statistical methods and recursive methods while AI based methods include Artificial Neural Networks (ANN), machine learning etc. Theory of Evidence based methods include belief functions, transferable belief models etc. Figure 15.2 shows the use of AI in IoT decision making.

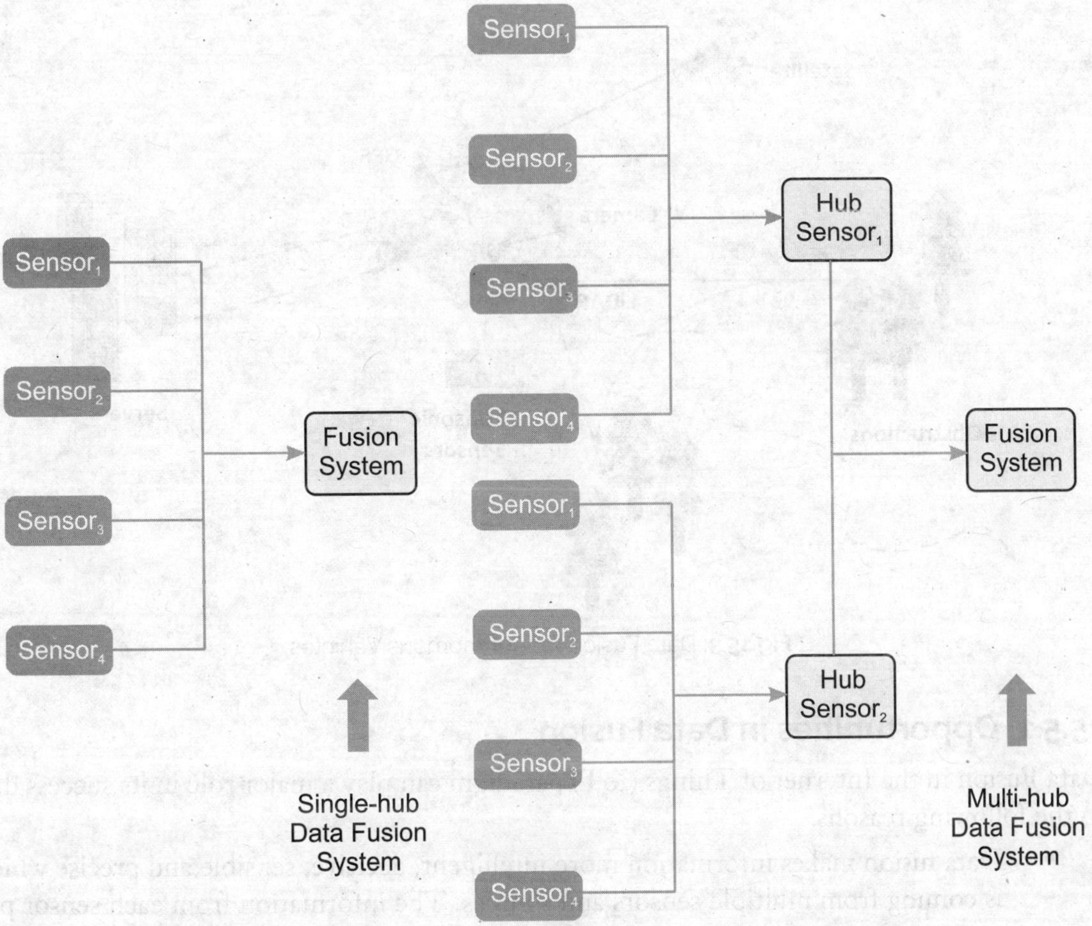

Fig.15.1: Single-hop and Multi-hop Sensor Data Fusion

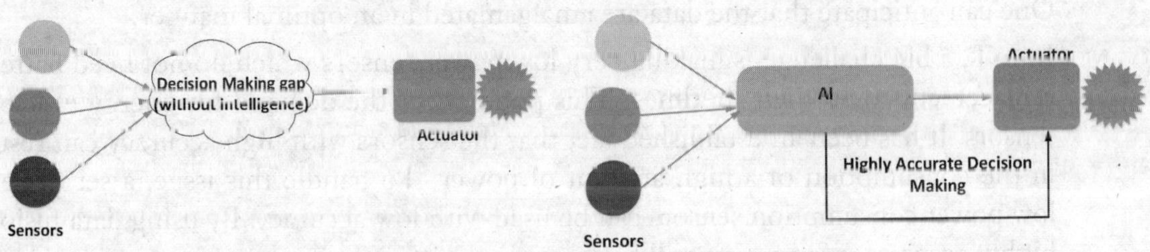

Fig.15.2: Use of AI in Decision Making

Similarly the data fusion for autonomous vehicles is shown in Figure 15.3.

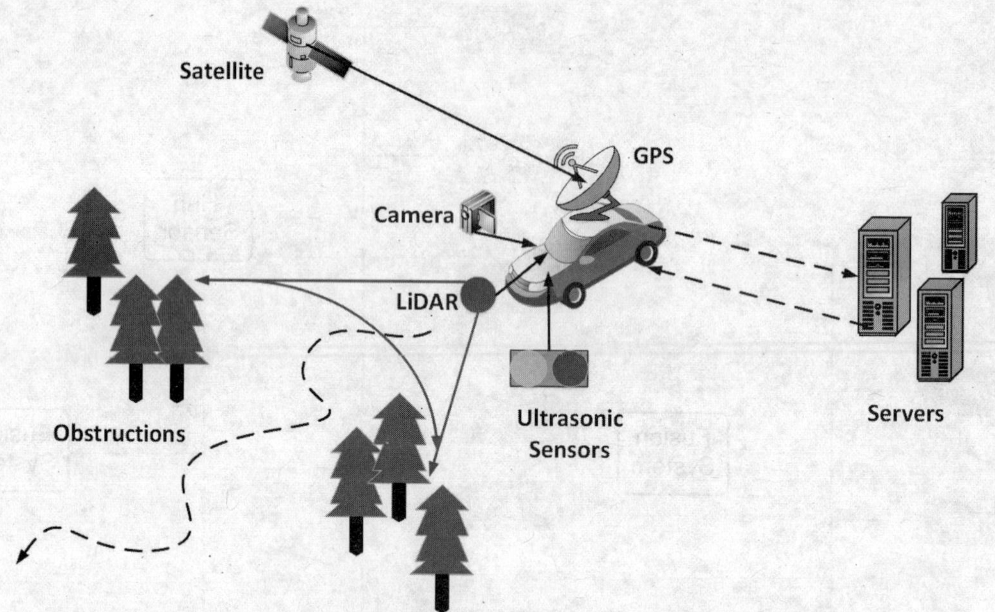

Fig.15.3: Data Fusion for Autonomous Vehicles

15.5.1 Opportunities in Data Fusion

Data Fusion in the Internet of Things (IoT) paradigm can play a major role in its success due to the following reasons.

- Data fusion makes information more intelligent, decisive, sensible and precise which is coming from multiple sensors and sources. The information from each sensor per se may not make much sense.
- A statistical benefit of fusion is obtained by computing the N independent observations. One can anticipate that the data are amalgamated in an optimal manner.
- In IoT, a big challenge is making very low power sensors which do not need battery replacements over their lifetimes. This popularizes the demand for energy efficient sensors. It has been an established fact that the sensors with high accuracy can result in the consumption of a high amount of power. To handle this issue, a set of very low power consumption sensors can be used with low accuracy. By using data fusion, highly accurate information will be created.
- Data fusion can be helpful in handling the big data issues of IoT because we are fusing data from many sensors into more precise and accurate information.
- Another critical advantage of data fusion is that it helps to hide the critical information or the semantics which are responsible for the fused results. Examples of this are in military applications, some critical medical areas and in intelligence buildings.

15.5.2 Challenges in Data Fusion

Data Fusion has multiple challenges ahead which are listed below.

- Data Imperfection: Sensor data is imprecise at times. It can be inaccurate and uncertain. This behavior is not infamous in wireless sensor networks. The imperfection must be dealt with effectively with the use of data fusion algorithms.
- Ambiguities and Inconsistencies: Impreciseness is not the only factor responsible for data inconsistencies. The environment in which a sensor is operating is largely responsible as well. Outlier detection, replacement and data imputation are vital in IoT environment.
- Conflicting Nature: The conflicting nature of data can give rise to counter-intuitive results. The problem of conflicting data is visible more in evidential belief reasoning. The data fusion algorithm must take critical care while treating conflicting data.
- Data Correlation and Alignment: This problem is more common in Wireless Sensor Networks (WSNs) and can result in over or under confidence in a data fusion algorithm. An alignment problem which is also known as a sensor registration problem occurs when sensor data is transformed from every sensor's local frame to a common frame prior to fusion.
- Trivial Features: In IoT environment, applications may consist of several hundreds and thousands of sensors sensing different parameters. These sensed values in large setups such as smart cities and industrial plants consist of trivial and nontrivial data. Processing of trivial data may affect the data fusion accuracy. Thus most relevant features need to be selected before data fusion.
- Dynamically Iterative Process: Data fusion is not a static process in nature. However, dynamically iterative needs regular refinement of the estimates in a fusion environment.

It is still difficult to say that a perfect data fusion algorithm exists. In IoT, environment information fusion can be used in various areas to enhance the IoT ubiquitous aspect. These areas are environmental monitoring, healthcare, crisis management, monitoring, controlling, tracking, intelligence gathering and many more.

15.6 Smart Parking

Smart Parking is a parking strategy that combines technology and human innovation in an effort to use as few resources as possible such as fuel, time and space to achieve faster, easier and denser parking of vehicles for the majority of time they remain idle.

Smart parking and its sister approach, intelligent transportation, are based on the fundamental ecological principle that we are all connected. Parking and transportation are both essential in the movement of people and goods. The smart parking and intelligent transportation vision and overlapping technologies are steadily developing into one integrated stream.

Nowadays, the Internet is turning more and more dynamic, dense and heterogeneous. To support such a real-time service, conventional system architectures cannot satisfy any more drivers. Endless parking conflicts are happening every moment and we have to reconsider the system from all different perspectives, as a smart parking ecosystem. An essential smart parking ecosystem includes two flows: information and traffic. Figure 15.4 shows the smart parking ecosystem. The traffic flow happens on the path-way to find parking, as shown in the lower in Figure 15.4. Vehicle drivers receive parking availability information, steer to their desired parking areas and then park. When there are many drivers looking for a parking space, a competition occurs and results in cumulative parking conflicts. Parking behaviors also vary considering the information drivers have and how long they are cruising on the street. Once a vehicle arrives in or departs from a parking space, the parking availability information changes and is advertised to other drivers looking for a parking space. The parking information, from the moment when they are detected by sensors to the moment when they appeared on driver's terminals, is called the information flow, shown in Figure. 15.4.

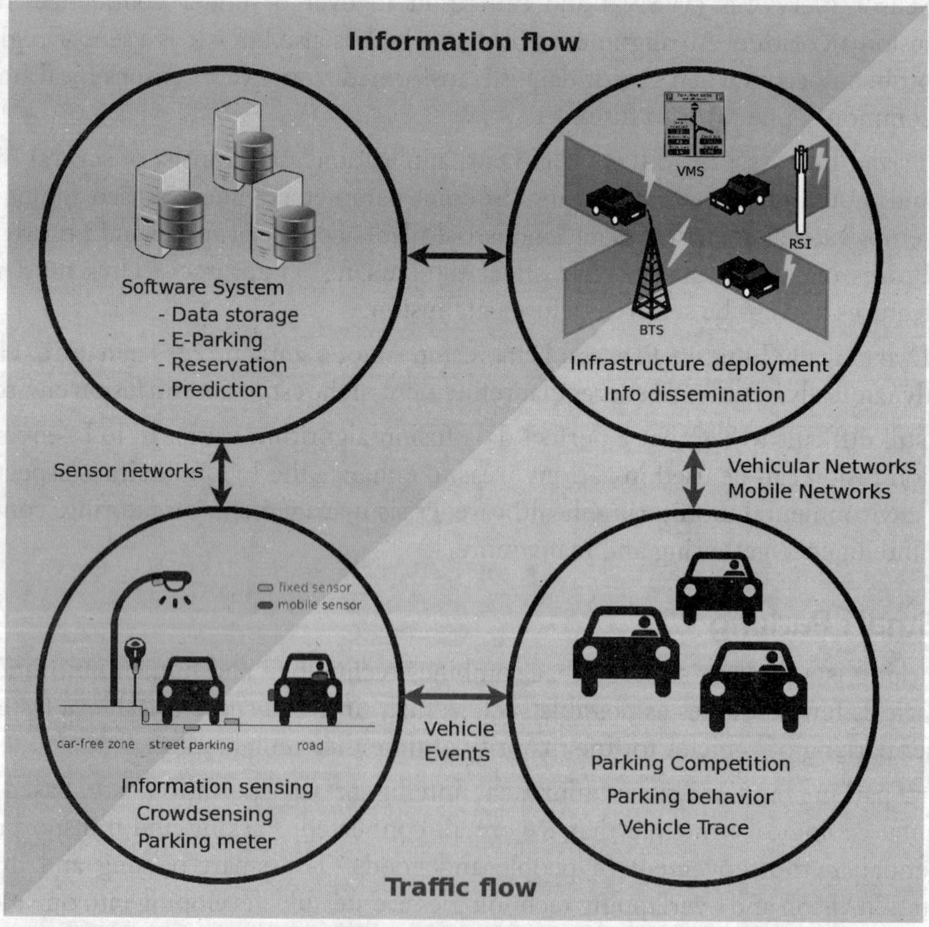

Fig.15.4: Smart Parking Eco-system

To get the occupancy status of parking spaces, sensors are installed on on-street parking to detect vehicular events. Then, sensors form a network and send the latest information to data storage devices. Drivers can obtain the latest information from Variable Message Signs (VMS) or their handheld smart devices that exchange messages with Road Side Infrastructure (RSI) or Base Transceiver Stations (BTS).There are several challenges in smart parking. Following factors should be taken into consideration while smart parking systems are deployed.

Robustness of sensor devices – Sensor devices are embedded systems that process sensed data into useful information and always evaluate their own health status, i.e., lifetime or malfunction, to inform system administration of any problem.

The stability and timeliness of sensor networks – The sensed information on sensor devices shall be collected through wireless networks. When there are lots of sensor devices, the spectrum is often limited and a transmission scheduling is needed. When a vehicle parks on a sensor-equipped parking space, it might block the radio communication and the status change will not be broadcasted on time.

The quality and agility of city service – Smart parking system uses sensed information to offer real time parking information to drivers. The system has to manage all of the parking resources, maintenance and payments. It has to efficiently filter parking information through driver's interests. If the drivers' interests are not well defined, the system shall be able to adapt and still provides a minimal level of service quality.

The user-centric information dissemination and assignment – Currently all the smart parking apps provide the same information to all drivers, but real-time parking availability data is useful only when the driver is very close to the parking location. Hence, the information shall be broadcasted to drivers considering their mobility and location.

Uncertainty of driver's behavior and traveling traces –Driver's behavior is strongly related to the information they have from smart parking systems, personal preferences and the city street layout. Before getting driver's data, their behavior can only be obtained from payment information or questionnaires.

The functional layers in smart parking are **information collection, system deployment** and **service dissemination.**

15.6.1 Information Collection

Information collection takes a technical overview of all the existing sensing techniques to identify parking spaces status. Two major research focuses are on the identification and transmission of vehicular information. The former involves various stationary and mobile sensors, including their detection methods and installation. The latter explains how sensors and cities' infrastructures collaborate together to gather information efficiently. There are two emerging urban services namely crowdsensing and gaparking, applied in smart parking. Both of them consider citizens as parking detectors that contribute to accessible parking information on the Internet. Information collection involves information sensing, sensor connectivity, parking meter, crowdsensing and gaparking.

A. Information Sensing

Information sensing relies on sensors to collect real-time parking availability information. Stationary and mobile collections are two types of methods. The former instinctively adds sensing ability on parking spaces. When the occupancy status changes, a sensor can detect a vehicle's presence or absence and updates the information in a short time. The latter takes advantage of the vehicle's mobility to collect information along the route with fewer sensors. Mobile sensors can detect the occupancy status when they pass through a parking space, so the information might not be updated for a long while. In ParkNet, a smart parking system, taxi cabs collect data from GPS receivers and ultrasonic sensors and then transmit it over a cellular uplink to the central server. Such a mobile parking sensor system requires much less installation, yet needs a longer average inter-polling time, to wait, 25 minutes for 80% of the cells in the business downtown area with 300 cabs. Different sensors have distinct manners to detect a vehicle's presence.

Passive infrared sensors receive heat radiated from the human body and are often used collaboratively with other sensors to know if a driver parks and gets off his/her car. Active infrared sensors measure the distance to any obstacle in front. Infrared sensors are very sensitive to sun and any kind of environmental object so that the sensing accuracy is not so good. Similar to infrared sensors, ultrasonic sensors use sound instead of light and work better in outdoor environments. Ultrasonic sensors provide a more complex signal pattern with a possibility of multiple detections in fixed or mobile scenarios. Accelerators measure the instantaneous ground vibrations. Since vehicles are usually the heaviest objects on the street, accelerators can infer that a vehicle comes and parks, with the aid of other sensors, e.g., optical sensors, which detect the change in light. Optical sensors must be installed where light can be obscured by a parked vehicle. However, optical sensors are vulnerable to any light source and transient staying objects, so their accuracy is still questionable. Magnetometers are, so far, the most common stationary parking detection sensors, especially for municipal deployment. It measures the current magnetic fields and detects huge metal object's presence. Its signal pattern is easy to read and precise but cannot support multiple detections. It is also more expensive than the above mentioned sensors. Alternatively, installed magnetometers along the driving pathway and compared the different counts between any two adjacent sensors to know roughly how many vehicles are parked between them.

Cameras and acoustic sensors provide a much more complicated signal pattern than ultrasonic. Both of them require image and sonar processing in order to extract the desired information from the background noise. Nevertheless, they have aroused certain research interests because of some extra information, concerning criminal scenes or personal privacy. Inductive loops and piezoelectric sensors are both contactive and installed on road surface. Inductive loop technology is considered mature and is widely used for traffic surveillance. It simply detects if a vehicle is passing. Piezoelectric sensors are similar to inductive loops but able to read more detailed information from the pressure exerted on it. Such kind of contact sensors require an intrusive installation and they are easy to be worn-out because of their frequent use. RFID is often proposed in smart parking payment solutions. As the popularity of electronic toll collection (ETC) increases, many vehicles, equipped with RFID tags, can be detected by RFID readers installed on parking spaces. Laser rangefinder is often used to build a 1/2/3D map, especially for environmental perception. Normally installed on vehicles, it emits a laser beam and calculates the time of flight to measure the distances from different objects in order to know if there are parked vehicles. Intelligent robots cruising on the street can also be used to recognize available parking spaces.

Mobile crowdsensing via smart phone is the most economical way to obtain parking availability information from drivers themselves. QR codes might be installed on parking spaces to help drivers identify and pay their parking spaces. When a driver ends a parking session, the system will announce that his/her parking space is now available to other drivers looking for parking. However, this system cannot control if drivers do pay their parking spaces since QR codes cannot detect vehicles' presence.

B. Sensor Connectivity

Once networked sensors are installed on parking spaces, they can form a network to send out their messages. There are two typical communication methods: either short-range, such as Bluetooth/BLE, 802.11ah (Wi-Fi HaLow) and ZigBee/Z-Wave/DigiMesh, or long-range, like Sigfox, LoRa, Weightless, Ingenu and NB-IoT/LTE-M. The long-range communication benefits from the existing radio access network can communicate with infrastructures anytime and anywhere. Short-range communication is often implemented by WSN where messages have to be re-transmitted several times via relays, e.g., parking meters or other sensors, until they reach cities' infrastructures. The studies on WSN have been germinating for several years but few of them have been evaluated in an urban parking context considering lifetime, information delay and wireless link quality constraints.

1. Low-Power Wide-Area Network (LPWAN): Considering the rich functionality of 3G/4G is unnecessary for networked sensor devices, a long-range cellular link has to be adapted to the emerging IoT market. Long-range IoT communication technologies, namely cellular IoT, are designed for LPWAN. Because of their compatibility with the existing cellular networks, no extra infrastructure is required.
2. Wireless Sensor Network (WSN): Unlike LPWAN, WSN does not need a monthly fee per sensor. In order to coordinate a group of sensors, delay and mesh network's energy efficiency are the main challenge. The communication reliability in the range of 0 to 5 meters is good. If senders and receivers are both covered by parked cars, no communication is possible.

C. Parking Meter

Parking meters are used by municipalities as a tool to pay on-street parking. With the rise of networked sensors, parking meters are turned into parking helpers, which establish a link between drivers and parking data. Single-space and multispace meters are the two main automated payment machines. Multi-space meter manages several parking meters and can provide more functionalities than single-space ones. Parking meters are often used as relays for parking sensors. Thus, parking meters are not only basic payment machines but also transceivers, which can be integrated into existing relays and infrastructures for any communication devices. Parking meters might communicate with some mobile access points, such as taxis and buses, to enrich urban information and increase transmission opportunities.

Vehicular on-board units (OBU) can communicate with roadside parking meters in order to gather availability parking information and find a parking space. Drivers, who park their cars on on-street parking spaces, can easily extend their parking time and pay from the Internet. The payment information will be updated and showed on parking meters. Besides, parking meters have an internal clock and are able to turn off themselves during parking time so as to reduce energy consumption. Some big companies work on service integration to enrich parking meters' functionalities and their interaction with drivers.

D. Crowdsensing

Crowdsourcing has been used in some smart parking applications, especially in gathering the sensed available parking information from smart phone users. Thus, a new term crowdsensing came. The most common way is to design a smart parking app and motivate users to voluntarily share information, namely participatory crowdsensing. Three high-level conclusions can be drawn by mobile sensors: if there was still space in the area, if the area is full, or if the area should no longer be full. Five different spaces were determined to generate individuals' behaviors, such as parking time and probability. Drivers, who are not participating in crowdsensing and not using the decision support application, would still benefit from this application.

E. Shared parking - Gaparking

Gaparking takes the ideas of gap and parking to share one parking spot to more than one motorist at a different time. Principally, parking spot owners register their spare parking spots on a website through an app with proposed price and service time and then drivers bid one appropriate space that meets their needs. Some commercial car parks might join to sell their parking spots as a single person. ParkingAuction, Mobypark and JustPark are the most popular gaparking apps. Gaparking inherits the business model of Uberisation (shared economy) which allows peer-to-peer transactions between individuals' needs and services. It provides adequate parking and reduces excessive land use by optimizing personal resources.

15.6.2 System Deployment

System deployment deals with the software system exploitation and the statistical analysis of the collected data. Software generally involves E-Parking, reservation, guidance and monitoring information for administration and users. With the collected data, an analysis is often performed by data scientists to study drivers' behavior so as to improve the system performance and help municipalities make a better urban planning. System deployment involves the software system, information management, E-parking, guidance and data analytics.

15.6.3 Service Dissemination

Service dissemination investigates the relationship between information and social features. Two major research focuses are information dissemination and parking competition caused by individual behavior. Information dissemination is mainly related to communication techniques between vehicles and information. Municipalities can choose where and how to install urban infrastructure according to their planning and budget. Parking competition always happens when more than two drivers contend the same parking space. With the information assisted smart parking service, drivers' decisions are even more complicated to predict. Thus, studies on parking behaviors are important while designing a smart parking system. Service dissemination includes dynamic pricing, strategies, infrastructure based information, infrastructure free information, parking choice and vehicular activities.

15.7 Energy Management in Smart Cities

Energy management in smart cities involve energy efficient solutions like light weight protocols, scheduling optimization, predictive models for energy consumption, cloud based approach, low-power transceivers and cognitive management framework. Energy harvesting solutions include ambient energy harvesting and dedicated energy harvesting. Ambient energy harvesting includes RF sources, wind, sun, heat and vibration. In dedicated energy harvesting, energy sources are intentionally deployed near IoT sources. Amount of energy harvested depends on sensitivity of the harvesting circuit, distance between the device and the source and environment.

15.8 Conclusion

This Chapter gives a detailed description of smart cities. The characteristics of smart cities, various smart city frameworks and challenges in smart cities are explained. Data fusion, opportunities in data fusion and challenges in data fusion are described in this Chapter. Smart parking which is an important element of smart cities is described in detail. Various aspects of smart parking like information collection, system deployment and service dissemination is well explained. Finally energy management in smart cities is also discussed in this Chapter.

16 CONNECTED VEHICLES

16.1 Introduction

Connected vehicles are vehicles that use any of a number of different communication technologies to communicate with the driver, other cars on the road (vehicle-to-vehicle [V2V]), roadside infrastructure (vehicle-to-infrastructure [V2I]) and the "Cloud" [V2C]. This technology can be used to not only improve vehicle safety, but also to improve vehicle efficiency and commute times. Automated and connected vehicle technologies are among the most heavily researched automotive technologies. The vehicle technologies currently available are only a fraction of what is being developed for the future. The technologies for autonomous cars, connected cars and advanced driver assistance systems may overlap.

As emerging technologies from the consumer electronics and IT technology fields crossover to the automotive domain, modern vehicles are being equipped with powerful sensors and networking and communication devices that can communicate with other vehicles and exchange information with the external environment. A connected vehicle is evolving to have devices that can be connected to other devices within the vehicle itself and/or devices, networks and services outside the vehicle, including other vehicles, the home, office, or surrounding infrastructure. The way in which we interact with our vehicles is rapidly changing, driven by the increased use of mobile devices, cloud-based services and advanced automotive technology. In particular, the machine interface between automobiles and humans must allow for the seamless integration of several types of personal devices that support various software and hardware standards to allow drivers to use their smart phones while driving. Therefore, the future vehicle will have the capability of surround sensing and can form connections between vehicles, as well as between vehicles and surrounding infrastructure. This will lead to increased requirements for information and communication technology and ultimately, cars will become a part of the Internet in the near future.

The future mobility of the automotive industry requires new applications and technologies related to electric powering, automation, and connected services. Internet-integrated vehicles are already on the roads and it is predicted that the percentage of Internet-integrated vehicle services will jump from the current figure of 10% to 90% by 2020. The advances in cloud computing and the Internet of Things (IoT) have provided a promising opportunity in vehicular software and services in the automotive domain. Academia and the automotive industry are responding by exploring reliable and efficient connectivity solutions. In recent years, the demand for high-speed mobile Internet services has dramatically increased. Hence, the requirements and market demand for IoT device-connected cars will continuously increase. However, IoT-based vehicular data clouds must be efficient, scalable, secure and reliable before they can be deployed on a large scale. Existing algorithms and mechanisms are unsatisfactory to meet the necessary requirements simultaneously.

IoT-based vehicular data clouds are expected to be the backbone of the system, with the goal of making driving safer and more enjoyable. However, research into integrating the IoT with vehicular data clouds is still in its infancy and the existing study into this topic is highly insufficient. To ensure that vehicular data clouds are useful, numerous services such as road navigation, traffic management, remote monitoring, urban surveillance, information, entertainment and business intelligence need to be developed and deployed based on vehicular data clouds. Numerous challenges still exist such as security, privacy, scalability, reliability, quality of service and the lack of global standards. Due to the complexity involved in implementing vehicular clouds and integrating various devices and systems with vehicular clouds, a systematic approach and collaboration among academia, the automobile companies, law enforcement, government authorities, standardization groups and cloud service providers is needed to address these challenges. Though there are many challenges, IoT and cloud computing provide tremendous opportunities for technology innovation in the automobile industry and will serve as enabling infrastructures for developing vehicular data clouds.

One of the most important applications of IoT technology is the development of smart homes, smart offices, smart cars, etc., in a smart environment domain. There are two immediate driving forces bringing IoT connectivity to vehicles. One is for the connected vehicle to communicate, via the mobile network, with the connected house and the other is to adjust any connected devices in the home remotely. The mobile network plays a significant role in reliably and securely transferring relevant data from the vehicle to the house. The IoT technology enables linking physical objects such as different devices and sensors, with virtual objects, which exist through Internet connections, with increased comfort and safety. A seamless communication from the home to vehicle and to other parts of life is now expected. This is leading to smart phone connectivity with the vehicle and the connectivity of the vehicle with the cloud, etc. However, limitations exist regarding the evolution of cellular connectivity once the necessary components are embedded in the vehicle.

Nowadays, there is a growing demand for continuous access to the Internet in vehicles to provide improved safety, comfort, mobility and entertainment. As more people spend a considerable part of their lives in their vehicles, drivers will increasingly demand access to applications such as Google Maps and YouTube using the familiar interfaces in their car. Additionally, as mobile devices continue to grow in usage, people are creating secondary interface experiences related to, but not necessarily attached to, their vehicles, making this type of device a prime choice for any vehicular application. Moreover, they expect to have the same connectivity in their vehicles as they have at home and at work. Therefore, future automotive IT infrastructure and interaction specifications should follow on from general human–computer interaction guidelines with the understanding that there will be a high heterogeneity required to manage these contexts.

Even when end users can communicate with the IoT via multiple modalities, one of the most common ways to interact with electronic devices is through a graphical user interface (GUI). However, graphical interfaces can be confusing and difficult to use when users employ different interfaces in several environments. As the main modality that humans use to communicate with each other, speech can be one of the most convenient means of interaction. In terms of vehicle safety, the user interface is designed with connectivity in mind, significantly enhancing the possibilities of such technologies as speech synthesis and speech recognition. A recent advance in speech recognition is the adaptation of natural language understanding technology, thereby improving the efficiency of human-computer interactions. Speech interfaces are attracting more attention, and therefore, speech recognition technology is becoming an integral part of interacting with IoT devices. In the near future, speech interface technology will enable the end users to naturally speak to their household devices instead of pushing the buttons or clicking the icons on a GUI.

Vehicles have become a sophisticated and pivotal piece of the IoT and have always been an extension of us, integrated into our lifestyles and daily tasks as a reflection of our human experience. With the Internet technologies, the vehicle is able to interact with other connected ecosystems such as the smart home, providing seamless mobility. Drivers increasingly want to stay connected to their homes while driving and enable seamless home automation links to Internet-enabled smart devices, such as lights, home security systems, automatic garage doors and more. They want to experience an interaction to open a garage door and to turn on a light on the dashboard of their vehicles or through voice control when they are a certain distance from home.

16.2 Levels of Automation

Fully automated, autonomous, or "self-driving" vehicles are defined by the U.S. Department of Transportation's National Highway Traffic Safety Administration (NHTSA) as "those in which operation of the vehicle occurs without direct driver input to control the steering, acceleration and braking and are designed so that the driver is not expected to constantly monitor the roadway while operating in self-driving mode." There have been multiple definitions for various levels of automation, for the sake of standardization and to aid clarity and consistency, NHTSA has adopted the SAE International definitions for levels of automation. These definitions divide vehicles into levels based on "who does what, when."

Level 0: The human driver does all the driving.

Level 1: An advanced driver assistance system (ADAS) on the vehicle can assist the human driver with either steering or braking/accelerating.

Level 2: An ADAS on the vehicle can control both steering and braking/accelerating under some circumstances. The human driver must continue to pay full attention ("monitor the driving environment") at all times and perform the rest of the driving task.

Level 3: An automated driving system (ADS) on the vehicle can perform all aspects of the driving task under some circumstances. The human driver must be ready to take back control at any time the ADS requests the human driver to do so. In all other circumstances, the human driver performs the driving task.

Level 4: An ADS on the vehicle can itself perform all driving tasks and monitor the driving environment essentially, do all the driving in certain circumstances. The human need not pay attention in those circumstances.

Level 5: ADS on the vehicle can do all the driving in all circumstances. The human occupants are just passengers and need never be involved in driving.

16.3 Vehicle-to-Everything (V2X) Paradigm

V2X communication technology allows vehicles to communicate with each other, infrastructures as well as other parties. It is considered as a vital role in realizing future Intelligent Transport System (ITS). Information Centric Network (ICN) proposed as the a substitution for future Internet rely on its naming design is likely to associate with V2X well in contrast to conventional TCP/IP solution. Vehicle-to-Everything (V2X) covers the communications between vehicle-to-vehicle, vehicle-to-infrastructure and vehicle-to-pedestrian as shown in Figure 16.1.

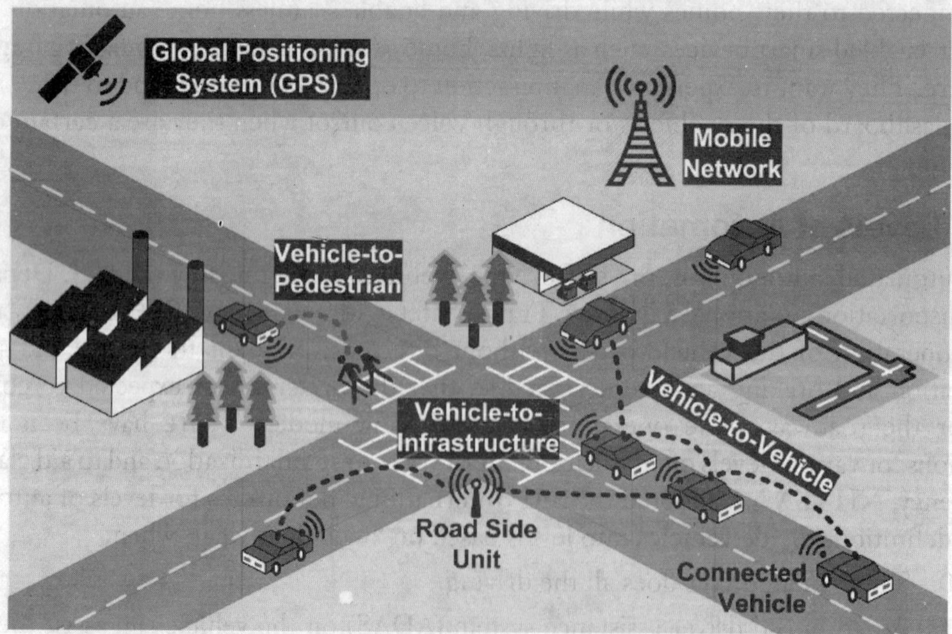

Fig.16.1: V2X Communication

This promising wireless technology enables vehicles to share diverse information such as their current speed, location with other vehicles in vicinity and remote infrastructures in practical complex traffic condition. V2X is considered as a vital role in realizing future Intelligent Transport System (ITS) where different technologies are integrated to provide optimized traffic management, safety ensuring, mobility for traveling. Although V2X technology greatly benefits to safety and travel efficiency, its applications raise new challenges at the same time. On one hand, V2X communication faces various expectations that requested by different features of applications. On the other hand, V2X has to overcome physical wireless problems caused by the highly mobile vehicle environment.

Conventional TCP/IP was designed for early Internet that handles a single conversation between two entities, cares about where data resides focusing on maintaining end-to-end connection between endpoints and centric hosts can hardly fit in V2X scenario where the network is primarily used as a tool for diverse contents dissemination instead of IP's inherent point-to-point communication. Furthermore, V2X is a new wireless paradigm with its content widely distributed over the network should no longer restricted by a single source provider but IP can only identify endpoints' address is not helpful for content distribution. IP also confines the mobility for the increasing wireless devices. Thus, a novel approach with native support to improve such issues is desired.

Content-Centric Networking (CCN) as one of Information-Centric Networking (ICN) architecture proposed for future Internet is an ideal alternative since CCN cares about the data itself not its location thus removes IP address restriction. Data are hierarchically named directly to be transmitted instead of embedded into a conversation, so as to eliminating the obstacle of supporting mobility and enabling scalable efficient data dissemination with low traffic requirement by its in-network caching. Therefore, CCN copes well with V2X content distributed background. However, it is not straightforward for CCN to adapt to vehicular environment. Several aspects have to be reconsidered to combine these two seamlessly. Recent research attentions have been paid to how data should be properly named to be identified and delivered, how and when data should be forwarded to the consumer in high dynamical topology.

16.4 Vehicular Ad-hoc Network (VANETs)

VANET has its mobile pattern of higher velocity, traveling path fixed and predictable. Based on Dedicated Short Range Communication (DSRC)/Wireless Access in Vehicular Environment (WAVE) as standards for PHY and MAC layers, VANET communication is able to archive high throughput with low delay. Thus, a variety of applications covering different aspects have emerged.

Safety applications include emergency braking, lane change warning collision avoidance and hazard notification. Efficiency applications include congestion management, electronic toll collection and parking availability. Commercial applications include Internet access live video stream. Comfort applications include weather information, autonomous driving and journey time estimation. However, VANET has its unique features to be taken into account.

High dynamic topology: This is caused by the high speed of vehicles and limit transmission range. Vehicles moving at 40km/h in urban and 100km/h on highway while radio coverage is only hundreds of meters which results in vehicles join and leave networks frequently thus network topology is constantly changing and partitioned.

High transmission and computation capability: Vehicles are equipped with on board devices and able to provide continous power in terms of computation and data storage that means hardware issue are not constraints.

Unstable connectivity: The inherent wireless transmission natures enlarged by high dynamic vehicles. In such a context, connectivity is therefore frequently disconnected and intermittent, the link duration trends to be very short.

Large scale: Each vehicle acts as a node in the network. This means the entire network can expand to the degree of roads coverage that includes a large number of participants.

Predicable mobility pattern: As vehicles have to follow roadways, that is to say the movement of nodes is limited to road layout. With refer to GPS system and road map nodes' future location can be predictable.

16.5 Information-Centric Networking (ICN)

ICN represents a general trend of future Internet architecture that evolves from the today's host centric, end-to-end, IP focused architecture to a content centric and distributed one. CCN and Named Date Networking (NDN) are the typical instances of the broad ICN umbrella. This book uses CCN and NDN interchangeably.

CCN basically changes the definition of network service from transmitting data to a certain destination address to requesting data identified by a given name from potential providers. As CCN focus on the named data itself instead of where data resides, the identified name is the key for both Interest packets and Data packets as shown in Figure 16.2 are the two kinds of data in NDN. Interest packets containing the content name are generated by consumers for requesting desire content and this Interest packets disseminate in the network to be received by intermediate routers then routers figure out proper outgoing face to forward this Interest accordingly. Once, Interest hits the providers having corresponding data, they reply with Data packets that travel back to consumer following the reversed forwarding path left by the Interest packets. Meanwhile

Data packets are cached at intermediate routers along the way for future reuse by potential consumer with same Interests.

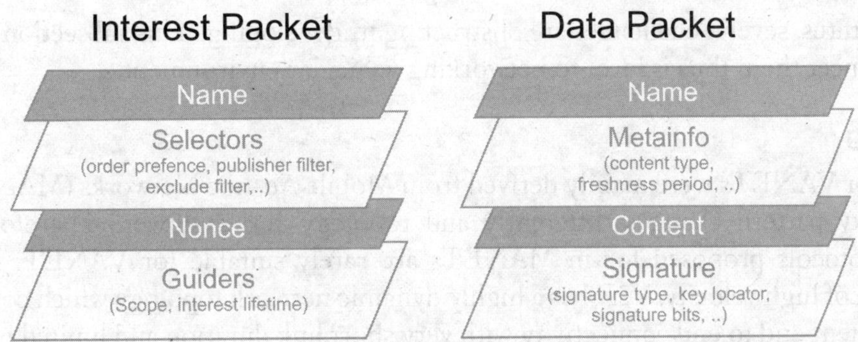

Fig.16.2: Packets of NDN

There are three components in each NDN router: *Pending Interest Table (PIT)* maintains an entry list of unsatisfied Interests that will be used for Data packets routing, *Forwarding Information Base* (FIB) keeps a list of faces where unsatisfied Interest should be forwarded to and *Content Store* (CS) caches Data packets arrived at this router for subsequent reuse. Figure 16.3 shows forwarding in NDN.

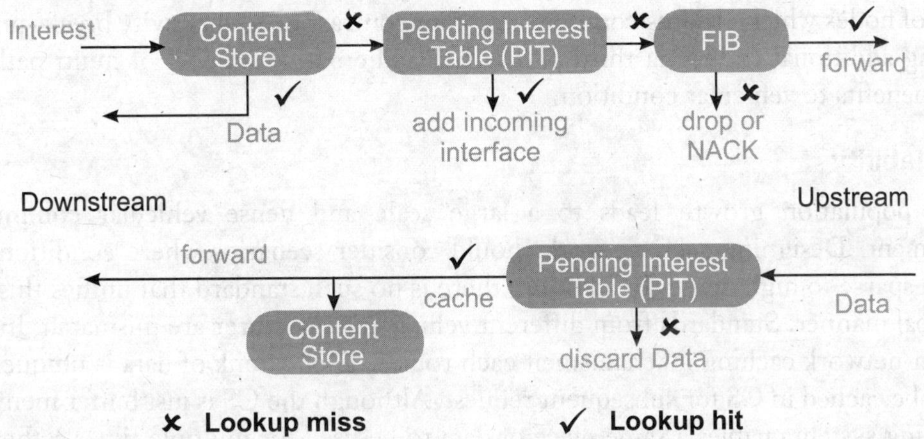

Fig.16.3: Forwarding in NDN

Consumer sends out an Interest packet, it arrives at NDN router. Firstly, a lookup will be performed in CS to match the Interest. If a match is found, the router sends back the Date via the incoming face. If not, a further lookup acts in PIT. At this point, if a match is found, the interest is discarded and only the incoming face of the Interest is recorded in PIT. If not, a new entry of incoming face is created in PIT then router forwards the Interest to the potential providers according to the FIB. An Interest does not match any of these tables will be dropped or trigger the node to discovery alternate routes.

16.6 CCN for VANET

Although VANET plays an important role in V2X communication due to its high mobile and wireless natures, several challenges are obstructing its developing. This subsection argues how CCN can meet them thus is ideal to networking vehicular environment.

(i) Routing

Routing for VANETs were mainly derived from Mobile Ad-hoc Networks (MANET) where the mobility pattern changes differently and topology varies slower. Therefore, existing routing protocols proposed for in MANETs are rarely suitable for VANET. Due to the vehicles are of high velocity, V2X has a highly dynamic network topology which contributes to an intermittent end to end connectivity with very short link duration and limited transmission range. Every communication cannot avoid the IP address or topology location which is a major obstacle to support mobility.

While routing and forwarding in CCN are based on the name of content rather than the location of content, it tremendously improves mobility. Routers advertise name prefix of individual content across the network in help of building each router's FIB not conventional IP address. There is no IP address exhaustion and management issues. Furthermore, in CCN the global unique name of content always remaining the same regardless the speed or direction change of nodes which ensures communication in contrast to connectivity breaks problem or tunneling additional traffic via third party of IP. The native support of multi-path routing greatly benefits to vehicular condition.

(ii) Scalability

Vehicle population growth leads to a large scale and dense vehicular communication environment. Designing such network should consider scenarios where condition changes between sparse to high dense. In addition, there is no such standard that unifies this network in a global manner. Standards from different vehicle manufacturer are mismatch. In CCN, it has an in-network caching mechanism at each router. Each chunk of data is uniquely named that can be cached in CS for subsequent request. Although the CS is just buffer memory, with the naming system enables a same piece of data to be used for multiple times rather than IP routers which are not able to reuse it after forwarding done. That is to say, when network size increases, the in-network caching functionality can greatly reduce the traffic load from a centric host because contents are widely distributed as cached replicas across the network. VANET can benefit from such advance when vehicle number rises at urban or during peak hours.

(iii) QoS

A network that guarantees less delay, minimum retransmission and stable connectivity is ideal for vehicular communication. One such will eventually enhance user experience regardless the blooming of application of all kinds. However, it is a challenging job for VANET designing. NDN is operating on top of unreliable packets delivery. Different from today's architecture transport layer, NDN shifts transport protocols into applications, supporting libraries. To ensure reliable transmission, a consumer that is not satisfied within given timer will resend the interest packets. Congestion control is taken care by each NDN router, it manages the interest forwarding rate to balance network traffic load. Caching functionality shorten the retransmission path from initial producer to previous hop where data lost which is idea for VANET because of the vehicular features so as to further avoid bandwidth being consumed by repeating transmission therefore it surely improves QoS in VANET.

16.7 Three Layered Architecture

The in-vehicle networking architecture is a three layered architecture. This architecture is also known as "Body and Brain" architecture. Figure 16.4 shows the Body and Brain architecture.

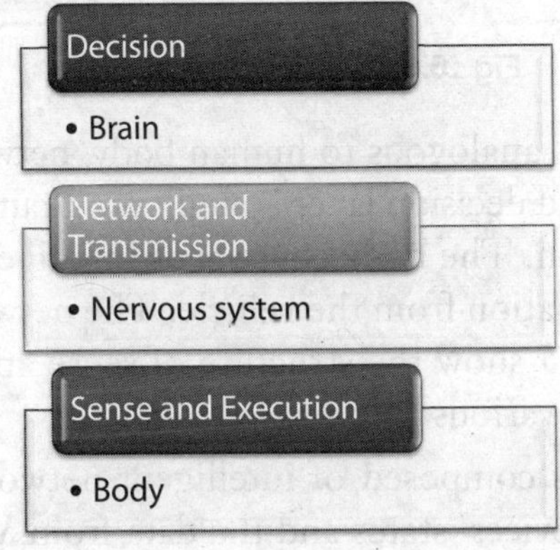

Fig.16.4: Body and Brain Architecture

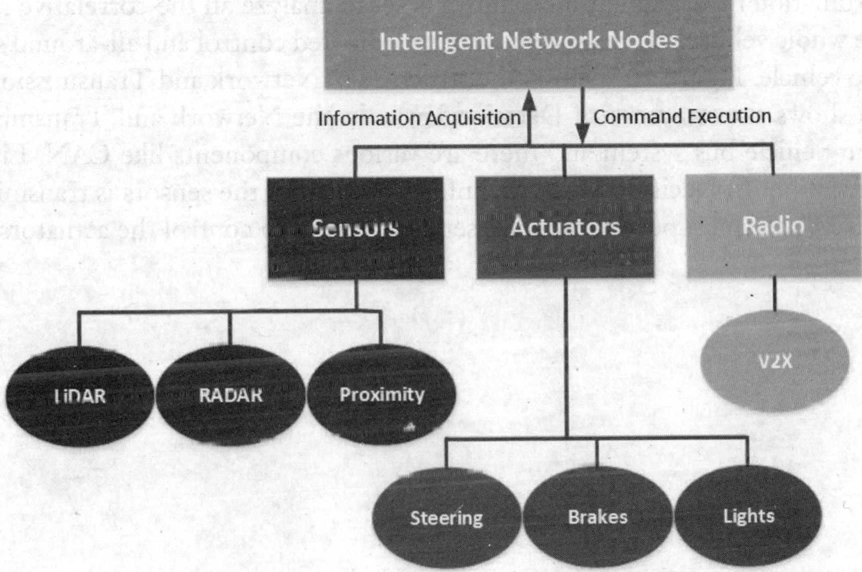

Fig.16.5: Structure of Sense and Execution Layer

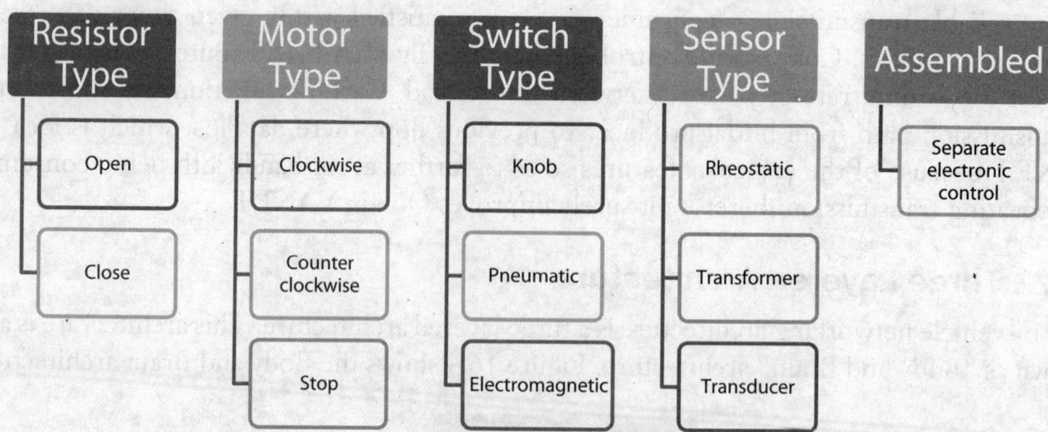

Fig.16.6: Classification of INNs

The sense and execution is analogous to human body, network and transmission layer is analogous to nervous system and decision layer is similar to brain of a human being. The brain manages the actual coordination. The body consists of Intelligent Networking Nodes (INN) which constantly collect information from the vehicle. The network based transmission forms the nervous system. Figure 16.5 show the structure of sense and execution layer and Figure 16.6 shows the classification of various INNs.

Sense & execution layer is composed of intelligent network nodes, which obtain both in vehicle electric/electronic devices' states and the data from V2X, achieve real-time online diagnosis and implement the control command to them. Network & Transmission layer for information transmission between sense & execution layer and Decision layer. In Decision layer, central coordination management mechanism is set to analyze all the correlative relationship between the whole vehicle's devices, achieving coordinated control and all-around supervisory of the whole vehicle. Figure 16.7 shows the structure of Network and Transmission layer and Figure 16.8 shows the structure of Decision layer. In the Network and Transmission layer, there is an in-vehicle bus system and there are various components like CAN, Lin, Flex-ray for communication. In Decision layer, the information from the sensors is transmitted to the administrative node and supervisory nodes send command to control the actuators.

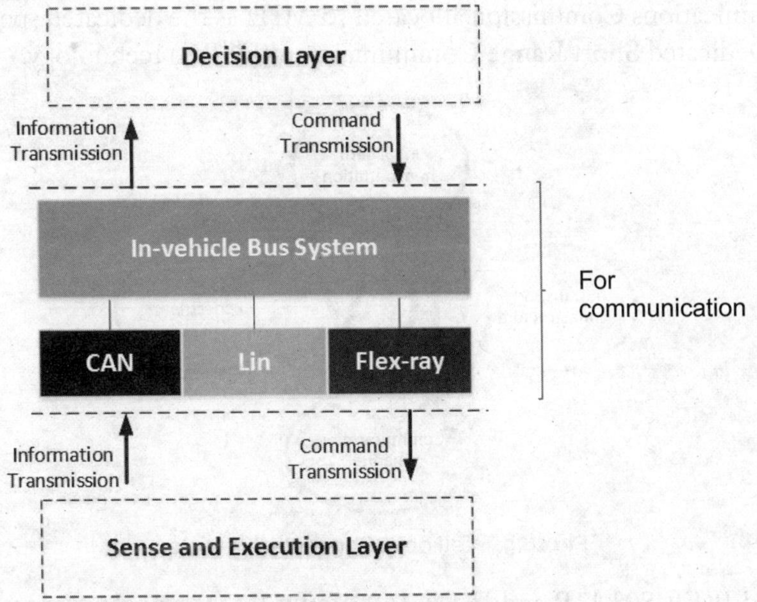

Fig.16.7: Structure of Network and Transmission Layer

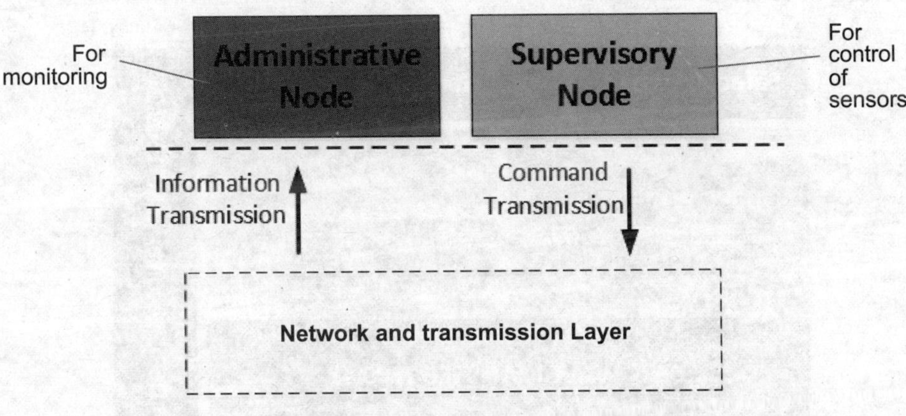

Fig.16.8: Structure of Decision Layer

16.8 Intelligent Connected Vehicles

With the development of the communication technology, more and more entities are connected to the communication network and become one of the elements in the network. Over recent decades, in the area of intelligent transportation, pedestrian and transport infrastructure are connected to the communication network to improve the driving safety and traffic efficiency which is known as the ICV (Intelligent Connected Vehicle). It can be considered as the confluence of intelligent transportation, transport infrastructure, pedestrian and communication channel as shown in Figure 16.9. The U.S department of Transport and

Federal Communications Commission allocated 75 MHz as the dedicated spectrum for ICVs. It is based on Dedicated Short Range Communication (DSRC) technology.

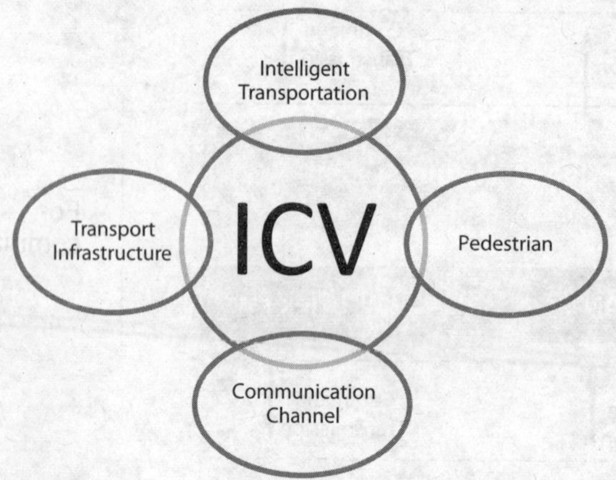

Fig.16.9: Intelligent Connected Vehicle

IEEE developed IEEE 802.11P and IEEE 1609 as DSRC standards. Society of Automotive Engineers (SAE) came up with SAE J2735 and J2945 as DSRC standards. Figure 16.10 shows the architecture of DSRC.

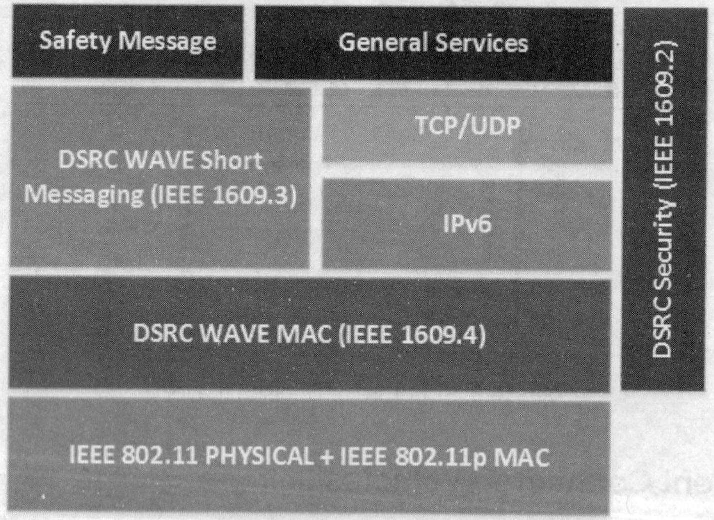

Fig.16.10: Architecture of DSRC

At the bottom are the IEEE 802.11 Physical and IEEE 802.11p MAC. The DSRC WAVE MAC is on the next top layer. On the top of it is the DSRC WAVE short messaging protocol and the regular IPv6 and TCP/UDP. The top most layers consist of safety messages and general services. Security is spread through DSRC WAVE MAC layer up to the top most layers.

The IEEE 1609 family provides with various standards for vehicular communications as follows.

- **IEEE P1609.0**- This is a draft standard for Wireless Access in Vehicular Environments (WAVE) architecture.
- **IEEE 1609.1-2006** – This is a trial use standard for Wireless Access in Vehicular Environments (WAVE). This is a protocol from resource manager point of view.
- **IEEE 1609.2-2006**- This is a trial use standard for Wireless Access in Vehicular Environments (WAVE). This is for security services for applications and management messages.
- **IEEE 1609.3-2007**– This is a trial use standard for Wireless Access in Vehicular Environments (WAVE). This is for networking services.
- **IEEE 1609.4-2006**- This is a trial use standard for Wireless Access in Vehicular Environments (WAVE). This is the protocol for multi-channel operations.
- **IEEE P1609.11**- This is the Over-the-Air Data Exchange protocol (OADE) for Intelligent Transportation Systems (ITS).

The phases of ICV development can be classified into 3 phases. In phase 1, it is considered to have facilities for infotainment service with remote information processing. It is based on 3G/4G technologies. In phase 2, the focus was on Intelligent Transportation Service (ITS) and is based on 4GLTE or DSRC technology. In Phase 3, the vehicles are connected to the cloud. Figure 16.11 shows forward collision warning in Vehicle-to-Vehicle (V2V) communication.

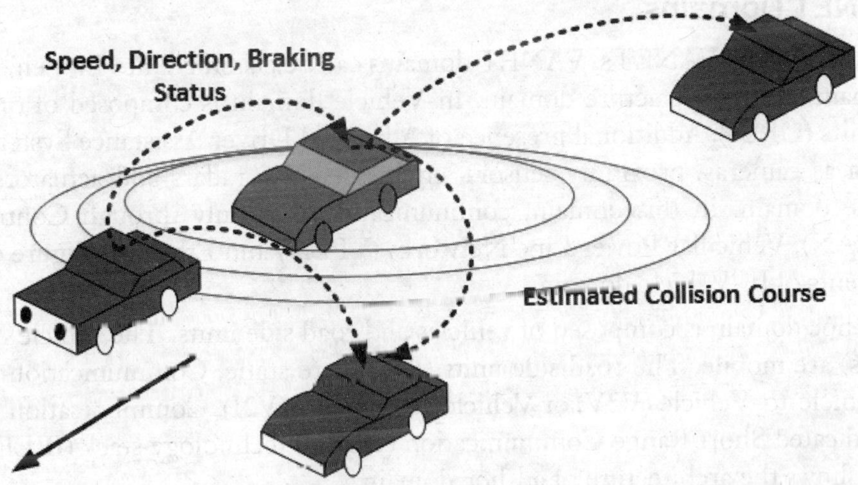

Fig.16.11: Forward Collision Warning in V2V

Consider the forward collision warning in Figure 16.11. All the vehicles have information regarding speed, direction and braking status of other vehicles. Based on this information, they can estimate the collision course so that they do not collide with each other. Another application is in vulnerable road user safety (V2P) which is shown in Figure 16.12.

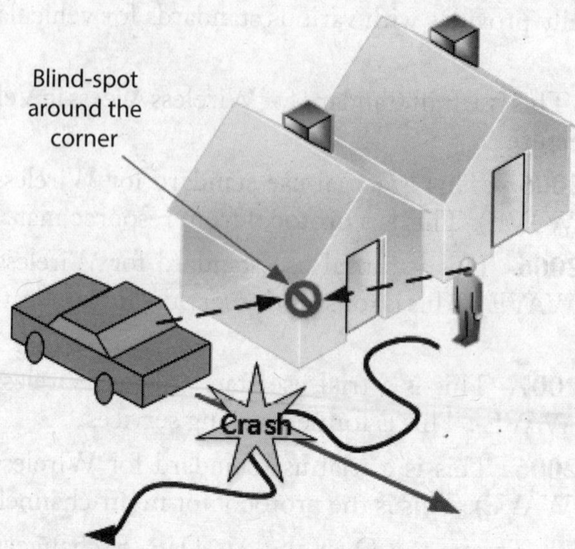

Fig.16.12: Vulnerable Road User Safety (V2P)

The figure is an example for blind spots on the road. When the vehicle and user tries to cross, there is a chance of hitting each other. This happens because they were not in line of sight of each other. Intelligent Connected Vehicles takes care of these type of situations and avoids accidents.

16.9 VANET Domains

The core of ICV is the VANETs. VANET domains can be classified into In-Vehicle domain, ad-hoc domain and infrastructure domain. In-Vehicle domain is composed of one or more on-board units (OBUs). Additional presence of Advanced Driver Assistance Systems (ADAS) sensors such as cameras, proximity sensors, engine sensors, radars and actuators are there in In-vehicle domain. In this domain, communication is mainly through Controller Area Network (CAN), Vehicular Power Line Networks (VPLN) and Ethernet. Figure 6.13 shows the components of In-Vehicle domain.

The ad-hoc domain is composed of vehicles and road side units. The vehicle's on-board-units (OBUs) are mobile. The road side units (RSUs) are static. Communication mode may be either Vehicle-to-Vehicle (V2V) or Vehicle-to-Internet (V2I). Communication takes place through Dedicated Short Range Communication (DSRC) technology stack (IEEE 802.11p). Figure 6.14 shows the architecture of ad-hoc domain.

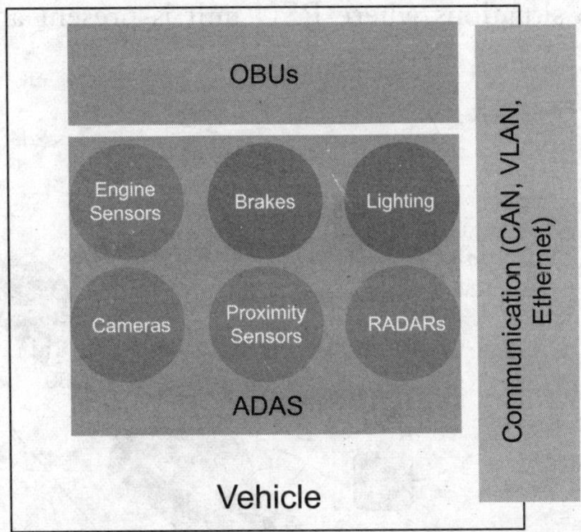

Fig.16.13: Components of In-Vehicle Domain

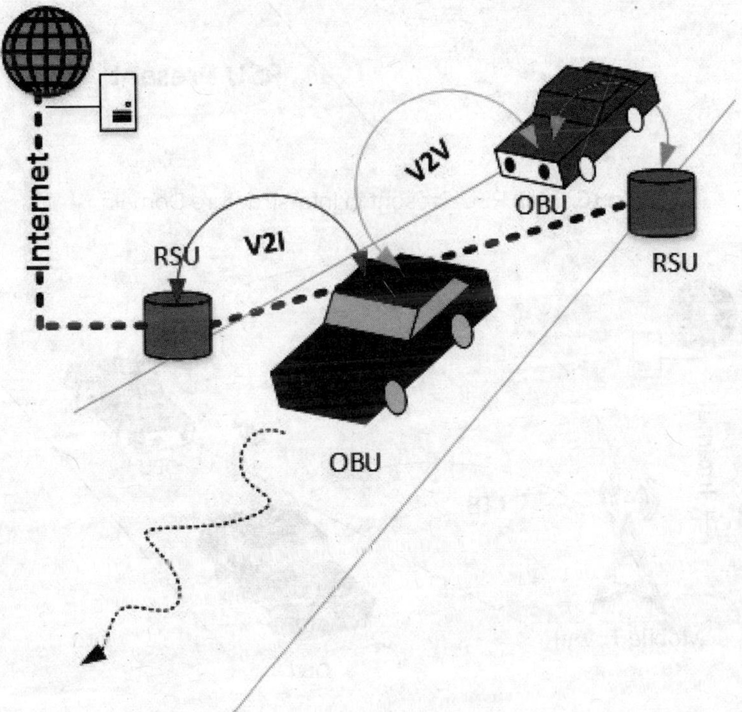

Fig.16.14: Architecture of Ad Hoc Domain

In infrastructure domains, Road Side Units (RSUs) are connected to Internet by means of gateways. In the presence of RSUs, The vehicles may communicate to the Internet via Vehicle-to-Internet (V2I) interfaces. In the absence of RSUs, the vehicles may communicate with each other or the Internet through cellular networks such as 3G, 4G, LTE etc. Figure 16.15a and

Figure 16.15b shows two situations where RSU unit is present and absent respectively in infrastructure domain.

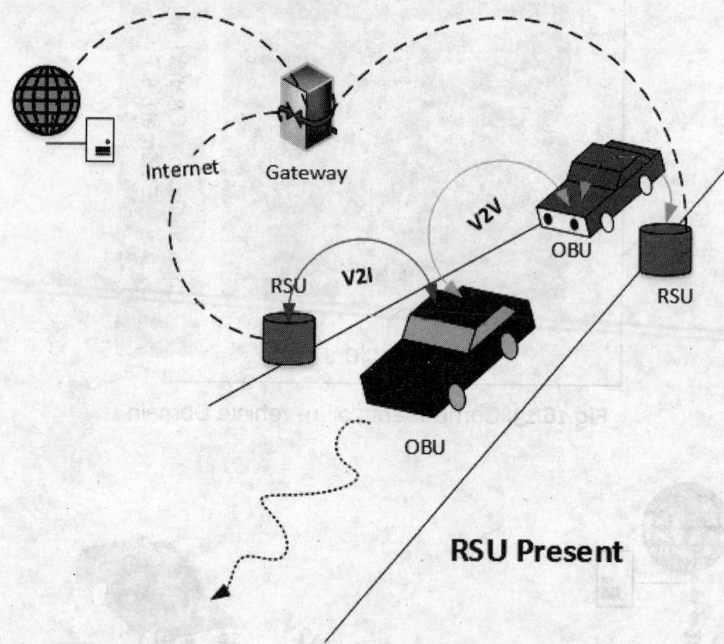

Fig.16.15(a): RSU Present in Infrastructure Domain

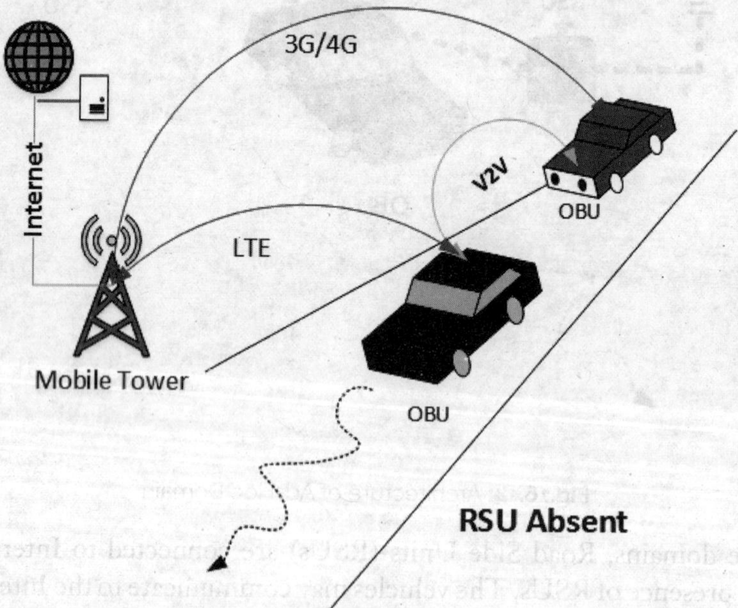

Fig.16.15(b): RSU Absent in Infrastructure Domain

16.10 Benefits of V2X Communication

There are several benefits for V2X communication which are listed below.

Mobility management functions allow the driver to reach a destination quickly, safely and in a cost-efficient manner. This includes current traffic information, parking lot or garage assistance and optimized fuel consumption.

Vehicle management functions that aid the driver in reducing operating costs and improving ease of use. This includes vehicle condition and service reminders, remote operation and transfer of usage data.

Breakdown prevention can be prevented because the technology is connected to a breakdown service, with a back end algorithm predicting breakdowns and an outbound service intervening via phone, SMS or push notification.

Safety functions are available that warns the driver of external hazards and internal responses of the vehicle to hazards. It helps the driver to drive in low-visibility or unfavorable conditions and prevents the vehicle from crashes.

Entertainment functions involving the entertainment of the driver and passengers are present like smart phone interface, WLAN hot spot, music, video, Internet, social media, mobile office etc.

Driver assistance functions involving partially or fully automatic driving are present. This includes operational assistance or autopilot in heavy traffic, in parking, or on highways.

Well being functions involving the driver's comfort and ability and fitness to drive are also present with connected vehicles. For example, fatigue detection, automatic environment adjustments to keep drivers alert, medical assistance etc.

16.11 Challenges of V2X Communication

Although the connected car offers lots of benefits and excitement to the drivers, it also faces drawbacks and challenges. A major issue with the connected cars is hacking. The more it is connected to the Internet, the more it becomes exposed to being penetrated from the outside. If the service and help can be provided from distance by car-makers, through that channel, hackers can access and control the car as well.

Reliability is also a major concern. Cars, sensor and network hardware will malfunction. The system has to deal with incorrect data, as well as faulty communications, such as denial of service attacks.

Privacy is another dimension, both with hacking and with other uses. Sensitive data gathered from the car such as the location, driver's daily route, apps that are used, etc. are all susceptible to be hacked and used for unauthorized purposes, as well as being used by businesses and government.

A simple failure in the system, whether in the connected car, or elsewhere in the network, while on the autonomous drive can cause fatal consequences.

16.12 Conclusion

This Chapter gives a detailed description of Connected Vehicles and its associated technologies. Different levels of automation in connected vehicles, Vehicle-to-Everything (V2X) paradigm, Vehicular Ad-hoc Networks (VANETs), Information-Centric Networking (ICN), CCN for VANET, three layered architecture of V2X, Intelligent Connected Vehicles (ICVs) and various VANET domains are well explained. Finally benefits of V2X communication and challenges of V2X communication are discussed in this Chapter.

17 INDUSTRIAL IoT

17.1 Introduction

The Industrial Internet of Things (IIoT) is the use of Internet of Things (IoT) technologies in manufacturing. Also known as the Industrial Internet, IIoT incorporates machine learning and big data technology, harnessing the sensor data, machine-to-machine (M2M) communication and automation technologies that have existed in industrial settings for years. The driving philosophy behind the IIoT is that smart machines are better than humans at accurately, consistently capturing and communicating data. This data can enable companies to pick up on inefficiencies and problems sooner, saving time and money and supporting business intelligence efforts. In manufacturing specifically, IIoT holds great potential for quality control, sustainable and green practices, supply chain traceability and overall supply chain efficiency.

A major concern surrounding the Industrial IoT is interoperability between devices and machines that use different protocols and have different architectures. The nonprofit Industrial Internet Consortium, founded in 2014, focuses on creating standards that promote open interoperability and the development of common architectures.

Industrial Internet of Things (IIoT) can be considered as the intersection of Internet of Things (IoT) and Industry 4.0 as shown in Figure 17.1. Industry 4.0 is a name for the current trend of automation and data exchange in manufacturing technologies. It includes cyber-physical systems, the Internet of things, cloud computing and cognitive computing. Industry 4.0 is commonly referred to as the fourth industrial revolution.

Industry 4.0 creates what has been called a "smart factory". Within the modular structured smart factories, cyber-physical systems monitor physical processes, create a virtual copy of the physical world and make decentralized decisions. Over the Internet of Things, cyber-physical systems communicate and cooperate with each other and with humans in real time, and via cloud computing, both internal and cross-organizational services are offered and used by participants of the value chain.

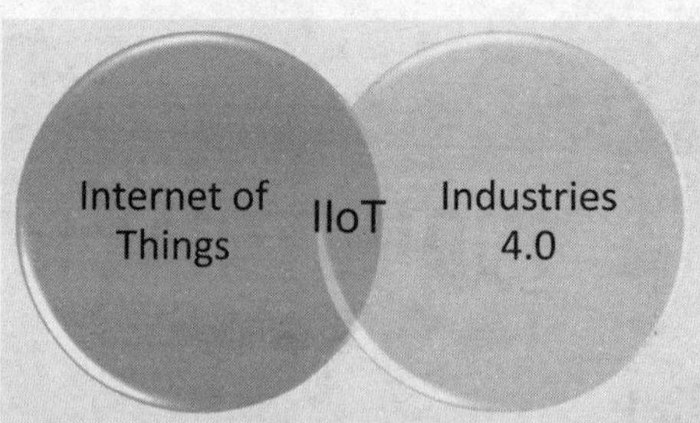

Fig.17.1: Industrial Internet of Things

Industrial Internet of Things (IIoT) is also known as Enterprise IoT while Internet of Things is known as Consumer IoT. Enterprise IoT is not equal to Consumer IoT. But there are some common aspects for both. Figure 17.2 shows the relationship between IIoT and IoT. IIoT is supported by huge amount of data collected from sensors. It is based on "wrap and re-use" approach than "rip and replace" approach.

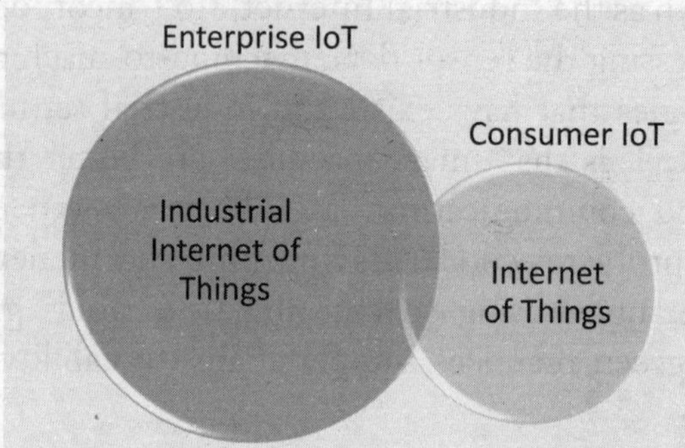

Fig.17.2: Relationship between IIoT and IoT

The first industrial revolution came with the mechanized production. With mass production came the second industrial revolution. Internet evolution and automation paved the way for third industrial revolution while fourth industrial revolution came with Industrial Internet of Things (IIoT). IIoT is a network of physical objects, systems, platforms and applications. These networks can communicate with each other, external environment and other people. The acquisition of IIoT has led to the availability and affordability of sensors, processors and other technologies which facilitates capture and access to real-time information.

17.2 IIoT Requirements

The IIoT can be characterized as a vast number of connected industrial systems that are communicating and coordinating their data analytics and actions to improve industrial performance and benefit society as a whole. Industrial systems that interface the digital world to the physical world through sensors and actuators that solve complex control problems are commonly known as cyber-physical systems. These systems are being combined with Big Data solutions to gain deeper insight through data and analytics.

Imagine industrial systems that can adjust to their own environments or even their own health. Instead of running to failure, machines schedule their own maintenance or, better yet, adjust their control algorithms dynamically to compensate for a worn part and then communicate that data to other machines and the people who rely on those machines. By making machines smarter through local processing and communication, the IIoT could solve problems in ways that were previously inconceivable. As innovation grows so does the complexity, which makes the IIoT a very large challenge that no company alone can meet.

At its root, the IIoT is a vast number of connected industrial systems that communicate and coordinate their data analytics and actions to improve performance and efficiency and reduce or eliminate downtime. A classic example is industrial equipment on a factory floor that can detect minute changes in its operations, determine the probability of a component failure and then schedule maintenance of that component before its failure can cause unplanned downtime that could cost millions of dollars.

The possibilities in the industrial space are nearly limitless: smarter and more efficient factories, greener energy generation, self-regulating buildings that optimize energy consumption, cities that can adjust traffic patterns to respond to congestion and more.

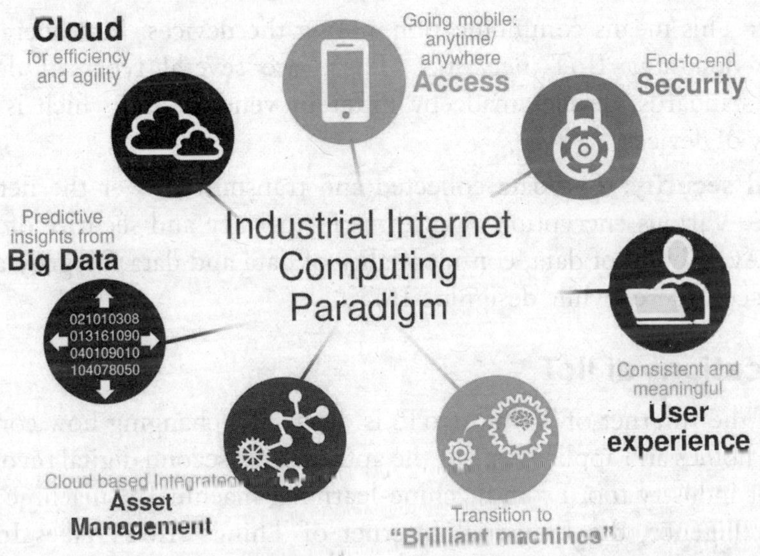

Fig.17.3: IIoT Requirements

The IIoT requirements are cloud computing, access (anywhere, anytime), security, Big data analytics, UX (user experience), assets management and smart machines as shown in Figure 17.3.

Service management in IIoT refers to the implementation and management of the quality of services which meets end user's demand. Service is a collection of data and associated behaviors to accomplish a particular function or feature of a device or portions of a device. Services can be of two types namely primary service and secondary service. Primary services are the basic services which are responsible for the primary node functions. The auxiliary functions which provide services to the primary service are termed as secondary service.

17.3 Design Considerations

To use an IoT device for industrial applications, the following design objectives are to be considered.

Energy: It is defined as the time for which the IoT device can operate with limited power supply. There is power constraint for IoT devices and the more the IoT device could work with little power supply, the more energy efficient is the IoT device.

Latency: It is defined as the time required for transmitting the data to the Cloud or other processing centers. While designing IoT devices and network, latency should be kept in mind and latency should be reduced as low as possible.

Throughput: It is defined as the maximum data transmitted across the network in unit time. Design consideration should keep in mind the increase of throughput.

Scalability: The IoT devices connected to the network may increase day by day. The network should be scalable to accommodate these devices.

Topology: This means communication among the devices. Interoperability is a major concern while designing IIoT networks. There are several types of devices operating with different standards, devices made by different vendors etc. which is a challenge for interoperability of devices.

Safety and security: The data collected and transmitted over the network should be safe and secure. Various encryption algorithms for privacy and security of data need to be implemented. Availability of data, confidentiality of data and data integrity are other factors that need to be considered while designing IIoT.

17.4 Applications of IIoT

The growth of the Internet of Things (IoT) is drastically changing how consumers interact with their cars, homes and appliances, but the aptly named second digital revolution has major implications for industry too. From machine-learning, machine-to-machine communication to artificial intelligence, the Industrial Internet of Things (IIoT) takes IoT technologies and directly applies them to industrial concerns and in the process improves efficiency and productivity.

While consumer-focused IoT solutions have dominated headlines in recent years and the relatively long life cycles of industrial equipment has limited growth in this sector so far, major firms and manufacturers are beginning to embrace IIoT on a big scale, attracted by the opportunity to drive down costs and increase competitiveness. We will see the application of IIoT in various fields like manufacturing, healthcare services, transportation, logistics, mining, firefighting etc.

17.4.1 Manufacturing Industry

Manufacturers and industrialists in every sector have a significant opportunity at hand where they can not only monitor but also automate many of complex process involved in manufacturing. While there have been systems which can track progress in the plant but the Industrial IoT (IIoT) technology provides far more intricate details to the managers. IIoT finds application in manufacturing in the following areas.

1. **Digital/connected factory**: IoT enabled machinery can transmit operational information to the partners like original equipment manufacturers and to field engineers. This will enable operation managers and factory heads to remotely manage the factory units and take advantage of process automation and optimization. Along with this, a digitally connected unit will establish a better line of commands and help identify key result areas (KRAs) for managers.
2. **Facility management**: The use of IoT sensors in manufacturing equipment enables condition-based maintenance alerts. There are many critical machine tools that are designed to function within certain temperature and vibration ranges. IoT Sensors can actively monitor machines and send an alert when the equipment deviates from its prescribed parameters. By ensuring the prescribed working environment for machinery, manufacturers can conserve energy, reduce costs, eliminate machine downtime and increase operational efficiency.
3. **Production flow monitoring**: IoT in manufacturing can enable the monitoring of production lines starting from the refining process down to the packaging of final products. This complete monitoring of the process in (near) real-time provides scope to recommend adjustments in operations for better management of operational cost. Moreover, the close monitoring highlights lags in production thus eliminating wastes and unnecessary work in progress inventory.
4. **Inventory management**: IoT applications permit the monitoring of events across a supply chain. Using these systems, the inventory is tracked and traced globally on a line-item level and the users are notified of any significant deviations from the plans. This provides cross-channel visibility into inventories and managers are provided with realistic estimates of the available material, work in progress and estimated the arrival time of new materials. Ultimately this optimizes supply and reduces shared costs in the value chain.
5. **Plant Safety and Security**: IoT combined big data analysis can improve the overall workers' safety and security in the plant. The Key Performance Indicators (KPIs) of health and safety, like the number of injuries and illness rates, near-misses, short-term and long-term absences, vehicle incidents and property damage or loss during daily operations can be monitored. Thus, effective monitoring ensures better safety. Lagging indicators, if any, can be addressed thus ensuring proper redressed health, safety and environment (HSE) issues.

6. **Quality control**: IoT sensors collect aggregate product data and other third-party syndicated data from various stages of a product cycle. This data relates to the composition of raw materials used, temperature and working environment, wastes, the impact of transportation etc. on the final products. Moreover, if used in the final product, the IoT device can provide data about the customer sentiments on using the product. All of these inputs can later be analyzed to identify and correct quality issues.
7. **Packaging optimization**: By using IoT sensors in products and/or packaging, manufacturers can gain insights into the usage patterns and handling of product from multiple customers. Smart tracking mechanisms can also trace product deterioration during transit and impact of weather, road and other environment variables on the product. This will offer insights that can be used to re-engineer products and packaging for better performance in both customer experience and cost of packaging.
8. **Logistics and Supply Chain Optimization**: The Industrial IoT (IIoT) can provide access to real-time supply chain information by tracking materials, equipment, and products as they move through the supply chain. Effective reporting enables manufacturers to collect and feed delivery information into ERP, PLM and other systems. By connecting plants to suppliers, all the parties concerned with the supply chain can trace interdependencies, material flow and manufacturing cycle times. This data will help manufacturers predict issues, reduces inventory and potentially reduces capital requirements.

17.4.2 Healthcare Service Industry

Medical diagnostic consumes a large part of hospital bills. Technology can move the routines of medical checks from a hospital (hospital-centric) to the patient's home (home-centric). The right diagnosis will also lessen the need of hospitalization. Industrial Internet of Things (IIoT), has an extensive applicability in numerous areas, including healthcare. The full application of this paradigm in healthcare area is a mutual hope because it allows medical centers to function more competently and patients to obtain better treatment. With the use of this technology-based healthcare method, there is an unparalleled prospect to improve the quality and efficiency of treatments and accordingly improve the health of the patients. Some of the applications of IIoT in healthcare service industry are given below.

1. **Simultaneous reporting and monitoring**: Real-time monitoring via connected devices can save lives in event of a medical emergency like heart failure, diabetes, asthma attacks, etc. With real-time monitoring of the condition in place by means of a smart medical device connected to a smart phone app, connected devices can collect medical and other required health data and use the data connection of the smar tphone to transfer collected information to a physician. Center of Connected Health Policy conducted a study that indicates that there was a 50% reduction in 30-day readmission rate because of remote patient monitoring on heart failure patients. The IoT device collects and transfers health data: blood pressure, oxygen and blood sugar

levels, weight and ECGs. These data are stored in the cloud and can be shared with an authorized person, who could be a physician, your insurance company, a participating health firm or an external consultant, to allow them to look at the collected data regardless of their place, time or device.

2. **End-to-end connectivity and affordability:** IIoT can automate patient care workflow with the help healthcare mobility solution and other new technologies, and next-gen healthcare facilities. IIoT enables interoperability, machine-to-machine communication, information exchange and data movement that make healthcare service delivery effective. Consequently, technology-driven setup brings down the cost, by cutting down unnecessary visits, utilizing better quality resources and improving the allocation and planning.
3. **Data assortment and analysis**: Vast amount of data that a healthcare device sends in a very short time owing to their real-time application is hard to store and manage if the access to cloud is unavailable. Even for healthcare providers to acquire data originating from multiple devices and sources and analyze it manually is a challenge. IoT devices can collect, report and analyses the data in real-time and cut the need to store the raw data. Moreover, healthcare operations allow organizations to get vital healthcare analytics and data-driven insights which speed up decision-making and is less prone to errors.
4. **Tracking and alerts**: On-time alert is critical in event of life-threatening circumstances. IoT allows devices to gather vital data and transfer that data to doctors for real-time tracking, while dropping notifications to people about critical parts via mobile apps and other linked devices. Reports and alerts give a firm opinion about a patient's condition, irrespective of place and time. It also helps make well-versed decisions and provide on-time treatment. Thus, IoT enables real-time alerting, tracking and monitoring, which permits hands-on treatments, better accuracy, apt intervention by doctors and improve complete patient care delivery results.
5. **Remote medical assistance**: In event of an emergency, patients can contact a doctor who is many kilometers away with a smart mobile app. With mobility solutions in healthcare, the medics can instantly check the patients and identify the ailments on-the go. Also, numerous healthcare delivery chains that are forecasting to build machines that can distribute drugs on the basis of patient's prescription and ailment-related data available via linked devices. IoT will improve the patient's care in hospital. This in turn, will cut on people's expense on healthcare.

17.4.3 Transportation and Logistics

The Industrial Internet of Things (IIoT) has the potential to revolutionize the transport industry. It provides access to new data streams and has made self-driving vehicles a reality. IIoT holds the potential to reduce pollution, optimize the mobility of people and goods and save lives. Here are some of the key applications of IIoT in transport.

1. **Fleet Management**: This can be used by businesses, transportation carriers and governments. It enables intelligent tracking and monitoring of vehicles through data from GPS sensors. Vehicles can be routed and scheduled automatically. Monitoring of driver behavior and vehicle performance and compliance can be done. Fleet management through IoT results in benefits such as increased safety, improved productivity and time and cost savings.
2. **Transport Logistics**: This is especially helpful for long-haul cargo operators and last-mile delivery providers. Containers and packages can be tracked and environmental conditions monitored through on-board sensors. Speciality shipping services to track cargo that is temperature-sensitive, hazardous or extremely valuable is possible with IIoT. Prevention of theft, product damage, successful delivery, scheduling and placement can be automated. Using IIoT for transport logistics ensures that products are delivered to the right place, at the time and in the right condition. It minimizes human intervention and reduces fuel costs.
3. **Smart Toll Collection**: Enables real-time financial transactions. IIoT automates revenue collection, bill generation and toll metering. Pricing based on demand or time of the day is possible in smart toll collection. Monitoring and assessing of vehicle parking and traffic flow can be identified using IIoT. Smart toll collection enables governments to create accurate billing records and reduce traffic congestion.
4. **Railways**: Control and collision avoidance systems enable automatic braking of trains. IIoT sensors monitor train speed in real time. Automatic scheduling and re-routing of trains is another application of IIoT. Sensors can track and monitor conductor behavior. Using IoT for trains ensure safety, controls speed and reduces fuel consumption.
5. **Smart Parking:** Sensors can detect whether a space is occupied or not in real time. Drivers can be provided with pictures of available parking spaces. It helps increased utilization for car parks. Smart parking enables more organized parking, reduces traffic congestion and benefits local authorities through higher revenues.
6. **Roadways:** IIoT enables traffic reduction by automatically monitoring and controlling traffic lights. IIoT is helpful in finding structural problems in bridges, tunnels and roadways. It analyses traffic flow to determine traffic status and improve routing. Smart lighting and security monitoring for urban streets is another application of IIoT in roadways. Using IoT solutions helps improve the safety of motorists, cyclists and pedestrians by decreasing traffic congestion and preventing accidents.

17.4.4 Mining

Monitoring air quality and the presence of gases is a big concern in the mining industry – for both economic and human safety reasons. Yet, technology is not being deployed in ways that make meaningful differences in this area. The common story in the industry is that a person is sent out every hour to traverse the mine, manually read sensors and document the status of oxygen levels, dangerous gases and escape routes. This information is then recorded on white boards at a central location, and a mine manager performs a standard analysis on the data to make decisions on how to regulate oxygen levels inside the mine.

Without any real-time monitoring and data-driven automated responses to changes in conditions, this antiquated methodology does little for the safety of miners and requires an individual to be placed in a potentially hazardous situation. Additionally, the ability to achieve significant energy cost savings from the more efficient management of fans and venting systems is limited.

IIoT can automate air and dangerous gas monitoring and generate related alerts and "ventilation on demand". It can creatively accomplish this in a way that makes the mines safer for workers as well as brings economic benefits to the operators.

17.4.5 Firefighting

Fire prevention and fire safety equipment are undergoing a revolution with Industrial Internet of Things (IIoT). Connected to low power wide area (LPWA) or even cellular networks, fire safety IoT stands to enhance prevention, speed up response times and keep first responders safe when walking into the fire. IoT's data capabilities provide more information for teams planning evacuations, rescues and fire suppression. Despite improved safety equipment and training, the greatest danger fire-fighters face is all the unknown factors they must deal with when they arrive on scene. For example what's the layout of the building?, how much longer does it have until it collapses?, how many people still are inside? where is the best place to enter and exit? etc.

The longer it takes to assess, enter and navigate a burning building, the higher the probability of property loss, injury and loss of life.

Imagine if technology could assist with these unknowns, allowing firefighters to act with greater confidence. As Fire Rescue points out, many departments already employ smart technology, such as thermal cameras. But what if leaders on the ground or even consultants miles away could see what firefighters using cameras and other navigational tools see in real-time? IoT networking makes this possible.

Networks linking a suite of IoT technologies can be set up at any fire site so as to communicate and share data to keep your team safe. With fire engines acting as the wireless hotspot for each IoT linked device in a fire department's inventory, the captain on scene can monitor team and individual movement through the fire and direct each member accordingly.

Often, IoT can integrate with existing alarms, personal safety devices and fire suit technology with minor adjustments to make the changeover process easier for fire departments on a limited budget. In particular, tracking technology promises to keep firefighters safer by reporting each team member's exact location directly to the shift commander. While GPS-based trackers may not work inside a concrete or steel structure, there are other options.

Lightweight RFID-based trackers that can reveal a team member's location at any time can be embedded in any suit to communicate continuously with the linked network. By monitoring each team member's location at all times in conjunction with linked thermal cameras, commanders can begin to map out the response location and offer precise guidance for the team's movement. As equipment is easy to lose in a smoky environment, different tools can be similarly tagged and tracked to prevent loss or to enable retrieval either during or after a fire.

17.4.6 Smart Dust

The concept of tiny sensors the size of a grain of sand, with the ability to detect everything from chemicals to vibrations, was first thought up in the early-1990s, but little progress was made in the following years turning this intriguing idea into a reality. However, interest in this nascent technology has grown recently, with research firm Gartner predicting smart dust will trend in the next five to ten years.

Applications of these connected smart dust particles in the IIoT are virtually endless, from oil exploration companies spreading smart dust to monitor rock movements to small sensors all over factory equipment continually looking out for changes and problems.

At the moment, smart dust sensors are still out of reach, primarily due to the difficulty in miniaturization and the prohibitive cost of producing huge quantities. However, they are slowly but surely becoming cheaper to manufacture, so it may not be long before billions upon billions of miniscule smart dust particles populate the world.

17.4.7 Drones

Unmanned aerial vehicles, or drones, have quickly become one of the most talked about products in the tech space, thanks to their many useful applications. In the near future these machines could play a significant part in the IIoT by acting as either a sensor or by providing a connection between sensors and data collection points.

Drones may not yet be seen as a fully fledged connected IIoT device, but they can carry all range of sensors and are autonomous machines capable of gathering massive amounts of valuable data. Construction companies can use drones to undertake daily land surveys and feed this data into software to ensure construction is on schedule and send an alert if anything looks out of place or improperly built. But drones are no mere data collectors, with the devices potentially being able to quickly act on the data they collect and communicate with other drones in the IIoT to work together to overcome problems.

17.4.8 Futuristic Farming

Far from the factory floor, in countless farms around the world, is where the IIoT could make the biggest difference. Utilizing the latest technologies is nothing new for the agriculture industry, but implementing smart, connected IIoT projects enables farmers to make use of the massive amounts of data generated on their farms.

The large size of many farms makes manual surveys ineffective and difficult, leading farmers to turn to IIoT solutions. Oyster farmer Ward Aquafarms, with the help of telecoms firm Verizon, deployed an IIoT program to maximize productivity and ensure the quality of food in the supply chain, using satellite imaging and IIoT track-and-trace technology to monitor farming operations all the way from harvest to delivery.

In areas like precision agriculture, real-time data about soil, weather, air quality and hydration levels can help farmers make better decisions about the planting and harvesting of crops.

17.4.9 Aerospace

Aerospace companies have mainly introduced IIoT solutions on the factory floor for tracking tools and parts, with some beginning to expand the number of on-board IoT devices. An airplane that knows when it's going to encounter maintenance problems before they actually happen would save a significant amount of man-hours and money for airlines. Taleris, a joint venture by General Electric and Accenture, is at the forefront of developing IoT solutions for airlines, aimed at minimizing delays and disruptions by analyzing data collected from sensors on airplanes.

Uptake of these IoT technologies in the aerospace sector has been slow, as cost-savings are not easy to estimate, but as the benefits of these systems become apparent, interest from airlines will grow. The widespread usage of analytics programs that have the ability to monitor aircraft proactively not only improves turnaround times for airlines but also helps meet customer needs more effectively.

17.4.10 Energy Networks

Energy companies can expect to see their operations fundamentally altered when IoT is fully embraced in their sector. Spikes in energy consumption around major TV broadcasts and weather events have long troubled utility firms. But with effective energy demand management through the IIoT, the need for investment in both energy networks and power plants is reduced.

Smart meters are one example of the industry's move towards IoT technologies, although at the moment they only record usage amounts and timings. Utility firms could potentially provide price information to these meters, which could in turn interact with other IoT devices to use energy at the most efficient time.

New oil and gas pipelines are fitted with sensors that detect leaks and alert repair teams, so issues are fixed before they can cause problems and the number of blackouts and brownouts are kept to a minimum. Any improvements the IoT can achieve in energy supply management will become increasingly valuable as utility companies look for the most effective ways to deal with multiple energy sources in a decentralized network.

17.5 Benefits of IIoT

IIoT has improved connectivity among devices, improved efficiency, upgraded scalability, reduced operation time, remote diagnosis and cost effective. Connected ecosystem is an advantage with IIoT. Traditional supply chains in industries are linear in nature. To shift the business focus from products to outcomes, new ecosystem should be followed. Digital ecosystems progress at a much faster rate than physical industries. Hence, it can quickly adapt to the changes in the external environments.

Integration of digital and human workforce is another benefit of IIoT. In IIoT, machines become more intelligent. Hence the automated tasks can be done in the industries at lower costs and higher quality level. When humans work with machines, the outcome will be higher overall productivity. IIoT will reform and redefine the skills of the workers.

IIoT will create new job opportunities. The creation of new composite industries such as precision agriculture, digital healthcare system, digital mines etc. will lead to the development of new job opportunities. Highly automated machines will require lesser number of unskilled workers, but will require skilled experts with digital and analytical skills.

Reformation of robots is another advantage. In IIoT environment, robots are featured with 3 capabilities namely sensing, thinking and acting. They will be reformed with the ability to carry out repetitive tasks. Robots will be more intelligent but will work under the supervision of human beings. Robots can be reprogrammed to perform new tasks.

17.6 Challenges of IIoT

The primary challenges in IIoT include identification of objects or things, manage huge amount of data, integrate existing infrastructures into new IIoT infrastructure and enabling data storage. There are several safety challenges which include worker health and safety, regulatory compliance, environmental protection and optimized operations. Challenges related to hazards include handling, storing or using hazardous substances, oxygen deficiency, radiation and physiological stress.

Standardization is another challenge. Standardization plays an important role in the development of the system. The goal of standardization is to improve the interoperability of the different systems or applications and allow the products or services to perform better. The problems related to standardization are interoperability, semantic interoperability, security and privacy and radio access level issues.

Other important concerns related with IIoT are information security and data privacy protection. The devices or things can be tracked, monitored and connected. So there are chances of attack on the personal and private data. For example, in healthcare industry, the medical data of a patient must not be tampered or altered by any person in the middle. Another example is in the food industry where the deterioration of any food item being sent to the company must be kept confidential as it will affect the reputation of the company.

Though IIoT provides new opportunities, new factors may cause hindrance in the path to success such as lack of vision and leadership, lack of understanding of values among management employees, costly sensors and inadequate infrastructure. For example, meeting the challenges of costly sensors can be improved by miniaturization, performance of sensors, cost and energy consumption. The challenges in operational efficiency can be improved through predictive maintenance, savings on scheduled repairs, reduced maintenance costs and reduced number of breakdowns.

17.7 Conclusion

The Chapter explains Industrial Internet of Things (IIoT) in detail. IIoT requirements and design considerations of IIoT is explained in this Chapter. Several applications of IIoT in various domains like manufacturing industry, healthcare service industry, transportation and logistics, mining, firefighting, smart dust, drones, futuristic farming, aerospace and energy networks are explained in detail. Finally benefits of IIoT and challenges of IIoT are discussed in this Chapter.

INDEX

INTERNET OF THINGS

DR. JEEVA JOSE

FEEDBACK FORM

1. Which topics from your examination point of view are inadequately or not covered in this book?

____

____

2. Is there any misprints/ mistakes/ factual inaccuracy in this book? If so, please specify.

____

____

3. What is your assessment of this book as regards the presentation of the subject-matter, expression, precision and price in relation to the other recommended books available on this subject?

____

____

4. Which competing books you regard as better than this? Please mention their author and publishers.

____

____

5. Any further suggestions/comments you would like to make for the improvement of the book?

____

____

PS: If needed, please attach a separate sheet.

Name : ____________________

College : ____________________

Address : ____________________

Email : ____________________

Mobile : ____________________

Please mail the feedback form at:

KHANNA BOOK PUBLISHING CO. (P) LTD.

4C/4344, Ansari Road, Daryaganj, New Delhi-110002

You can also email this feedback form at contact@khannabooks.com or Whatsapp at +91 – 99109 09320

BEST FEEDBACK WILL BE REWARDED SUITABLY